POP

WHEN THE WORLD FALLS APART

POP

WHEN THE WORLD FALLS APART

Music in the Shadow of Doubt

Edited by Eric Weisbard

An EMP Museum Publication

Duke University Press

Durham and London

2012

© 2012 EMP Museum
All rights reserved
Copyright acknowledgments for individual chapters
appear at the end of this book.
Printed in the United States of America
on acid-free paper ∞
Typeset in Scala by Tseng Information Systems, Inc.
Library of Congress Cataloging-in-Publication
Data appear on the last printed page of
this book.

CONTENTS

Eric Weisbard

Introduction

T he Pop Conference at Experience Music Project, the source of this collection (the third book to date, along with *This Is Pop* and *Listen Again*[1]), took place in April 2002, much more the spirit of *American Idol* (then in its first season) than the aftershocks of the previous September 11. The Pop Conference quickly found its voice as an expression of what Kevin Dettmar has called "pop-positive criticism" (a play on "sex-positive feminism"). All sorts of writers gather each year to bring their passion, erudition, and laughter to bear on subjects that others ignore or castigate. Elsewhere, the topics on the agenda might be essentials: best-of lists and other canons. At EMP, the focus is the opposite. One never knows what will find its way onto the program: a Top 40 star reclaimed, a song's lineage traced through radically different incarnations, a seemingly random occurrence treated as central rather than deviant. We have fun each spring and go home rejuvenated.

Over the years, what started as a banquet has come to feel more like an oasis. When we reconvened in 2003, military operations in the Iraq War were under way. In 2006, Hurricane Katrina was on our minds, and the destruction of New Orleans, America's musical cradle. The recording industry steadily withered through the 2000s, paralleled by the loss of jobs in music journalism. Then the rest of the economy collapsed as well. As moods darkened, so did our conference themes. In 2006, the topic was, essentially, guilty pleasures, except that Drew

Daniel, a program committee member, shrewdly recast it as shame and "loving music in the shadow of doubt," a thornier subject than taste hierarchies. In 2007, the EMP gathering was titled "Waking Up from History," a Gen-X reference (Jesus Jones!) that nodded to our sense of living in some sort of embattled aftermath. And in 2008, at the urging of two other committee members, Joshua Clover and Ned Sublette, struggle took over: the theme became music in the mode of conflict—songs in the key of strife.

It is these last three years of conference proceedings, 2006 through 2008, that shape this book, which finds common ground in how pop lovers confront crisis—recognize cracks in the fundament and shake their stuff anyway. These are not marginal approaches to listening. After all, at the end of 2009, heavy metal sites gleefully reported that Metallica's album *Metallica* (also known as *The Black Album*), the release that brought the band into the mainstream in 1991, had just passed Shania Twain's *Come on Over* to claim the title of best-selling album of the SoundScan era. As a race between tortoise and hare, and between one musical mood and another, the contrast is striking. *Come on Over*, released in 1997, shot ahead quickly, combining a sentimental ballad, "You're Still the One," with endless upbeat affirmations: no artist is as fond of exclamation points in her titles as the author of "Man! I Feel Like a Woman!" *Metallica*, recorded during the first Gulf War, was a million copies behind it as of 2003: the year that the second military operation got under way. Since then, however, *Metallica*'s "Sad But True" lyrical disaffirmations have plodded ahead as decisively as the band's down-tuned guitar riffage, consistently attracting new cohorts of the "dead-end kids" Donna Gaines captured so well in her book *Teenage Wasteland*, also a 1991 title. "The Unforgiven," six minutes of a boy growing old scratching against rock in a lightless hellhole, might prove in retrospect the defining commercial statement of the past generation.

Can our analyses evolve to match? In the months following *Metallica*'s first release, the far bigger media story was *Nevermind*, Nirvana's blow for Generation X and the rock-and-roll dream: those instantly iconic cheerleaders with the anarchy outfits in the "Smells Like Teen Spirit" video applauded music as a rebellious force (an irresistible idea), even though Kurt Cobain's lyrics pronounced it all "less dangerous." One critical response to the disillusioning collapse of alternative rock was so-called poptimism: an impulse to celebrate commodified culture for its ability to represent the types of people left out of the rock rebellion paradigm. What would it mean, however, for poptimism to confront the calcified disillusionment of Metallica to the same degree as bouncy Shania?

This book gets at an answer by taking as its theme music in times of trouble: the role of pop at times when it seems that the world has fallen apart. Trouble, it must be noted right away, can be as much interior as exterior, as much a part of normal life as of extraordinary crisis, as much Metallica on permanent simmer as Nirvana boiling over. There is an old radical song, "The World Turned Upside Down," which began as a broadside in the English Revolution and gave title to the classic study of working-class social history by Christopher Hill. That kind of broadside, with its roots in carnivalesque rituals of social reversal and connections forward to "Summertime Blues," "Say It Loud," "Born to Run," "Blitzkrieg Bop," "Bring the Noise," and "Smells Like," presumes identification: the powerless finding representative voices. *Pop When the World Falls Apart* presumes *disidentification*, what the queer theorist José Esteban Muñoz describes as placing one's self in moments and objects not coded for you and accepting the often shameful consequences. The disidentifying subject, Muñoz writes, is neither rebel nor subservient, working "on, with, and against a cultural form."[2] Given a generation-long shift from industrial-era group consumerism to postindustrial economic gaps, queasy celebrity culture, and record business collapse, popular music is almost inherently something to be disidentified with now: emotionally claimed through, rather than in resistance to, personal or collective breakdown.

The first few chapters of this book hail the cracked-up self. The novelist and gawky dancer Jonathan Lethem, keynote speaker in 2007, salutes the wanna-be, the happy fake who ensures that pop, blessedly, remains "a kind of trick." If James Brown was no real musician, according to his trained sidemen, the rest of us (Fifth Beatles) have nothing to worry about. Greg Tate, as much of a self-confessed "sci-fi nerd" as Lethem but also a curator of négritude, traces a few vivid moments in a lifetime of his black rock efforts to keep space open for his "irreverent, neologistic, avant garde art-damaged ass." To the categories of wanna-be and nerd, Alexandra Vazquez's immigrant "softy polemic" adds the ideal of knowing nothing, being "comfortable being uncomfortable . . . entertained when left out of the conversation." Finally, David Ritz, king of the as-told-to memoir and a twelve-step veteran to boot, testifies to why he became a ghostwriter: putting the urge to express his self directly aside like a dangerous substance.

From the conflicted self we head out to reclaim for darkness and doubt the notoriously conflict-averse suburbs. Three chapters are set in Orange County: birthplace of fast food and Reaganite conservatism, a toxic home for Karen Carpenter, and then launching pad for Gwen Stefani. Tom Smucker, in old-school rock critic fashion, compresses libraries worth of social and cultural context to contrast the commercial requirement that Karen Carpenter project an inner life with Lawrence Welk's sanction to just blow bubbles. Smucker's EMP talk inspired Eric Lott to write his own take, in newer-school American Studies fashion. "What is worst in Carpenters' music," Lott posits, "may also be what is best about it"—a harmony so overstated it negates itself. Then Karen Tongson explores a later Orange County: an eighties breakdance nightclub (evoked, Stefani says, on her *Love. Angel. Music. Baby* solo album), based in an amusement park, once as pale as Disneyland, that wound up catering to queer kids, immigrants, and other suburban B-boys-and-girls looking for "a parcel of fantasy . . . as the cold world melted away."

Two subjects I very much hoped that this book would confront were the Iraq War and New Orleans after Katrina. Happily, J. Martin Daughtry and Larry Blumenfeld have delivered important and detailed accounts of how music joined these different battles. Daughtry makes his focus the act of listening in a situation where to hear at all is to risk being deafened. Here, airmen create soundtracks for self-produced videos of their bombing runs (only one way that music and violence are relentlessly interwoven), then cool down to "normal" Top 40. In New Orleans, by contrast, police drive through second-line gatherings, and Congo Square—the only place in North America where Africans were once free to drum—remains padlocked. Blumenfeld's investigative reporting probes at a jazz culture fighting for its life as a community culture, which is to say a popular culture. "Kill 'em with pretty," the Mardi Gras chiefs say. Not a bad way of describing the song that centers the next chapter, Israel Kamakawiwo'ole's version of "Over the Rainbow." Nate Chinen schools us to hear in the performance a plea for Hawaiian sovereignty from the land of rainbows, "a sense of anguish braided with uplift."

After exploring turbulences of self, suburbs, and sovereignty, we move on to tensions around the genres that constitute pop's "worlds." Music genres, cemented in a half century of Fordism and Keynesianism, as the entry of dispossessed groups, in particular African Americans, into consumer economies corresponded to heightened social and political clout, have become a much murkier category in postindustrial, postmodern, post–civil rights America. Diane Pecknold considers how a country song, "By the Time I Get to Phoenix," became the vehicle for Isaac Hayes's transformation into "Black Moses," a symbol of cultural nationalism, at the moment Hayes's world—Stax soul, played by integrated bands for integrated audiences—collapsed with the shooting of Martin Luther King Jr. Oliver Wang takes up soul from a radically different perspective: the retro-soul revivalists whose entire aesthetic is based on the conflict they have with how the music has developed since the late 1960s. Carlo Rotella examines Magic Slim, the Chicago blues master journeyman who somehow became the last orthodox player in a genre taken over by simulacra; his "substantive party music" was built to survive apocalypse. Finally, a University of Iowa writing program triumvirate, Brian Goedde, Austin Bunn, and Elena Passarello, fashion dramatic monologues from interviews with white hip-hop fans in the Tall Corn state.

No book on music in troubled times could avoid the theme of anger, which is often to say punk and metal. Yet when Michelle Habell-Pallán picks up the story of a classic punk rocker, Alice Bag, she draws gestural correspondences that the 1970s L.A. scene would not have recognized, connecting Bag's sharp elbows and loud lungs to Mexican *canción ranchera*, the *estilo bravío* of postrevolutionary women such as Lucha Reyes. Scott Seward, a hospital custodian, writes from the intellectual underclass about "middle of the road . . . death grunts," Heinous Killing's "Strangled by Intestines," Shinto texted Japanoise, and an album titled *Gothic Kab balah* about a mystic who lived four centuries back. Open the archive, as Habell-Pallán insists we do, and anything might come out. Kembrew McLeod's punk friends in Virginia didn't get mad when the alternative rock industry came calling in response to a bogus *Spin* feature on the scene in New Market, Virginia. (Reread name.) They got even, treating the label reps to one prank after another. Amazingly, the Dave Matthews Band was lurking, unsigned, a few burgs over. Forget real versus fake, McLeod's anecdote argues: credulity drives the whole enterprise of pop.

Ending the volume is what those in an earlier era of the CD reissues trade might have called a bonus track. Carl Wilson's Pop Conference presentation on the "guilty displeasure" of hating Celine Dion ranks among our best-received ever, and grew to be the basis of a book of its own, that received pop-cultural discourse as few music writers ever achieve, from glossy magazines to the Academy Awards runway and the *Colbert Report*.

Here, we include the original talk (notice how Hurricane Katrina finds its way in at a crucial turn), along with a postscript reflecting on the book's journey. "People who complain that thinking, writing, or talking too much about music 'ruins' it or is 'not rock 'n' roll' are getting it backward," Wilson insists. "Whether or not the music needs any discussion, discussion needs the music. Rock may not need discourse but discourse needs to be rocked." I hope that, through our annual gathering and books such as this, the Pop Conference continues to do its part.

Notes

1. Eric Weisbard, ed., *This Is Pop: In Search of the Elusive at Experience Music Project* (Cambridge: Harvard University Press, 2004); Eric Weisbard, ed., *Listen Again: A Momentary History of Pop Music* (Durham: Duke University Press, 2007).

2. José Esteban Muñoz, *Disidentifications: Queers of Color and the Performance of Politics* (Minneapolis: University of Minnesota Press, 1999), 12.

Jonathan Lethem

Collapsing Distance

The Love-Song of the Wanna-Be,

or The Fannish Auteur

When I dance these days, I don't bend so much at the knees as I used to. My knee-bends are more kabuki indications, representational rather than presentational, like Lou Reed's vocal range, like Muhammad Ali teasing a video crew with boasts of flurries of punches so fast you couldn't see them, even as he posed with his upraised fists completely still. Don't blink or you'll miss them—and you did. The dancing I do now enciphers in shorthand the drops and knee-bends of my twenties—these were moves that, once I'd learned them, I drove, so to speak, into the ground. My knees reminisce of old dancefloors in clubs in Berkeley and Oakland and San Francisco when I climb too many stairs, a sad involuntary pun on dancing about architecture.

Other ghosts rustle in my dancing these days, kinetic memory routines, muscle quotes of punk-rock ironized glam-kicks, Elvis Costello intentional-awkward heel-scoots and skids, a kind of sideways bunny hop and mechanical stop and restart that I appropriated from my friend Sari Rubenstein, and which always reminds me of both the B-52s and a certain beer-swollen wooden-plank dormitory living-room floor in Vermont. From that same scene my dancing self still periodically retrieves a mimicry of the solitary, ecstatic dancing of a young poet named Reginald Shepherd, who'd cascade his body side-

to-side to the Psychedelic Furs and Donna Summer, propelled by his hurl-
ing arms, as if caught up on the shuttle of some gigantic loom—for a
while I could only want to dance exactly like Reggie, and the phantom still
gains possession of me from time to time.

When I got to college I was already a dancer. In my freshman year of
high school I seized that role for myself, first, and definitively, at a Manhattan loft party full of hip adults to which my father had brought me and
my new girlfriend, my first girlfriend. When the dance floor filled, not
to be outdone by my father's friends, I began impulsively and spastically
showing off in the midst of the dancers, finding my own ready dance-
appropriating instinct available when I needed it to even begin—an image
is still fresh in mind of the shaved-bald black man in dashiki whose technique I glommed, or tried to: he bent at the waist, snapped his fingers and
shook his bright dome as if in a self-amused trance. His obliviousness to
our regard was what I wanted for myself, was what I wished to hijack on
behalf of my own craven pursuit of regard. I began immediately shaking
my head, not yet capable of observing the finer details, how that dancer's
headshaking must surely have been driven by less ostentatious but completely authoritative movements through his feet and hips, zones I'd yet
to learn to activate. Yet my ears were open, I wasn't deaf to the music, I
know I was in the kind of bodily rapture-in-sound where all real dancing
begins. Alas, I was trying to lead my dance with my head, like trying to
play a song's bass line on a pair of cymbals, or a triangle. Somehow I made
this my trademark, no one intervened to advise me otherwise, and so I
built my dancing body from the headshake downward, like a Cheshire Cat
begun at the grin.

At grown-up parties in Brooklyn hippie communes, I gradually worked
out my dancing on this basis, to the soundtrack of *The Harder They Come*
and to the Rolling Stones and to Marvin Gaye and to the first Devo record,
which I smuggled in and was allowed to play sometimes, earning in the
process a nickname from my father's best friend, Roy Pingel: he called
me the Headman. As the Headman I became the mascot dancer of a band
in my high school, three brothers and a bass player named Blake Sloane,
a blue-eyed soul group who called themselves Miller, Miller, Miller and
Sloane. Their hit song, "Funky Family," a Jackson-5-ish A-side, was probably the song to which the Headman laboriously discovered his body—
I danced to it at high school parties and alone in my room, wearing out
several copies of the Miller brothers' parent-financed 45. I was or wanted

Miller, Miller, Miller and Sloane. Photo by Leo Sorel.

to be Miller, Miller, Miller and Sloane's Fifth Beatle, the evidence of their groove, and so at our high school's auditorium but also at an opening slot at CBGB's I danced in some area closer to the band than the the rest of the audience of my schoolmates—who were as much their whole audience at CBGB's as they were in our high school auditorium—my vicariousness charted in real space. But I never pretended I was in the band—Miller, Miller, Miller and Sloane's perfect name spoke of the inalterable sense of their lineup.

The height of my dancing—the apogee, as I like to think of it—came in a club called Berkeley Square, in 1990 or '91. It was a day I'd spent free of my retail job, a day I'd spent at home discovering some new level of what my words could do—at the time I was writing a novel called *As She Climbed across the Table*, a book I associate with my learning to take command of my sentences, to make them dance the way I wanted them to. In the evening I went out dancing with some friends. In the middle of a strenuous sequence of songs Prince's "Kiss" came on, and in letting that song take me over, course through my body like a drug, with my dancing perhaps perfectly poised between savvy intention and callow frenzy, my knees and my head and what lay between all about as limber and aligned as my savvy and callow and frenzied sentences had been earlier that day, I found myself pretty sure that I was dancing, say, just about as well as anyone ever had. In fact I had the thought at that moment that there might be my equal at sentence writing roaming the earth, somewhere, might be even a few of them out there, and that the same could be said of my dancing, that I might not be the only dancer working at such a high level at this moment in the planet's history, but that certainly there was no one alive who could both write and dance the way I had that day. And I'm still almost convinced of it, I am.

The terms "jazz" and "rock and roll," as a great man once pointed out, are only blues musicians' slang for fucking. The whole history of pop, the half-century or more of intricate delirium is, in other words, a joke about fucking, but for me it is a joke I grew up inside, a joke that was also a day-dream, a shaggy-dog story, a surrealist fable like *Alice in Wonderland* or *The Phantom Tollbooth*, depicting an alternate reality of jokes taken with scrupulous deadpan, a world I wanted to climb inside and flesh out with my own yearning, a realm between audience and band that seemed as sacred as both and perhaps more sacred than either one. In other words, it's a bloody miracle I didn't turn out a rock critic. I'm still not entirely sure how I evaded the honor.

When I was younger it was hard for me to keep the future and the past from collapsing—I persistently mixed up astronauts and dinosaurs, for instance. It was hard for me, too, thanks to the bohemian demimonde in which I dwelled, the milieu of my parents and their friends, all of them with their astonishingly valuable and mistreated record collections, to believe, for instance, that Bob Dylan and Beatles were not about fifty or a hundred years old, as canonical as F. Scott Fitzgerald or Walt Whitman, as revered as Thomas Jefferson or Abraham Lincoln. The first time I learned there were human beings still alive—some of them my aunts and uncles—who still thought of rock and roll as "that noise," I laughed, feeling a kind of slaphappy disbelief. I was pretty sure everybody, for instance, knew that Paul wasn't "really" dead, but knew that some people had believed so, for a while. And the quest for the identity of the "Fifth Beatle," which seemed to me an allegory of authenticity and collective identity as deep as a Zen koan, represented an attempt to understand the world I'd been born into. The Fifth Beatle in particular haunted me like a ghost of crime, a Ross MacDonald investigation, where the façade of a life in the present peels away to expose the wild truths of the past, the impostures—some of them brave, some shameful—on which our contemporary reality was founded.

Who was "Murray the K"? What was payola? Do you mean to tell me that someone had to be paid to play rock and roll on the radio, that something unfair occurred, that the music had bought its way into our hearts? The idea of payola was in itself easy to conflate with the idea of "the hook," or the "irresistible hit record," or "Beatlemania" itself, the sense that pop was a kind of trick, a perverse revenge against the banality of daily life dreamed up collectively by ten or fifteen Delta bluesmen and a million or a hundred million screaming fourteen-year-old girls. Maybe if a rock-and-roll chorus, a killer hook was like a bullet or a drug or a virus—and payola therefore was a kind of gun or hypodermic needle, designed to penetrate a resistant culture—then we all lived in a world permanently drugged or psychedelically sick with fever, or dead and dreaming, like characters in a Philip K. Dick novel.

If so, I was grateful to live on the drugged, feverish, or dead side of the historical trauma. On the side of conspiracy theories stood Sutcliffe, Best, Epstein, Voorman, Preston, this sequence of suspects who were also victims, seeming to indict the magic circle of four heroes of some wrongdoing or at least misrepresentation. But these "Fifth Beatles" also seemed confirm the four in their status as iconic survivors—probably no one else deserved to be a Beatle, that might be the answer. And Bob Dylan, as Jimi Hendrix apparently knew, was your grandmother—full of gravelly authority and punitive conscience, nowhere near as fun, but titanically arresting—he was your grandmother in a wolf's costume for certain.

But soon enough I, too, was engaged in a kind of game of reverent skepticism, a weird pursuit of exposing the flimsiness of the cartoon world I loved, as if testing its authority. I remember the day I learned Ringo's drumming was "bad." So bad Paul had done some of it for him. Then—I recall it as if it was the very next thing I learned, like geometry leading to algebra—I read somewhere the beautiful thought that Ringo's role was to be our surrogate in the band, the Beatle who was also a fan of Beatles, in awe of the "real ones" from the nearest possible proximity. So maybe there was no Fifth Beatle, maybe there wasn't even a fourth! It was somehow inevitable to note next that George was given a free ride in the other songwriters' wake (yet you also could sense he was stunted or thwarted or cheated).

John explained bitterly that he wrote the hook to "Taxman," George's "best" song, just as Ray Davies was quick to note he helped his brother with "Death of a Clown," Dave Davies's greatest hit. So the sham notion of a "democracy of talent" within these great groups, with its analogous utopian implications for collective action, for a gestalt mind as depicted in Theodore Sturgeon's *More Than Human*, could dissolve into sour cynicism: the presiding genius probably could have done just as well with any other supporting cast. Or paradoxically, the reverse: the urge to pronounce the solo careers so thin and cheesy that the magic was proven to be in the lucky conjunction of a bunch of ordinary blokes, raised temporarily above their station as much by history and our love as by any personal agency: if there wasn't a Beatles we would have had to invent one, and perhaps we did. Maybe the search for the Fifth Beatle was always destined to end, like the list of Time Magazine's Person of the Year, with the conclusion that the Fifth Beatle is YOU. For evidence, one only needs to listen to *The Beatles at the Hollywood Bowl*—here was music content to ride like a froth of sea foam atop a tsunami wave of adulation and yearning for, well, itself. What were little-girl screams if not the essential heart of Beatles' true sound, the human voice in a karaoke track consisting of the band itself? Getting by with a little help from my friends, indeed. Oh, and Dylan? A study of his sources reveals he was always just the guy who happened to be smart enough to steal Jon Pankake's record collection— literally a music writer's daydream run mad.

Our urge to expose the trick is bound up in our mad love at being tricked, a kind of revenge of the seduced, and simultaneously a projection of our knowing selves into the space between the singer and the song. Jim Morrison and Michael Stipe, unmusical jesters, posturing poets, charlatans—yet imagine their bands shorn of them, and maybe you're left with only forgettable garage rock outfits, nobody Chuck Berry couldn't hustle up in time to play a quick gig and then steal back out of town. In fact, I watched the Chuck Berry documentary *Hail! Hail! Rock 'n' Roll!* again recently and was struck by it as a kind of masochistic orgy of deconstruction, a taunt to the audience's regard for this so-called art form. Here's Keith Richards, hastening to expose the very Stones themselves as nothing but an accretion of Chuck Berry licks, and here's the man himself, so unimpressed by what his followers have wrought that he can't even seem to pay full attention. The film is constructed as a detective story, a series of clues leading to Johnnie Johnson, the piano player whose chords Berry transposed to create his great hooks, so that all of rock and roll is revealed as inconsequential at its birth, a handful of copped stride-piano flourishes. Berry presents a nihilistic face, utterly destructive of his own legend, and by the time of the climactic concert, the hapless and poignant Julian Lennon is brought out for our inspection as a good-enough John substitute—"He looks and sounds just like his father," Berry asserts, and we're horrified to find ourselves in agreement. Then Robert Cray is celebrated by Berry as looking just like *him*—like Chuck Berry. As these ersatz figures parade we're pretty sure the film has confirmed the triple collapse of, at least, Beatles, Stones, and Berry, and as the depressingly complacent middle-aged audience confirms, there's nothing left to do but party.

As the men who play on stage with him will hasten to explain to you—and believe, they did so to me, to a man, from the young and the old in his last road band, to former star performers like Fred Wesley, James Brown is, sadly, *not a musician*. Those devoted and long-suffering players, all of whom also revere their boss as a creator and star beyond all comparison, have confessed how they always sniggered into their sleeves during his agonizing and agonized organ solos. Here was the Godfather of Soul, the unmistakable pioneer of our whole rhythmscape, derided as a kind of fake by his own collaborators, a half-assed Beethoven propped up by his orchestra.

In this role, weirdly, Brown's greatness is actually confirmed, since the notion of Brown as a kind of charlatan-presider over music he could never play himself exactly describes his role as bridge between the clown-jazz figures of Louis Jordan and Cab Calloway and the hip-hop musicians whose world he brought into being, as the scatting, grunting foreground presence against a landscape of sonic astonishments. The showman whose exhortations and shouts of surprise at the virtuousity of the soloists mark him as an MC or DJ who inserted himself into the band, a figure of pure will and egotism, distinct from the audience in terms not so much musical as Nietzschean. He'd better be able to dance like a motherfucker to dare to take that half-vicarious role in our steads—dance, or else scream, or suffer, or make us suffer, or even better, all of the above. This too is where the figure of the punk from hell, the Iggy Pop or Sid Vicious whose authority derives from his ineptitude, spontaneity, embarrassment, and pain, can weirdly seem an allegory for the whole history of pop itself—

these three chords, these cheesy riffs, this off-key singing, this doggerel poetry, all of it, somehow, a bluesman's or jazz man's joke taken way too seriously.

A real music would have some modesty, and we'd have a proper reverence for its history, a proper sense of its distance from ourselves. Our pop life, then, may be exactly described by the collapse of musical expertise into raw expression—even when it makes use of expertise and skirts collapse. The collapse of singing into screaming, even when it's only the possibility of screaming, or the audience's screaming, or the guitar's.

This too is why our pop life seems at every possible turn surrounded by the gestures of the pretender, the charlatan, those who dwell in the ocean of the vicarious in which these tender artifacts, these hit records and the stars who make them, swim: the maker of mix tapes who believes he is in some way to credit for the beauty of the music, and who is somehow believed by his lover, the child stars and karaoke stars and American Idols whose degraded and ludicrous projection guiltily thrills us, the lip-synchers and air guitarists and mirror stars, the singers of those off-key Studio One covers of Motown songs, transcribed from the radio with the lyrics wrong, yet always somehow the equal or surpasser of their originals, the one-shot bands, the garage bands, the party bands that luck into a contract, even, that horror, the *critics'* band, Lester Bangs or Yo La Tengo. Even, dare I say it, this present furshlugginer enterprise of scholarship and enshrinement, those of us who stand here because we've kidded ourselves our dancing or our writing, or both, makes us something like rock stars, somehow fit to slip into Wonderland—we Fifth Beatles, we happy fakes. We're a bunch of smartasses, you and me, but that's just to cover our embarrassment at how much we believe. For this whole story really is a naked egalitarian dream, isn't it?

Greg Tate

Black Rockers vs. Blackies Who Rock,

or The Difference between Race and Music

F irst time I ever saw the term "Black Rock" was back in 1972. My mother was given a stack of new Stax Volt albums by a friend who worked at the label and these included the Bar-Kays' album of the same name. That record was filled with some remarkably taut and complex psychedelic guitar solos and some still-bitching acid-soul arrangements of originals and chestnuts by many of the same Memphis musicians who would grace Isaac Hayes's *Shaft* soundtrack that year as well. I was already a veteran fan of Black psychedelia by that point, having been mesmerized by Norman Whitfield's productions for Temptations and by Sly Stone's late sixties hits like "Dance to the Music" and "Hot Fun in the Summertime." Without quite knowing why, I adopted all these things as *my* music, the way teenagers will—largely because there was something in them, and in jazz by the following year, which corresponded to my previous interests in science fiction novels, horror movies, and the black liberation movement. My older sister, who would soon exile herself from the States for twenty years and join an African liberation movement in Angola called the MPLA, had music she considered hers too and it was called Motown; my mother, who was a member of and helped form an African American cultural center in our hometown of Dayton, Ohio, also had her own hot picks—Nina Simone, Otis Redding, and the speeches of Malcolm X being what

she kept on heavy rotation during my wonder years. Later she would introduce me to Fela and to reggae through the politically de rigeur soundtrack
to *The Harder They Come*. My younger brother Brian, who would later become one of Washington, D.C.'s first hardcore Black punks, also discovered music he felt quite attached to in the seventies, by Led Zeppelin,
Queen, and Sparks—the last of which is the only music I've ever heard
that has made me want to do violence to another human being.

In any event the paradigmatic changing of the guard in soul presaged
by Sly Stone and in jazz by Miles Davis set the tempo for much of my
serious music researches in the seventies. Possibly because I was in transition from sci fi nerd to Black Music Nationalist I was drawn to whatever I thought was avant-garde Black pop back in those days. Largely this
meant a favoring of bands over singers, instrumental improvisations over
songs, and Miles Davis over everybody, even God, Jesus, the Devil, and
my mama. Around the same time I became an avid reader of what we'll
lovingly call the Whiteboy Rock Criticism Tradition as portrayed in *Rolling Stone* and *Creem*. The strange thing is that I probably enjoyed reading
rock criticism as much or more than I did listening to most rock music
in the seventies. Partly this was because I quickly became a jazz and funk
snob after discovering music I could call my own—music that spoke to
my existential condition as a nascent Black bohemian nationalist book-
worm growing up ensconced in Washington, D.C.'s upper-middle-class
upper-northwest Gold and Platinum coasts of the seventies. This being
the post–Black Power seventies when class differences were rendered all
but invisible by an all inclusive hyperblack communalism, I never felt like
my music wasn't the music of my working-class peers at Paul Junior High
and Coolidge High School. In point of fact at Coolidge the two biggests
thugs at the school were also the biggest David Bowie and Kiss fans—this
reflecting, I'd later discover, a longstanding and still standing tradition
in the Black community of hardcore street hustlers, pimps, and players
being devout audiences for well-turned cross-dressing musical caba-
ret. That these two schoolyard bullies would later also become devout,
tambourine-rattling, Bhagavad Gita–peddling Hare Krishna is a riddle to
which perhaps only *The Autobiography of Malcolm X* may provide answers.
Everybody's got a little light under the sun.

Up until punk and Prince broke in the early eighties I largely kept up
with white rock music through whiteboy rock criticism, mainly because
by the time Miles retired in 1976 and George Clinton abandoned Funka-

delic for Parliament in 1977, the only music which I was proud to call my own was D.C. go-go, the Sun Ra Arkestra, and the new avant-garde jazz coming out of New York from the transplanted likes of David Murray, Butch Morris, Art Ensemble of Chicago, Oliver Lake, and Julius Hemphill. This avoidance of all things popular changed somewhat when reggae and dub rushed in to fill the void left after African American rockheads got subsumed by discomania. I got suddenly hip to Bob Marley, Peter Tosh, Steel Pulse, Black Uhuru, Black Slate, Aswad, U-Roy, Linton Kwesi Johnson, Dennis Bovell, Judy Mowatt, and so on.

The first time I ever saw rock criticism matter to anyone in the business of actually producing Black rock was in 1984 when Prince released the *1999* album with his "All the Critics Love You in New York" joint on it. This scathing recognition of the critical establishment would later be echoed in the text of the music by Public Enemy in the songs "Bring the Noise" and "Don't Believe the Hype." By the time *1999* came out I was a critic living in New York, writing things that provoked Chuck D to denounce me from the stage as a "*Village Voice* porch monkey" and for the Red Hot Chili Peppers' Flea to command his audience to beat my ass if I was found in attendance. I was, and pointed myself out, but unfortunately no one stepped forth to deliver the requested critical beatdown.

Now the point of all this is that when Vernon Reid called me one fine August morning in 1985 to help him call a meeting about the plight of the Black Rocker I didn't know there was such a creature in such a crisis. What I did know then and still feel now is that Blackfolk like me who grooved to whiteboy rock criticism still felt that whiteboy rock critics often didn't get it right when it came to writing about Black music. It was largely this belief that compelled me, Nelson George, and Barry Michael Cooper to try and become music critics at the *Village Voice*.

We all came to realize that the culture of rock criticism practiced at the *Village Voice* under Dean Robert Christgau's capo regime was the only place where young Black intellects such as ourselves could have written our best work on the Black music we loved in the 1980s. Largely this is because high-handed, no-holds-barred, and radical cultural criticism did not have a place in the Black popular press of the period, even though it was bursting out of the pores of Black feminist and gay literary culture of the seventies and eighties, and had been a strong feature of pre–civil rights era Black journalism dating back to the 1890s. Point being that, as a Black writer serious about Black popular music discourse, rock criticism was the only club that would have my irreverent, neologistic, avant-garde-art-damaged ass at the beginning of my career.

. . . . .

So everybody talks about Blackies Who Rock but nobody does anything about 'em. Or at least nobody did until that fateful Friday the 13th back in August of 1985 when Vernon Reid gathered Craig Street, Konda Mason, Geri Allen, Melvin Gibbs, and yours truly together to listen to Sir Reid gripe about the plight of the Black rock musician in a post-punk MTV hairband crossover R&B world that acted like we were all supposed to get lighter skin, a perm, and sound like Prince, Michael Jackson, and Lionel Richie knockoffs.

Somewhere around the second hour we got the idea that he needed to stop bitching and we become a proactive musical action group with a firebrand manifesto and a self-determination race music agenda à la Chicago's AACM —they of Great Black Music, "Ancient and to the Future" fame. The first political act of the Black Rock Coalition was to throw an Xmas season social molotov we called, with D.C.'s Troublefunk in mind, our "Drop the Bomb Party." The BRC's first official poster for the jam featured a screaming Little Richard emblazoned over the Japanese symbol of the rising sun. GOOD GOLLY MISS BANZAI-A-WHOOOOO.

"Rock and roll is black music and we are its heirs!" we so proudly declared in our first Black Pantherish platform manifesto. This at a time when manufactured racial and sexual ambiguity, in the style of those canny supermacho supersavvy crossover queens Prince and Michael Jackson, seemed the only way for a Black man to get a song with a long guitar solo on the radio. These were also of course those long gone daze when rock was corporate music's king and major record companies and radio got to pretty much make or break rock and roll careers. We defined white rock as whitefolk having the industry-supported freedom to pimp any derivation of Black music they chose and be promoted to the widest possible demographic imaginable à la jazzy Sting, vogueing-ass Madonna, and jungle-juking nigger-knocking Guns N' Roses.

We further went on to declare that Black music, contrary to popular beliefs held at the time held by the major labels' Black departments (yet another happily bygone product of a bygone age), was a music to be defined by far more than whatever Anita Baker, Lionel Richie, and good ole Luther Van were doing. For some reason this sly and provocative bit of reasoning got us labeled troublemakers and considered somewhat toxic by several prominent pop musicians then trying to make an untroubled living in a tribally segregated music market. For this reason the membership of the early BRC was filled with more civilians than veteran musicians—a working-class and professional-class coterie of students, teachers, city adminstrators, and investment bankers, all drawn by our bold program of a full-frontal black cultural assault on rock hegemony. Best part about this more-real-folk-than-apolitical-artiste phase of the BRC was finding out you weren't the only Black nerd who listened to Bowie and read Marvel Comics assiduously.

Now the second best part about the early daze of the BRC did not turn out to be shooting at those turkeys in a barrel known as A&R men, colored and non. No, the second best part was putting on multiband festival style shows at (blessed be that defunkt and hallowed hall) CBGB's. Three-day affairs featuring innovative upstart bands nobody had ever heard of and nobody ever will, like the Deed and the Uptown Atomics. These events also made predominantly audiences from Brooklyn, the Bronx, and Harlem swell the joint like it was the 1930s Savoy Ballroom during the Chick Webb versus Cab Calloway battle of the bands era.

We also in this time instituted the notion of Black Rock as a genre with a historic orchestral repertory through the creation of our Black Rock Orchestra—a roving conceptual ensemble whose repertoire over the last twenty-five years has come to comprise the composers James Brown, Public Enemy, Abbey Lincoln, Max Roach, Sly Stone, Jimi Hendrix, Mandrill, War, Grace Jones, X-Ray Spex, John Coltrane, Arthur Blythe, Joan Armatrading, Big Mama Thornton, Sister Rosetta Tharpe, Stevie Wonder, P-Funk, Robert Johnson, Elizabeth Cotton, Art Ensemble of Chicago, Robert Pete Williams, Nona Hendryx, Betty Davis, Nina Simone, and Earth, Wind & Fire, etc., etc. Future programs are set to cover the musics of Fela, Chaka Khan, and Sun Ra. Making us about the most historicizing freeform formalist interventionist canon-formation-ing furthermuckers in the history of live as opposed to virtual Afrofuturizm. . . .

The eclectic and Afrocentric nature of our rock canon versus others you may have encountered is due to the fact that the BRC was formed by people who grew up in the post–Black Power seventies when all the Blackfolk you knew who loved music listened to everything from Pharoah Sanders, Eddie Palmieri, and Johnny Guitar Watson to Yes, Joni Mitchell, and the Rolling Stones on a daily basis, and you could hear all of it on the radio and in concert without much hardly trying. I recently shocked the hell out of the Roots' Questlove by telling him that back in the day it was pretty normal for a typical concert bill to feature Weather Report, Last Poets, Betty Davis, and Bobby Womack on the same bill. What shocked Ahmir even more than the lineup was the fact that the audiences of the day actually liked all those things at the same time—as if today the audience for such a show would show up repping for opposing genres.

One of the saddest ironies of hip-hop of course is that a genre built on the broadest array of global, historic, technological, and stylistic sonic sources imaginable has come to produce a young Black popular listenership with, largely speaking, the narrowest musical taste imaginable. There are many superstructural explanations for this closing off of the young Black American musical mind that one could cite—the educational system, the political economy of broadcast media, hypercapitalist artificial scarcity, age-old American anti-intellectualism, the death of rhythm and blues, and so forth. All relevant and likely true, though I also think there's an existential, endangered species element in there as well: a primal, erasure-anxiety future-shock-ridden response to the recognition that hip-hop is the only place that being Black and loud, or as the old folks used to say "loud and niggerish" (as in "Stop being so . . ."), still matters as a racial marker in American life and as one that can be racially, sonically, bodily owned by young American Blackfolk in the public sphere.

It's for this reason I believe that the most liberated, liberating, and electrifying movement going on in hip-hop culture today is not musical or sonic but choreographic—a project of self-definition through organized freestyle group movement that actually has little to no chance of ever securing much in the way of corporate support (a few recent and rather lame Hollywood dance movies notwithstanding). At any given moment in African diasporic history I think the most creative inventive and rebellious spirits of their generation gravitate toward mediums where they can have the maximum amount of unlicensed, libidinous self-determination and blast forth from the head of the next zeitgeist. For the current generation (meaning young Blackfolk born after 1977), I think those zeitgeist mediums are turning out to be vernacular group dance, the international visual art system, and the most polyglot arenas of alternative rock. The recent critical and relative market appeal of race-forward alt-rock bands such as TV On The Radio, Santigold, Bloc Party, M.I.A., Dragons of Zynth, and Apollo Heights echoes if not predicted an emergent American racial zeitgeist that has become clear after the election of Barack Obama—that victory itself a testament to how much terrain Black nerds can now freely occupy and even flourish in within domains of cultural and political influence once considered the sole province and patrimony of guess who, yes that's right, him, the goddamned White Man.

The critical distinction between these bands and the definitive Black musical nerds of my generation, namely Bad Brains, Fishbone, and Living Colour, is that [suddenly everyone leans forward, pregnant pause for effect, milk the tension] they seem to have absolutely no interest in becoming musical virtuosos who can play anything three times better than anybody Black or white within a ten-thousand-mile-square radius. This indeed represents a paradigmatic shift. For as long as I can remember every conceptual breakthrough in Black music has been accompanied by a new superhuman evolution in technique and virtuosity of some kind— hip-hop in fact brought us five new standards for prowess—breakdancing, turntablism, beatboxing, MC-ing, and spraycan writing—wholly new mediums for human mastery with no room for squares or the mechanically inept anywhere in there. I don't think this has ever been a virtuosity for virtuosity's sake thing but a virtuosity of expressive necessity—to say everything that demanded to be spoken about Black consciousness in any given era when the social space allowed Black bodies, minds, spirits was otherwise infinitely more circumscribed. All these folk I mentioned also lack a definitive low-end—they are also, whatever else they are doing, not kicking much bass. Their Black sonic modernity is soulful and vocal in ways not far removed from seventies alt-soul but is also removed from any requirement to make the church say amen. In this way these acts and their predominantly whiteboy'n'girl congregations do echo the racialized artist-audience ratio of most well-known jazz musicians of the past forty years, neo-bop and free.

My best friend's father was a high school basketball coach who loved to say, "They don't pay niggas to sit on the bench." A truism of the pre-nineties sports industry, this brash retort means Black athletes only got paid gazillions to produce physically verifiable miracles—a notion somewhat still true throughout professional American sports, the past decade of the New York Knicks notwithstanding. What's relatively fascinating about the Black nerds movement in rock is that they have vital contemporary things to say about Black consciousness and Black expressivity in this historic moment that do not radically elevate or aesthetically transform the alt-rock genre but do shift it in palpable ways by being themselves, Black, free, and intellectually sexy. What they do all bring to the table that most certainly seems rooted in Black music tradition is a very refined and highhanded sense of individuality and self-definition largely lacking in contemporary Black pop's more conservative modes of jazz, hip-hop, gospel, and soul. What they are all virtuosos at is being completely themselves in music and performance, which by today's standards of cookie-cutter Black pop success is damn near a revolutionary act.

. . . . .

Addendum: In my experience, there are two kinds of colored folk: Black Rockers and Blackies Who Rock. The distinction is between those who'd gladly join the Black Rock Coalition or openly claim Afro-punk affiliation, and malcontents who're such badass renegade punk-rock furthermuckers that they'd never join the only club that would have them, and would rather badmouth your mama in print.

I've had to think about this again recently for two reasons. First came Ann Powers's astute and timely *L.A. Times* response to Sasha Frere-Jones's mock-lament in *The New Yorker* about the whiteness of indie rock, wherein Ann informs us that the indie "scene" — largely defined as the five bands that at any moment five paler-skinned critics say matter — has never been more integrated, more *infested* with people of color who all serve as some critic's "darkling": Bloc Party, TV On The Radio, M.I.A., Santogold, Lightspeed Champion, Apollo Heights, Earl Greyhound, Saul Williams, Dragons of Zynth, the Dears, the Noisettes, or Yeah Yeah Yeahs. (Hell, yeah, I'm even claiming Karen O's half-Korean, half-glamazon behind, just because.) Now, most of these people I would say fall into the category of Negroes Who Rock: Black people whose rock trip is more aesthetically than racially motivated, identified, or contextualized. Being a Black bohemian nationalist Libra from the seventies, I'm down with whatever kinda proracial, aracial, transracial rock 'n' roll negroid you wanna be, so long as you're out there spanking that ass.

Howsomever: The second reason I've been musing about race rock of late is because of good brother Bad Brains bassist Darryl Jenifer's recent interview in *Stop Smiling*: a far more problematic text for this pundit than Frere-Jones's coy teapot tempest. This would be the one where Frere Jenifer gets drawn into some low-rent divide-and-conquer slamming of the BRC and Afro-punk, where he says he's always considered himself more punk rock than Black. Cool, all good, if that's your thing, man. But yo, Darryl: claiming the BRC and by default any African American self-determination movement evinces a "slave mentality" seems roughly akin to claiming that the sixties set Blackfolk back four hundred years. WTF, Darryl? So solidarity and pan-African collectivism in the pursuit of justice is okay for Rasta, but not Rastus? Furthermore, why even bother claiming Jimi Hendrix didn't directly influence you like these "black-rock type dudes" you now disparage? So what? At this stage of history, that's like saying you're not affected by the air you breathe. You live in the same post-Hendrix noise continuum as the rest of us, bruh. And there's no escaping it.

But whatever, I was about to let it all pass—water under the bridge and all that—because it's Darryl, and Bad Brains are the sonic symphonic architects of hardcore, and Dr. Know played on BRC events from damn near the giddy-up—except then the low-rent bee-atch bushwacker interviewer, one Daemon Lockjaw or some such, decides that Darryl's given him license to proclaim that the BRC has put on bands *only* because they were Black—as if the history of rock, like the history of America, isn't the history of mediocre Caucasoids being put on just because they weren't colored. Now never mind that both BRC and Afro-punk ain't no cult-nationalist social clubs, but just a means to present Black bands who rock to Black people who care worldwide—never mind that I've yet to see much advantage to anybody's career come from being associated with either group. Attack the cultural politics of BRC all you want, but don't even try and diminish damn near a quarter-century of music and struggle with some offhand, unsubstantiated, random race-baiting piffle. I'm like, "Give me names and dates, you low-rent sniveling neocolonialist wankster, then let's go settle this like gentlemen down a blind alley somewhere." But then I thought, no, in this year of the Obama, I want to be a healer, not a death-dealer/fearless vampire killer—I want to be audacious with my hope for the future of *all* Black Rockers and Negroes Who Rock Out, divisive diseased duppy conquistadors be damned! And thanks to YouTube, I have become very optimistic about the prospects for same.

People frequently ask me, "Greg, how do you do it—how do you keep up with all this new music, you crusty, fifty-year-old Harlem hermit, you?" Well, having hip, wide-open-eared young people in your life—like my twenty-seven-year-old daughter and the prescient, erudite *Vibe* staffer Linda "Hollywood" Hobbs—helps, but what helps even more is YouTube.

Verily, I declare that 2007 will go down in Tate musical history as the year I spent more time with YouTube than my iPod. The beauty of this site—and I drop this pearl more for my fellow Net-aphobic quinquagenarians than anyone else—is that anytime anybody said some newjack was hot to death (Lil Mama, Lil Wayne, Arcade Fire, the Decemberists, Estelle, Santogold, Silversun Pickups, Lupe Fiasco), I could just click in and do a quick, discerning survey. Because for sure, who but Davids Byrne and Bowie (along with my man Christgau) have maintained the time-consuming desire or inclination after the age of forty to obsessively seek out reams of whole new music *albums*? On the other hand, who doesn't have time to dip into a music video? For all those getting up there in dog years like *moi*, you can now go down the Top 20 list of all those artists and albums in this year's Pazz & Jop that you ain't never heard of, run 'em through YouTube, and in twenty minutes be straight for the year so far as being caught up on "new" music goes.

That said, I've also pursued other, more nostalgic, more classical passions at the site: vintage clips of Marvin, Curtis, Gladys (with and without the Pips), Phyllis Hyman, Marilyn McCoo and the Fifth Dimension, the Friends of Distinction, the Delfonics, and Chic. Plus Inner City (see "Good Life"), and 2 Puerto Ricans, a Black Man & a Dominican (see "Do It Properly"). Plus Otis Rush, Son House, the Bar-Kays, and Ronnie Laws. I was also glued to ten-minute chunks of hour-long Cecil Taylor solo piano concerts, and ten-episode Miles Davis concerts in his '69 *Bitches Brew* prime. Not to mention the Coltrane Quartet killing "Vigil" in '65, or Charlie Parker grinning at Buddy Rich. Or Ella, Sarah, Andrew Hill, Art Ensemble of Chicago, Joe Henderson, Tony Williams with Stan Getz in '71, Don Cherry with Sonny Rollins in '59, the entire Les McCann/Eddie Harris *Swiss Movement* concert, and yeah, Jimi Jimi Jimi James James James, plus forty years' worth of the P-Funk All-Stars, Bad Brains (still my heroes), Fishbone, and the Wu-Tang Clan in Paris. In a nutshell, YouTube is where Real Black Music still lives, people: all kinds of Black music, in the most high-tech, twenty-first-century frame imaginable.

Of course, YouTube also has that clip of two girls gone wild for feces, but what could define American democracy more than Marilyn McCoo and Cecil Taylor sharing the same space as that shit? This is the best justification yet for the very invention of the Internet.

That said, Black Rockers (or Negroes Who Rock) need our *own* Pazz & Jop, and really our own *Village Voice* and our own Grammies, and of course our own extraterrestrial galaxy far, far away. If only because I'd love to show and tell the good news to all those other Black people who *don't* rock, but are maybe open to hearing something musical from American-raised colored folk other than Beyoncé, Rihanna, Jay-Z, or Soulja Boy. Because such folk need—nay, *deserve*—to know how stupendously, consistently genius MeShell Ndegeocello's *The World Has Made Me the Man of My Dreams* is, or how tantalizingly terrifying Game Rebellion's (FYI: the heir apparent to the Bad Brains/Living Colour/Public Enemy/Rage Against The Machine mantle) *In Search of Rick Rubin* mixtape is, or what a galvanizing comeback the Family Stand's *Super Sol Nova* became. Or what a stone-cold genius freak singer-songwriter Lightspeed Champion must be to have crossbred Elvis Costello, Arthur Lee, and Jim Henson. Or what a super-stylish punk-rockitude stage animal Noisettes bassist/singer Shingai Shoniwa beez, or what a noisefest Trent Reznor cohort and word magician Saul Williams devised for *The Rise and Liberation of Niggy Tardust* (with all due praises to local guitar hero Jerome Jordan for that pun, tho'). Finally, praise those fools Apollo Heights for finally getting that album out and going head to head with MeShell for album title of the year with *White Music for Black People*, maybe the best Zen koan to come out of the whole rock 'n' roll nigra experience, like, ever. (Speaking of Zen, somebody toss ECM a bone for finally, thirty-three years late, rereleasing Bennie Maupin's gorgeous Afro-Buddhist gem *The Jewel in the Lotus*, featuring his Herbie Hancock Sextant bandmates; ditto to the Norwegians for also rebooting Dewey Redman's *The Struggle Continues*, both of which, alas, still sound like the future of jazz rather than the jazz of Xmas past. Honorable mentions need also go out to Maya Azucena's *Junkyard Jewel*, Imani Uzuri's *Her Holy Water*, and Felice Rosser for her band Faith's *A Space Where Love Can Grow*.)

Finally, there's Feist, neither Black nor a non sequitur here. Like Joni Mitchell back in the day, she came into my life through other Black people—not *Rolling Stone*, *Spin*, *Pitchfork*, or whatever. Specifically, she came through my partners/bandmates Jeremiah (a New England Conservatory–trained opera singer turned twenty-first-century soul man) and D-Maxx (a Brooklyn MC turned interdisciplinary performance artist), both of whom threw Feist on the van system during a Burnt Sugar road trip and chatted her up like she was the second coming of *something*, and made me reckon with her wry, jazzy, and whimsical (no easy combo) storytelling prowess. Then, just today, as if to prove my suspicion that

Feist is so white she's Black (as my aceboon AJ once said about Andy Warhol), our MySpace page got a friend request from one Joseph Démé, a singer in Burkina Faso who has Feist high up in his otherwise quite pan-Africanist list of friends. Like Joni before her, Feist's strange charms also extend to soothing the Original Man.

Now, I'm still trying to figure out the hoopla over lcd Soundsystem, but I remain quite comfortable holding down the minority opinion on that one up in this piece. Maybe I'll give those YouTube testimonials one more shot. . . .

Alexandra T. Vazquez

Toward an Ethics of Knowing Nothing

To know nothing is an accusation forced upon certain critics, typically those who will never be consulted as experts. Many are leveled with this charge at an early age during their earliest experiences in a record store. Suspiciously there for too long in sections that might not match up with their outsides, these nascent theorists are asked versions of the same question: "What are you doing here?" Later, there are material implications. Those who know nothing go unnoticed, underpublished, underemployed. They sit at the seminar table uncalled on. They simply won't do as reliable sources. And yet, to be a nonexpert—a position that can be forced and/or chosen—is a location of possibility: you can get involved with the connoisseur's discarded objects, throw stones from the journalistic outside, enjoy the hung-over delirium of Sunday morning conference panels. Knowing nothing is not for everyone: it requires you to be comfortable being uncomfortable, open to the unpredictable, entertained when left out of conversation, secure with what you can't know, and quite often, broke.

To be a music critic is to dedicate yourself, monklike, to a life of knowing nothing. Think of all those times you weren't ready to hear something, or when a particular sound comes into your life *only* when you have gone through a bit of training. It is why João Gilberto is better appreciated with age. There are all those encounters with unfamiliar sounds that have a tendency to produce the most obvious sensations of knowing nothing. It is during these moments that some—those who feel only discomfort in igno-rance—react with fear and violence. Remember, for example, the mob antics of the Disco Sucks riots. It is no wonder that the music industry attempts to anesthetize such reactions by distributing "World Music" in cartoonish, kid-friendly packaging so as not to disturb the geographical status quo.

Forgive the reiteration of what we all know, or should know, to be true. Although "living with music" (as Ellison put it) means to be open to the unheard-of, to be caught unawares and struck dumb, musical criticism has produced some of the most intense discourses of mastery out there.[1] A knowing everything. My refusal to belabor the foregoing is a selfish one, for I can trace a direct correlation between my involvement with music criticism and a sudden development of acid reflux. While the different manifestations of knowing everything about music might all be gener-alized as means to power, I'd rather not reduce their reasons for deploy-ment. Sometimes knowing everything is a strategy, say, when you flex your knowledge of stereo equipment in front of a group of unsuspecting boys. Nor do I underestimate how knowing everything might offer pro-tective cover on a dance floor or in front of a classroom.

I'd nevertheless like to point out a few forms that knowing everything can take in musical criticism. There is the temporal condition: knowing everything as shaped by time constraints that require fast opinions. Jour-nalistic deadlines quite literally contour conditions of living and thinking. One's job can depend upon knowing everything (or at least pretending to) about a something (of which they often know nothing) by press time. There is what I like to call the capital gain model. Some will skillfully per-form legible erudition to secure resources. Those who have this dexterity are able to land jobs and win grants. There is the evidence safeguard mode that gives those with seemingly unchecked access to musicians and musi-cal spaces some pretty heavy insularity from critique. They are equipped to use the horse's mouth and/or the experience of "being there" to keep your doubt in check. Finally, there is the attempt to subjugate commodi-ties as proof of a knowing everything. Collectors' collections are virile ex-tensions of musical cunning. And just as plastic guards their LPs, you are not allowed to touch them—lest you get them dirty, imprint yourself, or put them back in the wrong place.

And yet, throughout time there has always been a rumbling of crit-ics—a hum you could imagine coming from underground rivers—that has long anticipated and responded to this mastery. These critics might not be legible or cited enough or published, but that is often because they do not waste time asking for inclusion.[2] They run deep under the landscape, keeping their currents steady, always doing the work. They keep on from unmarked graves. Federico García Lorca made a poetics of knowing nothing, never quite settling on how to put what he heard as *duende* to the page. In 1933, Lorca delivered his "Theory and Play of the Duende" from a podium in Buenos Aires. The dawn of his famous lecture was a reckoning and disclaimer: "As simply as possible, in the register of my poetic voice that has neither the glow of woodwinds nor bends of hemlocks, nor sheep who suddenly turn into knives of irony, I shall try to give you a simple lesson in the hidden, aching spirit of Spain."[3]

Lorca models a kind of knowing nothing that gently acknowledges the insufficiency of his voice; it lacks the grain long earned by objects, plants, and animals. At the same time, he humbly sets up who and what he isn't as entities that probably know better: woodwinds and hemlocks and sheep are perhaps better equipped to approximate what the spirit sounds like. As the lecture proceeds, he allows what he hears to be affected by nature, the supernatural, history, forces beyond his control. Lorca's unfinished project of transcribing the "hidden, aching spirit" of Spain, song, and self made him a dangerous figure: his poetics of knowing nothing made him an unknowable figure. Perhaps it was this ambiguity that produced the violent paranoia that robbed him (and us) of his life before he reached his fourth decade.

I now turn to a few other examples that have helped me to get at (and will hopefully get you at) the sophisticated mechanics behind knowing nothing about music and what such mechanics might make possible, not for only criticism but for the larger project of open-heartedness. Textual examples like Lorca's are far from exceptional. They are a voluminous and powerful rush of water always and forever present. In this essay, however, I signal a few examples of knowing nothing found in the everyday life of listening. This softy polemic will unfold in three interconnected parts.

Listening Wrong

A moving image I sometimes encounter on the subways of New York, where I live, is two young people who split up the listening devices of their portable music players as they ride. One gets the right, the other the left.

The earphones might be inserted so that the connective wire will cradle their faces, pressed together. Or, ignoring instruction, one will put the right earphone in the left ear and vice versa for some shoulder-leaning and much needed sleep on the way to school. Most of the time they are teenagers, and I'll see them working out dance moves both together and apart. They will take the opportunity to work out some lyrical complexity and go into negotiations about "what they said in that part." They listen in unison or they will carve out their own aural world, even in such intimate interdependence. There are all kinds of forms these wired connections will make, say, between older and younger siblings, aunts and their nieces, young lovers who'll use the divide of the earphones to cop some serious feel before curfew. The music will usually come from a CD player, an imitation MP3, an iShuffle. Perhaps I betray my affective locations, but I find the phenomenon acutely present on the opposite track of Strayhorn's A train: that which delivers the populace to Brooklyn.

To my mind, there are some wonderful signals here. Sure, there's a send-up to certain audiophilic protocols of listening and collecting; a corruption of that "desire to achieve high-quality reproduction."[4] For many of us, low-quality reproduction has always been part of our processes of listening. Whether we've lacked the proper equipment, limped along with a rotten channel, or discovered the wonders of silicone gel for busted speakers, using devices in ways that might not be intended is a necessity and a choice. And if you think I'm wrong, try and dream up Kingston's Hellshire beach on a Sunday.

Issues of portability extend beyond convenience. On the train, they don't, or can't, or won't lug 160 gigabytes because, counter to the persnickety accusations of today's youth harboring Freudian death wishes against the album format, and with it, their critics, they listen to not as much with greater care. This is something that countercollectors have been doing for time immemorial. There is another lesson here: we cannot participate in the categorical derision of one-hit wonders. It is a phrase that can demean and make small vital recordings and people at once, particularly those hits and bodies perceived as accidental blips on popular music's radar. And while there are the well-rehearsed (and often justifiable) arguments about the totalitarian functions of repetition, these critics between the earphones do much to extend repetition's softer side. Dance routines that might have been worked out in living rooms (that is, if they even have them) are brought into public space. They reignite your slow dance memories of past, present, and future. They make new, mobile versions of fireside chats by gathering around sound together.

More than anything else, I'm attached to this vision of listening as an actual mode. It decenters the idea of an individual's "total" sonic experience. Through split headphones, some might say that they listen wrong because they listen fractured. But this is what compels me most about this listening mode: they supplement stereo's binary. These agents of listening actively imagine the other side of sound as they move through the city.

The Other End of the Line

While the telephone has had a lengthy career as a featured cameo in song, it is stunning to see its current persistence in so much music. A return to Michael Chanan's work, however, reminds that this presence is far from accidental. In the first pages of his *Repeated Takes*, Chanan reveals the mutually formative relationship between the telephone and the phonograph by tracing Bell's and Edison's claims to invention within one year of another. While accounting for the multiple persons and histories that made such inventions possible, Chanan reveals that Edison came to the phonograph by way of tinkering with Bell's telephone. Edison had initially wanted "to extend the reach of the telephone line by producing a device to repeat the signal, on the same principle as his successful telegraph repeater." In other words, by way of his desire to expand the geographical distance of telephonic communication, he discovered a way to record sound. An early version of the phonograph sprang from this experimental play.[5]

As Avital Ronell drives home, "the possibility of a telephone was never fully dissociated from musical strains."[6] These musical strains have been a strong presence in the gamut of popular music. The phone as object and site of drama has been recently utilized by the likes of post-teen papis Aventura and Wisin y Yandel. It could be argued that much of Bachata's universe happens on the phone. There are too many precursors to mention: Erykah Badu's "Telephone," Electric Light Orchestra's "Telephone Line," that "Maldito Telefono" by Los Zafiros, and the bouncy mambo "Un Besito por Telefono" by the Orquesta Riverside. From Guinea, we have Bembeya Jazz National's twist on "Telephone." How about Jorge Ben's falsetto in "O Telefoni Tocou Novamente"? And who could forget Millie Jackson's 1982 cautionary tale "Mess on Your Hands"? And no, I'm not interested in chalking this telephonic presence up solely to the proliferation of certain technologies—an argument that could fall prey to systems theory, which to my mind requires not having feelings.

Instead, let me use some pedestrian evidence to briefly gesture to the presence of music in global telecommunications. Note the musical entice-ment found on calling cards specific to geographical region (see the illus-trations accompanying this chapter). Calls to the Dominican Republic might be given more swing with the "Perico Ripiao" card. With the Los Tigres del Norte phone card, "Los Jefes de Jefes" (the Bosses of Bosses), your call to Puebla could be connected with more swagger. And my per-sonal favorite, the "Dale Pa' Ya" card, bearing a hispanophone redaction of something like "go 'head." Through the transnational sign of the accor-dion, the card offers a shadowy and ethnically ambiguous outlet that adds some oompah to your calls, be they to Mexico, the D.R., Venezuela, and Colombia. One would assume that these cards are made to speak (or sing) to particular immigrant populations, using music as a lure for purchase. Perhaps these graphics curb some of the rage that occurs when the call won't be put through—especially when used from a microbio-infested-payphone.[7] Ronell argues, "To this day the telephone still houses back-ground music, as if to deaden the pain."[8] On these cards and in those songs, I would say that music is made of the telephone to remind of the painful necessity of (and reasons for) being apart.

Knowing nothing allows a lingering in that which is immeasurable and unbindable to argument. Here and everywhere I mean the intense upheaval of bodies all over the world, how those bodies come to hear the ones they've left behind, and how the left behind must imagine their loved ones in places they have little sense of. It gives one the time to reflect on how much staying in touch *must* take place in song, because there might be something more satisfying about it. To sing of the telephone might be a way to emotionally round up what can't be made felt from the cabins of a call center/Western Union office. Perhaps it provides a soundtrack behind financial remittances, as a way to include all the love, conflict, relief, pain, and pleasure that lie behind them. There's something in these songs that are up-front about the impossibility of ever being together in any kind of easy way, because after all, everyone's lives must also attend to the chal-lenges of the everyday. Knowing nothing about the other side of the line is a way to deal with not being in the same place at the same time.

With this in mind and ear, I'd like to turn to the song "Comunícate"

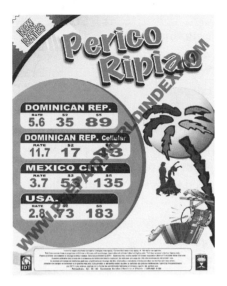

(clockwise from above) Perico Ripiao;
Los Tigres Del Norte; Dale Pa' Ya

(Communicate) by Manolito Simonet y Su Trabuco, a group among the stellar cohort of internationally popular Cuban dance bands founded in the early 1990s. A phone rings as a bass and horns heavy flourish kick-starts the song. As the jam begins to roll itself out, we are given the time to get on the dance floor (in the mind or in the club) and prepare ourselves for a story at once. The patient, pelvic dip-dip of Eduardo Mora's bass guitar grounds Simonet's tightly orchestrated arrangement. We hear Ricardo Amaray Macías croon-speak into the telephone line, frustrated, yet ready to deliver the lament to come:

Halo? Halo?	Hello? Hello?
Comunicando	Communicating
Hace una hora que te estoy llamando	I've been calling you for over an hour
Me llamó el teléfono	I call you up
tratando de inventar comunicación	Trying to invent some communication
hace buen rato que no hablo con mi amor	It's been a good while since I've talked to my love
lo necesito pide a gritos el corazón	I need to says my screaming heart
comunica comunícate	Communicate, get in touch with me
Comunicando	Communicating
hace horas que te estoy llamando	I've been calling you for hours
comunica comunícate	Communicate, get in touch with me
Comunicando	Communicating
comunica comunícate	Communicate, get in touch with me
hace una hora que te estoy llamando	It's been an hour that I've tried to call you
si no comunico perder esta ocasión	If I don't get you, I'll lose the chance
de decirte niña que te estoy llamando	to tell you, baby, that I'm calling you to say
que lo tuyo y lo mío es amor	that what we've got going is love
te llamaré todo el dia preguntaré si me amas	I'll call you all day and ask you if you love me
insistiré esa línea aunque me suena ocupada	I'll insist even if the line is busy
te llamaré todo el dia preguntaré si me amas	I'll call you all day and ask you if you love me
pero si no me respondes te llamaré todo la semana . . .	But if you don't answer me, I'll keep trying all week long . . .

Part of what might be enacted in this song are those special challenges of trying to get in touch with someone across shoddy national optics. In Cuba, it is a well-known condition that telephone calls are not the quick, caller-ID'd, and voicemail-able entities familiar in the United States. Phone calls are instead processes. Second, third, and fourth tries can and do take place, over several days. Perhaps the song reveals the point of view of migrating musicians from the Americas, especially Cuba, who have had a long and historical relationship to being on the road. We might imagine all that time spent trying to call home. It could simply be the view of one of those controlling boyfriends that we'll roll our eyes at.

But to speculate on what this song might mean to its writer, arranger, and performers would not only be an impossible, but arrogant exercise. And no, I haven't interviewed anyone that's a part of it. Nevertheless, there is something tender in Macías's vocal crooning—something about his interpretation that feels like love sickness from a faraway place. That said, I'd like to stay very vague about distance here. I'd also like to draw away from a lyrical reading, and use the space I've got to underscore the piano tumbao after this first section of the song.[9] The tumbao does too many things: it encapsulates the frustration of all those failed attempts to get in touch. It is a break that allows the absent presence on other end of the line to make some noise. It is a generous moment in the song—a bountiful convention found in timba—where the band gives way to those who listen and dance. The keys are ground out in such a way that you, the dancer, are given only one place to go, and that's down. How you get there and however long it takes is up to you. It is a space that reminds us that we need to give some room to the other end of the song and telephone line to do its own thing. As it recedes, we hear a breathless Macías cry: "Sube" (Get up).

Take Your Time, Do It Right

I'll conclude with a flashback from the "Music and Performance from the Hispanophone Caribbean" seminar that I taught several years ago inside faux-Gothic walls. In the second week of class—the one that always seems to fall on that unfortunate anniversary—I brought in a recording of the national anthem as sung by the blind Puerto Rican singer José Feliciano during game 5 of the 1968 World Series between the Pirates and the Tigers. It is a version and pedagogical tool I was introduced to by Jason King in 2003.[10] Together, we listened along as he gently thrummed the opening chords on his guitar. As he sang this standard of being and belonging,

Feliciano's voice gently wavered, offering itself as a gift to the audience in Detroit's Tiger Stadium. In Feliciano's rendition, "the rockets' red glare" never sounded so earnest.

Beyond the date and location of the recording, I did not give the students any context for Feliciano or his performance. I will often refuse to front-end context in the classroom because it gives students the room to create their own idiosyncratic relationships to what they hear. After gearing Feliciano's version, I asked them to describe the performance. Folksy. Sincere. Like a country singer. These were the bulk of the descriptives. But when I called on a visibly moved Mariel Novas—and I am using her first and last name because she is already shaping the future of Dominican studies—she said, after a lengthy pause, very strongly and very seriously: "I thought it was really beautiful." When I asked why she said, "Because, you know, he made it his own." She rounded out her statement in such a way that it was caught between a question and an assertion.

It was difficult to follow up this moving uncertainty with accounts of Feliciano's actual reception that day. I handed out copies of the *New York Times*, *Washington Post*, and *Los Angeles Times* articles that all reported the massive booing and indignation Feliciano was subjected to after the performance. Receptive violence was waged for his having dared to alter the standard. Newspapers and televisions around the country were inundated with phone calls from outraged viewers. The effect of his adaptation made headline news in all the major newspapers:

> "I'm young enough to understand it, but I think it stunk. It was non-patriotic."
>
> "It was a disgrace, an insult. I am going to write to my senator about it."

Needless to say there was some devastation in our classroom given the disconnect between what they had heard and what these callers had heard. There was a collective damage palpably felt around this seminar table of mostly second-generation immigrants, a strong handful who were the first in their family to go to college.

In a postgame interview given behind first base with his dog Trudy by his side, Feliciano was asked to label his "kind" of performance. Refusing this taxonomic exam, Feliciano responded, "I guess people call it soul, but I don't call it nothing myself." Calling it nothing made it more difficult to know and understand. He refused to have his relationship to the anthem to be contained by this push to genre-classify him and it. Instead, he offered the following:

> I just do my thing—what I feel. . . . I was a little scared when I was asked to sing the anthem. I was afraid people would misconstrue it and say I'm making fun of it. But I'm not. It's the way I feel. America is young now, and I thought maybe the anthem could be revived now. This country has given me many opportunities. I owe everything I have to this country. I wanted to contribute something to this country, express my gratification for what it has done for me. I love this country very much. I'm for everything this country stands for. When anyone kicks it, I'm the first to defend it.[11]

Lest we think this day was left on anything but a reparative note, after class, Mariel approached me to say that she might have to miss lecture next week. When I asked why, she told me that she and her mother were due to get sworn in as citizens. And—very concerned now—that it might be hard for her to get back to class in time because her dad would have to drive her back from Boston. That is, if he could get the rest of the afternoon off. Plus they were going to have a party and the whole family was invited and everything. I think she wanted to be reassured that this was a moment in life where one needs to be with family, to miss class, to hold a mom's hand. Of course, I did my best to do just that. But for students like Mariel, because her commitment to learning which is to say, her commitment to listening—is at such an intensity, she felt the need to clear it with me again via email.

This immigrant condition and condition of possibility is something we might ourselves be intimately familiar with. It is also the kind of story we might hear all the time. It reminds us that we must be open and recognize the kind of work and the kinds of intense feelings one has to negotiate in the space of a seminar, reading, nation, and song. And that this is part of why certain folks will never be consulted as experts, why they will never be useful for the American Experience, the series and otherwise. Because they might need a little more time to say something about what they hear. That sometimes we can only say, "it's beautiful," without knowing why.

Notes

1. Here is just one moment in Ellison that gets us to the tune of knowing nothing: "One learns by moving from the familiar to the unfamiliar, and while it might sound incongruous at first, the step from the spirituality of the spirituals to that of the Beethoven of the symphonies or the Bach of the chorales is not as vast as it seems. . . . Those who know their native culture and love it unconditionally are never lost when encountering the unfamiliar." Ralph Ellison, "Living with Music," in *Living with Music: Ralph Ellison's Jazz Writings*, ed. Robert G. O'Meally (New York: Modern Library, 2001), 14. I am also clearly under the influence of Ronald Radano and Philip V. Bohlman here, specifically, their astute coinage of the "metaphysics of ownership"—a phrase they use to describe those (failed) attempts to discipline music and musical commodities. See their "Music and Race: Their Past, Their Presence," introduction to *Music and the Racial Imagination* (Chicago: University of Chicago Press, 2001), 6.

2. I often open the *Historia de la Musica Cubana* simply to take in the picture of the rounded features, soft gaze, and pearl necklace of its author, Elena Perez Sanjurjo. I love to imagine her in the archives, giving a lecture, notating a musical score. Perez Sanjurjo's resume and work has all the signs of knowing everything and yet she is never cited as much as she should be.

3. In the lecture, Lorca does not provide a definitive definition of *duende*, a quality found in the music in the actual and spiritual Andalucía. Nor will I for an endnote's sake. For Lorca, *duende* "is a power not a work. It is a struggle not a thought. . . . it is not a question of ability, but of true, living style, of blood, of the most ancient culture, of spontaneous creation." And perhaps most evocatively, Lorca echoes Manuel Torres's assertion that "All that has black sounds has duende." Federico García Lorca, "Play and Theory of the Duende," in *In Search of Duende*, ed. and trans. Christopher Mauer (New York: New Directions Bibelot, 1998), 48–49. He once called his work on deep song "a labor of preservation, friendship, and love" (1). Nathaniel Mackey is one of the forces responsible for highlighting the vitality of Lorca's writings on music for English-speaking audiences. For a beautiful reading of Lorca (as an opening into the work of Wilson Harris) see Mackey's "Limbo, Dislocation, Phantom Limb: Wilson Harris and the Caribbean Occasion," in *Discrepant Engagement: Dissonance, Cross-Culturality, and Experimental Writing* (Tuscaloosa: University of Alabama Press, 1993), 162–79. See also his contribution "Cante Moro," to the seminal volume *Sound States: Innovative Poetics and Acoustical Technologies*, ed. Adalaide Morris (Chapel Hill: University of North Carolina Press, 1997), 194–212.

4. *Oxford English Dictionary*, s.v. "audiophile."

5. Michael Chanan, *Repeated Takes: A Short History of Recording and Its Effects on Music* (New York: Verso, 1995), 4–5.

6 Avital Ronell, *The Telephone Book: Technology, Schizophrenia, Electric Speech* (Lincoln: University of Nebraska Press, 1991), 282.

7. *Microbios* (literally, microbes) are a catch-all for invisible germs. They are a particular source of contagion paranoia for many Latin/a American populations.

8. Ronell, *The Telephone Book*, 282.

9. There have been a few critics out there who actually do know everything. One of them was Helio Orovio, who tragically passed away, too soon, in 2008. His indispensable *Cuban Music from A to Z* defines tumbao as "best translated as 'groove.' It refers most often to the basic pulse of a composition, with characteristic aggregate rhythms, pulses, emphases, and syncopations. . . . Alternately, tumbao can refer to the most typical patterns played on particular instruments, especially the conga drum." Helio Orovio, *Cuban Music from A to Z*, trans. Ricardo Bardo Portilla and Lucy Davies (Durham: Duke University Press, 2004), 215. Rest in peace.

10. Some years ago at New York University, I had the opportunity to be in the audience as Jason King, an associate professor in the Clive Davis Department of Recorded Music, gave an undergraduate lecture that walked through multiple versions of "The Star Spangled Banner" to the students to illustrate the different relationships to citizenship that music can perform.

11. See "Singer's 'Soul' Anthem Produces Controversy," *Los Angeles Times*, October 8, 1968, B6; "Fans Protest Soul Singer's Anthem Version," *New York Times*, October 8, 1968, 54; "'Soul' Anthem Raises Furor," *Washington Post, Times Herald*, October 8, 1968, A3.

David Ritz

Divided Byline

How a Student of Leslie Fiedler and a Colleague
of Charles Keil Became the Ghostwriter for
Everybody from Ray Charles to Cornel West

I am a proud member of the high church of low funk,
the church of Jimi Hendrix, a nation of inordinate
music worshippers, passionate to the point where we
don't know what to do with the love, so we talk about it,
analyze it, try to understand it, worship it. By worship, I
don't mean mindless worship, but worship that entails
a battle and a struggle and much ambiguity, doubt, and
equivocation. I do what I do because of a spirit that moved
through me when I was a young boy. Hopefully I will
be an honest witness to that spirit. But be careful about
people who are witnesses because they tend to proselytize, and today I do intend to proselytize. I think I am
in possession of a truth, my truth, and like a witness in
church I am looking to convert and win you over. There
won't be an altar call at the end—though I'm tempted—
but I have an agenda; I'm here to testify.

A testimony is simply a story and like any kind of story,
has its own form. In Hollywood they say a screenplay has
three acts: beginning, middle, and end. The Tuscan poet
called it hell, purgatory, and heaven. At the twelve-step
churches I've been attending for twenty years, they call
it then, now, and how. My testimony will begin, then, in
hell—my childhood. My childhood is about music and

one artist in particular: Billie Holiday. My dad is an intellectual—he's alive and well at ninety-four—and the culture that he brought into our home was the culture of New York Jewish intellectuals of the twenties and thirties. He worshiped at the shrine of Engels and Marx, Einstein and Freud, Kafka and Dostoevsky. I was excited by his learning, but even more excited by his music—Ellington, Basie, and Billie Holiday. My mom, who was not intellectual or musical, also loved Billie Holiday.

My parents' marriage was miserable, but the soundtrack to that marriage—the songs of Billie Holiday—was magnificent. So the three of us were strangely joined by the poignant, heartbreaking intimacy of Billie's blues. Some kids take teddy bears to bed; I took Billie Holiday records to bed. The expression of her pain assuaged my pain. Music became a nutrient, a spirit that turned despair to beauty.

Billie also led to me ghostwriting. In 1956, when I was twelve, her autobiography, *Lady Sings the Blues*, was released. I read it immediately and loved it. She was talking to me—directly to me—painting a picture of a world I found wildly exotic. On the cover I saw the credits: "As told to William Dufty." "Who's he?" I asked my dad. "He's the guy who the wrote the book." "No, Billie Holiday wrote the book, she's talking to you, you can feel her." "Well, she probably doesn't know how to write a book, so she hires this guy who writes it in her voice." "Does that guy get to go over to her house?" I asked. "I suppose so," my dad answered. I decided that's the job I wanted.

That's the job I have, but it would be twenty years before I became a ghostwriter. I went to the University of Texas in Austin and had a traditional education with great teachers—William Arrowsmith, who taught the Greek plays, and Roger Shattuck, who taught Proust. Then I went to graduate school. My dad had grown up with Leslie Fiedler, who got me into the State University of New York at Buffalo, where he was teaching. I loved the school: it was the era of Robert Creeley, Charles Olson, John Barth, and Archie Shepp, who was teaching jazz. I liked Fiedler enormously. I had known him all my life, began reading him at about the time I read *Lady Sings the Blues*, and loved his muscular prose, genre jumping, and Jungian riffs. In fact, the critics I loved, like Fiedler, closed the gap between art and criticism. They were artists themselves. That's what I wanted to be: an artist-critic with a voice of my own.

During graduate school I realized I really didn't want to get a Ph.D., I wanted to write about music. I wrote an essay on soul music for the magazine *Salmagundi* and with my pal Charlie Keil, who gigged in the American Studies department at SUNY Buffalo, taught a course on pop music. My philosophy teacher, Lionel Abel, another character from my father's generation, told me I was just too enterprising to be an academic. "The academy will never contain you," he said. "You're a go-getter, a hustler, and you need to keep hustling."

So I started hustling as a freelance journalist. That was murder. Write eighteen articles to try to pay the rent. I needed a book advance. I went to the library and saw there had been no books written on Ray Charles. I knew a couple of guys who had been in his band and I asked them to whisper in Ray's ear that I was worthy. Keep in mind that the book I had in mind was Robert Caro on Robert Moses or Richard Ellmann on Joyce, Wilde, or Yeats. My Ray bio would win me the Pulitzer Prize and literary fame.

My agent, though, stopped me cold. "Are you sure you don't want to do an as-told-to book?" he asked. "What's that?" I wanted to know. "Well," he said, "he talks and you write." I realized that's like the Billie Holiday book I read as a kid. Then I remembered *The Autobiography of Malcolm X*, another big autobiography I dug—only I never thought of it as an as-told-to book, despite its having been written by Alex Haley. Ghostwriting just wasn't on my mind. During college and graduate school, no one even mentioned ghostwriting. I rejected the idea. I said, "No, I'm gonna go see Ray Charles, tell him I'm the one to interview him, tell him I can't do the book without him, but this will be *my* book." "Well," my agent said, "the book you have in mind is worth maybe $25,000. If you do a book with Ray, though, it might bring in $100,000 and he'll give you a taste that will be more than $25,000." That made me stop and think. But even then I refused. I saw it as hiding behind someone else's voice. I had to project my own voice. Then, though, my agent asked a question that shook me to the core. "Which book would you rather read—a book told in Ray Charles's voice about his life, or a book written by a scholar about Ray Charles?" The answer was obvious—*of course I'd rather read Ray Charles's own voice.* Then my agent added, "Write the book you want to read—not the book you think you should write." I was nailed.

It was very difficult meeting Ray. The guy who protected him was a slippery Cab Calloway cat with a gun. He wouldn't let me in. That made me want to get in even more. I called Western Union and asked if I could telegram in Braille. Yes. What were the chances of anyone else in Ray's office being able to read Braille besides him? The telegrams became my pitch letters. I told him that I loved him and his artistry, knew all his music, and simply had to work on his book. Every day I'd compose a different telegram. Finally he called. I got in. We met. I sold him. It was on.

Now I became a ghostwriter writing Ray Charles's autobiography. The central problem, though, was this—I had no idea how to do it. My agent said it's simple: he talks and you write. So I began taping him and transcribing the tapes. Yet when I read the transcriptions, something was wrong. His voice wasn't there. That's when I realized that the eye hears differently than the ear.

Example: the word Ray loved most was *motherfucker*. He used it as an adjective, adverb, noun, and even verb—as in mother*fuckit*. The word was employed creatively in his spoken language, but on the page, used repetitively as he used it in his speech, it overwhelmed. It gave the impression that his vocabulary was impoverished—which it wasn't—and his mind weak. Meanwhile Ray was a brilliant man with an extraordinary language. So what do I do? I realized that I had to create a character, I had to sculpt, had to do what a novelist does, what a poet does. I had to make magic. How else could the reader feel Ray as I was feeling him?

How, then, do you make magic? I don't know. If I had a formula, I'd reveal it. All I know is that the process of making that magic took a couple of years. First I had to embrace Ray's speech, hear his speech with my heart as well as my head, had to incorporate the way he cut off words, had to break down his form of idiosyncratic metrics. I began to hear music in his speech: his vocal style came out in his talking style. He was one of those people, like Louis Armstrong, with a conversational way of singing. Conversely, he had a musical way of conversing. I, too, had to make music. There was also the difficulty of engaging him. One time, sitting next to him on a plane about to fly from L.A. to New York, I looked forward to a long uninterrupted interview. When I mentioned all the time we had to talk, Ray turned to me and unapologetically said, "I wouldn't talk to my mama now if she came out the grave." I wanted to die. But that's the gig. Figuring out when you can hang, when you can't hang, when to get in the limo, when not to get in the limo, when do I get to ask when you lost your virginity or whether you're homosexual.

I cut my teeth on Ray and it was rough, but I loved it because for me it was better than being with Mozart.

Another thing about the ego of ghosts: A. E. Hotchner, who wrote a celebrated bio of Ernest Hemingway, *Papa Hemingway*, had written the autobiography of Doris Day. He entitled it *Doris Day, Her Own Story*, by A. E. Hotchner. That excited me and I envisioned—*Ray Charles, His Life Story*, by David Ritz. That way, my name gets to be big and I'm listed as solo author. But the publisher said you are not A. E. Hotchner—he's a big shot; you're not. Then I suggested could it be Ray Charles *and* David Ritz. The publisher said fine. The publisher also allowed me to write an afterword so I could raise my own voice and tell the world, *Look at me, I'm here, too.*

The book came out. Good reviews, good sales. I was certain that Mick Jagger and Stevie Wonder would call me up to do their books. But they didn't. Nobody called. I was stuck. I chased after Aretha, but she wasn't interested. So I wrote a novel about a ghostwriter who chases an Aretha character (who looks like Diana Ross) and gets to have a love affair with her. Good reviews, lousy sales. I wrote other novels, but nothing sold well enough to guarantee a career in fiction.

Then in 1978 Marvin Gaye put out an album called *Here, My Dear*. The record destroyed me. I played it every night, memorized every lick. Fortunately, a reviewer in the *L.A. Times* massacred it, misunderstanding the work entirely. I thought that if I answered the critic, Marvin might read my defense and call me. My scheme worked. Marvin and I became friends. He had read the Ray Charles book and wanted to do a similar book with me. Another great ghost project. If Ray was the consummate business guy, Marvin had no sense of business at all. He was unmanageable. He said, "Meet me in Hawaii," only to wind up in England, only to leave London for Ostend, Belgium. I chased him around the world, leaving behind my poor wife and twin babies.

It was in Ostend where we wrote "Sexual Healing," another example of the art of ghostwriting. Up until that time, I had never written a song. When I saw a book of s & m art-porn on his coffee table, I said, "Marvin, this is some sick shit here. What you need is sexual healing." "What does that mean," he asked. I answered, "Finding someone who loves you and wants to please you. Sex doesn't have to hurt. Sex can heal." He asked me to write a little poem with that idea in mind. I did. He took the words and fashioned them into a melody. In a few minutes time we were done. I had given him a voice—words that went with his life—in a way not unlike the words I gave Ray Charles in Ray's autobiography.

"Sexual Healing" changed Marvin's life. He came out of exile, returned to America, and was murdered by his father. At the time of his death, I had a mountain of taped interviews with Marvin, but I had not begun to write the actual autobiography. Since I couldn't do an as-told-to book, I had to write a biography. That became *Divided Soul*. I got to live the life of a sole author. I went on a long cross-country promotional tour, appeared on television and radio shows, had signings. Afterward, having had a taste of this recognition, I asked myself, *Do I want to write another independent biography?* The answer was no. I decided that I like ghosting better. I did it naturally, I enjoyed it thoroughly, and came to a conclusion different from anything I had learned in the academy: namely, maybe my central passion isn't to discover my own voice but to help other people discover theirs.

I began considering the art of ghosting on a spiritual level: you love someone enough to shut up and listen. I was inspired by a wonderful Brazilian movie called *Central Station*, with Fernanda Montenegro. In the movie, her character works in front of the huge train station, writing postcards for people who are illiterate. When I saw the film, I thought to myself, *That's me; that's my job; and what a great job it is!*

After I had ghosted B.B. King's book, someone told me he had just read it. "Yes," I said, "I wrote it." "No," the person argued, "it was done by B.B." I pointed to my name on the cover proceeded by a "with." At that point, any kind of cover credit was okay with me. The reader was astonished. I was pleased. He had the impression that B.B. was talking to him, not me. I'd done my job.

I also began realizing that ghosting involves literary criticism in the broadest sense. In my interviews with B.B. King, Etta James, or Grandmaster Flash, I scrutinize and sculpt. Everything I am comes through. These people move through me, just as I move through them. My spirit and theirs are joined. The reason the B.B. King book is the way it is is because I love Robert Johnson, Son House, and T-Bone Walker, just as B.B. loves them. So naturally I'm asking B.B. all sorts of questions about those artists. I'm interested in addiction, so of course I'm going to ask about addiction. I'm all over the book. I can't be otherwise.

A friend said that he wouldn't know how to have conversations with famous artists. He wanted to know how I did. I said it was easy. I tell the artist that I love her or him and demonstrate my willingness to listen. That's about it. I open up a space that allows love to grow in me and in them. The spirit that began with Billie Holiday is still the spirit I feel today. How to get someone to open up and tell you the truth? Create intimacy by being vulnerable. Talk about your own life. Elicit by example. Know that love leads to intimacy. As a loving person, express loving curiosity.

But what happens if the artist gives you false information? I was at a conference in Austin where a gentleman attacked me for being a hack because I didn't have any power over the people I was working with. "You just put these books out, they don't have to be true. What power do you have over the people you work with?" My answer was guilty as charged. I have no power. When my collaborations begin, I give away all power, knowing that the more you give, the more you get. When power as an issue is off the table, trust is more possible, more prevalent.

What happens, though, if the artist is putting out exaggerations and even deceptions—and the ghost knows it. My answer is, let them. I think autobiography, at its heart, is mythopoetical. Ask me my life story today and I'll give you one version. Ask me tomorrow and I'll the spin the story in a different direction. The nature of autobiography is arbitrary and personal. You're participating in a mythopoetical construct. It's poetry, not literalism.

Take *Lady Sings the Blues*, for whose fiftieth-anniversary edition I recently wrote a new introduction. Most Billie Holiday scholars hate it. They say it's inaccurate. But Billie Holiday is entitled to her own myth and, as a fan, I'm happy to read that myth. This is Billie as she regarded herself in 1954. As a human document, it's invaluable. Would that we had more such documents!

I'd like to conclude by playing David Ruffin's "Walk Away from Love," a record released at the beginning of the disco era that I've been listening to for three decades. Ruffin was a great talent who died young and took his story with him. We'll never know that story—at least not how he knew it, felt it, and lived it. "Walk Away from Love" makes me mindful of the many stories I missed. In 1985, I met Ruffin in L.A. during the Temptations' reunion tour. We connected immediately; he told me he wanted to do a book. "I gotta tell my story," he insisted. For a number of reasons, I walked away. Years later, he died a sad and lonely death. It broke my heart.

So in thinking of Ruffin, I'm reminded of Lester Young and Ben Webster and Billy Preston and Tupac Shakur and thousands of other artists whose self-styled stories died with them. In short, ghosts are required; ghosts are vital; without them, history is lost and beautiful tales remain untold.

Tom Smucker

Boring and Horrifying Whiteness

The Rise and Fall of Reaganism as Prefigured

by the Career Arcs of Carpenters, Lawrence Welk,

and the Beach Boys in 1973–74

In 1973, toward the tail end of Ronald Reagan's second term as governor of California, in the year that the ceasefire in Vietnam was signed, the draft ended, and *Roe v. Wade* became law—in short, in the year the 1960s came to an end, the Carpenters released *Now & Then*, one of the greatest pop music explorations of whiteness in the last half century. Not only because of the music— four hit singles, including "Yesterday Once More," and a tepid yet significant oldies medley—but because of the album cover. Part photograph, part painting, a hyperrealistic southern California suburban street, no pedestrians, just a big red car driving by with the windows rolled up and the Carpenter siblings inside; a portrait of rock stars in their Ferrari *and* a snapshot of average Jane and Joe pulling into the family driveway. Here it is: suburban democracy, social isolation in community, the mobile domesticity of the inside of a car, and the consequence that Karen Carpenter's once-in-a-generation voice sometimes suggests, sometimes obscures, and sometimes reveals: a complicated inner life as well.

Even without her death from anorexia—a disease of underconsumption, not of excess or overconsumption like the aesthetically and commercially correct deaths of

Billie Holliday, Charlie Parker, Elvis, Morrison, Hendrix, Joplin, and in their own way, the assassinated rappers—the Carpenters were all about the relationship between control and subjectivity. Brother Richard's production and orchestration were evocative, elaborate, and precise—no Wagnerian Wall of Sound: this was Phil Spector filtered through Brian Wilson filtered through the Beatles filtered through Bacharach and David. Sister Karen's singing was simple yet profound, Patti Page filtered through Pat Boone filtered through Mama Cass, filtered through . . . well, here's where Karen was unique. Her diction and delivery were direct, often guileless, while her vowels and lower register were enormous, the female equivalent of Brian and Carl Wilson's expansive Beach Boys falsettos.

It was early seventies music, and *Now & Then* was its culmination. Its statement: maybe Phil Spector, Brian Wilson, and Mama Cass went too far. Karen's voice held that at a maybe. Although they were *the* recognizably Republican rock act of the seventies, and were invited by Richard Nixon to the White House (to sing for Willy Brandt), and developed a depoliticized, sentimental, privatized white aesthetic that helped set the stage for Reaganism as a national phenomenon, theirs was an aesthetic that Reaganism could never absorb. Because, in their own Downey, California, way, just like their Laurel Canyon contemporaries Crosby, Stills, and Nash and Carole King, the Carpenters refashioned but did not reject the 1960s.

"Yesterday Once More" and the medley that followed it on *Now & Then* evoked the early sixties. And although that suggests that something might have gone wrong in the latter sixties, Richard's production referenced, even as it refined, late sixties rock. The oldies radio format emerging at the time was often understood to be a revival of the 1950s. The film *American Graffiti*, released three months after *Now & Then*, was set in the summer of 1962, yet almost all the music on the soundtrack comes from the later fifties. But the Carpenters were nostalgic for the early sixties. The songs on their medley were originally released from 1962 to 1965, a significant specific chronology that we will return to when examining the Beach Boys.

National Reaganism, as it evolved after Reagan's two terms as governor of California, would leap past the civil rights movement, the Vietnam War, and the rise of feminism, reaching back to the future for a new morning in America. It proposed a storyline with a happy ending—the 1980s— that explained our recent history as a correctable, mistaken excess but left the boundaries of that mistaken history unclear. Maybe it included FDR, Teddy Roosevelt, even Woodrow Wilson and maybe not, but it certainly included Jimmy Carter and LBJ and so stretched back at least to 1963.[1] That cut-off date effectively eliminated the careers of the Beatles, the Beach Boys, and Bacharach and David, the three acknowledged influences on the Carpenters' sound.

When Karen Carpenter sang that early sixties rock 'n' roll "can even make you cry / Just like before / it's yesterday once more," she's singing about an emotionally accessible yesterday that's not sufficiently back in the past that she's not sufficiently upbeat about to have arrived at real Reaganism. In political terms you might say their oldies medley and their single recall the presidencies of JFK and early LBJ,[2] the single in its sorrow maybe even the moment after Kennedy's assassination. And so that makes them too attached to their memories of melancholy and too grounded in the rock tradition to move all the way forward into Reagan's conservative revival.

Control and precision—often assigned as white musical values—and elaborate pop production that implies a kind of mass affluence, locate the Carpenters' soft rock in the suburban world abstracted on the *Now & Then* album cover. Karen's voice itself projects a kind of affluence—it's rich—but there's real drama in the struggle of that voice to come to terms with its own implications. Sometimes Richard's studio work displays that voice in a context that allows the examination of a vast, and in some ways narcissistically indulgent well of loneliness, while simultaneously registering a jaunty satisfaction with its comfortable surroundings. Sometimes the reworked oldies or jazz lite contain that voice inside the wrong set of restrictions. But Karen's vocals never lose their identity and so glue together the failures and successes to make all this music signify a world where people grapple with an inner life even when they fail, a world that demands and frustrates subjectivity.

Low on prestige and originally marketed as such, and critically evaluated as too boring for evaluation in their heyday, the songs have seen time enhance their power as cultural markers.[3] There's the immediate, almost tactile presence of Richard's impeccable production and Karen's artlessly sensuous voice—not because of any conspicuously implied sexuality, but because it takes pleasure in itself. There's the dignity in their refusal to mask a suburban aesthetic in the ersatz cowboy and arcadian mythos gaining traction in Los Angeles at the time. And along with that, perhaps, nostalgia for the mass affluence of the lift-all-ships post–Second World War economic boom that was drawing to a close as the Carpenters hit their mid-seventies peak. Below that lies the tale of Karen's struggle, even martyrdom, reimagined to fit the norms of rock, or feminism, maybe queer theory—Karen as counterpoint to Janis. Mixed with that might lie our own conflicted longings for control; the pleasures of identifying with music that sort of wants to and yet refuses to break free. And below that the guilty pleasures of a homogenized universe that was white because it excluded people who weren't, the world of suburban white flight after Watts. An enclave that Carpenters music suggests is under siege, including from its own inhabitants' desires.

. . . . .

Around the same time as *Now & Then*, Lawrence Welk was struggling to reclaim his evening hour on television. Dropped in the spring of 1971 by ABC because his audience demographic skewed too old, Welk went on tour playing stadiums with his entourage to build momentum for what would become a successful return to nationwide TV via syndication, and then after his death, as a public television presence via videotape while pieces of his musical family, as it's called, performed and continue to perform live in Branson, Missouri, middle America's wholesome alternative to Las Vegas. But in reality, his days as a cultural power were doomed by a shift in the world he inhabited, a shift he helped set in motion, a shift that Carpenters music exemplified and examined.

Welk was never a recording star; he was a successful live dance band leader in the upper Midwest, followed by ten big years at the Trianon Ballroom in Chicago in the 1940s, after which he moved on to Los Angeles, where he developed the most popular show on local TV, and from there advanced to the national networks with his weekly variety show perched atop the ratings from 1955 to 1971. He was not an innovative musician but a self-taught master of audience maintenance and construction. Like the Carpenters' music, Welk's is considered very white, and it is also about control. But the control is social, not psychological. He was the musical embodiment of the great internal migration of white people out of the middle of the country in the middle of the last century who gathered in L.A.; he exemplified their ascendancy to power as a national cultural force, and their understanding of that ascendancy. The Carpenters were Welk's metaphoric offspring, maybe grandchildren, so to speak, who grew up in the postwar, suburbanizing world this migration was drawn to and helped create.

In spite of Welk's reputation as a paternalistic moralist who kept an eyeball on the private lives of his cast, he doesn't work as the musical template for postsixties psychic belt-tightening. He was a dance band leader who played Champagne Music. Dancing and booze—OK for Catholics, off limits but intriguing for many Protestants in the upper Midwest back then. In other words, when this guy was coming up he was in the business of selling fun.

And that was central to the in-migration to Los Angeles, and the nationwide migration to the suburbs, even when that migration only happened in North Dakota or New York City in people's living rooms while they watched TV or in their cars while listening to the radio: the idea of postwar fun. Growing up in this suburbanizing world meant growing up in a society that was both more centralized and more autonomous and more committed to the pursuit of pleasure than the old small-town, rural world that Welk evoked and left behind as soon as he was able.

Welk brought along the bits and pieces of those left-behind worlds of Yankton and Omaha and Chicago so his audience could affirm their roots while affirming their new cosmopolitan world. The Carpenters and their fans grew up in that new world, the new world of a new generation in Yankton and Omaha and Chicago as well.

Under Welk's accommodating baton the ethnicities, or maybe genres, were gathered in: there was the Irish tenor, the accordion-playing polka guy, the tap-dancing African American, the Mexican singer, the Dixieland instrumentalist, the country singer—but there was no music from the rock era. Welk's music was less white than the Carpenters'—he called Nat King Cole his favorite singer and devoted a tribute show to him, and referenced Duke Ellington and Louis Armstrong—but it was music about mainstream social cohesion. A white task for sure in a social structure where whites dominate. Hence the touches that were reassuring to his audience and appeared incomprehensible to those with a different idea about the function of music: the matching Day-Glo suit coats for the band, the identical, buttoned-to-the neck dresses when the ladies sang ensemble. This was an extended musical family, and Welk knew how to project that visually as well as musically on TV.

And then there was the overly familiar repertoire with the simplified arrangements. Again, these were intentional signifiers of cohesion that

appeared to outsiders as mistakes, or examples of lack of taste or imagination. To insiders they were reassuring reminders of already familiar
music, and in their own way a response to the problem of repetition in the
age of mechanical reproduction, solved elsewhere by bebop (improvise),
disco (elaborate), punk (compress), and hip-hop (compile). The simplifi-
cation aided the process of amalgamation, and acknowledged the song's
status as a memory.

And so to rock era music consumers, Welk appeared to have no inner
life and could and can feel incomprehensible, sleazy, hypocritical, zombie-
like—in my experience more horrifying to rock fans than scaremongers
like Black Sabbath, Alice Cooper, Marilyn Manson, the Sex Pistols, Public
Enemy, N.W.A. But that's because his music wasn't about an inner life.
His music was about helping his audience define their social boundaries.
It was a prerock, pre-1955 musical aesthetic, with a huge, but aging audience.

Below that age, an attachment to Lawrence Welk usually rests on something like the phrase, "I used to watch it with my grandmother." That's
not a guilty pleasure or a strategic exercise of taste, that's a suspension of
aesthetics for valid reasons of sentiment. And perhaps a momentary par-
ticipation in Grandma's memories of social cohesion, real or imagined.
Which doesn't mean that Welk had no inner life, or couldn't recognize
good jazz; it just wasn't what he was trying to achieve, or at the end of the
day, decided was important.

Halfway through his memoir *Wunnerful, Wunnerful!*, Welk describes a
moment in 1931 when, newly married, and failing to make it in Chicago
with his band, he throws caution to the wind and takes his wife to see
Louis Armstrong:

> Fern was just mystified by the whole evening. Armstrong was playing
> in a smoky basement club with low ceilings and recessed lights. The
> room was filled, on this particular night anyway, with an enthusiastic
> crowd of eager Dixieland jazz lovers. I was in seventh heaven listen-
> ing to his artistry on the trumpet and I could hardly sit still. "Isn't this
> wonderful?" I shouted to Fern above the storm of applause at the end
> of one number. She just smiled, a little uncertainly, and shrugged her
> shoulders.[4]

So he retreats to Yankton, South Dakota, realizing "that what seemed
like the greatest music in the world was just a lot of noise to her" and

wanting "to succeed so I could give her the things she really wanted." And give his audience, or the audience he was seeking, what it wanted.

If Welk has an analogous figure for the generations that came after him it would be the DJ, including the one at a wedding party who plays a little Elvis, the Supremes, the Village People, Shakira, Sinatra, Carpenters, "Rapper's Delight," and Garth Brooks, with the exact combination depending on the audience. Here the music also draws the social boundaries, but only for one night, or only for one subculture. Every wedding is a little different.

The Carpenters used a DJ persona, with mock Top 40 early sixties patter, as recreated by their lead guitarist, Tony Pelusi, to string together their oldies medley on *Now & Then* and when they performed live in concerts. A crowd pleaser that underscored the nostalgia for the lost social cohesion of a bygone era that was encoded in the medley, and in a way, in everything the Carpenters recorded.

DJ-shaped performance would reach its apotheosis with disco, where the turntable, rather than the baton, defined a new community. The interplay between subjectivity and social cohesion in classic disco is a topic too complex to take on here,[5] but it's worth noting the extraordinary hostility from rock audiences that disco generated in its heyday, not unrelated to the rock reaction to Lawrence Welk. And then also worth noting how successfully Michael Jackson, Madonna, and Lady Gaga among others, have fused rock and disco to fuel their careers. The Welkian aspects of disco, as it turned out, did not erase its utility as a mode of personal expression, in fact that would become a necessary strategic component for those with the widest cultural ambitions.

We expect rock era music, even very white music,[6] to describe or at least make reference to an individual inner life. And that makes an all-encompassing culture, even a multiethnic one like Welk's, more complicated: too many separate subjectivities. Attempts to create a rock canon do not produce one artist who can play it all, or would want to. The event DJ exhibits expertise in the selection of appropriate original recordings, but with original artists expressing original subjectivities; the disco or hip-hop DJ displays an inventive, stimulating eclecticism, drawing the ever-fluid boundaries of a milieu, but we aren't really interested in the inner life of that DJ.

In hip-hop that expression of the inner life would return with the elevation of the MC, and the relegation of the DJ to the background as producer. In shock-jock and then right-wing talk radio the DJ's angry subjectivity would replace the music altogether.[7] The interplay between the DJ and individual subjectivity would ebb and flow throughout the pop culture and politics of the last half of the twentieth century and beyond.

. . . . .

Like Welk, Ronald Reagan would appear to rock era voters who didn't get him as an empty suit, a cipher, a bad B movie actor and failed fifties TV host, hyped by hidden powers to improbably ascend into the presidency. And so they would misperceive or miss the potent and coherent Reagan narrative, agenda, and ideology, and miscalculate Reagan's appeal as a politician. Others would see the same blank screen, and like watching Lawrence Welk with Grandma, opt for his imagined idealized past and promised future as a way out of the dismal Carter era combination of stagflation, Iranian embassy hostages, and unresolved social turmoil.[8]

Many detractors and most admirers would eventually understand him as a nuanced partisan and experienced, intuitive tactician, yet biographers on both sides would agree that if Reagan had an inner life, it was hidden from everyone but Nancy. Patriot, warmonger, great communicator, Teflon president, son of an alcoholic, or old-school gentleman—he was, all agreed, hard to get to know.[9] Less interesting to analyze than Nixon and easier for his opposition (on the left and on the right) to dismiss to their eventual dismay, in 1973 he was preparing for the presidency promising to reestablish an optimism and social order that Lawrence Welk could no longer sell on network television. The Carpenters' circumspection and nostalgia might have looked like a part of this larger cultural and political current, but it would also turn out to be a part of its undoing.[10]

. . . . .

Among the covers on the Carpenters' 1973 medley were Jan and Dean's "Dead Man's Curve" and the Beach Boys' "Fun, Fun, Fun," both from 1964. Irony is not a perspective associated with the Carpenters, but there is a certain emotional or aesthetic distance entwined into the homage of the medley versions, as if to admit "this stuff is great, but it is from the past, and isn't what we usually perform. One rarely rocks out now." That would change within a year.

In 1974, the original "Fun, Fun, Fun" would appear on *Endless Sum-*

mer, an anthology of twenty Beach Boys songs from 1962 to 1965 that would shoot into the Top 10, sell a million copies, stay on the charts for three years, and establish the group as the number one concert draw in America. It would also call into question much of their music *after* 1965, and suggest a recalculation of the whole late sixties era from 1965 to 1973, including the work of the Carpenters.

1965 had been the pivot: the year the Vietnam War and the draft got hot, the year of the passage of Medicare and the Voting Rights Act, the rebellion and burning of Watts, and electric Bob Dylan booed at Newport — in short, the year the optimistic early sixties concluded and the complicated late sixties began, the year rock 'n' roll turned into rock. The singles that would show up eight years later on *Endless Summer* had gone out of fashion in '65, and the Beach Boys struggled to stay hip in the new and commercially successful hippie style.

Why did white pop ideas about hip shift so quickly in 1965? (And then why did they shift back again in 1974?) In the mix was the progression of studio recording technology and technique, the impact of art-schooled British pop stars, and the boomer bulge on its way through college. Alongside that was the psychological and social disjuncture in the United States caused by the escalation of the increasingly unpopular war in Vietnam; race relations in a "North" where job and housing segregation replaced voting rights as the point of contestation; and a tipping point on changing attitudes about sex and gender. The New Deal, Camelot, Great Society national narrative and public consensus of the last quarter century collapsed. For many, the opposite of what they had previously believed to be true seemed to be the case — about race, U.S. foreign policy, gender roles, and high and low culture. "When the truth is shown to be lies," as Grace Slick began Jefferson Airplane's first big hit in 1967.

Lyrics developed double meanings, or hidden meanings, or didn't make sense but sounded like they had a hidden meaning. The clarity of the early sixties fell away. "Something is happening but you don't know what it is," applied to audience and singer alike. Psychedelic or just stoned reality lay below normal white reality, as a sometimes noble and sometimes nutty pale imitation of W. E. B. Du Bois's Black double consciousness.

This was the long late sixties of 1965–73, and the Beach Boys, unlike white acts who appeared on the public radar in the latter sixties, such as Jefferson Airplane, the Byrds, and the Mamas and the Papas, navigated this terrain with a string of hits that stretched back to 1962 about subjects that were no longer a part of the zeitgeist. In the late sixties it was their baggage. After 1974 it was a blessing.

The reclamation of the cultural signposts of teenage summer in 1974 sent the Beach Boys back to their own past, where, it turns out, Brian Wilson had populated many of his adolescent anthems with protagonists with an inner life, sometimes a rather gloomy one if you gave a closer listen. The post-sixties reconnection to the surf, car, and summer metaphors did not demand a disconnection from rock era subjectivity because Wilson infused that subjectivity into his early subject matter and spread it across his later work, but it did produce a puzzle that had to be worked out by the Beach Boys and their hagiographers (myself included) in print, on tour, and on record. At their most nimble, they bridged the gap of '65, and in the process drew attention to the continuities as well as breaks before and after. Other times the gap proved too wide to negotiate.[11]

The successful repackaging of their early sixties work on *Endless Summer* signaled a shift away from the end of the late sixties, which mirrored the end-of-an-era political events of 1973, an understanding that pop music could absorb only so much middlebrow profundity, a desire, at the dawn of punk and disco, to reclaim the ecstatic elements of rock endangered by the soporifics of the early seventies, and a new ability in the culture to revisit and rethink the early sixties. *Summer* was not a slap-dash best-of, but a judicious choice of big and small hits and album cuts that could segue toward the psychological and musical explorations of *Pet Sounds* in 1966 and beyond while respecting the parameters of surfing, cars, and summer. The double album cover illustration showed unsmiling, long-haired, bearded Beach Boys peering through the flowers, waves, surfboards, and sand. It was the middle seventies coming to terms with the early sixties through the lens of the late sixties.

Therein lay a problem for Reaganism. For although the aesthetic, critical, and financial success of *Endless Summer* could be understood as a slap in the face of progressive rock pomposity and counterculture posturing (and by extension, utopian left-wing political ambitions and critiques), it was still music that inevitably linked to the latter sixties and beyond (and linked back, as rock 'n' roll often does, to a racially integrated past, real or imagined, in this case the multiracial doo-wop of southern California).[12] It was performed live, to ever larger audiences on both sides of the Atlantic and Pacific, by Beach Boys in rock hipster garb and grooming, an act that validated the permanent establishment of the mass pop counterculture.

. . . . .

In the early seventies Reaganism was finishing its run in California and still in formation as a technique of national governance. Economic trends and international events propelled the public mood as the decade ended toward a politics of reinvigoration that would look for inspiration to some earlier, undefined national moment and sweep Reagan in a landslide to the presidency. The success of *Endless Summer* was both a preliminary articulation of this dynamic, and a warning that nonetheless, the 1960s were solidifying their cultural impact, and creating a public narrative of their own, the history of rock 'n' roll.

Reaganism and Reagan himself would confront this directly on two occasions. In 1983 Reagan's first secretary of the interior, James R. Watt, banned the Beach Boys from playing for the public on the Washington Mall for the Fourth of July, as they had for the last three years, and replaced them with Wayne Newton, because they "attracted undesirable elements." By this time they were billing themselves as America's Band, the benign ambassadors from southern California performing essentially from the *Endless Summer* playlist, which made Watt's claim absurd and hence newsworthy and hence worth some bankable notoriety. Reagan stepped in, told Watt he had put his foot in his mouth, and invited the Beach Boys to the White House; a year later, after another public miscue, Watt would resign.

But here's the point. If Watt could have gotten away with it, Reagan would have let him; the Reagans didn't like rock era culture of any kind. Realistic politician and show biz veteran, the president was quick to defend the Beach Boys and their fans, and eventually threw Watt, but not his policies, overboard. The cultural boundary of Reaganism had now been adjusted up to at least 1965, and was creeping ever forward (as well as backward to the doo-wop past). That reopened the debate that Reaganism had claimed to settle: what went wrong in 1965? The answer could no longer be, "Everything."

And then, in late December of 1983, after a long alcoholic decline, Dennis Wilson drowned in Marina Del Ray, and was buried at sea in Santa Monica Bay in early January, after the family received a civilian dispensation from the Reagan administration. A sad bit of Beach Boys biography perhaps, a small humanitarian gesture, or a just a smart political calculation. And proof that Reaganism had failed to consolidate the ambitious cultural control that matched its political agenda. A sign the zealots and some of their opponents that rose to power after Reagan would ignore. Dennis Wilson was buried at sea, but that did not diminish his cultural resonance as the only Beach Boy who was a real surfer, and as it turned out, that still matters.

If Reaganism had reset the national clock back to a time of personal and social rectitude and uneven, unregulated free market affluence—as events showed—that affluence and its contradictions would once again lead forward back to the time of subjectivity. Going back to Lawrence Welk led forward back to the Beach Boys and then led forward back to the Carpenters. Where, their career as a whole suggests, we enter a suburban cul-de-sac, which the Carpenters would struggle to escape from and maintain, trapped and supported by their nuclear family. While Lawrence Welk and his larger musical family fled southern California for Branson, Missouri.

Lawrence Welk led forward to the Carpenters. The Carpenters led back to the Beach Boys, and where that led is a longer, and more complicated discussion.[13] Let's just say for now that it led in more than one direction, including to and through the Carpenters. But it did not lead back to Lawrence Welk. Unless, of course, you chose to and were able to impose a rectifying culture through the power of the state—a chore inaugurated by the Watt wing of the Reagan administration, and a pattern of imposed and failed cultural repression that repeated for another twenty years,[14] as partisans attempted to kick the country back to 1955 and stubbed their toes on the existence, in fact, the history of rock 'n' roll.[15]

The presidential election campaigns of 2008 would produce new leaders, on the left and on the right, propelled in large part by these dynamics. Barack Obama was not just our first African American president, he was our first biracial or really multiracial president: black, white, Indonesian, Hawaiian, wrapped in cool confidence. In short, a multiplicity of subjectivities contained inside a large persona. Sarah Palin was the first right-wing national politician comfortable with contemporary pop culture, in part due to her Pentecostal religious roots, able to project self-confidence and an inner life. Both were post-Reagan, but not post-rock.

Notes

1. "The press is trying to paint me as trying to undo the New Deal. I'm trying to undo the Great Society," Dinesh D'Souza quotes from Reagan's diary in D'Souza's admiring analysis *Ronald Reagan: How an Ordinary Man Became an Extraordinary Leader* (New York: New Press, 1997), 60. But D'Souza sets up this quote with an explanation of how "FDR's broader vision of an activist government outlived him and established the foundation for the Great Society." Once you go back to 1960 to correct things, how do you resist going back to 1944, and then back to 1929 and then . . .

2. For our purposes, with a focus on 1965 as the important break, culturally and politically, between the early sixties and the late sixties, LBJ's presidency then also breaks into the early, optimistic passage of the Civil Rights Act and the War on Poverty and the late divisive, unsuccessful escalation in Vietnam, the eruptions in big city ghettos, and the white backlash personified by George Wallace.

3. *The Rolling Stone Record Guide* (1979; rev. ed., New York: Random House, 1983) rates all Carpenters albums; in the 1979 edition, all are awarded one star out of five except for the *Singles* compilation, which receives three. By 1983 most of the albums, including *Now & Then*, had been downgraded to zero stars.

4. Lawrence Welk with Bernice McGeehan, *Wunnerful, Wunnerful! The Autobiography of Lawrence Welk* (Englewood Cliffs: Prentice Hall, 1971), 93. Welk would later return for a triumphant ten years performing at the Trianon Ballroom in Chicago before jumping to southern California.

5. Disco could deemphasize the human voice to spotlight the dance groove—think "Fly Robin Fly"—and also shape and promote the careers of singers with defined personas like Donna Summer, Sylvester, and Gloria Gaynor. See Tom Smucker, "Disco," in *The Rolling Stone Illustrated History of Rock & Roll* (New York: Random House, 1992), 561–72.

6. Country music, working out of a different combination of expressiveness and control than the Carpenters, can reach an almost unbearable tension in the singing of someone like George Jones. But both paths can dead-end in melancholy.

7. Some radio talkers came out of the raconteur tradition, some came out of the newsroom, and some were drawn directly to the format once it took shape. The premier shock jock, Howard Stern, transmuted from a classic rock DJ. The premier Obama era nemesis, Glenn Beck, who found a home on Fox News, began as a Morning Zoo Top 40 DJ. Rock culture could create a format and a stance for white male reaction on the right, different in temperament, and I would claim, in perspective, from Reaganism, and contemporaneous with Palinism.

8. See Lou Cannon, *President Reagan, The Role of a Lifetime* (New York: Public Affairs, 1991), 450–51.

9. Besides D'Souza, see Peggy Noonan, *When Character Was King: A Story of Ronald Reagan* (New York: Viking, 2001). Both D'Souza and Noonan worked in

the Reagan White House, consider it their Camelot, and quote other admirers and biographers about Reagan's inscrutability. Also see the book by Reagan's daughter Patti Davis about her reconciliation with her father during his final struggle with Alzheimer's, *The Long Goodbye* (New York: Knopf, 2004); it makes the same points from her left-liberal perspective. Davis is also quoted by Noonan in her book. Cannon makes the same observations in his biography.

10. In 1968 Welk released *To America with Love* as an album and a single (Ranwood R-814). The flip side of the single was the album cut "Let's Make America What It Used to Be." Most of the lyrics on that song would not be out of place, with some judicious tweaking, at a Pete Seeger concert, except for the title. Rock 'n' roll, or rock, or sixties culture did not want to make America what it used to be. That worked as politics, but not as culture. Of course, ten years later Bob Seger would be singing about "Old Time Rock & Roll" and "days of old," but that's another, longer, story.

11. So now there are two very different versions of the same album. The 1967 *Smiley Smile* includes the original ambitious singles "Good Vibrations" and "Heroes and Villains" and some minimalist, stoner takes on other bits and pieces that were also originally intended for the more ambitious *Smile*. The 2004 *Smile* is a fresh recreation and completion of the original and lives up to its ambitions, and certified Brian Wilson as a pop genius. Both are great, and taken together, reflect the stresses placed on late sixties rock.

12. Mike Love, the cousin who didn't go to Hawthorne High School but to the more interracial Dorsey High, gets the most credit for adding doo-wop into Beach Boys' music, but Brian quotes "Gee," which many cite as the first doo-wop hit, on *Smile*. "Barbara Ann," usually considered a Beach Boys song, was originally an early sixties doo-wop hit for the Regents out of the Bronx, reworked by Jan and Dean, and then reworked again by Dean and the Beach Boys for the *Beach Boys Party* album. Doo-wop shows were integrated, on the stage and in the audience, at the El Monte Ballroom in East L.A.

13. There have been three presentations of the Beach Boys' career, sometimes in competition, sometimes part of a single whole. One favors their early sixties work, adds some doo-wop covers, and includes their number one 1980s single (written without the aid of Brian Wilson), "Kokomo." This is the aesthetic of the Mike Love–Bruce Johnston touring group, and most of the big hits CD compilations. Another is displayed by Brian and his touring group and is organized around his publicized tragedies and triumphs and latest compilations and emphasizes Brian as *auteur*. This is also the organizing principle of the box set *Good Vibrations*. The third, and the most ambitious, was presented in the 1970s concerts when Carl and Dennis Wilson were still alive, and was probably organized by Carl. It connected the Mike and Brian polarities along with other contributions from the band and successfully navigated a coherent presentation of the band's first fifteen years.

14. September 11 temporarily disgorged some classic Reaganistic cultural re-

pression into the Bush administration. Besides engineering the Patriot Act, Attorney General John Ashcroft, before he was forced out of office, managed to entrap, raid, and then jail the hippie comic Tommy Chong for selling bongs, legal in California, but illegal in Pennsylvania. See www.akatommychong.com, the website for the documentary film made about the case. The prosecuting attorney general for western Pennsylvania who jailed Chong, Mary Beth Buchanan, appointed by Bush and replaced by Obama, also seized thousands of DVDs of the documentary in a second raid.

15. After Reagan, the Republicans, led by Newt Gingrich, would make their grandest miscalculation during Clinton's second midterm election, when in spite, or maybe because of the Lewinsky scandal, Clinton's approval ratings remained at 65 percent, and the Democrats actually gained seats in the House and did not lose any in the Senate, defying historical precedents and professional prognosticators, including Al Gore. See Sean Wilentz, *The Age of Reagan* (New York: Harper, 2008), 394–95.

Eric Lott

Perfect Is Dead

Karen Carpenter, Theodor Adorno, and the Radio, or If Hooks Could Kill

FOR TOM SMUCKER

> The only philosophy which can be responsibly practised in face of despair is the attempt to contemplate all things as they would present themselves from the standpoint of redemption. Knowledge has no light but that shed on the world by redemption: all else is reconstruction, mere technique. Perspectives must be fashioned that displace and estrange the world, reveal it to be, with its rifts and crevices, as indigent and distorted as it will appear one day in the messianic light. To gain such perspectives without velleity or violence, entirely from felt contact with its objects—this alone is the task of thought.
> —Theodor Adorno, *Minima Moralia*

The Carpenters seem made to order for what Theodor Adorno in a famous essay called "the fetish-character in music and the regression of listening."[1] Nothing in the smooth, reified, even fetishistic sheen of songs such as "Close to You"—a brand of Los Angeles vernacular sentimental poetic production for the airwaves—suggests the potential for authentic aesthetic experience or expression. The apparently unbroken surface of this industrially manufactured sound, however, is in fact riven by longing, constriction, and discomfort, and I will argue that it constitutes a kind of negative dialectic of the L.A. that had so revolted Adorno during his exile there in the 1940s and early 1950s. In this sense Karen and Richard Carpenter provide an excellent test case for Adorno's ideas about structural listening and the fate of aesthetic responsiveness in the age of radio (one of Adorno's first activities upon his arrival in the United States was of course his work with Paul Lazarsfeld's Princeton Radio Research Project). In *Dialectic of Enlightenment* (an L.A. story if ever there was one), Adorno and Max Horkheimer use the parable of Homer's Sirens to theorize sonic experience in capitalist society, the only options being dogged sublimation (the rowers' stopped-up ears) or beauty without consequence (Odysseus strapped, motionless, to the mast);[2] it is tempting to suggest that by the time the Carpenter family moved to Downey, California, in 1963, the agon of Odysseus and the Sirens had been reduced to the upbeat oblivion of surfers and the Beach Boys. Yet when the Carpenters hit it big in 1970, deuce-coupe Fordism was already undergoing significant strain, and the contradictions of capital, urban space, cultural abundance, the nuclear family, and female power were registered—hideously, magisterially— in music calculatingly designed for the car radio and the quadraphonic sound system. The Caucasian blues of "Superstar," "Rainy Days and Mondays," "Goodbye to Love," "Hurting Each Other," and others project the suburban whiteness of Downey—known for its aerospace industry, its surfing, its pioneering fast-food chains, and its racist police force—into a soundscape of pain and self-negation, whose real-life counterpart came in Karen Carpenter's notorious death from anorexia at the age of thirty-two. Read right, in other words, the Carpenters' music speaks symptomatically of the "damaged life" Adorno espied in L.A.'s endless summer.[3]

It is amusing, I'll allow, to catalogue some of the ways in which the Carpenters story suggests a willfully antiliberatory ethos, political, personal, and musical. The brother-sister duo looked almost freakishly alike, their visages on album covers and in photo shoots frozen into the same rictus of compulsory cheerfulness. This aura of sibling sameness is often represented pictorially and musically as a marriage of true talents, an endogamous involution that further resists the incursion of difference. The motivating product behind—or consequence of—this imaginary is a series of hit songs overdetermined by repetition, calculation, sameness: the same sweet bummer vibe in song after song of lost or unrequited love, set to arrangements that blur one into the next, featuring Phil Spector–like choruses of background vocals made up solely of Karen

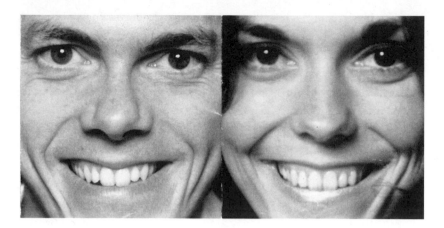

Compulsory Cheerfulness

and Richard Carpenter's multiply overdubbed voices. One of their first big hits, "We've Only Just Begun" (1970), was originally a bank commercial jingle—at a single stroke fulfilling exponentially Adorno's nightmare of culture-industry commodification. By all accounts, Richard Carpenter and his lyricist, John Bettis, not infrequently wrote to a precise formula. Richard and Karen both insisted that their stage show perfectly reproduce—without variation from show to show in a punishing touring schedule—their already overcalculated recordings. Their record company, Herb Alpert and Jerry Moss's A&M Records, was careful to market the group only in terms that conformed to the public's perception of them as bland and square.[4] In 1973 the Carpenters accepted Richard Nixon's invitation to perform at the White House during a state visit by the West German chancellor Willy Brandt and basked in the president's description of them as "young America at its best," thus officially becoming the musical face of Nixon's "silent majority" (Coleman, *The Carpenters*, 143). The group dominated early-seventies easy-listening FM radio formats, which had been built on the kind of administrative audience research Adorno decried in his work with Lazarsfeld.[5] If to Adorno standardization was the watchword and the death knell of cultural forms produced by industrial means, the Carpenters embraced those means perhaps more fully than any bestselling pop band of their moment.

The fetish-character of the Carpenters sound is evident all across the hits they carefully packaged in 1973 as *Singles 1969–1973*, which sold many millions of copies upon its release. In the very first notes of the album's brief opening snippet of "Close to You" comes a piano-and-vibraphone iso-morphism whose crystalline ring sounds like a perfectionist's manifesto. (Since the song in its entirety closes the album, the placement of this little excerpt out front, an interesting packaging move in its own right, makes the record go in a self-enclosed circle, ending where it begins.) The cordoned-off "classical" piano-and-strings segment that opens the group's dolorous cover of the Beatles' "Ticket to Ride" could have given Adorno the fatal heart attack he suffered the year they recorded it; nor is the band above studio tricks such as the overamplified closed hi-hat strikes that begin each verse of "Superstar," only to recede deep into the mix. The absurdly incongruous fuzz-guitar solo on "Goodbye to Love" is so deliciously overwrought that you can hear the guitarist's pick tortur-ing the strings. And the Herb Alpert/Tijuana Brass horns that come out of nowhere in the middle of "Close to You" sound like nothing so much as a gold-plated gear-shift thrown in to drive the tune into a new key. Even these obvious examples of Richard Carpenter's gifts as an (over)-arranger understate his ability to turn calculated simulation into a brand: the "Herb Alpert" horns I just mentioned were played by Chuck Findley, since Alpert himself wasn't available the day of the session.[6]

Meanwhile, Karen Carpenter's voice is unmatched in its ability to sum-mon a languid melancholy that is somehow at the same time evacuated of personality. This is what Robert Christgau was referring to, I think, when he spoke long ago of "Karen Carpenter's ductile, dispassionate con-tralto."[7] Aside from the self-mortgaging "We've Only Just Begun," the un-convincingly upbeat "Top of the World," and the infantile "Sing," all the songs on Singles are downers—full of rainy days, Mondays, fugitive rock-star lovers, so-longs to love, embraces of loneliness, nostalgia for better days, romantic skepticism, pain, and longing. Yet you never get the sense that the persona being crafted is really going through anything; as Roland Barthes says in "The Grain of the Voice" of the baritone Dietrich Fischer-Dieskau, "Everything in the (semantic and lyrical) structure is respected and yet nothing seduces, nothing sways us to *jouissance*." The art is, as Barthes could with justice have said of Karen Carpenter, "inordinately expressive (the diction is dramatic, the pauses, the checkings and releas-ings of breath, occur like shudders of passion) and hence never exceeds culture: here it is the soul which accompanies the song, not the body"— an effect of breath, not the grain of the voice. "The lung, a stupid organ," writes Barthes, so unlike the throat.[8]

Fetishized, segmented, voided: a perfect case, one would think, of Adorno's contention that to broadcast (and by extension record) music in the commercial culture industries is to make it impossible. Adorno's work on aesthetics and the radio came at the intersection of three closely related concerns: a post-Hegelian philosophy of music, both serious and popular; a philosophical and methodological critique of the culture industry and its own commercial research practices as well as prevailing U.S. trends in social research; and a critical encounter with U.S. cultural life, first in New York City and then in Los Angeles, in which German fascism seemed recapitulated in laissez-faire leisure society. The conjuncture of at least these matters put Adorno on high-minded lookout for art forms that in their structural integrity could produce part-and-whole dialectics that resisted the wholly administered tendency of modern Western societies and the increasingly one-dimensional political economies that characterized them. The administrative research of Lazarsfeld's radio project, as David Jenemann splendidly documents in *Adorno in America*, struck Adorno as "sneering empiricist sabotage" that, instead of examining radio programming in the context of a total social situation of production, distribution, and consumption in whole social fields structured in precisely identifiable if contradictory ways, took audience likes and dislikes at their word, among other things mistaking values for facts—a conspiracy of bean counters complicit with the logic of social domination.[9] The radio as Adorno found it upon his arrival to the United States in 1938 not only used aesthetic forms to sell products but thereby turned those forms themselves into commodities, canceling their aesthetic value and binding them and their listeners ever more firmly to the everyday harmony of unfreedom. It was the task of criticism to expose this:

> Chesterfield is merely the nation's cigarette, but the radio is the voice of the nation. In bringing cultural products wholly into the sphere of commodities, radio does not try to dispose of its culture goods themselves as commodities straight to the consumer. In America it collects no fees from the public, and so has acquired the illusory form of disinterested, unbiased authority which suits Fascism admirably. The radio becomes the universal mouthpiece of the Fuhrer. . . . The gigantic fact that the speech penetrates everywhere replaces its content, just as the benefaction of the Toscanini broadcast takes the place of the symphony. (*Dialectic of Enlightenment*, 159)

This is doomy, no doubt; but here and elsewhere Adorno's insistence on the dialectical rehearsal of the entire situation of entertainment reception is, I would argue, crucial to any lasting sense of aesthetic possibility. I have argued elsewhere that, contrary to thinking of aesthetics as a ruse or repository of ugly political animus—antidemocratic investments in "standards" or normative notions of taste, for example—we should pursue its democratic reclamation. The problem with aesthetics is not (pace Terry Eagleton) that it's a bourgeois illusion but that it's too often a bourgeois reality; we ought to be arguing for more of it for more people, not less of it for the few.[10] To the extent that the culture industries debase aesthetic possibility, Adorno is there, with no little sympathy I might add, to suggest why. "The customers of musical entertainment are themselves objects or, indeed, products of the same mechanisms which determine the production of popular music. Their spare time serves only to reproduce their working capacity. It is a means instead of an end. . . . Popular music is for the masses a perpetual busman's holiday."[11] For working people beaten down by the same political economy that sponsors (in every sense) their leisure time, the labor of aesthetic responsiveness takes a backseat to escape and distraction—which in turn delivers them each Monday to the same labor routine. Inducing relaxation because its products are patterned and predigested, according to Adorno: "The culture industry perpetually cheats its consumers of what it perpetually promises. The promissory note which, with its plots and staging, it draws on pleasure is endlessly prolonged; the promise, which is actually all the spectacle consists of, is illusory: all it actually confirms is that the real point will never be reached, that the diner must be satisfied with the menu" (ibid., 139) However much Adorno's approach could slide into somewhat moralistic condemnations of everything from jazz to astrology, it would be silly to discount the pressures he outlines on the creation of a genuinely popular aesthetic—just as Adorno's framing of such pressures here will return to animate—and haunt—the work the Carpenters produced in the 1970s.

If that work depends on the techniques or at least commercial requirements of repetition, standardization, and the other culture industry attributes that Adorno relentlessly critiqued (e.g., "On the Fetish-Character in Music," 306; *Dialectic of Enlightenment*, 136), might it be worth looking further into their shape and resonance and effects in the contexts that produced and embraced them? I am inspired here by Adorno's remarks about "immanent criticism" in his essay "Cultural Criticism and Society," written in Los Angeles in 1949. There Adorno argues that the contradictions or inadequacies of form or meaning in artistic products may dialectically suggest the social forces that deformed them—by indicating how "untrue" they are to the social field they claim to represent. The forms themselves are not untrue, writes Adorno, but rather their pretension to correspond to reality: "Immanent criticism of intellectual and artistic phenomena seeks to grasp, through the analysis of their form and meaning, the contradiction between their objective idea and that pretension. It names what the consistency or inconsistency of the work itself expresses of the structure of the existent."[12] What is worst about the Carpenters' music, in other words, may also be what is best about it; in so fully giving form to one wing of the culture industry of its time, the group might be said to have "produced the concept" (à la Althusser) of turn-of-the-seventies southern California unfreedom.[13] On this view, it is less important to note the ways the Carpenters amount to a sort of sonic servitude than to look into how they cognitively map through aesthetic inadequacy the culture and subjectivity of one aspect of their historical moment. "A successful work, according to immanent criticism," Adorno writes, "is not one which resolves objective contradictions in a spurious harmony, but one which expresses the idea of harmony negatively by embodying the contradictions, pure and uncompromised, in its innermost structure" (32). I'd like to try to show that the Carpenters, while seeming to opt for a "spurious harmony," are all about its negation.

The sort of dialectical treatment Fredric Jameson describes, which would aim, "not so much at solving the particular dilemmas in question, as at converting those problems into their own solutions on a higher level, and making the fact and the existence of the problem itself the starting point for new research," is, I would contend, something to which the Carpenters have not as yet been subjected.[14] This is not strictly true: there is the brilliant and corrosive 1987 Todd Haynes short film *Superstar*, which features Karen and Richard played by Barbie and Ken dolls (as Karen gets sicker the doll's face is gradually whittled and sanded away) and which Richard managed to suppress in 1990 (though it's now easily available on the Internet); there is Sonic Youth's 1990 song "Tunic (Song for Karen)" (more on which anon), an equally brilliant meditation on the singer's fame and physical frame; and there is the 1994 tribute compilation, *If I Were a Carpenter*, of Carpenters songs covered by bands like Sonic Youth (an incredible reading of "Superstar") and Babes in Toyland, which on the whole attempts to retrieve the group's dark side. For that matter, Ray Coleman's biography of the Carpenters is full of (usually oblique) testimony by fans and friends alike concerning the pain and emptiness of its principals' inner lives and music. The present attempt draws on these readings to analyze further the ways in which something was very wrong in Downey.

I say "in Downey" rather than "in the Carpenter family" because the deformations that beset the family—and they were many—were endemic to the post–Second World War suburban settlement. Downey, incorporated in 1956, lies in southeast L.A. at one of the busiest intersections in 1950s America: the crossroads of U.S. Highways 19 (the through route from Laguna Beach to Pasadena) and 42 (the road from L.A. to San Diego). Once the Interstate Highway System (officially authorized, probably not coincidentally, the year of Downey's incorporation) had been completed, Downey was bordered by federal Highways 710, 105, 605, and 5—perfectly plotted, that is to say, on the postwar map of state-sponsored highway construction under Eisenhower that helped push-pull suburban/inner-city racial and class formations into being. (Downey is cheek by jowl with relatively isolated Watts.) Eric Avila's *Popular Culture in the Age of White Flight* offers an excellent account of the way in which this dialectic of chocolate city and vanilla suburb came about. Studying such institutional formations as Hollywood, Disneyland (opened in 1955), Dodger Stadium (built in time for the 1962 season), and the freeway system, Avila shows how mid-century L.A. was self-consciously made into a white or white-dominated city.[15] As in other U.S. conurbations, housing in Los Angeles was concertedly racially redlined by a host of agencies and activities, not least among them the New Deal's Home Owners' Loan Corporation and Federal Housing Authority. Disney's choice of Orange County's Anaheim for the location of Disneyland certified the sanitized suburban ethos he meant to foster there. Dodger Stadium was set down atop a working-class Chicano neighborhood in an attempt by city fathers to "renew" the historic downtown area. Key to this entire system was the freeway, whose supplanting of an extensive, demographically diverse, public streetcar system cemented the new urban regime of privatized, racially segmented living. (As California historian and activist Carey McWilliams put it in 1965, the "freeways have been carefully designed to skim over and skirt around such eyesores as Watts and East Los Angeles; even the downtown section, a portion of which has become a shopping area for minorities, has been partially bypassed.")[16] The figurehead for these developments, Avila observes, was Ronald Reagan, who aided the House Un-American Activities Committee in its quest for "subversive" influences in Hollywood, emceed the televised opening ceremonies at Disneyland, and appeared on live television to promote the building of Dodger Stadium (*Popular Culture*, 7). Reagan was of course governor of California from 1967 to 1975, precisely the years of the Carpenters' ascendance.

The Carpenter family parachuted into this context from New Haven, Connecticut, in 1963, partly to get to better weather and partly to bolster Richard's budding musical career (Richard was seventeen, Karen was thirteen). What they encountered in Downey was a city like the whole of L.A. on the cusp of post-Fordism, poised between the suburban commute and the service shopfloor and the entertainment business on one side and factory work (Karen and Richard's father, Harold, worked in industrial printing) on the other. The very first Taco Bell had just opened there (in 1962; the fourth-ever McDonald's had gone up there in 1953) and suburban homes and aviation factories had recently replaced the area's farms. Two years after the Carpenters' arrival, the 1965 uprising in next-door Watts made spectacular protest against the racial entailments of the area's suburban splendors. The Carpenter family's response to the cumulative force of the above structures, as we will see, was to circle the wagons into a highly strung, centripetally focused family unit that more or less ravaged its members, however upbeat they appeared on the surface. On the face of it, the kids reveled in clean-cut postwar L.A. youth culture: Karen's lifelong affinity for burger joints (until the onset of her illness) and both siblings' love of cars (Richard to this day remains a collector), while certainly not unique to Downey, are hardly coincidental. Of course L.A., perhaps more than any other city than Detroit, is the urban monument to the automobile. The Beach Boys memorialized that fact in "Little Deuce Coupe," "Fun, Fun, Fun," and at least a dozen others, great songs that undeniably capture a moment and an ethos of suburban white abundance and mobility. The Carpenters picked right up on this soundscape, similarly sublimating the blackness of car music such as Ike Turner's "Rocket 88" even as they offered a broadly whitened defense against it in the musical context of the late 1960s. If they turned it to the account of a very different sound, it's worth noting that, like the Beach Boys' Brian Wilson (and what the hell, the rest of them too), each of the Carpenters in their own way caught the wave of catastrophe brought on by the ebullient sense, and sound, of plenty.

How this seeming paradox might have come about—that in a land and moment of abundance the result was constriction, loss, self-denial, and horror—has too often and too easily been ascribed to the bottoming out of the sixties into helter-skelter madness and murder, the now canonical (almost postcanonical) script to be found in (say) Joan Didion's dispassionate odes to dispassion and disaffection, *Play It As It Lays*, *Slouching Towards Bethlehem*, and *The White Album*. Not in the Carpenters' backyard did it happen this way, those moderate Republican friends of music bizzer (and sometime boyfriend of Karen's) Mike Curb, leader of the popular whitebread middle-of-the-road singing group the Mike Curb Congregation, chair of the California Republican Party during Reagan's tenure as governor, and later himself the state's lieutenant governor. So what was it? Clues exist everywhere in the Carpenters' music: the sense of (suburban? automotive?) isolation conveyed in "Close to You," an apparently dreamy evocation of intimacy which is in fact its opposite—"just like me / they long to be / close to you." The sense there, too, of personal interchangeability, or the everyday monotony of routine and repetition that defines "Rainy Days and Mondays" (which "always get me down"), the latter a weekly certainty certain to give the singer, as she sings, "what they used to call the blues" (don't they still?); or again, the fragile (and rather frightening) hope articulated in the forced antidepressant "Top of the World" that, like the sudden joy of today, "tomorrow will be just the same." We're treading on pins and needles, here, and it's not a little ominous. Whence the will to melancholy in a willfully upbeat world? Did the Carpenters intuit something about the culture that produced them?

In my view, the Carpenters songs that thematize and, as it were, self-reflexively theorize their sound are the ones that speak most interestingly to the underside of El Dorado. "Superstar," for example, these days surely the Carpenters' signature song, limns the story of a groupie longing for the eponymous guitarist to come back to her:

> Long ago, and, oh, so far away
> I fell in love with you before the second show.
> Your guitar, it sounds so sweet and clear,
> But you're not really here, it's just the radio.
> Don't you remember you told me you loved me baby?
> You said you'd be coming back this way again baby.
> Baby, baby, baby, baby, oh, baby,

I love you, I really do.
Loneliness is such a sad affair,
And I can hardly wait to be with you again.
What to say, to make you come again?
Come back to me again, and play your sad guitar.[17]

All somewhat ludicrous—she fell in love that fast? she forgot she's listening to the radio?—until you consider that this is nothing less than a set
of reflections on the culture industry itself: its promissory note that never
delivers, its illusory compensation, its perpetual confirmation of frustration. "It's just the radio": one hell of an indictment of the commercial universe that it was Richard and Karen Carpenter's every ambition to enter.
Presence of guitar is here absence of star, ironic commentary indeed on
what I've noted about the withholding quality of Karen's voice, to say nothing of her gruesome disappearing act. The song appears to work like this:
girl falls in love with guitar superstar, and they have a brief moment in
the flesh; she later hears him on the box, which makes her feel even more
abandoned and wanting than she already did; she longs for his return so
she can hear him "play [his] sad guitar" in person once more. One big culture industry circle, the outcome of which is frustration and even a desire
for further sadness, which Adorno argues was guaranteed to happen in
the first place ("On the Fetish-Character in Music," 313–14). And as for
one's demeanor in the face of that frustration and sadness? "The pathos
of composure justifies the world which makes it necessary" (*Dialectic of
Enlightenment*, 151).

But there's more. A dialectic of the live and the commercially repro-
duced here structures the responses of the singer, who is also a listener
like us (in serial regress, we listen to her as she listens to the guitarist;
her experience is a stand-in for ours). The live is itself, of course, commercially mediated, otherwise the guitarist wouldn't be a superstar; but when
his sounds take to the airwaves, an evacuation—of presence, of flesh—
occurs. This is in the nature of radio, as Allen Weiss has written, this
is how it works: "Recording and radio—through a sort of sympathetic
magic—entail a theft of the voice and a disappearance of the body, a radical accentuation of the mind/body split, with its concomitant anguish."[18]
The crush that the radio fosters is by definition unrequited: that is what
this song says. Some understanding of this on the singer's part may be
why she desires the superstar to come back and play his guitar for her—

he's less a person now than a *sound*. If, as Weiss argues, "Recording produces an exteriorization and transformation of the voice, a sort of dispossession of the self" (*Phantasmic Radio*, 32), we can observe here not only the guitarist's but also the singer's dissolution into sound, the flat magic of lyrical repetition in her multiply articulated desire, as in some *fort/da* game of the soul, that the superstar come back again, the very word "again" repeatedly punctuating the insistence of desire, until articulation fails: "Baby, baby, baby, baby, oh, baby." The attempt to cling to an absence by such means only ensures the fate of all such radio-produced evacuations: "Radio-phonic airspace is a necropolis riddled with dead voices, the voices of the dead, and dead air—all cut off from their originary bodies, all now transmitted to the outer international and cosmic airwaves only in order to reenter our inner ears" (ibid., 79).

Meanwhile, a similar decomposition-by-culture-industry occurs in the song "Yesterday Once More." As the early-seventies reclamation of 1950s Americana—think *American Graffiti* and *Happy Days*—kicked in, the Carpenters produced a song (this one by Richard Carpenter and John Bettis) that addressed this nostalgia with striking self-consciousness:

> When I was young
> I'd listen to the radio
> Waitin' for my favorite songs
> When they played I'd sing along
> It made me smile.
> Those were such happy times
> And not so long ago
> How I wondered where they'd gone
> But they're back again
> Just like a long lost friend
> All the songs I loved so well.
> Every Sha-la-la-la
> Every Wo-o-wo-o
> Still shines
> Every shing-a-ling-a-ling
> That they're startin' to sing's
> So fine.
> When they get to the part
> Where he's breakin' her heart

It can really make me cry
Just like before
It's yesterday once more.[19]

Once again the substitution of sound for "friend" via the radio. And here again, this time in the nostalgic embrace of oldies (or their recreation in current music), the industrial production of sound establishes a closed circuitry of repetition—of the past, of former feelings, of period musical refrains themselves (so commercially familiar that the singer can short-hand them with a "sha-la-la-la")—summed up in the title's "once more." Not least, the singer's allegedly happier times are marked by the tears of musically induced heartbreak. Culture industry seriality: all is unchanging, and invariably downcast, in the radio's orbit. I am arguing that the Carpenters' music depends on a soundscape of structured disappointment and disillusion, but also that this soundscape offers them an occasion to reflect on and willfully perpetuate that disillusion. As succeeding lines of "Yesterday Once More" have it: "Lookin' back on how it was / In years gone by / And the good times that I had / Makes today seem rather sad / So much has changed."

The self-annihilation the Carpenters, particularly Karen, enacted by way of radiophony is eerily evoked in such songs. In retrospect, it is as though they lived the sublating maxim expressed in one of their titles, that "All You Get from Love Is a Love Song." Yet it must be said that the Carpenters' intended response to an administered world they espied even in their own music was homeopathic—a striving for perfection and extreme exertions of studio (and stage) control; I think you can hear it (and its essentially negative outcome) in the music. Sound quality was prized so far above performance aura that the Carpenters' stage show (until they made drastic changes to it in 1976) was widely considered a dud.[20] (Check them out on YouTube: Richard sits inertly at the keyboard, Karen sighs into the mike like a willow in a mild breeze.) The word "perfection" peppers the accounts of their studio methods and output. A revealing 1971 article captures their compulsive meticulousness:

What the Downey pair will do tonight is put the finishing touches to [the song "Hurting Each Other"], adding things none but the best-trained ears will even hear. But Richard hears, and Karen hears, and they are perfectionists. . . . To the average listener the song was already complete, and even those of us watching and listening were unable to perceive why the Carpenters would suddenly stop, say "no, that's not right," and start over again. . . . With a technician standing by, the Carpenters entered the sound booth and the 16-track tape containing their latest release was started. It will sound like 12 to 15 voices on the radio Friday, and all of them are Richard's and Karen's.[21]

The nonchalance of the Carpenters' music is belied by a straitjacketed production ethic that undermines the desired effect; it sounds manufactured, airless, the swelling vocals less like rock 'n' roll background singers than the Mormon Tabernacle Choir, which, come to think of it, may not have been far from the desired effect.

The article from which I just quoted was aptly called "Can't We Stop?" and it rightly suggests the out-of-control, compulsive quality of perfection's lure for the Carpenters. Again, this has its dialectical counterpart in the Carpenter family unit and the destructions it wrought, or for which it provided the scene. For whatever combination of reasons, that family was an impacted, armored horror show in the guise of suburban rectitude (but aren't we all). Allow me just to telegraph the dimensions of the Carpenter family lockdown. Agnes Carpenter ruled the household with more vigor than warmth. The family ethos dictated that Karen and Richard live at home with their parents—not only when they first became stars at nineteen and twenty-three, respectively, but also for many years after. When they did move out, Karen and Richard bought a house and lived together. Even then, one tiptoed around Agnes's dictates. Richard complained bitterly for years that Karen had adopted Agnes's mother-function, policing in particular his romantic life (she broke up more than one of his relationships).[22] The aura of incest that hung over the group was conveyed pictorially on album covers, on stage in the hand-holding they indulged at certain moments during their shows, and musically in the marriage-minded "We've Only Just Begun," which of course they sing with, if not exactly to, each other. (As Richard put it in 1988, "I called her K.C., and she called me R.C. It seems as if we did everything together. We loved cars and went bowling and listened to Spike Jones, Nat King Cole and Elvis, among many others. More than brother and sister, we were best friends.")[23] After Karen's death, and only after it, Richard got married—to his cousin Mary. Both siblings appear to have had obsessive-compulsive disorder, and both became drug addicts, though in Karen's case the consequences were deadly. One might say they responded in kind to an administered world, and it killed them.[24]

In 1979, Richard successfully kicked an addiction to Quaaludes in a Topeka, Kansas, rehab facility; Karen for many years took as many as one hundred Dulcolax laxative pills a day, together with syrup of Ipecac and thyroid medicine to speed up her metabolism. Later in her short life this five-foot-four woman fluctuated between 106 and 77 pounds; her heart was so stressed by this regime that when in early 1983, after extensive psychiatric treatment, she managed to gain a considerable amount of weight, she suffered a fatal heart attack. The point of all this for me is not the usual Hollywood Babylon fable. When she wasn't in the bathroom Karen obsessed over her needlepoint, and Richard mostly washed his cars. Rather, Karen met the culture industry on its own terms, and lost. Operating at the intersection of show-biz spectacle and her mother's severe strictures on female power and autonomy, she strove to eliminate imperfection until there was no life left. Internalizing the business's murderous pressure on the female image, K.C. tore at herself to preserve an imagined innocence that amounted only to self-negation. Her fleeting romantic relationships were invariably unsatisfying, and her only marriage was abortive. Quite a good drummer as well as singer, she was implored by Richard to abandon the drums, crimping her musicianship and putting her out front, where her paralyzing self-consciousness was only redoubled. She made every attempt not to grow up, surrounding herself with her beloved stuffed animals and Disney paraphernalia. When, with Richard in rehab, she attempted a solo record with famed producer Phil Ramone (veteran of recordings with Bob Dylan, Bruce Springsteen, and scores of others), she did try on a more embodied, adult image, with songs like "Remember When Lovin' Took All Night" and "My Body Keeps Changing My Mind." The result was so ridiculously unconvincing that A & M refused to release it—yet one more moment of negation and waste that amounted, if only unconsciously, to an immanent critique of the industry norms the Carpenters had so embraced.

Enter Sonic Youth, whose "Tunic (Song for Karen)," released seven years after the singer's death, acutely renders the culture industry death drive I have tried to capture in this essay.[25] After a drilling, discordant opening, we find Karen in heaven, reflecting on celebrity, selfhood, music, body image, and—Agnes, her mother:

Dreaming, dreaming of a girl like me
Hey what are you waiting for—feeding, feeding me
I feel like I'm disappearing—getting smaller every day
But I look in the mirror—and I'm bigger in every way
She said:
You aren't never going anywhere
You aren't never going anywhere
I ain't never going anywhere
I ain't never going anywhere

Fed on Hollywood dreams, Karen, as they say in the business, "blew up"—got as big as stars came in the 1970s. This, as "Tunic" rightly suggests, produced a series of self-alienations. It made it impossible for her to have a healthy relation to her size. The body that disappeared in radiophony and in commercial spectacle was also always outsized and therefore a problem in the flesh. At the same time, the song speculates, whether because of anorexia or fame, the singer felt dwarfed ("smaller every day"), a feeling contradicted by the mirror, which doesn't so much return the singer to her "self" as invert its image. And these dissociations are founded on the installation of Agnes in Karen's head as internal admonitor.

The only way out of this, the song asserts, is posthumous. "I'm in heaven now," Karen says, "I can see you Richard / Goodbye Hollywood, Good-bye Downey"; and she seems happy with "all [her] brand new friends," among them "Janis" (Joplin), "Dennis" (Wilson, the just-deceased Beach Boy, most likely—an inspired choice since he too was a drummer), and, inevitably, "Elvis." Karen's ambition ("dreaming, dreaming") has taken her to the ultimate firmament.

Hey Mom! Look, I'm up here—I finally made it
I'm playing the drums again too
Don't be sad—the band doesn't sound half bad
And I remember, Mom, what you said
You said honey, you look so underfed

Looking down from the house band of heaven: not a bad fantasy of omniscient restoration, complete with drum set. The result is a version of the Carpenters' "Top of the World," with K.C. literally "lookin' down on creation." Where in that song it was love that had lifted her, here it is death.

Convincing first-person testimony of anorexia nervosa reveals precisely this: a withholding that delivers plenitude: "Anorexia nervosa isn't an attempt to make yourself suffer; it's an attempt, from a postlapsarian vantage point, to recapture Eden by revealing it; with pain you feel, with shivering cold, warmth becomes real and wonderful again. Food becomes delicious and gratifying. . . . It isn't that I wanted to be a child again. It's that I wanted to feel the way I felt when I was a child in this asocial life, centered on my home."[26] This is indeed, as Adorno would have it, contemplating things from the standpoint of redemption. It draws on the tradition Joan Jacobs Brumberg describes as "anorexia mirabilis," which descends from the examples of fasting saints, though, as Gillian Brown observes, it is also taken with the Romantic imperative to self-expansion.[27] Brown's work directs us to the contradictory relations among consciousness, self-determination, and subjection to be found in the case of Karen Carpenter. The anorectic refusal of food amounts to a paradoxical attempt at self-assertion and self-maintenance; as Brown has it, "the anorectic projects a self that expands through its material reduction" ("Anorexia," 190). The assumption of power and control is produced by the anorectic as a disappearance; mastery takes the form of self-subjection, for as long as it lasts.[28] Thus is "alienation absolutely identical with self-possession" (196), which, I have argued, is the Carpenters' distaff contribution to a critique of the culture industry. In this radical form of self-proprietorship—dispossession itself—is a kind of antihumanism that shines in every note the Carpenters put on record.

This is, finally, the "health unto death" of which Adorno acidly wrote in *Minima Moralia* (58). Karen Carpenter withdrew from feeding (and thus the mother) and musical coimplication (and her brother) into self-possession in extremis—slow starvation and a bad solo record. It may be that these were among the "libidinal achievements" Adorno speaks of as being demanded of an "individual behaving as healthy in body and mind," which can be performed "only at the cost of the profoundest mutilation":

> The regular guy, the popular girl, have to repress not only their desires and insights, but even the symptoms that in bourgeois times resulted from repression. Just as the old injustice is not changed by a lavish display of light, air and hygiene, but is in fact concealed by the gleaming transparency of rationalized big business, the inner health of our time has been secured by blocking flight into illness without in the slight-

est altering its aetiology. The dark closets have been abolished as a troublesome waste of space, and incorporated in the bathroom. What psychoanalysis suspected, before it became itself a part of hygiene, has been confirmed. The brightest rooms are the secret domain of faeces (*Minima Moralia*, 58–59)

Not long before Karen died, the regular guy and the popular girl managed to release (in June 1981) their all too fittingly titled comeback album *Made in America*. It was too little too late: there was nothing left to eat but the menu, and Karen found only in heaven the only perfection there is.

Notes

1. Theodor Adorno, "On the Fetish-Character in Music and the Regression of Listening" (1938), in *The Essential Frankfurt School Reader*, ed. Andrew Arato and Eike Gebhardt (New York: Urizen, 1978), 270–99.

2. Max Horkheimer and Theodor W. Adorno, *Dialectic of Enlightenment*, trans. John Cumming (1947; New York: Seabury, 1972), 32–37.

3. Theodor Adorno, *Minima Moralia: Reflections from Damaged Life*, trans. E. F. N. Jephcott (1951; London: Verso, 1974).

4. Ray Coleman, *The Carpenters: The Untold Story: An Authorized Biography* (New York: HarperCollins, 1994), 163. See also Barney Hoskyns, *Waiting for the Sun: Strange Days, Weird Scenes, and the Sound of Los Angeles* (New York: St. Martin's Press, 1996), 230–31.

5. Joseph Lanza, "'Beautiful Music': The Rise of Easy-Listening FM," *The Popular Music Studies Reader*, ed. Andy Bennett, Barry Shank, and Jason Toynbee (New York: Routledge, 2006), 161; see also Lanza, *Elevator Music: A Surreal History of Muzak, Easy-Listening, and Other Moodsong* (New York: Picador, 1994), 167–82.

6. "Chuck didn't play it that way at first, but I worked with him and he nailed it," said Richard. "A lot of people thought it was Herb—Bacharach thought so, too. But it's the way Findley is playing it." Quoted in Daniel Levitin, "Pop Charts: How Richard Carpenter's Lush Arrangements Turned Hit Songs Into Pop Classics" (1995), in *Yesterday Once More: Memories of the Carpenters and Their Music*, ed. Randy Schmidt (Cranberry Township, Pa.: Tiny Ripple Books, 2000), 219. Originally published in *Electronic Musician*.

7. Robert Christgau, *Rock Albums of the '70s: A Critical Guide* (New York: Da Capo, 1981), 75.

8. Roland Barthes, "The Grain of the Voice" (1972), in *Image—Music—Text*, trans. Stephen Heath (New York: Hill and Wang, 1977), 183.

9. David Jenemann, *Adorno in America* (Minneapolis: University of Minnesota Press, 2007), 1; see also 45, 53–54. For an excellent account of Adorno in Los Ange-

les, see Nico Israel, "Damage Control: Adorno, Los Angeles, and the Dislocation of Culture," *Yale Journal of Criticism* 10, no. 1 (1997): 85–113.

10. Eric Lott, "The Aesthetic Ante: Pleasure, Pop Culture, and the Middle Passage," *Callaloo* 17, no. 2 (1994): 546, 547.

11. Theodor W. Adorno (with the assistance of George Simpson), "On Popular Music" (1941), in *On Record: Rock, Pop, and the Written Word*, ed. Simon Frith and Andrew Goodwin (New York: Pantheon, 1990), 310.

12. Theodor W. Adorno, "Cultural Criticism and Society," in *Prisms*, trans. Samuel Weber and Shierry Weber (1967; Cambridge: MIT Press, 1981), 32.

13. Louis Althusser, "On Levi-Strauss" (1966), in *The Humanist Controversy and Other Writings*, ed. Francois Matheron, trans. G. M. Goshgarian (London: Verso, 2003), 26–27.

14. Fredric Jameson, *Marxism and Form: Twentieth-Century Dialectical Theories of Literature* (Princeton: Princeton University Press, 1971), 307.

15. Eric Avila, *Popular Culture in the Age of White Flight: Fear and Fantasy in Suburban Los Angeles* (Berkeley: University of California Press, 2004); see also Cotten Seiler, *Republic of Drivers: A Cultural History of Automobility in America* (Chicago: University of Chicago Press, 2008), 1–16, 69–104.

16. Carey McWilliams, "Watts: The Forgotten Slum," *Nation*, August 30, 1965, quoted in Avila, *Popular Culture in the Age of White Flight*, 213.

17. Leon Russell and Bonnie Bramlett, "Superstar" (Embassy Music Corp./ Cherry River Music Co., 1971).

18. Allen S. Weiss, *Phantasmic Radio* (Durham: Duke University Press, 1995), 32. See also, more generally, Susan J. Douglas, *Listening In: Radio and American Imagination* (Minneapolis: University of Minnesota Press, 2004).

19. Richard Carpenter and John Bettis, "Yesterday Once More," (1971).

20. For an account of the absurdity of those changes, see Ray Coleman's 1976 *Melody Maker* article, "Carpenters über alles!" in Schmidt, *Yesterday Once More*, 137–43.

21. Dan Armstrong, "Can't We Stop? Putting the Finishing Touches on a Carpenters Record" (1971), in Schmidt, *Yesterday Once More*, 57.

22. See, for example, the revealing comments in Coleman, "Carpenters über alles!" 140–41.

23. Richard Carpenter, "Karen Was Wasting Away . . . I Had a Drug Problem . . . And We Couldn't Help Each Other," *TV Guide* (1988), in Schmidt, *Yesterday Once More*, 193.

24. These more or less standard biographical details come from Coleman, *The Carpenters*, the biography authorized by Richard Carpenter.

25. Sonic Youth, "Tunic (Song for Karen)," *Goo* (Geffen, 1990).

26. "Norma," quoted in Hilde Bruch, *The Golden Cage: The Enigma of Anorexia Nervosa* (Cambridge: Harvard University Press, 1978), 71.

27. Joan Jacobs Brumberg, *Fasting Girls: The History of Anorexia Nervosa* (Cam-

bridge: Harvard University Press, 1988), 44–45, 47–48; Gillian Brown, "Anorexia, Humanism, and Feminism," *Yale Journal of Criticism* 5, no. 1 (1991): 190. Brown's essay is brilliantly useful in the present context; for Brumberg's interesting remarks on Karen Carpenter, whose illness brought major public attention to anorexia, see *Fasting Girls*, 17–18.

28. See also in this connection Judith Butler, *The Psychic Life of Power: Theories in Subjection* (Stanford: Stanford University Press, 1997).

Karen Tongson

Agents of Orange

Studio K and Cloud 9

> The goal was to make a record that had that feeling I got when I'd
> go dancing at Studio K at Knott's Berry Farm. You don't feel that
> anymore . . . I wanted to make a record where every song sounds
> like a single . . . and every single would be someone's guilty plea-
> sure, even if they hate me.
> —Gwen Stefani, describing her debut solo album,
> *Love. Angel. Music. Baby.*, December 2, 2004

It may not immediately be legible to the naked ear,
but Stefani's *Love. Angel. Music. Baby.* is an interpretive sonic archive, not only of the Orange County suburbs broadly defined, but of a particular place, time, and
people: of the youth who attended Studio K at Knott's
Berry Farm in Buena Park, California, from 1984 to
1991.[1] The synthetic grain of 1980s pop is unmistakable in Stefani's album. As Krissi Murison in the vener-
able Brit music magazine *NME* notes: "All the best bits
of the decade of decadence are here—Salt-N-Pepa's cartoon rap ('Crash'), Madonna's breathless purr ('Cool') and
camped-up Prince sexperimentalism ('Bubble Pop Electric'). . . . Like a more clued-in Material Girl, Gwen Stefani has looked to the youngsters and realised that if the
Thatcher/Reagan years can work in rock clubs . . . they
can certainly work on the charts."[2] What gets lost in an
equation structured entirely around Stefani's productions in a global music marketplace, as Murison's review

makes us acutely aware, are the local, suburban practices of *consumption* rendered historically in the final product.[3] Stefani herself characterized dancing at Studio K as a sound capture of a moment in time in which the weekly Top 40 ruled, and "every song sounds like a single."[4] But what did Studio K *actually* sound like? How do we get from the pop eclectic, mid-eighties teen sound of amusement park nightclubs to the chart-friendly postmillennial pop baubles that made Stefani stand in for an Orange County sound in a global pop imaginary? What exactly was Studio K? And for whom did it truly resound?

Knott's Berry Farm itself has no official corporate archive of Studio K, despite the fact that the club remained open for seven years (from 1984 to 1991) and redefined the park for a brief moment in history by tapping into a new demographic of local teens, expanding upon what was no longer, by itself, a lucrative market of families with young children.[5] Very few traces of Studio K remain in municipal archives. The Orange County Archives in Santa Ana, California, holds about a dozen photographs and photo proof sheets documenting the teen scene, but this is the extent of their holdings on the regional phenomenon that was Studio K. Stefani's album, *Love. Angel. Music. Baby.* is perhaps the definitive (if profoundly interpretive) sonic archive of that moment. Otherwise, most traces of Studio K reside in the memories of those who created it, those who DJed there, and those who attended the club during its heyday.[6] Finding what is left of Studio K requires following the ephemera and tracking the public intimacies of a suburban teen club culture through its "remote" reenactments online on blogs, on web communities like OCThen.com, or on social networking sites like Myspace.com.

The relocations I trace in this essay—of sounds, memories, archives—transpose the concept of "remote intimacy" from Jennifer Terry's work about militarized gaming cultures. I believe that these networked forms of intimacy among strangers online, which Terry links specifically to a post-9/11 world of surveillance and militarization, can also be refigured to describe a form of engagement practiced by suburban subjects scattered across time, as well as space. As I argue in my book *Relocations: Queer Suburban Imaginaries*, remote intimacies in the analog age were practiced through the shared consumption (or some would say overconsumption) of broadcast television and popular music, as well as by "hanging out" live, at differently situated chains (like Denny's or Dairy Queen), or even at amusement venues like Knott's. Sometimes the resonance of these activities and of these shared popular objects is only discovered be-latedly, recreating intimacies in the present based on the shared, remote gestures—some experienced in isolation—in the past. I would venture to describe such asynchronous echoes as remote intimacies across time.[7]

Stefani's album could serve as an ideal example of such remote inti-macies: the songs she listened to on the radio and at Studio K forged the sound for her first solo album, one that calls forth different temporal layers of local sonic archives for disparate audiences scattered across time and space. Our postdigital age not only enables these remote intimacies across time through the various forms of conversation, networking, and convergence offered by communications technologies and the memories and shared archives it activates, but also, importantly, literalizes and re-inforces the spatial "remoteness" structuring these intimacies. Indeed, connections actually happen "remotely"—on message boards, social net-working sites, even on virtual community sites. Some recollections of the theme park clubs, Studio K at Knott's and Videopolis at Disneyland, are decidedly more innocuous and nostalgic, whereas others hint at the sexual scenes improvised in these family venues. A blogger incarcerated at the Salinas Valley State Penitentiary in Soledad (who uses the moni-ker "Prisoner David"), shares a tale of being transported from his cell to Orange County's theme park clubs through the echoes of The Cure's "Just Like Heaven" on a local college radio broadcast: "The song took me back to my adolescent days when I just got my license to drive. . . . Friday nights at Studio K in Knott's Berry Farm. Saturday in Videopolis in Dis-neyland. Paying off the wino old man, a fixture on the sidewalk in front of the liquor store to score us some beer. Strawberry Hill for the Ladies."[8] Another commentator going by the pseudonym Gavin Elster, meanwhile, responded to a thread about Disneyland's Videopolis with a more explicit tale: "Videopolis! . . . I was one of those elements they tried to keep out. I remember being stopped and asked to leave twice. Once for dancing with another guy and another time for having spikes in my jacket. It was inter-esting to see aspects of club life seep into the park. It was a time when you could get a blowjob in the Fantasyland restroom. I guess I have Eisner to thank for that hummer."[9]

Locating materials about Studio K from beyond the recesses of my own youthful memory as an immigrant, Inland Empire kid dazzled by what might be found there, proved difficult and required following the actual "threads" of these remote intimacies through public and sometimes anonymous conversations conducted on community websites. Thwarted by official corporate and civic archives, I was ultimately able to track the proverbial breadcrumbs scattered across Internet message boards to live encounters with the club's founders and DJs at resort venues like the Pirate's Dinner Adventure in Buena Park—a spectacular theme dinner-theater nestled among the new Korean restaurants and old Denny's coffee shops in strip malls all along Beach Boulevard, just down the street from Knott's Berry Farm. It was at the Pirate's Dinner Adventure in the summer of 2008 that my research assistant, Alex Wescott, and I met Gary R. Salisbury, the Knott's entertainment executive who created Studio K. I tracked Mr. Salisbury down after daily visitations to a thread titled "Cloud 9 and Studio K" inspired by a former avid club-goer, Stephen L. Becker on OCThen.com (a site that focuses on "Memories of Orange County, California").[10] Becker plans to create a tribute site to the two clubs, which were open concurrently at Knott's. His reminiscence about Saturday nights at the park prompted numerous responses about "the K and 9."[11] Among the respondents to the thread about Studio K and Cloud 9 was Gary R. Salisbury, former director of entertainment at Knott's Berry Farm from 1985 through 1989. When he created Studio K in 1984, Salisbury was the entertainment manager at the park. On February 17, 2008, nearly a year after I began visiting the thread in search of further information, Mr. Salisbury offered this post:

> I was the one who came up with the concept of Studio K.
>
> This concept was proposed in a memo dated February 11, 1984. I still have this memo framed in my office.
>
> We opened Studio K on Memorial Day Weekend 1984. The success was overwhelming. She was credited with bring in an additional $2.5 million per year.
>
> I also ran Cloud 9, but Cloud 9 never did near the numbers that were attributed to Studio K.
>
> The name Studio K came from a contest sponsored by Knotts [sic] prior to opening. The winner received a year pass to the park. I have the original plans in my office and they refer to this facility as: Teen Dance Area.
>
> I am also the person who suggested that Studio K be torn down when we approached the 90's. I could see that her days were numbered. She was now bringing in the wrong type of crowd.

She had a good life. WHAT A RIDE!!!
Gary R. Salisbury
By Blogger show40, at February 17, 2008 12:14 AM

I contacted Salisbury through his blogger I.D. and scheduled an interview after verifying with the Knott's Media Relations office that he was, indeed, the founder of the club. This information was not supplied through any corporate documentation, but instead someone at the Media Relations office "asked someone else" and called me back to confirm. Mr. Salisbury is now the marketing and entertainment director at the Pirate's Dinner Adventure on Beach Boulevard (a thoroughfare also known as California State Route 39, the road that originally connected Orange County to Los Angeles), a mere one block north of Knott's Berry Farm. On August 14, 2008, in the shadow of Knott's towering thrill rides, Mr. Salisbury not only shared his recollections about founding Studio K, but he also volunteered some of the paper and video documentation never archived by the Knott's corporation, such as the memo to executives pitching the idea for the club, along with his aforementioned paper plans for the "teen dance area."

As Salisbury comments on the OCThen.com website, Knott's Berry Farm already had an entertainment venue that featured dancing (initially meant for the ballroom variety) called Cloud 9. Cloud 9 was located in the northern portion of the park in the "Roaring Twenties" theme area. I asked Salisbury why it was necessary to create a new club space for Studio K rather than simply converting Cloud 9 into the space he envisioned. As he explained, Cloud 9 was enclosed and located deeper in a less immediately accessible area of the park. Because of its location, security and fire safety measures were always a concern. The extreme crowding in the enclosed space of Cloud 9 threatened to become a fire hazard and aggravated patrons to a degree that would often ignite conflagrations of another character.[12] Furthermore, "Cloud 9 was just the name of a facility" (in Salisbury's words) that staged all of the park's numerous other forms of entertainment regardless of genre, including such fare as hypnotists, magicians, "The Berry Sisters," a capella groups and other forms of "old-time" amusement featured (in "Roaring Twenties" fashion) at seaside resorts of that era.[13] Even in its guise as a popular evening dance venue for teens, featuring alternative rock and new wave, "Cloud 9 never pulled the numbers of Studio K," according to Salisbury, typically drawing an addi-

MEMORANDUM

Date: February 11, 1984

To: Joe Meck

From: Gary R. Salisbury

Subject: Fiesta Village Teen Dance Area

The new dance area which would be located at the site
of the old Animal Farm is being proposed to take advantage of the current teen entertainment trends to increase
the Park attendance in this market.

The concept is to develop a dance area that simulates the
new Southern California teen dance clubs that are geared
toward the youth market. These clubs utilize recorded
music, which research shows is preferred over live bands
by todays teens. Soft drinks and snacks are served and
an area with tables and chairs is provided for those
wishing to view the dancing. Our dance area must include
all the elements found in these clubs plus, by utilizing
special effects such as fog, lazers, and video, we will
offer much more.

We will highlight a special area to feature one of the
fastest growing, crowd gathering, entertainment attractions
of the '80's - break dancing. Break dancing is a form of
street dancing which due to several major motion pictures,
is a style of dance that has been sweeping the nation. By
showcasing break dance teams, I feel that we can generate
a great amount of public awareness of the new area and
generate added attendance at the gate.

GRS:kc

Salisbury's memo to Joe Meck re "Fiesta Village Teen Dance Area."
Courtesy of Gary R. Salisbury.

tional 250–500 guests to the park at its peak. Studio K, however, would be a new concept altogether in Salisbury's eyes, a rebranding of the entire park by offering open-air entertainment that could bring numbers directly to the entry gate in a very literal way: the new venue for Studio K would be located adjacent to the entrance at the site of what was formerly a petting zoo and animal farm (to add an Orwellian twist befitting its opening in 1984). To enter Studio K, patrons would have to be "teenagers, nineteen and under, with a Studio K club card that would allow them to enter both the park and the club after 5pm or 6pm for the price of only $8."[14] Knowing Knott's could never compete with the affordable five-dollar cover charge for other underage clubs further a field in Hollywood, Salisbury lobbied for this alternate entrance fee to boost overall park attendance, making all of the park's attractions more accessible to the thirteen-through-nineteen age demographic with Studio K's incentive pricing.[15] By contrast, the price for an admission pass to Videopolis, Disneyland's competing teen club which opened over a year later, required a lump sum of forty dollars for a seasonal "Videopolis Pass."[16] Studio K was open seven days a week during the summer, and weekend nights year round to cater exclusively to the youth and teen market. Salisbury was given the additional challenge of doubling Cloud 9's revenue numbers, which Studio K accomplished with ease in its heydey during the mid- to late 1980s, pulling over one thousand teenage patrons on some summer evenings.[17]

By the time of Studio K's opening on Memorial Day weekend in 1984, as the nation approached Reagan's reelection, break dancing had become thoroughly domesticated: "You could buy several how-to-do-it books as well as even more numerous how-to-do-it videotapes. All over the suburbs, middle-class housewives and professionals could take classes at their local Y's and dance centers."[18] And yet, as numerous scholars have rightly insisted, break dancing, even in its most popularized forms, cannot be abstracted from the racialized conflicts over the privatization of public space as a consequence of Reagan's postindustrial economic policies.[19] Faith in the marketplace to provide quick solutions to resource impoverishment captivated many break dancers themselves, who, "Like practitioners of sports, graffiti and rap music" (as Robin D. G. Kelley reminds us), "were not only willing to work within the marketplace, but actively promoted the commodification of the form as an alternative to dead-end wage labor."[20] The break dancing crews' willingness to harness the marketplace for financial mobility in a bleak, postindustrial landscape converged with the amusement park executives' efforts to profit from what began as a subcultural phenomenon in controlled venues like Studio K. Yet break dancing crews were never even officially hired to perform at the club. As Salisbury remarks, "We relied on the spontaneous expression of break dancing in a space we created to be suitable for an activity that was all the rage both nationally and internationally. We didn't think we needed to hire any professionals to do it."[21]

Salisbury's budget-savvy appeal to spontaneity may have ended up yielding more than he bargained for. What actually happened at Studio K—the provisional communities and the improvisations practiced by its patrons, and by the DJs who were asked to double as entertainers as well as a security element in the club—frustrates any tidy narratives about the lamentable absorption of what may have began as subcultural forms into the controlled and controlling environment of the suburban amusement park. Indeed, a reading that would foreclose such reparative possibility would correspond quite well with the same corporate and development-driven interests that believed in effectively corralling "delinquency" within a *cordon sanitaire*.[22] In the end, Studio K far exceeded its maze-like rope lines, strict musical playlists, and even the boundaries of the park itself. While his memo to Meck focuses on his desire to capitalize on the "break dancing craze . . . sweeping the nation" as a justification for opening Studio K, in our conversation Salisbury offered a more personal reason for bringing a new "teen dance area" into Knott's Berry Farm. Like so many pleasure-seeking suburban youth who would commute to Los Angeles in search of fun, Salisbury's teenage daughter would regularly make the forty-five-minute drive from Orange County to dance at a club called the Odyssey on La Cienega Boulevard in Los Angeles: "My daughter was driving up to Hollywood to go dancing every night, and I knew the name of the club, so I went up there to check it out and as soon as I walked in, all these light bulbs went off in my head and I thought, 'Wow. Wouldn't this be a great thing to put into an amusement park?!?'"[23]

Salisbury was stopped at the door and questioned by the bouncer about his interest in an underage club with only a five-dollar cover. He explained his curiosity about the Odyssey "as a dad whose daughter was driving to who knows where," and achieved admittance.[24] Captivated by the environment he discovered in the city through his daughter, Salisbury quickly hatched the concept of a club at Knott's Berry Farm to which the youth of Orange County would not be required to make an odyssey, so to speak: a venue with "security around, away from a busy boulevard, in an enclosed area with supervision, where there'd be other things to do like rides. Plus parents could drop the kids off and pick them up."[25] Even in Salisbury's rhetoric, we see how an Orange County ethos that combines security with commerce, and mixes amusement with reassurance, influenced the entertainment executive's plan to reinvigorate the park's atmosphere. Salisbury hoped to allay parental concerns and avert any potential mishaps with meticulous organizational planning. In much the same way amusement parks will recreate urban environments like the streets of San Francisco in a sanitized form (to use Disney's California Adventure Park as but one example), Salisbury envisioned a way of bringing urban excitement to The Farm without compromising its promise of family entertainment.

In his interview with me, Salisbury insisted that the executives' primary concern was not so much to curb any specific "gang activity" associated with certain styles of music or dancing in the venue, but rather to limit any dangers posed by unleashing "a huge teen population . . . from this area down here, which is kind of a mixed area" into the club.[26] He added that "musical format was tremendously important" to this principle of crowd control, especially when admitting throngs of libidinal teens, without commenting further on what he meant by the phrase "mixed area," or the specific concerns such an assessment of the local culture may have inspired in Knott's execs. Like much of the region, Buena Park—site of Knott's Berry Farm and the topographical center of southern California (the city's official motto is "Center of the Southland")[27]— underwent dramatic demographic shifts in the 1980s concurrent with Studio K's height of popularity. For example, a cumulative increase in the South Asian population in Buena Park gave rise to a shopping and restaurant district called "Indian Village" in the 1980s—a name shared with an attraction at Knott's Berry Farm's Ghost Town, albeit referring to Native Americans and the "Wild West."[28] From the 1980s onward, the "Center of the Southland" also experienced an upsurge in the Korean, Chinese, Filipino, and Vietnamese populations, keeping pace with north Orange County's growing Latino population.[29]

While Salisbury himself tried to keep his comments about the racial demographics of the region and the club's attendees to a minimum during our conversation, since he and Knott's Berry Farm's corporate organization did not collect any official demographic data (only sales revenue information),[30] the pervasive anecdotal discourse about Studio K on blogs, in interviews with attendees, and even in books mentioning Disneyland's competing club, Videopolis, suggest that at the very least, *perceptions* about the racial dynamics of the club began to influence its regional reputation. In his OCThen.com post quoted at length earlier, Salisbury offers an aside about "the wrong type of crowd" eventually leading to Studio K's demise. A former club-goer at both Studio K and Videopolis (who prefers to remain anonymous) observed in an email interview that "[Disneyland's] Videopolis was full of white kids in mostly 'New Ro' [New Romantic] or trendy fashions. K was full of Hispanic kids in red and blue bandanas and baggy jeans. I guess you could call it 'gangy' clothing . . . but we were too young to know the implications of all that."[31] Contrary to Salisbury's market research, then, which emphasized the universalized popularity of the break-dancing phenomenon, the gathering of racialized bodies at Studio K resulted in scopic reinterpretations of the venue and its patrons within sensationalized local imaginaries about "gangs." Whether or not these "gangs" (or at least the patrons attired in "gangy" fashions) were exclusively "Hispanic" is also disputable.

In a chapter titled "The Tragic Kingdom," in David Koenig's unofficial history of the Magic Kingdom, *Mouse Tales: A Behind-the-Ears Look at Disneyland,* he alludes to several violent incidents at Knott's Studio K that gave the planners of Disney's own dance club pause: "When the Videopolis dance area opened in 1985, officials knew they would see more large groups of teenagers at the park, including more gangs. They had seen it happen at Knott's Berry Farm with its two similar dance clubs Cloud 9 and Studio K. And just days before the unveiling of Videopolis, bloody clashes broke out between dozens of Hispanic and Samoan gang members at Knott's and then at Magic Mountain."[32] Within a year of its opening, Studio K acquired a far edgier reputation than its executives imagined, albeit one they always feared, in part because of the repopulation of Buena Park by communities of color, notably Asians and Pacific Islanders who didn't quite live up to the innocuous, nerdy image propagated in John Hughes films of the era. Whether or not Koenig's reporting of "violent clashes" at Studio K and Cloud 9 stems from fact or clever counter-marketing on Disney's behalf matters very little. Studio K's "street rep" had been established with the youth of the region, even though their parents took some time to figure it out. Adolescents and teens continued to attend the club in droves into the late 1980s and early 1990s.

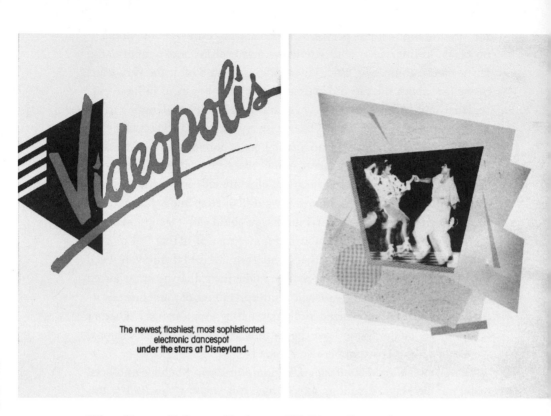

Videopolis press kit front and back cover, Walt Disney Corporation.

The newest, flashiest, most sophisticated
electronic dancespot
under the stars at Disneyland.

This sense of something "real" happening in a space that was manufactured for their innocent entertainment only added to the venue's appeal for some, especially in contrast to the more noticeably restricted and automated Videopolis at Disneyland. Unlike Studio K, Videopolis (launched a year after Studio K in 1985) rarely featured live DJs: only a predetermined playlist of recorded music, a live cover band that played Top 40 hits for thirty minutes nightly, and an assemblage of futuristic video screens playing MTV hits the rest of the night.[33] It also employed its own theme song "Videopolis (Going to the Top)," which used such lyrical boasting as "Gonna use my very best moves / Show what I can do / Dance to the drum / 'Cause the music's so hot, hot, hot . . ." to pump up its crowds.[34]

Marciano Angel Martinez, now an L.A.-based AIDS activist, artist, and queer about town, offers this succinct remark about what differentiated the crowds at Videopolis from Studio K: "The nerds went to Videopolis, and the cool kids were at K."[35] Stephen Becker, the former Knott's club goer whose inquiries on OCThen.com ultimately led to the creation of a Myspace group devoted to Studio K and Cloud 9 called "KBF locals," commented on the rivalry between Disney's Videopolis and Studio K, and the classed and racialized stereotypes that adhered to it, pitting Disney's "sophistication" against Knott's lack thereof: "There was 'teenage tension' between the Knott's crowd and the Videopolis crowd.... From what I could tell, Studio K was the place for the non-yuppie crowd to spend weekends. Videopolis was more of the 'money' crowd."[36] Whereas regular patrons of Videopolis and Disney historians like Koenig read an underlying violence threatening to rupture the "diverse" image of Knott's Studio K, Becker and other devotees of the Knott's venues looked upon this aspect of Studio K as an added incentive to their patronage: "The Knott's crowd was FAR MORE diverse than the Disneyland crowd . . . EVERYONE was treated equally at Knott's clubs. There was a lot of subscene activity happening on the weekends, including Domination and Submissive [sic] behavior: [some] people were walked around the park or parts of it, with leashes on, etc. etc."[37]

A former Studio K and Cloud 9 DJ from 1985 to 1991, Craig Gregg (who transitioned from male to female in 2000, and now goes by the name of Bridgette "Mixtress B" Rouletgregg), also reminisced about the eclectic scenes that collectively ruled the platforms and dance floors at Studio K:

> It was the kids who had mohawks, and the boys who wore more make-up than the girls, and dressed in black and danced really weird and did drugs, and dropped acid, and smoked pot, or brought razor blades, who came. And they came in part because the DJs were so badass. We [as DJs] collaborated and actually helped to make the crowd diverse. We had all types of ethnic backgrounds . . . Latino, Black, Asian and White kids and all the little subcultures within those groups. We'd play all the different genres they followed and appreciated. Some would intermix, some would clash and throw down about dance styles. The experience at Studio K offered everything—class, stigma, style. And we [DJs] knew how to work all of it.[38]

Contrary to the historian Eric Avila's reading of suburban amusement parks then—one that scripts the undoing of the vibrant classed, immigrant sexual cultures of the "urban industrial democracy" into a narrative about the theme park's structural suburbanization (including automobile-focused transportation and the "centerless development" pioneered by Disney and Knott)[39]—attractions like Studio K actually became expressive venues for emergent forms of classed, immigrant sexual cultures in the *sub*urban, postindustrial world of the Reagan-era eighties.

Even a club as closely regulated as Disneyland's Videopolis had its share of controversy, not the least of which was an infamous lawsuit brought by three gay UCLA students who were prevented from couple-dancing there in 1988. The three young men, Christopher Drake, Eric Hubert, and Jeffrey Stabile Jr., were told by a Disney guard that "touch dancing is reserved for heterosexual couples only" at the club, and filed suit with a national gay rights legal fund lawyer, Leroy S. Walker.[40] Disney eventually settled the suit and lifted its ban on same-sex dancing, but Videopolis closed shortly thereafter in 1990.[41] If we are to believe narratives about the class divide between Studio K and Videopolis shared by Stephen Becker and the other club patrons I interviewed, the sheer fact that the gay "couple-dancing" controversy at Disneyland occupied newsprint and entangled legal resources only reinforces the perceived socioeconomic differences between the clubs' milieus.[42] Disneyland and the Walt Disney Company's complex relationship to its gay patrons and employees is well documented, insofar as organized, institutionalized forms of grievance and agitation (by its gay employee union, for example) is woven into local histories, and even scholarly books and journals.[43] The documentation of Knott's queer scene, meanwhile, is far more anecdotal and ephemeral, with nary a legal case to cite as official evidence of its existence. Instead, we only hear its patrons' inclinations in echoes and whispers through music across time and space. Playing upon its setting, Orange County, the nascent form of suburban expression practiced by queers and youth of color at Studio K transposed the very principles of security, spatial isolation, and a service-driven economy—as well as the weekly Top 40[44]—into their repertoires of rebellion.

Like Rouletgregg, Salisbury himself attributed the vibrant life and enduring afterlife of Studio K to the club's DJs, albeit in his comments their role as protectors of the club enterprise was paramount. Asked to address Studio K's reputation as a hot spot for club kids of color (leading to its conflation in the regional imaginary with gang activity), Salisbury returned to the topic of musical formatting and his youthful DJs' street savvy as a perceived firewall to any conflicts that would arise at the club: "Your DJ is so important because he can control that crowd. He's got to know there's a problem area. He's got to see 'there's something going down here' and change that music so that it mellows out."[45] Rouletgregg seconds Salisbury's statement with a cheeky programming example from back in the day: "Erasure breaks up gang fights pretty quick, you know? It just makes you wanna hug."[46] Her reference to the gay band Erasure and the impulse to "hug it out" in the afterglow of their infectious synth-music and falsetto vocals also underscores what came across as the relatively unremarkable and peaceful coexistence of queer or questioning youth and youth of color with the much ballyhooed "thug" element at Studio K. Indeed, the lines among these scenes often blurred at Studio K, even in the decades before "homothugs" came to consciousness as an object of interest in contemporary queer studies.[47] Young queers of color found themselves poised within these multiple worlds that were sometimes apportioned according to musical taste cultures. Marciano Angel Martinez offers this rendering of the scene at Knott's: "There was the Latino/Asian mini-truck crowd. Islanders (Samoan and other) were, at the time, interchangeable with the mini-truck crews. The KROQ [alternative radio station] crowd was all melded. The blacks and Latinos were there . . . but tended to go to Cloud 9. Throughout the evening those of us who had 'crossover appeal' usually went between the two clubs a few times."[48] In multiple recollections (including Gwen Stefani's famous aside about the club), "the hits," and in particular "the kind you can dance to," ignited a special chemistry among the disparate scenes at Studio K. Rouletgregg in particular recalls mixing Soft Cell's hit "Tainted Love" (1982) with the theme from *Sesame Street*: "All the kids—all the little death rockers—would go arm in arm and bunny hop . . . they were young enough to appreciate it, and old enough to have the freedom to be silly."[49] Couple-dancing at Disneyland be damned: the kids at K wanted a chance to move together *en masse*.[50]

Despite the Knott's executives best efforts to produce a family-friendly environment by monitoring the DJs' playlists, going so far as to outright ban rap and hip-hop (further deracinating the break dancing phenomenon by extracting it from some of its musical contexts), the club's teens and DJs, some of whom were older teens themselves, ultimately figured out a way to circumvent and thwart The Farm's security measures.[51] Rouletgregg, for example, contradicts Salisbury's account of the musical formats sanctioned and actually played at the teen club, admitting that "Studio K was a little more hip-hop, funk, soul, and rap-based. . . . Gary basically just opened the doors and said 'Do with it what you want.'"[52] Nevertheless, in

Studio K dance floor, circa 1989. Courtesy of the Orange County Archives in Santa Ana, California.

the remembrances offered by both Salisbury and Rouletgregg, there were certain limitations on *how* rap and hip-hop could be mixed into the DJs' sets. Rouletgregg, like many of the other DJs at the venue, improvised mixes to maneuver around the club's purported safety ban on rap by creating mash-ups that embedded samples and recognizable instrumental or sung vocal riffs from rap hits with more melodically driven Top 40 dance hits:

> We couldn't play any hardcore rap, and I remember being frustrated about not even being able to play radio hits like "Push It" by Salt-N-Pepa or "Wild Thing" by Tone Loc. It was 1987, '88. I was doing mash-ups live out of necessity. I wanted to play rap music. I wanted to play funky-ass shit. I wanted to throw down and groove because this was what the

kids wanted to hear. They wanted the freshest hits and they wanted you to do it with style or else you'd have 3,500 kids on the floor shaking their heads, sayin' "Uh-uh." . . . One of my favorite mixes involved playing the "you want it, you got it" vocal hook of Young MC's "Bust a Move" with Janet Jackson's "What Have You Done for Me Lately?" That would get the crowd going.[53]

The DJs' musical improvisations at Studio K were in keeping with an ethos of "making-do"—a special alchemy of making something out of nothing—enacted by the youth of the southern California suburbs on a regular basis, be it through musical playlists or through retooling commercial and private spaces as their playgrounds. Indeed, the stories Rouletgregg and others have shared about the forms of DJ culture at Knott's converge with some of the larger spatiocultural narratives that also informed break dancing's emergence in postindustrial urban landscapes. Tricia Rose offers the definitive argument about the nascent hip-hop generation's reinvention of the streets, sidewalks, and evacuated buildings of urban America as social environments for youth of color in the wake of the nation's postindustrial privatization.[54] The suburban equivalent of this spatial repurposing also transpired in regions like southern California from the 1980s onward, albeit without a city-based public culture of streets and sidewalks as their canvas. Rouletgregg's stories, among those of others, bring to light some of the shadow economies and other forms of queer/of color, *sub*urban sociability that transpired in and around Buena Park and Knott's Berry Farm.

The DJs' unofficial resumes, itemizing their service-industry day jobs alongside their gigs at local clubs, provide a detailed socioeconomic mapping of Orange County's overlapping cultures of service and amusement. As an older teen, Rouletgregg worked full time by day at Pacific Bell and began DJing at night, picking up various gigs in Orange County as well as in Los Angeles at a club called Dreams of L.A. in Silver Lake (which has since become the indie music venue Spaceland). Rouletgregg's entry into the Knott's DJ circuit was facilitated by her time at a local community college, Cyprus College, where Craig Gregg met Dale Clark (a radio DJ at the college) who offered Rouletgregg regular work spinning at a club called Bentley's housed at the Holiday Inn in Buena Park.[55] As DJ Craig Gregg, Rouletgregg gained momentum working in the Orange County scene, especially at some of the area's signature clubs staged in unmistakably suburban venues such as Holiday Inn ballrooms, or in backyards at house parties produced by groups of local teens. The backyard party scene in particular, with its queer variant known as T-parties, took place throughout the southern California region in Orange County, the Inland Empire, the San Gabriel Valley, and South and East L.A. Its more hetero-normative histories have recently been commemorated in multimedia archival projects like the Los Angeles–based PBS station, KCET's *Webstories*.[56] Elaborating on why southern California is amenable to this kind of DJ and party culture, one of the project's authors, Gerard Meraz, remarks, "The planning of our streets with its city grids and post-war middle class homes allow many residents to enjoy a backyard with an orange tree and enough space to throw a party."[57] Though not through corporate intention, Studio K at Knott's started to overlap significantly with the backyard scene driven by the "greater Eastside" that was just reaching its apex in the early 1980s, as DJs combined suburban, radio-friendly, Top 40 pop with other genres like "Hi N-R-G, new wave, rock-a-billy, ska, reggae, funk [and] freestyle."[58]

Another of Knott's legendary Studio K DJs, and one of its very first—Tony Gonzalez—was also spinning backyard parties and at the Bentley's club at Holiday Inn with Craig Gregg. Gonzalez began working his way up the service ranks at the park, first as an usher at Knott's Goodtime Theater, before he was tapped by Salisbury to open Studio K: "Tony was working for five dollars an hour as an usher and he was doing some of the music at Cloud 9, so I offered him ten dollars an hour to run Studio K and he couldn't believe it. I offered him that money because I really had to trust him to run that operation from the ground, which he did. He was amazing with the crowds."[59] Other favorites at Studio K and Cloud 9 include the DJs Todd "Hot Toddy" Payson and Mike Martin, the latter of whom went on to become a radio DJ at KIIS-FM—a station that has boasted of being "Los Angeles' number 1 Hit Music Station" since the Rick Dees era in the 1980s. As their circulation in different suburban work and play scenes might suggest, the DJs' role as entertainers and security at Studio K was not limited to the confines of the club.

Rouletgregg in particular confesses to partying with some of the other DJs and their shared fans: "I did associate with the locals . . . a preppie group, a ska group, a surf group, a brainiac group. I had lots of different little cliques around me because I played such different kinds of music. I would also make them bring me music. That British EBM [Electronic Body

Music] band, Nitzer Ebb, was introduced to me by one of the regulars. I re-member one girl brought me an import of Nina Hagen's 'New York, New York' so I played it for her at the club." The circuits of musical exchange and sociability Rouletgregg describes are at once, utterly mundane and yet remarkable for the way in which they model the uses and limitations of suburban space, be it the unofficial listening parties thrown at the houses of kids whose parents were out of town for the weekend, or even the more organized repurposing of backyards and hotel meeting rooms in an effort to fashion alternate social environments for youthful experimentation.

In personal interviews with some of the club attendees who identified themselves as either "queer" or "questioning" during the Studio K era (from 1984 to 1991), the gender-bending pop landscape of the 1980s itself also helped give the amusement park clubs an aura of stylistic experi-mentation, despite the fact that much of the music was not of an "under-ground" origin, but culled from pop radio (Rouletgregg's rare import deviations aside).[60] Judith Ann Peraino's Listening to the Sirens, a remark-able and sweeping account of queer identity and music "from Homer to Hedwig," illuminates the context for some of the sentiments expressed by Studio K's queer and proto-queer clubgoers: "The play with androgyny and irony in much of 1980s new-wave pop opened mainstream doors to queer identities, at least as a source of cutting-edge fashion and provoca-tive sensibility."[61] Referring to his own queer awakenings at Studio K, Marciano Angel Martinez also cites new wave and "New Ro'" as a cata-lyst: "Just the way that guys were allowed to wear make-up, and dress in their New Romantic finery made you imagine. Even if that wasn't your scene. And you also had to know as a 'Homo Thug' that there had to be others at Studio K like you . . . whatever you were into. It set into motion the idea, the possibility."[62] The capitalist-driven eclecticism, then, of the Top 40 charts in the 1980s—one that encouraged DJs to manufacture sonic proximities between British neo-bubblegum like Wham's "Wake Me Up before You Go-Go," industrial-lite exhortations about s & m (and the Hegelian dialectic), like Depeche Mode's "Master and Servant," and the Hot, Cool and Vicious female rap of Salt-N-Pepa's "Push It"—materializes as another historical moment in which capitalism and gay identity are en-twined around the dissolution of traditional family structures and envi-ronments. To make this claim is not to celebrate capitalism as the agent of transformation and queer emergence, but rather to track the relations between queers, racialized subjects, and objects and spaces that may have been meant to shore up the family's defense against the kind of "social instability" (to use John D'Emilio's phrase) these milieus represented in Orange County, while enabling different configurations of sociability altogether.[63] As Marciano Angel Martinez reflects, "I heard songs like 'Tastes So Good' by File 13, 'Sex Dwarf' by Soft Cell, and Hillary's 'Drop Your Pants!' These were songs we only heard on KROQ when we were alone late at night. To hear them manifest in some place outside of your head (or your room), where there were other people dancing to the same music which isolated you from others . . . well, it was liberating to know you were not the only freak."[64]

Ultimately, the latch-key quality of Studio K as a space of amusement in which parents could deposit their children "safely" in the care of broadcast media (like the weekly Top 40), and an amorphous community of other adult supervisors, actually made the suburban amusement park an amenable habitat for nascent efforts to fashion the "affectional communities" D'Emilio calls for in the conclusion of his essay on "Capitalism and Gay Identity."[65] Conceptualized in 1979–80, and published in 1983 (a year before Studio K's opening), D'Emilio's essay speaks out against the ethos of privatization-driven, Reagan-era capitalism, urging us instead to work toward alternate forms of community building: "As we create structures beyond the nuclear family that provide a sense of belonging, the family will wane in significance. . . . The building of an 'affectional community' must be as much a part of our political movement as are campaigns for civil rights. In this way we may prefigure the shape of personal relationships in a society grounded in equality and justice rather than exploitation and oppression, a society where autonomy and security do not preclude each other but coexist."[66]

Numerous critiques and friendly amendments to D'Emilio's thesis have multiplied in the decades since its watershed appearance in the early 1980s—not the least of which challenge the essay's emphasis on the urbanity of queer developmental history. In the interest of focusing on the historical moment his essay shares with Studio K, however, it behooves us to dwell on how the key terms of his proposed solution to the political dilemmas faced by gay activists were imbricated with the provisional communities already being formed in the classed and racialized youth context of the amusement park clubs. Indeed, the forms of sociability being enacted in Studio K anticipated, in many ways, the (in)formal strategies for undoing what we have come to think of as a set of primarily white, gay male priorities in building queer institutions.

Strikingly, "security" and "privacy" combined become the touchstones of a gay political project, but only the right to privacy has been invoked in legal fights to protect the private sexual practices of gay men—most notably, in the battles over sodomy laws in state and federal supreme courts throughout the 1970s and 1980s that culminated in *Bowers v. Hardwick* in 1986.[67] And yet couched in the conclusion to "Capitalism and Gay Identity" is an appeal to support "the rights of young people" as part of the project of "broaden[ing] the opportunities for living outside of traditional heterosexual units."[68] An innovation that Studio K offers in the genealogy of queer battles over rights is that it challenges us to think beyond private sexual practices as our only retort to traditional configurations of the nuclear family, presenting instead collective, improvisational models of affection—through dance, musical exchange, or merely hanging out together in motley assemblages—that unravel "security" with its seemingly innocuous impetus toward amusement.[69] Historically, D'Emilio has mapped the opportunities to disrupt the nuclear family on to what he calls a "social terrain," mostly gay and lesbian bars, and same-sex boarding houses like YMCAs scattered throughout the United States, but celebrated as "community building" in places like New York and San Francisco.[70]

Contrasting Videopolis's archive with Studio K's—the former documented in legal rights cases and sordid tales of Fantasyland blowjobs, the latter felt in the aftershocks of eighties pop and scattered in threads on tribute websites—underscores the documented disparaties that inform our competing claims for a *contemporary* queer agenda. Caught in the push and pull between a right to privacy, and the desperate quest to find something broader, potentially beyond "queer" itself, the suburban, racialized subjects of Studio K employed any means necessary to make something out of nothing. The question remains, then, whether or not a place like Studio K ultimately belongs to the genealogy of queer social terrain documented by D'Emilio and the many scholars who followed.

The club was not a bar (despite the creative smuggling of libations, or parking lot tailgating that may have lubricated social interactions there on occasion), but an entertainment venue in a family-themed amusement park. It was not exclusively a same-sex environment, despite the awkward, adolescent separation of spheres sometimes choreographed by group dance trends of the 1980s. Neither was the space grass-roots or community generated, but rather, manufactured for profit while keeping entertainment execs' amusement park safety records unblemished. Studio K, in other words, was a distinctly suburban space conceptualized around safety, convenience, and the automobile, a technology engineered for and inspired by the nuclear family's flight from the city. Its very lack of urbanity, its *suburbanness* in nearly every aspect, would seem to preclude it from queer histories of emergence. And yet Studio K, I would argue, necessarily belongs to a political genealogy of queer sociability, not in spite of what it lacks but because of how it exceeds the boundaries of what we are willing to call "gay and lesbian history." What we find there is utterly ordinary, but not in the way our imaginaries have been trained to expect ordinariness to manifest in the suburbs, especially in Reagan's county during the 1980s.

In a suburban world that the Cold War built not simply through industry, but in the flows of immigration wrought by its policies, Orange County's youth—queer and proto-queer, trendy and awkward, a couple of generations or less removed from the boat or the barrio—dismantled security simply by letting it amuse them. Orange County in general, and Studio K in particular, may ultimately end up meaning the same thing to and for queer and national imaginaries. It was and continues to be (to paraphrase its sonic archivist, Gwen Stefani) one of our guiltiest pleasures: a paradoxically well-ordered mess we want desperately to get rid of. It is proof of our embarrassingly provincial suburban origins, of our attachment to tacky objects like the weekly Top 40, as well as the cultures of convenience that are the source of both our employment and entertainment. The suburban sociabilities found there threaten to rupture the veneer of queer cosmopolitanism while actively thwarting even the most mainstream of LGBT political agendas. But they also call out our questionable, queer collusions with the hetero nouveau riche fantasies that buttress such a world. From the Pacific Island gangsters who strutted tough, to the brown, bunny-hopping Goths with smeared makeup, to the suburban B-boys-and-girls who longed to be discovered on its platforms, Studio K swelled with the ranks of those looking to claim their territory,

---

(opposite) Press photo proofs of Studio K, ca. 1989.
Courtesy of the Orange County Archives.

any parcel of fantasy that could be made their own. Maybe they were just looking for a sweet escape, a way of being in Orange County without feeling like they were. But on those endless summer nights, long before "the O.C." was catchphrased into being, the refrains of New Order would score a mess of bodies moving, wanting to be moved, as the cold world melted away.

Notes

1. The epigraph to this chapter quotes Ben Wenner, "Gwen Stefani Puts Out Her Own Album but Says No Doubt Will Go On," Arts and Entertainment section, *Florida State University News*, December 2, 2004, at www.fsunews.com.

2. Krissi Murison, "NME Review: Gwen Stefani: *Love.Angel.Music.Baby.*," *NME Magazine*, December 10, 2004, at http://www.nme.com.

3. We might also track Stefani's Japanophilia to an early object of trendy consumption during her suburban childhood, Hello Kitty: "Gwen was also interested in Japanese trends. Her father often traveled to Japan on business for his job with Yamaha Motorcycles. He would bring back souvenirs for Gwen. 'I loved Hello Kitty and all these different Japanese things,' Gwen remembered." Quoted in Katherine Krohn, *Gwen Stefani* (Minneapolis: Twenty-First Century Books, 2007), 15.

4. Wenner, "Gwen Stefani Puts Out Her Own Album."

5. Interview with Studio K creator and Knott's director of entertainment, Gary R. Salisbury. Salisbury notes that the club was credited for bringing in an extra $2.5 million in revenue a year throughout the mid to late 1980s.

6. When I interviewed the former Knott's entertainment director, Gary R. Salisbury, and asked if they statistically tracked or performed any market research to appeal to some of the specific patrons that attended Studio K and Cloud 9, Salisbury simply replied, "We knew the Goth and New Wave kids were coming because the DJs knew it. They knew it, and they would tell me. That's about as formal as we got." Interview with Gary R. Salisbury, recorded on digital audio, August 14, 2008, offices of The Pirate's Dinner Adventure, Buena Park, California.

7. Alexandra Vazquez heightened my sense of these reverberations created by popular objects across time and space in her paper for the American Studies Association Annual Convention in 2008, which discussed the intergenerational resonance of a Ted Nugent song shared by an older Cuban woman and a younger Cuban American woman from Dade County. Vazquez, "What I Brought Back Here," paper presented at the American Studies Annual Convention, Albuquerque, N.M., October 2008. Cited with the permission of the author.

8. PrisonerDavid.com is a popular website administered by "a California inmate currently serving 25 years to life." As his bio explains, "When Prisoner David is not in the law library seeking ways to prove his innocence, he writes about prison life

and can be heard on the Adam Carolla radio program." The post about Studio K appears in "Sleepless in Soledad," undated, at www.prisonerdavid.com.

9. This commentary appeared in response to a blog post on May 21, 2008, featuring photos of Disney's Tomorrowland circa 1986 (around the time Videopolis was situated near that area of the park), on a popular Disney-themed blog featuring "Vintage and Current Disneyland Photos" called "Daveland." See http://davelandblog.blogspot.com.

10. The article, dated October 26, 2007, is on the website *Orange County Memories*, at http://www.octhen.com.

11. Ibid., Ruben Sanchez, comment on August 17, 2008.

12. Salisbury interview, August 14, 2008.

13. See David Nasaw's classic account of seaside resorts opened up to the masses thanks to a masterful synergy among public transportation systems (such as ferries, buses, trolley cars), in *Going Out: The Rise and Fall of Public Amusements* (New York: Basic Books, 1993). Nasaw writes, "Because the nation's waterways had served as its main transportation networks until the triumph of the railroad in the mid-nineteenth century, almost every major and mid-size American city was located on or near a waterfront that could, with minor adjustments, be converted into a playland for excursionists. . . . In the late 1990s, the resort areas at the outskirts of the city, once the province of the wealthy, privileged or politically connected, were opened up to the city's working people as ferry boats, steamers and streetcar lines linked them to the central city" (80).

14. Salisbury interview, August 14, 2008.

15. Ibid.

16. Needless to say, not all the youth of the region had forty dollars to pay up front for a seasonal pass, despite the fact that its holders were entitled to regular admission to the park after 5 P.M. throughout the summer. Casual patrons were thus discouraged. Also, if you wanted to enter the park *before* 5 P.M., you would still have to pay the regular price for admission to Disneyland. The parks' competing admission prices are mentioned in an article by Randy Lewis, "Videoland in the Magic Kingdom," *Los Angeles Times*, July 5, 1985.

17. Ibid. See also a brief mention of Knott's attendance records in a *Los Angeles Times* article about Disneyland's efforts to match its competitor's success nearly a year later: "Disney was beaten to the punch last year when nearby Knott's Berry Farm embraced the teen market by building Studio K, which packs in 2,000 or more patrons on Friday and Saturday nights during the busy summer season." Quoted in Bruce Horovitz, "Seeking to Attract Affluent Adolescents Disneyland Will Open Teen Nightclub," *Los Angeles Times*, Orange County Edition, April 23, 1985.

18. Banes, "Breakdancing: A Reporter's Story," in *Writing Dancing in the Postmodern Age*, 131.

19. See Tricia Rose, "A Style Nobody Can Deal With: Politics, Style and the Post-

industrial City in Hip Hop," in *Popular Culture: A Reader*, ed. Raiford Guins and Omayra Zaragoza Cruz (London: Sage Publications, 2005), 401–16, originally published in *Microphone Fiends: Youth Music and Youth Culture* (London: Routledge, 1994). Rose elaborates on how "hip hop culture emerged as a source of alternative identity formation and social status for youth in a community whose older local support institutions had been all but demolished along with large sectors of its built environment. . . . The postindustrial city, which provided the context for creative development among hip hop's earliest innovators, shaped their cultural terrain, access to space, materials and education" (407–8).

20. Robin D. G. Kelley, "Looking to Get Paid: How Some Black Youth Put Culture to Work," in *Yo' Mama's DisFUNKtional: Fighting the Culture Wars in Urban America* (Boston: Beacon Press, 1997), 68.

21. Salisbury interview, August 14, 2008.

22. My Foucauldian-inspired formulation about the *cordon sanitaire*—literally, a "quarantine line"—is owed to D. A. Miller's classic account of Dickensian delinquency in *The Novel and the Police* (Berkeley: University of California Press, 1988): "The closed-circuit character of delinquency is, of course, a sign of Dickens's progressive attitude, his willingness to see coercive system where it was traditional only to see bad morals. Yet one should recognize how closing the circuit results in an 'outside' as well as an 'inside,' an 'outside' precisely determined as *outside the circuit*. At the same time as the novel exposes the network that ties together the workhouse, Fagin's gang, and the police *within* the world of delinquency, it also draws a circle around it, and in that gesture hold the line of a *cordon sanitaire*" (5, emphasis in original).

23. Salisbury interview, August 14, 2008.

24. Ibid.

25. Ibid.

26. Ibid.

27. See the City of Buena Park's official website, www.buenapark.com.

28. For more on the growth of the South Asian population in southern California, with specific reference to the Indo-Pak Bridal Expos held in the region starting in 1989, see Karen B. Leonard and Chandra S. Tibrewal's "Asian Indians in Southern California: Occupation and Ethnicity," in *Immigration and Entrepreneurship: Culture, Capital and Ethnic Networks*, ed. Ivan Light and Parminder Bhachu (1993; Rutgers: Transaction Publishers, 2004), 141–63.

29. The most recent census data for the City of Buena Park, taken in 2000, measured the city's Asian/Pacific Islander population at 21.6 percent (nearly twice the state average for California cities), and the Latino population at 33.5 percent. See the U.S. Census Bureau's State and County online database, http://quickfacts.census.gov.

30. "We just knew the trends and demographic because my DJs knew it, felt the crowd and could tell me." Salisbury interview, August 14, 2008.

31. Email interview with Anonymous "M," August 27, 2008—a thirty-six-year-old Caucasian female who resided in Anaheim and regularly attended both Videopolis and occasionally attended Studio K from 1988 to 1991. This interview subject currently resides in the Inland Empire.

32. David Koening, *Mouse Tales: A Behind-the-Ears Look at Disneyland* (Irvine: Bonaventure Press, 2006), 158.

33. Lewis, "Videoland in the Magic Kingdom."

34. Studio K also featured live entertainment, often teen-friendly pop acts of the 80s, including stars such as Tiffany, Debbie Gibson, and the Tongan freestyle-inspired band, The Jets. The Disney Publicity Department's press pack for Videopolis in 1985 focuses on the venue's "high-tech" appeal, especially its "90 television monitors . . . arranged in a video 'wallpaper' effect around the dance floor." See Press Pack, "Videopolis: The Newest Flashiest, Most Sophisticated Electronic Dancespot under the Stars at Disneyland," Fall 1985. The "Videopolis" theme song was posted August 2006 on a Disney enthusiasts blog, http://www.disneyfrontier .com.

35. Interview with Marciano Angel Martinez via email, December 17, 2008.

36. Interview with Stephen L. Becker via email, May 4, 2008. Capital letters in original. Becker's online group for former regulars at Studio K and Cloud 9, KBF [Knott's Berry Farm] Locals, can be found at http://groups.myspace.com/kbflocals. Membership is required to access the group's discussion boards.

37. Stephen L. Becker, interview, May 4, 2008.

38. Interview with Bridgette "Mixtress B" Rouletgregg, recorded on digital audio, August 18, 2008, at a private residence in Los Angeles.

39. Avila, "A Rage for Order: Disneyland and the Suburban Ideal," 110.

40. John Spano, "Dancing Gays Sue Disneyland Anew in Suit Similar to One the Park Lost," *Los Angeles Times*, Orange County Edition, February 26, 1988.

41. "It was the scene of controversy last September when gay men sued the park over the right to dance with one another there. Disney has settled the suit and lifted its ban on same-sex dancing." Mary Ann Galante, "For Teen-Agers, Closed Videopolis Limits Boogie Options," *Los Angeles Times*, Orange County Edition, November 4, 1989.

42. The Disney Corporation, unlike the more casual operation that seemed to be at work at Knott's Berry Farm, explicitly voiced its desire to lure "affluent teens" to Videopolis. Bob McTyre, the manager of marketing and entertainment at Disneyland leading up to Videopolis, remarked in a *Los Angeles Times* interview that their "first concern is to keep Disney a family place, but there are a lot of good kids in Orange County who want a place to go." Quoted in Horovitz, "Seeking to Attract Affluent Adolescents."

43. See Sean Griffin, *Tinker Belles and Evil Queens: The Walt Disney Company from the Inside Out* (New York: New York University Press, 2000) for a more expansive take on the Disney Company's relationship to gay and lesbian employees, and

cultural movements. For a more theoretical approach to these entanglements, see Arthur Asa Berger, "Of Mice and Men: An Introduction to Mouseology Or, Anal Eroticism and Disney," in *Gay People, Sex, and the Media*, ed. Michelle A. Wolf and Alfred P. Kielwasser (New York: Harrington Park Press, 1991), 155–65.

44. Top 40 formatting has gone through numerous conceptual transformations in the rock era, and has arguably been a significant format for regionalized America, if not the suburbs' definitive radio format—a distinction, some scholars argue, that belongs to its offshoot, "MOR" (or "Middle of the Road") Adult Contemporary. See Eric Weisbard's Ph.D. dissertation, "Top 40 Democracy: Pop Music Formats in the Rock Era," University of California, 2008. As Weisbard argues, "Top 40 persisted as a format long after the rock cohort had condemned it as 'square' and moved on to the burgeoning FM album rock format. It needs to be understood as a format of outsiders opting into the mainstream, far from the rock narrative's prizing of subculturalists opting out" (19).

45. Salisbury interview, August 14, 2008.

46. Rouletgregg interview, August 18, 2008. Erasure is an iconic gay band, and still regularly makes appearances at Pride Festivals throughout the world alongside some of the artists who they inspired, and who came of age during the Studio K era at Knott's, like queer female hip-hop artist, Melange LaVonne, who is based in the Inland Empire. For a list of LaVonne's musical influences, see www.melangelavonne.com. I also conducted an interview with her in the context of my blog about the Inland Empire, where she named another eighties British pop band, Tears for Fears, as her favorite rock band: "Tours of the Duty (Free) + an Interview with Melange LaVonne," February 17, 2007, at http://theinlandemperor.blogspot.com.

47. A groundbreaking essay on the aesthetic and social fantasies that combine queer eroticism with the "homeboy" aesthetic in the work of the Inland Empire/ Los Angeles artist Hector Silva is Richard T. Rodriguez, "Queering the Homeboy Aesthetic," *Aztlan: A Journal of Chicano Studies* 31, no. 2 (Fall 2006): 127–38. For more on "homo hip-hop" and its recent commercialization and spectacularization in the popular media, see Robin R. Means Coleman and Jasmine Cobb, "No Way of Seeing: Mainstreaming and Selling the Gaze of Homo-Thug Hip-Hop," *Popular Communication: The International Journal of Media and Culture* 5, no. 2 (May 2007): 89–108.

48. Martinez interview, December 17, 2008.

49. Rouletgregg interview, August 18, 2008.

50. A *Los Angeles Times* article published near the end of both Videopolis's and Studio K's respective runs focused on how teen dancing in the 1980s—particularly in the teen clubs of Orange County—abandoned the couple form. Dana Parsons, "Footloose and Partner Free: When It Comes to Dancing, Today's Teens Are Single-Minded in Their Devotion," *Los Angeles Times*, Orange County Edition, August 19, 1989.

51. Describing how he monitored Studio K's set lists, Salisbury declared: "We *didn't* have any rap in there, or hip hop . . . but then you get the songs that are partial rap and partial singing and we'd all have to make another determination." Salisbury interview, August 14, 2008.

52. Ibid.

53. Rouletgregg interview, August 18, 2008.

54. "While graffiti writers' work was significantly aided by advances in spray-paint technology, they used the urban transit system as their canvas. Rappers and Djs disseminated their work by copying it on tape-dubbing equiment and playing it on powerful, portable 'ghetto blasters.' At a time when budget cuts in school music programs drastically reduced access to traditional forms of instrumentation and composition, inner-city youth increasingly relied on recorded sound." Rose, "A Style Nobody Can Deal With," 408.

55. Rouletgregg interview, August 18, 2008. The story that Rouletgregg and other Knott's DJs have shared about their networks, the institutions they attended, and the venues in which they both worked and played bear some resemblance to Jeff Chang's account of the role black suburbia played in hip-hop culture of the late 1980s on the East Coast. See in particular his tracking of DJ networks through local community and vocational colleges in "What We Got to Say: Black Suburbia, Segregation and Utopia in the Late 1980s," in *Can't Stop, Won't Stop: A History of the Hip-Hop Generation* (New York: St. Martin's Press, 2005), 215–31.

56. Titled "Backyard Parties: A Brief History of DJ Culture in Southern California," the project contains materials with commentary from the personal collection of an early backyard party scenester, the DJ and local scholar Gerard Meraz, among contributions from others who participated primarily in the scene's East L.A. and South L.A. incarnations. The interactive project also includes archival video footage and MP3 "mixtapes." See http://www.kcet.org/explore-ca/web-stories/backyardparties.

57. Ibid., start page.

58. Ibid., 1980s page.

59. Salisbury interview, August 14, 2008.

60. Eric Weisbard, a popular music critic and historian, also draws several crucial connections between the evolution of Top 40, capitalism and gay identity, and multiple modalities of imperialism vis à vis Elton John's emergence as a bankable Transatlantic (and ultimately global) pop star in the 1970s. See the chapter "Madman across the Water: Elton John and the American Top 40," in his dissertation "Top 40 Democracy."

61. Judith A. Peraino, *Listening to the Sirens: Musical Technologies of Queer Identity from Homer to Hedwig* (Berkeley: University of California Press, 2006), 136.

62. Martinez interview, December 17, 2008.

63. D'Emilio, "Capitalism and Gay Identity," 109.

64. Martinez interview, December 17, 2008.

65. Particularly striking in light of Studio K's function as a safe holding place for youth in the evenings, is D'Emilio's call for "community- or worker-controlled daycare" and "housing where privacy and community coexist" (111).

66. D'Emilio, "Capitalism and Gay Identity," 111.

67. For a reading that situates the sodomy laws and the obfuscation of racialization within a longer history of queer liberalism, see David L. Eng's "Freedom and the Racialization of Intimacy: Lawrence v. Texas and the Emergence of Queer Liberalism," in *The Blackwell Companion to Lesbian, Gay, Bisexual, Transgender and Queer Studies*, ed. George E. Haggerty and Molly McGarry (Oxford: Blackwell Press, 2007), 38–59. See also Jasbir K. Puar's discussion of the "right to privacy" discourse and the occlusion of racialized bodies from the project of homonationalism in "Intimate Control, Infinite Detention: Rereading the Lawrence Case," in *Terrorist Assemblages: Homonationalism in Queer Times* (Durham: Duke University Press, 2007), 114–65.

68. D'Emilio, "Capitalism and Gay Identity," 110.

69. My evocation of "assemblages" here is indebted to Jasbir K. Puar, *Terrorist Assemblages: Homonationalism in Queer Times* (Durham: Duke University Press, 2007).

70. D'Emilio, "Capitalism and Gay Identity," 106–9.

J. Martin Daughtry

Belliphonic Sounds
and Indoctrinated Ears

The Dynamics of Military Listening

in Wartime Iraq

K-k-r-r-BOOM.
—Armor Geddon

I've never felt so alive in my life.

Explosions going off all around, fireballs rising into the sky, quickly replaced by black smoke, the already familiar smell of charred bodies, the Brad's guns exploding in your ears, TOW missiles whooshing through the air, not knowing where the enemy is and frantically trying to find him.
—A Day in Iraq

Zzzip.
P-e-e-e-w-w-w-w.
Crack . . . CrackCRACK.
—Armor Geddon

I heard a hiss about a split second before [the rocket-propelled grenade] hit me. [Afterward] I couldn't hear anything except a dull static-like humming in my ears.
—Blackfive

Glass and sound rain down on me. . . . I know it was bad, I have never heard anything so loud, and light debris is falling all around me. . . . What happened? IED? VBED? . . . What the fuck happened?
—The Questing Cat

Dadadadadada. Dadadadada.
—As related to Tim Pritchard

Whoosh.

Out of nowhere, there was a whistle and the thud of a mortar landing nearby. Captain Scott Dyer looked around, momentarily confused. He recognized the sound of the incoming shells
as 120 mm mortar rounds. At the same moment he heard rounds
pinging off the tank's two-inch-thick steel ballistic skirts. His first
reaction was surprise rather than fear. *So this is what it feels like to
be shot at.*
—As related to Tim Pritchard

K-k-r-r-BOOM.
K-k-r-r-BOOM.
K-k-r-r-BOOM.
—Armor Geddon

. . . . .

What does it mean for a being to be immersed entirely in listening,
formed by listening or in listening, listening with all his being?
—Jean-Luc Nancy

F rom the *Iliad* to *All Quiet on the Western Front*, descriptions of the
sounds of combat have been a prominent presence in literary depic-
tions of war; documentary accounts and oral histories are similarly
saturated with evocations of war's sonic dimension.[1] That sound is regarded as worthy of commentary should not be surprising: war has been
a noisy, grunting, clanging business throughout history. Since the advent
of explosive ordnance and, later, mechanized cavalry, the sounds of modern warfare have often exceeded the range of its shocking sights and nox-
ious smells. The distant thunder of cannon may be one's only indicator
that a battle is taking place beyond the next hill; the grinding rumble
of tanks usually precedes their appearance on one's street. The U.S.-led
military intervention in Iraq is no exception: from the first sorties of the
so-called Shock and Awe operation on March 21, 2003—a bombing campaign that was designed to be deafening[2]—the sonic dimension of the
Iraq conflict has been a source of intense preoccupation and consterna-

tion among civilians and military service members alike.[3] In the quotes above, gleaned from military blogs ("milblogs") and other published accounts of Operation Iraqi Freedom, service members struggle within the confines of written language to evoke the urgency, indeterminacy, iconicity, and omnipresence of what might be called "the belliphonic," the spectrum of sounds produced by armed combat.[4]

On and off for the past several years, I have been conversing with U.S. veterans and active-duty service members and, more recently, a group of Iraqi civilians about their memories of the ongoing conflict in Iraq, and about the centrality of sound to those memories. Their frank and detailed testimonies point to the exceedingly challenging listening conditions that emerge when people are forced to navigate through fraught environments in which the sounds of weapons are often coterminous with the speeding projectiles that produce them. At times, the resonant properties of sound produce situations in which the differences between soldier and civilian, native and foreigner, are almost completely elided. (To take an extreme example, the sound of an explosion that literally deafens would appear to be, in its overwhelming immediacy, unequivocal.) At other moments, the listening practices of these two populations radically diverge: the sustained exposure of military personnel to loud weapons sounds; the limited degree to which Americans new to Iraq are able to historically and culturally situate ambient sounds; the formal and informal training that service members undergo to discipline their ears; the noise-reducing headphones, iPods, and other technologies for mediating belliphonic sounds that are widely available to service members; military regulations that govern the use of these technologies—all of these conditions frequently converge to create a militarized "auditory regime" that overlaps with but is distinct from the more heterogeneous and informal listening practices that structure Iraqi civilians' experiences of the war.

In charting the activities of these individuals as they moved through the shifting environments of wartime Iraq, I have drawn a set of conclusions about their collective acts of listening that are commonsensical but (I hope) contributive—to those who, like the other authors in this volume, study various aspects of the sonorous world; to those who seek to better understand the phenomenology of modern combat; and to those who have a stake or an interest in the ongoing conflict in Iraq. First, I argue that people who live in conflict zones tend to develop sophisticated listening skills that allow them to extract an enormous amount of information from belliphonic sounds, information that increases their chance of survival and allows them to create rich narratives of battles that they can hear but cannot see. Second, these very sounds, while crucial sources of tactical information and narrative detail, often traumatize those who are exposed to them, both physically (through hearing loss, the most common injury in the Iraq war) and psychologically (with sound serving as a powerful trigger for post-traumatic stress). Third, by interrogating the act of listening outside of the aestheticized arena of the concert hall and the musical framework that this arena presumes—by investigating instead the extreme conditions of listening within the Iraq war and its immediate aftermath—we can learn something about listening in general, or at least can calibrate new questions about the dynamics of listening, the web of contingencies that enable it, its costs and its benefits, its ethics and its politics. The eventual goal of this research will be to compare and contrast the listening practices of the U.S. military and Iraqi civilian populations. While Iraqi perspectives are periodically mentioned within this essay, its scope is narrower, focusing on the sound-centered reminiscences of U.S. military service members who were stationed in Iraq between 2003 and 2008. This is my first public attempt to deal with some of these issues; as such, it only scratches the surface of a subject whose complexity is belied by the brevity of the thoughts that follow.[5]

Charting the Belliphonic

For people whose ears work, to witness war is to hear it. And to survive it is to have listened to it. Or better: to have listened *through* it. In post-Hussein Iraq, people listen through the war in three senses, all germane here. First, they are compelled to listen to the sounds of everyday life—voices, music, prayer, sounds produced by the natural world, sounds produced by electronic media—*through* an intermittent scrim of vehicular, weapon, and other sounds that are the byproduct of modern urban combat. The sounds of conflict in this scenario are coded as noise, as something to be bracketed out to the extent possible. Second, as I will discuss in more detail below, this mode of listening can be jettisoned instantly when people deem the sounds of the conflict to contain useful information. Here, the figure and ground of the previous scenario are reversed, and the sonic residue of violence is taken very seriously. Sound in this scenario can be regarded as an active participant in a network that sutures together weapons, perpetrators, victims, bystanders, architectural and open spaces—everyone, and every thing, within earshot, as well as many people and things that lie beyond the horizon of the audible.[6] The product of this network is the sensory experience of violence, an experience that, while always intersensorial, is often primarily auditory. The information-rich sounds of war both make possible and demand acts of tactically significant listening. *Through* the war—*by means of* the war, the witness is transformed into the diagnostician, the expert listener, the urban auscultator assessing the health not of a patient but of a neighborhood.

At the same time, in a temporal sense, to listen *through* the war is to have experienced war's evolution and fluctuations. Conflicts have circadian rhythms, as evidenced by the U.S. Army's standing orders to maintain heightened vigilance at dusk and dawn, when fighting in Iraq tends to be heavier. But cyclical motions such as these are nested within slower, less rhythmic changes. The belliphonic sounds of the Iraq war have mutated over time, with the emergence of flare-ups and cease-fires, with the introduction of new military technologies, with the erection and partial removal of blast walls in Baghdad, with the abrupt rise and gradual reduction of IED explosions, with the destruction and gradual reinstatement of the electric infrastructure, with the reintroduction of formerly prohibited vocal forms of sectarian expression and the introduction of new forms of mass dissent—in short, with changes in the strategy and tactics of insurgents, sectarian fighting groups, coalition forces, and the civilian population alike. This moment-to-moment mutability (which, incidentally, characterizes the sounds of any urban space) renders all metaphors that rely on stasis—all "soundscapes" and "acoustic environments"—inadequate, if not obfuscatory. This is not to say that we are surrounded by unalloyed sonic flux; we hear continuity amidst the cacophony that surrounds us. We are experts at discerning patterns produced by the repetition of sounds in a given place over a protracted time, and if many of these patterns are not as sustained as F. Murray Schafer's "keynote" sounds would have us believe, they are repeated, in identifiable permutations, often enough to make some tentative, temporally conditioned generalizations possible.[7] The service members who spoke with me had no trouble identifying a palette of sounds they associated with their tours of duty, sounds that constituted a semifluid "sonic situation" in which their acts of listening took place. The following taxonomic sketch reflects a number of the sounds that appeared most frequently in service members' testimonies, and the modes of listening that these sounds engendered.

Vehicular Sounds

Service members negotiating city streets in Humvees, Bradley fighting vehicles, Stryker armored combat vehicles, the newer mine-resistant ambush-protected (MRAP) vehicles, and, more rarely, Abrams tanks, must contend with the distinct background noise of their engines. An up-armored Humvee generates ninety-five decibels of engine noise; a tank's engine is significantly louder. A tank's engine noise combined with its thick hull renders all but the loudest explosions inaudible from inside. Bradleys, Strykers, and MRAPs also block out street sounds, albeit to a lesser degree. However, gunners and scouts, who stand in the hatches of these vehicles with their heads and upper bodies exposed, hear much more than those inside, and can be called upon to report on sonic and other events when the situation demands.

Helicopters accompany U.S. ground troops throughout the Iraqi theater, and contribute substantially to the auditory experience of everyone beneath them. The massive, twin-propeller CH-47D Chinook, a version of which has been in military service since the Vietnam War, produces a piercing, high-pitched whine from its turbine engines, along with the deep rhythmic beating of its rotors, a percussion so powerful that it enters the realm of the haptic: as it approaches, it is felt as well as heard. (One of my Iraqi interlocutors who lived in Baghdad said that multiple daily flybys of the Chinook "would make the plates vibrate off the table.") Other, smaller helicopters—Apaches, Blackhawks, Kiowas, the MH-6 "Little Bird"—all have their own signature sounds.

In Iraq, military and civilian listeners alike often code vehicular sounds as noise. At the same time, the sounds of vehicles are frequently read indexically—as indications that support has arrived, wounded are being transported, or surveillance is being undertaken. Additionally, the striking and at times overwhelming sounds of helicopters overhead have been interpreted by many of my civilian interlocutors as symbols, albeit inherently polysemic ones. "Tariq," an Iraqi dentist, read the sound of the Chinook as a troubling symbol of American panoptic control over Baghdad. By contrast, Tracy, a former civil servant in the Green Zone, heard helicopters as "the sound of freedom." But whether coded as noise or signal, index or symbol, the sonic presence of a mechanized military is undeniable.

Communication

Voices frequently penetrate the white noise of vehicular engines. Service members in vehicles frequently find themselves in a state of almost constant conversation, trading barbs and stories, commenting on traffic and events seen through their windows, and exchanging tactical information. Many service members on motorized patrols have headphones embedded in their helmets that also serve as communications systems, projecting the voices of their fellow team members in the vehicle as well as more distant interlocutors into one ear or another. Team leaders will often monitor two communications networks ("nets") simultaneously — one with each ear. The microphones that transmit voices pick up background noises as well, so that a Humvee driver communicating with a helicopter pilot might hear the pilot's voice mixed in with the wash of the helicopter's rotors.

For those service members who patrol Iraqi cities on foot, their own voices are mixed with the voices of local residents speaking primarily in Arabic, but also in English, Kurdish, and other languages, and in multiple dialects. Units that regularly engage with Iraqi citizens frequently travel with a "terp," an Iraqi interpreter working as a local contractor for the military. For most of the period from 2004 to 2008, interpreters commonly wore full face masks in order to shield their identities, thus reducing the risk of sectarian retaliation for their collaboration with coalition forces.[8] During this period, the multitude of non-English voices that service members heard were filtered and translated through the voice of the masked translator, a semiacousmatic voice hidden behind a screen of cloth. On house patrols, service members strain to make sense of the interpreter's voice, which overlaps with the foreign voice of the true interlocutor. Their mediated conversation takes place in a challenging auditory space, one often filled with a multitude of vocalizations: crying, supplication, angry shouts, and hollered instructions from one team member to another, along with instructions coming from communications systems, vehicular noises, and, occasionally, gunfire. The stakes of accurate communication, which, in many instances, could not be higher, only add to the challenges that service members, civilians, and interpreters face. And the politics of a situation in which heavily armed service members ask questions of unarmed (or disarmed) Iraqis, at times at gunpoint, surely inflects how these words are received.

Music

U.S. military personnel began listening to recorded music in large numbers in the First World War, when rugged field gramophones, including a model invented by Thomas Edison, were shipped to bases overseas in service of the belief that "song makes a good soldier, a better soldier; a tired soldier, a rested soldier; a depressed soldier, a cheery soldier."[9] Accounts of music-listening practices of the U.S. military abound, with particular emphasis given to the centrality of rock music to the experience of troops in Vietnam. Several scholars and a larger number of journalists have noted that the war in Iraq is the first major conflict to take place in the iPod era.[10] As Lisa Gilman, Jonathan Pieslak, and others have documented, for the entire length of the U.S. military engagement in Iraq, troops have relied upon music—in iPods, on boomboxes, on P.A. systems, and, in violation of military regulations that are seldom enforced, jacked into vehicles or headsets during missions—to attain the mildly altered state of heightened awareness and/or aggression necessary in order to be an effective warrior.[11] Nearly all of the combat servicemen with whom I spoke had constructed, in conversation with others, one or more MP3 "battle playlists," which helped them "pump up" (or "amp up," or "get psyched up," or "get into the right mindset" or "get in the zone") before missions.

The overwhelming majority of these servicemen claimed never to have listened to music while on a mission. However, one of my interlocutors admitted that within his company this was common practice. "Teflon Don," an army engineer assigned the extremely dangerous task of clearing Iraqi roads of live IEDs, explained:[12]

> We did most of our movement in mine-resistant trucks, with crew size ranging from one to six people, depending on the vehicle. Every vehicle we had played music while on mission. In my truck, we used a small set of portable speakers powered by four AAA batteries. . . . One truck in my platoon used intravehicle communication headsets to talk to each other while on mission; that squad wired an audio jack directly into the

vehicle's communication system so that they could play their iPod over the headsets. In all cases, music was playing only when it didn't interfere with mission. We understood music to be a privilege—one that could be lost if we abused it. More than that—we hunted bombs, and we used music to stay awake and alert. When we were creeping up on a suspected bomb, we didn't need any help staying awake.

Predictably, given the demographics of the enlisted ranks of the armed forces, metal and rap music were heavily represented, both on pre-mission battle playlists and on the more rare playlists for missions. But, as Teflon Don explained,

> What music we listened to on mission depended on who was commanding the vehicle and what our mood was like. We listened to a lot of country with one sergeant—artists like Travis Tritt, Steve Earle, George Strait, and John Michael Montgomery. I liked some of that, especially the songs about soldiers, and I added some of them to my playlist (including "Letters from Home," "Copperhead Road," and Lonestar's "I'm Already There"). We listened to classic rock and metal constantly—AC/DC, Black Sabbath, Van Halen, as well as newer and contemporary stuff: Nine Inch Nails, Guns N' Roses, Rage Against The Machine, Disturbed. I had my own pre-mission playlist that I would listen to while "suiting up" for a mission and preparing the truck. On night missions I liked to go out early, set up my machine gun turret and watch the sunset or the stars while the music played. That list included Project 86, Dropkick Murphys, and similar bands.

More surprising, perhaps, was the broad range of musical choices on a second set of playlists to which service members listen in order to "cool down" after a stressful day spent "outside the wire," in the combat zone. On these lists one encounters the songs of Enya, Bach's *Goldberg Variations*, smooth jazz compositions, and recordings in a wide variety of genres that are not commonly associated with the modern warrior. Teflon Don described his postmission playlist as consisting of "mostly melancholy songs":

> I must have listened to Dave Matthew's "Gravedigger" hundreds of times. Eventually, it became corrupted on my computer somehow, and my iTunes copied the corrupt file to my iPod. I never found a replacement song file before I left. The instrumental group E.S. Posthumus

had several tracks on this list. Their tracks were named for dead cities, and I found inspiration for my writing in them several times. Nickel Creek, Iron and Wine, and Ben Folds were all on this playlist.

The ubiquity of iPods and laptops has allowed all but the most remotely posted service members to download and trade music with one another, and in so doing fine-tune their playlists, at times on a daily basis. The salience of these evolving playlists in service members' testimonies speaks to their value for negotiating the rhythms of warfare. As one soldier explained to me, the battle playlist is the musical equivalent of amphetamines; the cool-down playlist, of barbiturates.

The sonic situation of the U.S. armed forces in Iraq has thus been suffused with recorded music to a degree unprecedented in the history of combat. Access to "mobile music" (along with videogames, movies on DVD, and videochats with friends and relatives at home) enables an experience of wartime that is more mediated, more virtualized, than ever before. Having said this, the testimonies of servicemen and women make it abundantly clear that no amount of music can drown out other sounds connected with the conflict.

Civilian Sounds

Even in peacetime, urban life is noisy. Urban life in wartime, as I hope to have demonstrated, is ineluctably noisier. Wartime urban life in places where the centralized electricity source has broken down is noisier still. With the disruption of local fuel production and distribution in the wake of the 2003 invasion, electricity plants throughout Iraq were forced to radically cut back on the production of power. Baghdad and other major cities throughout Iraq witnessed a proliferation of noisy gas- and diesel-powered generators—both small units supplying electricity to individual homes, and larger, louder units parked on neighborhood streets from which a group of residents draw power. According to my interlocutors, the tens of thousands of generators that ran in Baghdad from 2003 to 2008 (the number has since decreased somewhat) produced a pronounced white noise, which often drowned out the quieter ambient sounds of the city, and the quiet sounds of the insect and animal world in particular. Smaller towns were similarly marked with the drone, and smell, of diesel generators.

While traffic sounds are ubiquitous in modern metropolises, the sound of traffic is heavily inflected by local factors. In postinvasion Baghdad, for example, the generic rumble of engines, squealing of brakes, and honking of horns have been frequently punctuated by warning gunfire: Iraqi government troops, police, and U.S. military contractors have discovered that the quickest way to clear a congested intersection is to fire a few dozen rounds into the air.

With the widespread installation of twelve-foot concrete blast shields throughout the city beginning in April 2007, movement between majority Sunni and majority Shi'a neighborhoods—of people, of weapons, and, as an unintended consequence, of sounds—was dramatically curtailed. (Beginning in 2008, these walls began to be dismantled, a process that continues as of this writing.) Nonetheless, the local permutation of the global scourge of traffic noise contributes to service members' memories of a general sonic situation that also includes the sounds of crowds, amplified calls to prayer, public chanting and demonstrations, crying, laughing, dogs, hyenas, birds, and wind.

It bears mentioning that, while service members are regularly exposed to their own music through the ubiquity of MP3 players among the troops, Iraqi music was a marginal presence in the reminiscences of service members patrolling the city during the years immediately following the invasion. One U.S. army captain who was temporarily embedded in an Iraqi army unit mentioned that his Iraqi counterparts "were constantly listening to music" on FM radios and singing and dancing in small groups to pass the time. During the worst years of sectarian violence, however, music rarely seeped out of the security of private spaces and into the public sphere. As one of my Iraqi interlocutors explained it, anyone who performed or listened to music in public during this period (roughly 2004–7) ran the risk of having one's musical choices read as indexes of religious, political, or ethnic allegiance. Unless one was located in the center of a sectarian stronghold, in which case public music might be played as a demonstration of the strength of a neighborhood's allegiances, to play music was considered somewhat hazardous. In an environment where listening to the "wrong" music increased one's chance of provoking a sectarian attack, the aesthetic sphere encountered the political sphere—and was swallowed up by it. Under these conditions, the cautious turned off their music, or moved it indoors. Another Iraqi who lived in Baghdad during the same period agreed that music listening decreased during those years, but attributed this to different factors. The absence of music, he claimed, had less to do with the danger that music engendered, and more to do with the fact that, in the face of extreme violence, people lose the desire or energy to listen to music. According to this interpretation, life amidst the daily sounds and smells and sights of violence, life amidst the constant threat of violent death, created a state of abjection and vulnerability in which music became unthinkable.

Learning to Listen to the Sounds of Weapons

The sounds of military vehicles and urban life occasionally leap to the forefront of a service member's consciousness. A Humvee engine makes a strange noise and its driver listens intently to it in order to discern its condition. The sounds of angry crowds—or, conversely, an eerie reduction of the ambient sounds of the street—can cause experienced service members to prick up their ears as they scan their surroundings for evidence of an impending attack. And of course people in the most war-torn environments remain capable of being transfixed by the things that once caught their attention in peacetime: a call, a cry, a laugh, a snippet of a song, a dog's bark, the howling of the wind. But the service members whom I interviewed frequently referred to these ambient sounds as the sonic background *through which* they were actively listening for another set of sounds. The crack of bullets, the low boom of the IED, the whoosh of the rocket-propelled grenade, the arcing whine of the mortar—sounds that herald the immanence of corporeal violence, sounds that at certain volumes become a form of violence in their own right—are, for obvious reasons, the primary focus of the military listener's attention. The anticipation, experience, retention, and protention of weapon sounds are central activities within the phenomenology of urban conflict.

The degree of attention given to the sounds of weapons is radically dependent upon a number of factors, however, the most important of which appears to be proximity. In examining the importance of location to the perception of weapon sounds, we might profitably imagine, as a heuristic exercise, a striated landscape consisting of a number of roughly concentric zones that surround each military listener. These zones, I hasten to state, are not part of military discourse, but represent my attempt to synthesize the testimonies of military personnel regarding their common-sense assumptions about their listening experiences in Iraq.

Distant gunfire has been such a constant presence in the Iraq conflict that experienced service members claim they "no longer hear it." Only green troops new to the theater comment upon the popping sounds of distant weapons, and their more seasoned comrades tease them about their overly acute hearing. In the words of a soldier stationed in a small forward operating base outside Baghdad,

> You hear it so often it becomes background noise. It's different than the IEDs exploding or mortar hitting—you just don't even care about the shooting unless it's sustained or you can tell it's people actually shooting at each other back and forth. That background noise became inaudible to us almost. New units would show up, a visiting team of investigators, or somebody would show up, and they'd be like "Ooh! Didja hear that?" and you're like "What?" and they're like "That shooting!" and, "Oh, yeah, yeah, that's probably, you know, this neighborhood because they always shoot at noon, who knows?"

Distant gunfire becomes part of what we might call the zone of the "audible inaudible": a place far enough away that sound loses significance—and, along with significance, the illusion of presence. This act of rendering the audible inaudible, of failing or refusing to register sounds as such, points to the body's ability to train itself not to react to sonic energy it receives. In this sense, our conventional understanding of the experienced listener as an acute listener is turned on its head: experienced ears (or, perhaps more accurately, *indoctrinated* ears) are deadened to some sounds while attuned to others.

When the gunfire gets closer, however, experienced ears perk up; it is in the middle distance that service members pay attention to the unique sounds of particular weapons. For example, the AK-74, a popular firearm within the insurgency and sectarian militias, and the U.S. military M-16 both use 5.5 caliber rounds, and therefore sound almost identical to untrained ears. However, experienced listeners know that M-16s are designed to fire three-round bursts, while the AK-74 is most often used in fully automatic mode, so they can easily discern the one from the other. Having learned to decode these and many other acousmatic sounds, service members are able to construct rich narratives of battles that are fully within earshot but are not, or are only partially, visible. Service members cultivate and take pride in these listening skills. We might now imagine a second zone, more proximate than the audible inaudible, a zone in which gunfire is close enough to attract the attention of listeners but still too far to pose a physical threat. In this "narrativizable zone," experienced listeners will situate sounds in space, identify the weapons that produce them, and combine both bodies of data in the service of a story: the story of the unseen battle unfolding in one's ears. An army captain who served in Iraq in 2003 and 2004 explained that his narratives got more detailed as his knowledge about the surrounding neighborhoods, and the different fighting groups in those neighborhoods, increased:

> One of the things that we started noticing is we could tell if a police station was being hit or if they were shooting at the government building downtown, or if it was at the propane distribution spot, or wherever, based on where the stuff was coming from. Not necessarily whether it was incoming to us, but you could just tell, kind of what part of town, where it was hitting, and it helped us determine which little FOB [forward operating base] or mini-enclave of troops we had to send out [a message to] and say, "Hey, what's going on?"

The centrality of sound to memories of warfare is partially accounted for by the radical degree to which the identifiable sounds of battles such as these occupy the sustained attention of experienced listeners.

The sounds of weapons take on a much greater urgency when they signal the immanent presence of projectiles in the spaces in which service members find themselves. When gunfire is nearby, the narrative richness of its sounds collapses into the briefest tactical assessment: run *this* way; shoot in *that* direction. Close in, in what I'll call the "tactical zone," listeners train their skills of echolocation to determine the trajectory of bullets and locations of shooters. As one soldier described it,

> Beneath the engine sounds, transmission sounds, road noise, static over the radio . . . and ambient noises [over microphones] . . . everybody is very much in tune, listening for gunfire or rocket fire—and we had incidents of people firing rockets or mortars at us, and it was very much like the movies, cause you'd hear the whistling sound that goes by you and the first thing that pops in your mind is "Oh my god, somebody's shooting at us!" Secondly you say "Op, I heard the whistling

sound, and that means they missed, and it already went by us," and the third thing is "OK, where is that clown that just shot at me?"

Some of the most urgent information, however, is gleaned from the quietest sounds. The displacement of air made by a projectile on a near trajectory can herald itself as an exceedingly soft whizzing sound. Honing one's listening skills to discern, through the white noise, these subtle hisses and soft ricochets greatly increases one's chances of survival. In the words of a captain in the army infantry who served in Iraq in 2005:

> The gun being fired near you is . . . very loud, I mean there's almost a pain sensation involved . . . and that's probably within about fifty feet. Outside fifty feet, that's where the sound really changes depending on what direction it is, if it's being fired away from you or towards you and how close the bullet passes. If you can hear a "phiff" noise or a "zing," in and around you, the bullet probably passed within a few feet of you, probably about ten feet at the limit. And that's really nervewracking. Also, ricochets off your vehicle or anything near you—you know you hear it ricocheting and you usually get a "zing" noise like in the Western movies, and those aren't loud at all, sometimes you can't even— and then you're like "What was that?" and then you're like, "Oh crap, we're getting shot at" and everybody hits the ground, because somebody just heard a "ffft," you know, a "phip" or a "ffff." If they're shooting away from you, and you're away from the fire as well, you usually can't hear the bullet as it travels, but if it's being fired toward you, as it passes you or after it passes you, you can certainly hear the air being displaced.

At close distances, the volume of a bullet's displacement increases, but proximity is not the only factor governing these sonic shifts. A company commander who served in Mosul in 2005 and 2006 recalled that:

> I had a bullet go by my head that rang my ears for about two days. That was shot at me from maybe 100 meters or so, so fairly close, but that was not quiet at all. . . . At long distance, you might hear the splash on the Humvee or whatever, and then if it's really long, it's like [the snapping of] a high-tension wire. It's like a zip, I can't make the noise, but either it's like a zip, or, if it ricochets off the ground next to you, you can hear that, but you don't hear the report. And then different caliber weapons displace different amounts of air, but I think the range

matters a lot, and the caliber, but [also] where it hits: does it ricochet or does it hit the Humvee or does it go over your head? All of these things have different sounds, but some are soft and some were really, outrageously loud.

Amidst the chaos of combat, it is often impossible to perform the mental calculations necessary to determine the location of a shooter based solely on the sound of a bullet from the shooter's gun. In response to these difficulties, the U.S. military has begun to supply troops with artificial listening devices. One such device, the "Boomerang," consists of an array of seven microphones protruding from a metal pole and hooked up to a computer. The Boomerang has been mounted onto Humvees and other vehicles that patrol Iraqi streets. When a bullet passes within fifty feet of the device, the computer records the moment its passage was detected by each microphone, and based on the time and relative volume of the whizzing noise, it calculates the azimuth, height, and distance of the shooter. This information is delivered to the driver by a computerized voice. Augmenting the listening skills service members acquire over the course of their tours of duty, high-tech devices such as the Boomerang render the field of the sensible of the U.S. military increasingly distinct from that of all other parties to the conflict.[13]

We need to distinguish one more zone, even more proximate than the zone where sound acquires tactical significance: the space in which sounds produce physical damage, the "trauma zone." The physical injuries created by the loud sounds of weapons begin with hearing loss. Department of Defense regulations stipulate that all service members in the field wear in-ear hearing protection if they are exposed to continuous sound levels of 85 decibels and/or impulse sounds of more than 140 decibels.[14] Given that an up-armored Humvee can produce as much as 95 decibels of background noise, a burst from a 50-caliber machine gun is 160 decibels at fifty feet, and an IED, the most common weapon used in Iraq, can be literally deafening, most of the service members patrolling Baghdad fall under these regulations. While army audiologists claim that these plugs do not significantly impair one's ability to hear soft sounds, and in some cases actually enhance this ability, none of the service members I met who conducted foot patrols wore them fully inserted in both ears.[15] They preferred to risk their ears in order to discern the subtle sounds of bullets, footsteps, and distant voices that surrounded them. In the words of another captain:

On dismounted patrols if I wore an earplug I'd usually wear it in my right ear because that's where my rifle, if I'm shooting, is right closest to, but . . . as company commander I did not enforce that rule because I felt that my soldiers' ability to hear things when [they're] walking through fields or along canals or down city streets is more important than the possibility of hearing loss. You know, it's better to have some hearing loss than get shot and not have a chance to react.

This Odyssean bargain—trading ear protection for the unfettered ability to hear one's surroundings—surely accounts, at least in part, for the fact that hearing loss is the most common injury among service members who have served in Iraq. According to a 2005 study conducted by the *American Journal of Audiology*, hearing loss among soldiers deployed to Iraq between April 2003 and March 2004 is many times more prevalent than among soldiers at other posts, with over 15 percent of soldiers sampled reporting ringing in the ears.[16] For members of the Iraqi army, who have little to no hearing protection and fire significantly louder Russian-made weapons, the rate of hearing loss is certainly far greater. Lastly, while no statistics exist, civilians, although generally more distant from the sound of gunfire, surely are physically affected by the militarized noise in the city.[17]

Service members suffer hearing loss from repeated exposure to the sounds of their own weapons. (This well-documented phenomenon, known colloquially as "shooter's ear," has decreased over the course of the twentieth century as American weapons have become quieter.) But the most serious cases of hearing loss, involving punctured eardrums and the risk of permanent deafness, involve exposure to IEDS, the signature weapons of the Iraq conflict. For the first five years of the war, the IED was without dispute the most visible, audible, and influential weapon in the insurgent arsenal.[18] In addition to the destructive power of the explosion itself, the IED allowed the insurgents to exert a measure of control over the ears of the populace: the frequent low boom of an IED in the distance was incontrovertible sonic evidence that the insurgency was alive and well.

At the heart of the zone of physical trauma, when one is exposed to a nearby detonation of an IED or other explosive device, the distinction between the sound of the explosion and its destructive force breaks down completely. The detonation of an IED generates an irregular blast wave of compressed air that, at a distance, regularizes into a configuration that we perceive as sound. For those nearby, however, this very wave of acoustic energy is experienced as physical force. While medical studies are not yet conclusive, a growing body of evidence suggests that this wave of atmospheric pressure is one of the causes of closed brain injury, the signature injury for the ongoing conflict.[19] The lasting damage to the brain caused by a blast wave that, with distance, degenerates into an audible explosion, can in this sense be understood as a sound wound. It is here that the contention of music scholars such as Suzanne Cusick and Jenny Johnson— that the aural and the haptic are often experienced in a synaesthetic fusion that can be both viscerally thrilling and deeply traumatizing—is given its most frighteningly literal dimension.[20]

Although most of the acts of listening to the war in Iraq can be conceptualized in terms of the four zones of increasing proximity that I just outlined, these distinctions of distance lose much of their relevance when the discussion turns to psychological trauma. The psychological wounds inflicted by sound are profound, albeit poorly understood. What does seem clear is that, for many service members, sound serves as a powerful trigger for post-traumatic stress, and distant sounds as well as close-up sounds can have this effect. Several of my interlocutors related at length how far-off thunder and low booming sounds from construction sites forcefully generate visceral memories of IED explosions, causing them to freeze and wonder who had been injured. The published account of First Sergeant Russell W. Anderson Jr. describes an even more acute situation: "The anxiety attacks—[they're] unbelievable. Loud noises. I'm a hunter and I was on the gun range with my younger son and these people next to us started firing in rapid succession. I dove under the truck. I was so embarrassed. At least my son didn't see it. Anything can trigger [post-traumatic stress disorder]."[21]

Upon returning to American cities, service members are confronted with many urban sounds that resemble those they heard in Baghdad, rendering the possibility of flashbacks all the more likely. A car accelerating to pass you on an American highway can sound a lot like the beginning of a vehicle-borne IED attack in Iraq. Despite a large number of well-funded investigations, the depth and breadth of the PTSD problem—and the significance of the sonic for PTSD—remain poorly understood.[22] At the same time, it does not diminish the profundity of this problem to acknowledge that, for Iraq's permanent residents, a "post-traumatic" situation continues to be a distant dream; for the majority of Iraqis, the trauma of living in a combat zone, while significantly diminished since the peak years of civilian violence in 2006 and 2007, continues.

Auditory Regimes, Individual Experience

I would like to argue that the zones of listening that I have distilled out of service members' stories are in large part the manifestation of an informal, largely intuitive, but nonetheless powerful "auditory regime," a sound-centered habitus that structures the listening activities of military personnel in Iraq. To the best of my knowledge, this term was first theorized by Kate Lacey, who called for an investigation of the "hierarchically differentiated and competing *auditory regimes* analogous to [French film theorist Christian] Metz's scopic regimes (scientifically and technologically generated 'techniques of observation')," as part of her study of American radio listening practices.[23] The notion of historically contingent, technologically enabled listening practices has been circulating among music scholars for some time, however.[24] In describing what I would call the general foundation of all auditory regimes of musical listening, Richard Leppert wrote: "Listening, to belabour the obvious, demands a listener. But listen*ing* is not properly understood as a biological phenomenon, rather a historico-sociocultural one: the listener is framed by history, society, and culture."[25] It is with a similar awareness of the multiple domains that surround, frame, and partially structure any act of auditory perception that I deploy the term here.

I imagine the military's auditory regime coalescing around the full-spectrum sensory sensitization and desensitization that occurs during basic training; new technologies of listening and noise abatement; regulations governing the use of auditory technologies; and casual discussions among military personnel who find themselves thrust into extreme situations that both enable and demand particular forms of aural acuity. These widespread experiences and technologies, together with official and informal injunctions to maintain acute awareness of all sensory stimuli when on missions, combine to create a general sense of the methodology for— and value of—effective listening. At the same time, military audiologists, ear protection training programs, and formal and informal information sharing about the ways in which sounds can trigger post-traumatic stress serve as constant reminders that the auditory regime of active combat is an inherently risky system.

As I mentioned in the introduction to this essay, the dynamics of many of the listening experiences synthesized above appear to be shared, across space and time, by a wide spectrum of military and civilian survivors of war. The testimonies of Iraq War veterans resonate with conversations I've had with survivors of the first Gulf War; armed conflicts in Lebanon and Israel; the Iran-Iraq war; and violence in Pakistan. They also run roughly parallel to the stories that emerge in documentary and literary accounts of warfare throughout the nineteenth and twentieth centuries. This general background of continuity exists in tension, however, with the unique dynamics of the auditory regime that has emerged in wartime Iraq—dynamics engendered by topography, technology, and tactics, among other factors. In turn, any abstract "auditory regime"—in Iraq or elsewhere—is a construct distilled from the individual experiences of individual subjects: the decision makers and order followers and bystanders and victims who find themselves swept up into the conflict. In order to point toward the myriad individual lives from which all generalities are extracted, I want to turn now to a number of concrete acts of embodied listening as they were related to me by John Pullman (not his real name), a major in the U.S. Air Force, who served in Kirkuk in 2006.

I was introduced to Major Pullman by a friend of mine who teaches at the Naval Postgraduate School (NPS) in Monterey, California. I had asked my friend to lead his students, many of whom had recently served tours of duty in Iraq, in a discussion of the role that iPods and other MP3 devices were playing for troops serving in Operation Iraqi Freedom. Pullman was one of the students who volunteered to allow me to contact them with follow-up questions, and over the course of a long phone conversation, he told me stories about his memories of music, ambient noise, silence, and trauma in the theater of war. Pullman, whose original Air Force training qualified him to quickly repair runways that had been bombed by Soviet planes, was sent to command a large Air Force construction crew charged with repairing the roads pocked with craters from IED explosions. Upon returning from his tour of duty, Pullman rejoined his wife and children, with whom he relocated to picturesque Monterey for a stint at NPS. He is articulate, friendly, thoughtful, and quick to laugh. He also holds highly nuanced opinions about the decision to go to war, the geopolitics of the region, and the ideologies of the people he encountered while in Iraq. While he had experiences that troubled and saddened him—not least the death of some of his men—he does not see himself as having been irrevocably traumatized by the war.

Although Major Pullman—as a career officer, as a member of the Air Force on loan to the army, as a civil engineer and demolitions expert— is not representative of the core demographic for combat troops in Iraq, his recollections do touch on a number of themes that have arisen frequently in my conversations with other Iraq War veterans. I have chosen to present three of his stories that complement rather than exemplify the general trends I outlined above, in the hopes that they will add some nuance to the more structural account of the military auditory regime that I provided earlier in this essay. I hope these stories hint at some of the ironies, subtleties, and experiential richness that saturate service members' testimonies about their time spent in Iraq.

Listening through the Deployment:
The Importance of Music and Silence for Combat

Music was a prominent presence on Pullman's base. He and his airmen conducted much of their on-base work to musical accompaniment; they also spent much of their down time listening to their iPods and using their laptops to add soundtracks to videos they had shot "outside the wire." These videos would then be shared among the airmen, and with friends and family back home. Pullman disagreed, however, with the contention of several of my military interlocutors, that service members primarily used music to attain the altered state of consciousness necessary to be an effective warrior. While he acknowledged that this might be the case for infantry, with their "'charge the hill and kill, kill, kill' mindset," music was not such an on-the-ground necessity for his airmen: "Our guys being construction and engineers are trained to be a little bit more methodical and logical as we go about our business. I don't know if we were as easily swayed or prone to get into a mind-altered state," he said. While their engagement with music may not have produced the heightened affective extreme that other service members have described, he acknowledged that his airmen did value music for its galvanizing and invigorating properties:[26]

> Everybody in the military is a type-A personality, and particularly in a combat situation you want them arrogant and confident and feeling that they're bulletproof, and so yeah . . . we definitely used music to

further solidify the idea that we're gonna go out there and kick butt and take names, and the bad guy's not gonna get us, we're bulletproof—you definitely needed everybody in the correct mindset and in the game. Much is [the same] with sports as well . . . you get the adrenalin fired up and everybody's highly motivated and highly focused.

When prepping a mission, in the two or three hours spent loading up Humvees and other vehicles, the airmen under Pullman's command listened to music—mainly heavy metal, with AC/DC heavily represented, but also some "mainstream rap"—almost constantly. (Pullman explained the preference for metal as the result of ethnicity, age, and gender: "I think heavy metal was the most popular, just the demographic of the team I had, it was predominantly young, middle-aged white males.") Despite the fact that most of his airmen had iPods, the music played during these group activities was listened to communally, on a boombox that Pullman had purchased using organizational funds. Once his men returned to base, as they were unloading the trucks, the boombox was turned back on, but the playlist was altered:

> I wanna say that a lot of times we'd come back and again it was the de-mobilization phase . . . and a lot of times the guys would turn on more of the Top 40 radio playlist, whatever was popular and common. . . . It wasn't something to pump you up 'cause by this point everyone's coming down off the two-hour adrenalin rush, and we made it back safely, and nobody shot at us, or nobody hit us, or nobody got hurt. That was the big important part to it, when nobody got hurt, we'd play this music, and we predominantly chose the Top 40, because—I don't want to say it was benign—but if you psychoanalyze it, it was because it was American music and it was what we were comfortable with and it just fit: it wasn't sad, it wasn't overly happy, it was *normal*. And, you know, "situation normal," we're all back safely.

Not all missions ended this way. During his tour of duty, a number of the men serving under Pullman were killed. If a mission resulted in a casualty, the airmen turned the music off: "On those particular missions it was pretty much dead silence all the way home, and we would usually download the trucks in silence, and it was very quiet." Death and injury were marked by a lack of music. Similarly, listening to music signified death's absence, or at least its passage: within a day or so after a death, while the complicated process of mourning continued, the music-infused routine of "situation normal" returned to Pullman's company.

Pullman and the roughly sixty men under his command lived in an old Iraqi air hangar. The men built their own rooms using available materials. They lived three or four to a room; Pullman let them pick their own roommates. Within these semiprivate spaces, and on their iPods in public spaces, they were given complete freedom to choose their own music. Given that all of the men had laptops with CD-burning capabilities and Internet connectivity, they enjoyed a robust system of music downloading and hand-to-hand file sharing. Pullman remarked on the unprecedented agency that military personnel in Iraq had to design their own acoustic environments. "Everybody's got a laptop now, almost all my soldiers had laptops, everybody's got an iPod. . . . You can download what you want. It's not like Vietnam where you had a big clunky radio and only two English-speaking radio stations, and that's what you listened to." This freedom was curtailed, however, when music resonated in public spaces. Pullman would not allow his men to play "extreme" music on the company boom-box. "Some of the grunge heavy metal I don't care for, a lot of the profanity and proviolence music, some of the Snoop-Doggy-Dog-'let's-go-shoot-some-cops'" music was declared to be unwelcome. As in Teflon Don's bomb-dismantling company, music in public spaces reflected the taste of the commanding officer, and thus the hierarchy of the military order.

Creative Misprision: Listening to the Call to Prayer

The *adhan*, or Muslim call to prayer, figures prominently—centrally, even—in service members' reminiscences of their tours of duty in Iraq. In contrast to other more localized and ad hoc modes of vocal expression, the amplified and ritualized sounds of the muezzin's chant travel far, bathing American military installations and civilian neighborhoods alike in the sound of a human voice five times daily. For observant Muslims the adhan resonates within a powerful cultural matrix of temporality, theology, and topography to structure diurnal, spiritual, and social life: in the words of the ethnomusicologist Tong Soon Lee, the call does nothing less than "produce Islamic space."[27] Divorced from its religious context, however, as it is for the majority of U.S. troops, the call to prayer is regularly Orientalized, objectified, and understood as the sonic embodiment of an essentially exotic Arab East. Operating outside of the spiritual community that has assigned the call its rich symbolic resonance, some service members learn to appreciate it on their own terms, as an aesthetically satisfying performance. As a musically inclined army captain described it, the adhan is "sung, it's almost Gregorian. And of course musically I always thought it was interesting because they have quarter steps in their notes: quarter pitches, most people don't care but I'd always be amazed at the tonal quality of these, you know they're just preachers, the imams, but they have this amazing voice control, cause he's working all kinds of quarter steps, [when] most people [in America] don't even know the difference between a sharp and a flat."

Major Pullman and his airmen arrived in Iraq with a general awareness of the significance of the call to prayer for their Iraqi neighbors. With time, however, they also came to assign the adhan a significance that was purely tactical:

> Something else unique about the Middle East is prayer time, you would hear the mosques, and you knew that, OK, all the Muslims are going to be praying, so (1) no one's gonna be shooting at us for the next two minutes, and (2) we gotta watch out because people will pull over, and stop what they're doing and start praying and we don't need to run any body over or get in the middle of an accident because folks are stopping to pray. . . . If it was prayer time it was very convenient, and we would whip right through, and be out of their way in no time flat.

While Iraqi auditory regimes are not the subject of this article, I must point out that it is at moments like this where listening practices encouraged and enacted by members of the U.S. military appear to diverge most radically from those of the Iraqi civilian population. The act of creative misprision that allowed Pullman to read an expression of religious observance as a barometer of insurgent violence points, emphatically I think, to a discursive horizon at which the intersubjectivity of listening reaches its limit. It may very well be that a person for whom the adhan is a symbol of the presence of God and his blessing might refuse or otherwise be unable to occupy a stance from which the adhan is read as a marker for a narrow window of tactical opportunity. One does not have to essentialize difference to acknowledge, within this anecdote, at least the possibility that some practices of listening may be simply incommensurable, some interpretations mutually exclusive.

"I Love the Sound of the M-2 in the Morning":
On the Cathartic Aesthetics of Weapon Sounds

As I stated earlier, the military's auditory regime encourages service members to learn to echolocate, identify, and assess the narrative and tactical significance of the weapon sounds that surround them. Pullman's men, who were not engaged in active battles on a regular basis, were less accustomed to decoding the myriad furtive whiffing noises that bullets on near trajectories produce. Nonetheless, they did "see action," primarily in the form of the IED explosions whose effects they were assigned to mitigate. And they did, on occasion, fire their own weapons, either in defense or in warning.

Pullman recalled the thrilling experience of firing a large-caliber automatic weapon, in which the percussive force of weapon recoil fuses with sound and sight and the knowledge of one's destructive capabilities to create a full-spectrum sensory experience of power, violence, and heightened affect. In his recollection, the sonic dimension of the catharsis of gunfire was particularly pronounced:

> One of the neatest sounds, one of the most memorable sounds out there is a 50-cal [M-2] machine gun, [which makes] a very distinctive, commanding noise. . . . It's a very big gun, it's very intimidating, the noise is intimidating and the damage that the weapon can inflict is intimidating. We have those on our vehicles, and I think it has more of a psychological value than a real physical value. We always took them on our trucks, and we only had to fire the weapons once and you learn, and the bad guys learn that it makes a very loud, distinctive sound that is something to be respected and feared. And so, we took them with us more for the psychological value, and just hearing it would — bad guys would disappear quickly from hearing that noise.

The ballistics of the M-2 rendered it inappropriate as a projectile-throwing weapon on this battlefield. But the devastating sound of the machine gun's report made it an ideal *acoustic* weapon:

> I didn't let the guys shoot it at . . . targets because . . . it's such a big bullet that it has a tendency to travel *through*: through the vehicle, through the bad guy, out the other end, into the house in town, out through the mud-built houses, and through several houses so it was a lot of collateral damage that could happen so if we had to get into an engagement

the guys shot their M-16s or smaller weapons, but we always carried it because it was loud, and it was commanding, and it garnered respect.

This story highlights a fusion of violent efficacy and aesthetics that figures prominently in service members' testimonies of war. The "distinctive," "commanding" sound of the M-2, a string of percussive explosions accompanied by the sound of a cascade of brass cartridges clinking onto the ground, is inextricably bound together with the knowledge of the weapon's destructive force. (Surely the rush would not be the same if the bullets were silent, or if the "dadadadadadadada" sound was the result of a jackhammer.) The cathartic thrill of letting a noisy stream of bullets fly is one of the archetypal experiences that helps constitute the trope of the contemporary American warrior. Of course, what is a "neat" and "memorable" sound for the soldier is, by Pullman's admission, terrifying for the potential targets of the 50-caliber rounds. This is the Janus-faced aspect of all weapon sounds: that which tends to invigorate the shooter tends to frighten or frustrate the intended victim. In Pullman's story, his heightened awareness of the M-2 sound was coupled with the sense that the weapon was performing the valuable work of keeping him safe; adding this efficacy to the violent aesthetics of weapons being fired only heightened the affective power of the moment. Conversely, for the insurgents, at least according to Pullman's narrative, the painfully loud sound of the M-2, coupled with the immanent threat of death that the sound heralded, allowed the U.S. forces to dictate the crowd's behavior—to control bodies through sound. For both parties, the power of the sound and the power of the military were inseparable.

. . . . .

Music instrumentalized to lubricate the daily operations of a military unit. Silence mobilized to memorialize death. Sacred sounds inscribed with profane significance. Weapon sounds deployed as icons of military might. What do these stories tell us about the auditory regime of the U.S. military, the dynamics of listening in wartime, and the significance of the belliphonic in post-Hussein Iraq? Collectively, they point toward an affectively rich, emotionally charged situation in which members of the U.S. military learn to interact with and manipulate the sonorous world in a way that simultaneously participates in the mission of the military and produces a visceral sense of pleasure and (relative) safety. In each of these moments, the aesthetic and the political are fused together in such a way that to receive aesthetic pleasure is to serve as an effective warrior. Listening to music on base heightens coordination and reifies the military hierarchy; it also feels good, lessens fear, and helps the time pass more quickly. Listening to the call to prayer opens a window of opportunity to safely pass through dangerous zones; it is also accompanied by a feeling of relative safety and calm, and is remembered as hauntingly beautiful. Shooting the M-2 provides a nonlethal method for discouraging one's antagonists; it also sounds *awesome*. Listening experiences such as these, experiences that feel natural but that tacitly underwrite the interests of the military, are building blocks of the powerful habitus of the military auditory regime.

The intuitive, improvisational appearance of these acts—as voluntary, unplanned, seemingly unregulated instances of listening—belies the foundation of practice that enabled them. For all three moments of listening that Pullman described were, if not ritualistic, at least repeated, and all involved learned capacities that developed over time. It took repetition, reflection, and conversation for the service members in question to learn what music is appropriate for the tasks at hand, what significance to attribute to the call to prayer, how not to be overwhelmed by the sound of the machine gun. These moments also took place within a complex nexus of sounds (musical, vehicular, ambient, weapon-based), technologies (boomboxes, ammunition, Humvees, weapons), and people (comrades-in-arms, muezzins, civilians, combatants), all of whom were working through existential imperatives (to work, to mourn, to worship, to survive, to attack). When examined in the context of this network, and in light of the atmosphere of violence that surrounded them, these acts of listening emerge as anything but natural.

To conclude, I'd like to reflect on a question I imagine some readers have been asking; indeed, it is a question I continue to ask myself: why has an essay that radically decenters music in favor of discussions of bullet sounds and ambient noises been included in a volume of music scholarship? Phrased differently, what is the relation between listening to music and listening to the sounds of war? Or more pointedly, what is the relevance of "sound studies" like this one to music studies? I am tempted to make the somewhat iconoclastic claim that experienced military listeners concentrate on their sonic situations with all of the acuity and sophistication that Wagner afficionados deploy as they listen to *Tristan und Isolde*.

It is true that experienced service members are able to read significance into sonic differences much more subtle than those that distinguish a pre-Wagnerian half-diminished seventh chord's resolution from its harmonic function as the "Tristan chord." But in the end, comparing the concert hall to the combat zone does violence to both situations. Major Pullman's visceral thrill when listening to his M-2 notwithstanding, I'm not convinced that the similarities between listening to violent acts and listening to music (no matter how violent) outweigh the differences. The differences are important: indeed, they are quite literally the differences between life and death.

In the place of this contention, then, let me advance a more modest argument: one possible response to the questions I posed above is that grappling with the complex ways in which sound and violence are interwoven into wartime experience helps situate any discussion that we might have about the dynamics of listening to music in the combat zone, and hence about the significance of music for contemporary service members. We return to the perennial question: where does the meaning of music reside? If I tell you that many service members serving in the early years of the Iraq war loved the song "Bodies" by Drowning Pool (with its incantatory refrain, first whispered, then screamed: "let the bodies hit the floor, let the bodies hit the floor, let the bodies hit the floor"), how do we begin to make sense of this? Do we analyze the lyrics? The Spartan text of this song does take on a powerfully literal aspect (although one the lyricists may not have foreseen) when calibrated against the current conflict. Do we listen to the notes? One can make a convincing argument that the crushing power chords are iconically related to wartime actions, and that they invigorate service members and get them in an appropriately aggressive mindset for battle. Do we read this song as an emblem of service members' identities? Its popularity can easily be understood to be pointing to a large and vibrant taste community within the military. All of these interpretive moves are valid.

But until we focus on the actual situations in which acts of listening take place, until we focus on the fact that sneaking an iPod earbud underneath your headphones when you are on a mission reduces your ability to hear the whizzing of bullets and, hence, to survive; until we focus on the fact that service members are often listening *through fear*, listening with bodies that are coursing with adrenalin; or listening in exceedingly and unpredictably loud environments to stave off fear, or boredom, or homesickness; until we acknowledge that listening to music often precedes or accompanies the act of killing, or of being killed—in other words, until we consider the myriad situations in which listening occurs, and tally the costs and benefits of listening for the listener (costs and benefits which take on an existential dimension for service members in Iraq), a discussion of the meaning of a piece of music that focuses on our traditional hermeneutic (if musicology) or culture-contextual (if ethnomusicology) methodologies is in danger of missing the point. A growing number of scholars have begun looking beyond these methodologies toward new ways of theorizing embodied listening,[28] and this essay hopes to contribute to that conversation.

In stressing the physical conditions in which the act of listening takes place, I do not mean to suggest that these acts are solely the product of individual bodies and the spaces that envelop them. No one can occupy the exact location that I occupy, and so the waves that hit my cardrums, be they Mahler or M-16, are in some sense unique. But no act of listening is truly singular or fully autonomous. By focusing in this essay on the military's auditory regime and gesturing toward the presence of other less regimented structuring practices within the Iraqi civilian population, I have stressed the degree to which listening to the sounds of combat is not an automatic process that occurs identically for all people who have functioning ears, nor an individual process that depends solely on one's attitude and chemical makeup, but rather a socially conditioned process. Taken at the most literal level, this means (1) that the sounds of combat can and do mean different things to different people; but (2) that there is a structure to the field in which we decide what these sounds mean. Discerning the auditory regimes that give people a sense of what dimensions of (belliphonic or musical) sound are most deserving of attention, and what these sounds mean, is a key step to understanding the sonic dimension of war and the way that musical sound fits within it.

But even as these interpretive moves get us closer to an understanding of the role of music and sound in wartime, other considerations can push this understanding out of reach. One of them is this: the extreme nature of the auditory/haptic experiences of wartime exerts a potentially fatal pressure on our traditional vocabularies. Can the term "listening"—with its powerful connotations of intentionality, pleasure, and the quest to unlock hidden secrets—be applied to those who suffer hearing loss from an IED explosion? Or, to take up another fraught subject position, can "listening" be used to describe the experiences of those who are submitted to music against their will, be it through long-range acoustic devices on the battlefield or speakers in the interrogation chamber? Are there sounds that are too loud, or that are applied too violently, to "listen to"? Where does *listening* end and raw *exposure* begin? These questions, for me at least, destabilize the epistemologies that undergird music studies and trouble all assumptions about the essential relation between listening and aesthetic experience. By focusing on the conditions of listening, on what is at stake for those who listen, and on the violent margins where listening deteriorates into pain, or deafness, or death, we may need to come up with new vocabularies in order to approach an understanding of the dynamics of "belliphonic listening" or "auditory exposure" and the meaning that music can have for people in combat zones—and, in conditions that we now see are far from extreme, for ourselves. And by probing the ways in which service members and civilians, victims and perpetrators, central and peripheral figures listen, both to music and to the cacophonous, unpredictable world of the combat zone, we may make an incremental step toward learning how one can survive and act ethically in times and places that are warped by extreme violence.

Notes

1. This essay is an expansion of a paper delivered at the Experience Music Project annual conference, held in Seattle, Washington, in April 2008. Subsequent versions of the paper were presented later that year at Stonehill College and Carleton University; I'm grateful to my colleagues at these institutions for their insights and support. I would also like to thank Jason Sagebiel, Suzanne Cusick, and Siv Lie, who read versions of the manuscript and made valuable suggestions. My most profound thanks go to the members of the U.S. armed forces and civil service, and the many Iraqi civilians, whose testimonies form the central part of my work on sound in combat.

A piece composed in 2008, when combat operations were in full swing, this essay has been overtaken somewhat by recent events. In 2010, major U.S.-led combat operations in Iraq were officially brought to an end, and the majority of troops serving in Iraq were redeployed elsewhere. While the current situation in Iraq is far from peaceful, it is already markedly different from the historical moment that this essay describes.

2. Harlan K. Ullman and James P. Wade introduced the strategy in a paper titled "Shock and Awe: Achieving Rapid Dominance" (Washington: National De-

fense University Press, 1996). The strategy called for a show of overwhelming military force that would "dominate an adversary's will both physically and psychologically," in part through producing a combination of noise and lights that disorients the adversary and renders him "impotent and vulnerable." While a number of military strategists have claimed that Rapid Dominance was imperfectly implemented in Iraq, there is compelling, albeit anecdotal, evidence to suggest that the sonic dimension of the attack was consciously designed. Also, I have gathered ample commentary from Iraqi civilians about the overwhelming and debilitating effect of the attack, which was experienced by most Baghdad residents, gathered together in their homes, in auditory/tactile rather than visual terms.

3. "Service member" is the most widely accepted inclusive term for military personnel from all branches of the service. The more common "soldier" technically refers only to enlisted personnel in the army. In order to avoid offending my interlocutors who serve in the Marines and Air Force (I haven't interviewed anyone from the Navy, National Guard, or Coast Guard), and in order to avoid the cumbersome "soldiers, sailors, airmen and marines," I have settled on "service member," or occasionally "military personnel" in this essay. Any reference to "soldiers" in my text, outside of quotations, points to people serving in the army.

4. The largest clearinghouses of military blogs can be found at www.milblogging .com and http://www.mudvillegazette.com/milblogs. For a review of the history of milblogs and attempts by the military to censor them, see Noah Shachtman, "Army Squeezes Soldier Blogs, Maybe to Death," *Wired*, May 2, 2007, at http:// www.wired.com.

5. My work on listening within the context of the Iraq war is based on live and phone interviews with officers and enlisted men who have recently returned from tours of duty in Iraq; live interviews with a number of nonmilitary professionals who worked in Iraq for extended periods in various capacities; correspondence, live and phone interviews with Iraqi citizens who have fled Baghdad for Amman, Jordan, and the United States; as well as on critical readings of several dozen military and Iraqi blogs, documentaries and news footage, and several hundred videos posted by U.S. soldiers and self-proclaimed Iraqi jihadists.

6. Bruno Latour, *Reassembling the Social: An Introduction to Actor-Network Theory* (New York: Oxford University Press, 2005).

7. F. Murray Schafer, *The Soundscape: Our Sonic Environment and the Tuning of the World* (Rochester, Vt.: Inner Traditions International, 1993).

8. In September 2008, the U.S. military instituted a regulation forbidding interpreters from wearing face masks. Several months later, in response to criticism that the new policy put interpreters' lives at risk, it was largely reversed. For a full account of these events, see Ernesto Londoño, "Iraqi Interpreters May Wear Masks," *Washington Post*, February 13, 2009, A12.

9. Quoted in William H. Kenney, *Recorded Music in American Life: The Phonograph and Popular Memory, 1890–1945* (New York: Oxford, 1999), 194.

10. Press articles exploring the use of iPods in the war include Benjamin Suther-land, "Apple's New Weapon," *Newsweek*, April 27, 2009; Evan Serpick, "Soundtrack to the War," *Rolling Stone*, August 24, 2006; and Robert Mackey, "The Pentagon Adds iPods to Its Arsenal," *The Lede: The New York Times News Blog*, May 6, 2009, at http://thelede.blogs.nytimes.com. Actually, the Iraq war began well before iPods acquired their current global salience. When the Australian war artist and film-maker George Gittoes shot his groundbreaking documentary *Soundtrack to War* in mid-2003, the soldiers he interviewed were jacking portable CD players into the communications systems of their vehicles. (This practice was also widespread dur-ing the U.S. military intervention in Kosovo.) But by 2006, when I began conduct-ing interviews, the iPod had become ubiquitous; soldiers who didn't deploy with an iPod purchased one soon after arriving in Iraq.

11. Lisa Gilman, "An American Soldier's Ipod: Layers of Identity and Situated Listening in Iraq," *Music and Politics* 4, no. 2 (2010), at http://www.music.ucsb.edu; Jonathan Pieslak, *Sound Targets: American Soldiers and Music in the Iraq War* (Bloom-ington: Indiana University Press, 2009). See also George Gittoes's documentary film *Soundtrack to War* (Visual Entertainment, 2003), and Nate Anderson,"iPods at War," August 2006, at http://arstechnica.com. My discussion of iPod-enabled music listening in the military owes much to Tia DeNora's seminal work on *Music in Everyday Life* (Cambridge: Cambridge University Press, 2000). Just as DeNora's research subjects often used "self-administered music" as "a catalyst, a device that enabled [them] to move from one set of feelings to another over a relatively short time span" (16), so have soldiers "self-administered" music to achieve this goal throughout their deployments.

12. Teflon Don (a pseudonym) became one of the war's most eloquent mili-tary bloggers. His award-winning milblog, "Acute Politics," can be found at http://acutepolitics.blogspot.com.

13. Samuel Soza, "Shooter-Detection 'Boomerangs' Helping in Iraq," December 17, 2009, at the official homepage of the U.S. Army, http://www.army.mil.

14. See Thomas Helfer, Nikki N. Jordan, and Robyn B. Lee, "Postdeployment Hearing Loss in U.S. Army Soldiers Seen at Audiology Clinics from April 1, 2003, through March 31, 2004," *American Journal of Audiology* 14 (2005): 161–68.

15. A new electronically modulated set of earphones was introduced into the combat zone in 2008, and promises to change this landscape somewhat. The ear-phones, which are connected to a small device slightly bigger than an iPod, elec-tronically cancel out sounds above a certain decibel threshold, while actually ampli-fying softer sounds. These devices were not in circulation when my interlocutors served in Iraq, however, and so don't figure in their reminiscences.

16. Helfer et al., "Postdeployment Hearing Loss in U.S. Army Soldiers."

17. In 2008 I spoke to an Iraqi otologist who reported that his Baghdad clinic witnessed a marked increase in trauma-induced hearing loss among civilians of all age groups following the invasion. While this evidence is anecdotal and in need

of verification, it seems logical to assume that the civilian population would be affected by the same sounds that have deafened hundreds, if not thousands, of troops.

18. Since 2008, IED use has markedly decreased, and smaller "sticky bombs" have been ascendant.

19. For more information on the effect of primary blast waves on the human brain, see Katherine H. Taber et al., "Blast-Related Traumatic Brain Injury: What Is Known?" *Journal of Neuropsychiatry and Clinical Neurosciences* 18, no. 2 (2006): 141–45.

20. See Jenny Johnson, "The Luminous Noise of Broken Experience: Synaesthesia, Acoustic Memory, and Childhood Sexual Abuse in the Late 20th Century United States," Ph.D. dissertation, New York University, 2009; Suzanne Cusick, "Music as Torture / Music as Weapon," *Revista Transcultural de Música* 10 (2006), at the website of Sibe: Sociedad de Etnomusicología, www.sibetrans.com; and Suzanne Cusick, "'You Are In a Place That Is Out of the World . . .': Music in the Detention Camps of the 'Global War on Terror,'" *Journal of the Society for American Music* 2, no. 1 (2008): 1–26.

21. In Elise Forbes Tripp, *Surviving Iraq: Soldiers' Stories* (Northampton, Mass.: Olive Branch Press, 2009), 138.

22. Clinical literature unanimously presents sound as a trigger for PTSD. See, for example, Albert Rizzo et al., "A Virtual Reality Exposure Therapy Application for Iraq War Military Personnel with Post Traumatic Stress Disorder: From Training to Toy to Treatment," in NATO *Advanced Research Workshop on Novel Approaches to the Diagnosis and Treatment of Posttraumatic Stress Disorder*, ed. M. Roy (Washington: IOS Press, 2006), 235–50; and Carol S. Fullerton and Robert J. Ursano, eds., *Posttraumatic Stress Disorder: Acute and Long-Term Responses to Trauma and Disaster* (Washington: American Psychiatric Press, 2009). Studies of shell-shock immediately after the First World War speculated on the importance of sound as an instigator of anxiety (ibid., 243). But the exact nature of this relationship—and why some people are affected by sounds and others aren't—is more of an open question. Statistics for PTSD among Iraq War veterans are almost certainly lower than the actual number of veterans who experience acute anxiety and stress upon their return to civilian life.

23. Lacey's work was inspired by scholars of visual studies who "draw attention to the ruptures, discontinuities and multiplicity of viewing positions within and across historical moments and in relation to different techniques and technologies of spectatorship." Kate Lacey, "Toward a Periodization of Listening: Radio and Modern Life," *International Journal of Cultural Studies* 3, no. 2 (2000): 280–81. A dozen years earlier, Kaja Silverman employed the term, without explicitly defining it, to point to the structured sensibilities embedded in the sounds of films within a given period. Kaja Silverman, *The Acoustic Mirror: The Female Voice in Psychoanalysis and Cinema* (Bloomington: Indiana University Press, 1988): ix, 31, 38, 177.

24. See, most prominently, Peter Manuel, *Cassette Culture: Popular Music and Technology in Northern India* (Chicago: University of Chicago Press, 1993), and the discussion of "structures of listening" in John Mowitt, "The Sound of Music in the Era of Its Electronic Reproducibility," in *Music and Society: The Politics of Composition, Performance, and Reception*, ed. Richard Leppert and Susan McClary (Cambridge: Cambridge University Press, 1989), 173–97. More recently, Jonathan Sterne, *The Audible Past: Cultural Origins of Sound Reproduction* (Durham: Duke University Press, 2003); Emily Thompson, *The Soundscape of Modernity: Architectural Acoustics and the Culture of Listening in America, 1900–1933* (Cambridge: MIT Press, 2004); and others writing under the rubric of sound studies have written persuasively about socially structured listening practices.

25. Richard Leppert, "The Social Discipline of Listening," in *Aural Cultures*, ed. Jim Drobnick (Toronto: YYZ Books, 2004), 27.

26. Cf. Denora, *Music in Everyday Life*.

27. Tong Soon Lee, "Technology and the Production of Islamic Space: The Call to Prayer in Singapore," *Ethnomusicology* 43, no. 1 (1999): 86–100. Cf. Alain Corbin, *Village Bells: Sound and Meaning in the 19th-Century French Countryside*, trans. Martin Thom (New York: Columbia University Press, 1998).

28. See, for example, Veit Erlmann, ed., *Hearing Cultures: Essays on Sound, Listening, and Modernity* (New York: Berg, 2004); Sterne, *The Audible Past*; Thompson, *The Soundscape of Modernity*. Steven Feld's work on acoustemology is also an important antecedent: Feld, "Waterfalls of Song: An Acoustemology of Place Resounding in Bosavi, Papua New Guinea," in *Senses of Place*, ed. Steven Feld and Keith Basso (Santa Fe: School of American Research Press), 91–135; and Feld, "A Rainforest Acoustemology," in *The Auditory Culture Reader*, ed. Michael Bull and Les Back (2000; New York: Berg, 2003, 223–39.

Larry Blumenfeld

Since the Flood

Scenes from the Fight

for New Orleans Jazz Culture

In this place, there is a custom for the funerals of jazz musicians. The funeral procession parades slowly through the streets, followed by a band playing a mournful dirge as it moves to the cemetery. Once the casket has been laid in place, the band breaks into a joyful second line, symbolizing the triumph of the spirit over death. Tonight the Gulf Coast is still coming through the dirge, yet we will live to see the second line.

—President George W. Bush, televised address from Jackson Square, French Quarter, New Orleans, September 15, 2005

By mid-October, when the first real second-line parade after the flood rolled in the streets of New Orleans, in memoriam for chef Austin Leslie, President Bush was gone. His promised recovery assistance had yet to materialize. Jazz funerals and second-line parades would be invoked again and again in the name of recovery, yet nowhere as crudely as in Bush's address.

Yes, the glorious and exotic culture of New Orleans provided potent metaphor. Those jazz musicians, Mardi Gras Indians, and fancy-dancing second-liners made for instant B-roll and catchy human-interest characters in story after story of despair and destruction, repair and resilience. And they raised questions. Would the musicians return? Would they get new instruments? Could they find their groove and inspire good times again despite the pain? Largely missed was the fact that those at the center of New Orleans jazz culture were very much the foreground story. They held the keys to the larger questions of recovery. And, out of view of most cameras, they—and what they represented—weren't exactly welcomed back.

Second line parades are derived from traditional brass band funeral processions, a defining element of New Orleans jazz culture that transforms mourners into celebrants through music as it moves from dirge to uptempo rhythm once a body is "cut loose." The "second line" originally referred to those who followed the main line, the family and friends of the deceased, funeral directors and musicians. Second line parades, as they've come to be called, are four-hour Sunday afternoon affairs, sponsored by social aid and pleasure clubs, organizations that are direct descendants of Reconstruction-era black benevolent societies. The jazz funerals and second line parades referenced in Bush's speech in fact formed the first post-Katrina expressions of community, the earliest assertions of a right to return. A year later, those parades were threatened by Draconian fees and restrictions. The musicians who honor their dead in the processions Bush described occasionally faced arrest, cited with "disturbing the peace." And at Mardi Gras Indian gatherings (a closely related and no less significant tradition), the spectacle of black men standing fierce in eight-foot-tall suits of feathers and beads, doing battle by competing to be "prettiest," had more than once been overtaken by the sirens and flashing lights of NOPD cruisers. Tensions have long existed between the city's black culture bearers and its power brokers, but what's happened since the flood, what's still happening, is of a different order and begs consideration in a deeper, more urgent context.

There's a culture war going on in New Orleans—one with deep historical roots but also brand-new firepower and dangerous stakes. That conflict defines the tangle of issues woven into the rebuilding process (which has ended up meaning the creation of a "new" New Orleans more so than a recovery of the old one) and the matters of race and class underscoring them all. The story of how this culture war has played out provides a piercing look at New Orleans since the flood, as well as into how we really feel about traditions that have helped shape American music for more than a century. And it makes clear that New Orleans—a city built on culture, a city that to so many stands for culture—must be rebuilt through culture if it is to stand for anything at all—or just stand.

I know all that now, but I didn't when I began writing about New Orleans after the flood. In October 2005, I'd penned an angst-ridden essay for Salon about the cultural implications of the Katrina tragedy. Soon after, I spent a week researching a *Village Voice* article timed to precede the annual New Orleans Jazz and Heritage Festival, which, merely by virtue of its mounting that year, was a mighty symbol and not minor triumph of communal will and fundraising. I'd set out to document the reality confronted by the prime movers within the city's musical subcultures: the network of jazz musicians, the stable of brass band players and their closely aligned social aid and pleasure clubs and second-line dancers, the tribes of Mardi Gras Indians. I wanted to detail the situation from their eyes, outline their challenges, and evaluate the potential for communal loss or recovery.

As I researched, the dimensions of crisis in what has long been considered the birthplace of jazz grew larger and clearer: As historian Ned Sublette put it when I called in September 2005: "We're not just watching history disappear, history is watching us disappear." I sensed what he meant. As pianist and patriarch Ellis Marsalis explained in his living room in early 2006: "In other cities, culture comes from the top down. In New Orleans, it's the reverse: it springs from the street up. No neighborhoods, no culture." He was right. The culture of New Orleans depends on the integrity of its black neighborhoods, however troubled, lest it be turned into a tourist show or museum piece. And lest it lose its function, leaving a whole lot of people disenfranchised.

One nagging fact ignited my passion: after writing about American culture for twenty years, I was surprised to find many in my so-called jazz community oddly complacent about the cultural consequences of the flood, strangely unaffected by what has and has not happened in New Orleans in its aftermath. New Orleans was history to them, owed a debt of gratitude and proper credit (see episodes 1–4 of Ken Burns's PBS series, *Jazz*) but otherwise largely irrelevant to the present modern-jazz moment. I knew that wasn't true. New Orleans produced the first real jazz star, Louis Armstrong, and it is, I've come to believe, the only place left in this country with a real living jazz culture—one in which swinging music is elemental to the everyday lives of large swaths of ordinary people. Placed in stark relief since 2005 is whether that culture—which Burns's series famously cast as a signal of American values and virtues on the order of the Constitution—still carried currency when it comes to the issues Katrina raised: identity, race, poverty, and basic decency.

Possible Body

By March 2006, six months after the floods that followed the levee failures, New Orleans was two cities, so starkly in contrast it tested the mind's limits. One New Orleans inched toward renewal, the other was caught in what David Winkler-Schmidt of the local *Gambit Weekly* called "the horrible unending of not knowing."

Stick to the "Sliver by the River," the high-ground neighborhoods along the Mississippi's banks, and you might have thought the place was healing. Take a taxi from Louis Armstrong Airport to the French Quarter and you might easily miss the fading water line, fourteen feet high in some places, on the sides of buildings as you sailed down I-10. Sluggishly approaching its former self, the Quarter again boasted coffee and beignets, music in the air and mystery around each corner.

But the Gray Line Hurricane Katrina bus tour revealed miles of destruction, still stunning six months past the storm. And the Gray Line didn't even run through the devastation of the Lower Ninth Ward: houses impaled by cars or reduced to rubble that stretched as far as the eye could see. Signs tacked to lampposts voiced suspicions: "Saw Levee Break? Witnesses Wanted." Spray-painted notes from house-by-house search teams bore gruesome details, like the one marked simply, "Possible Body." Graffiti had been scrawled on the side of Fats Domino's house—"R.I.P. Fats. You Will Be Missed." Domino wasn't gone, thanks to a dramatic rescue. In fact, he had just released a new album, *Alive and Kickin'*, benefiting the Tipitina's Foundation, one of several aid organizations then feverishly working to help revive a culture in crisis. All of these groups were well meaning but none yet up to the task of finding, let alone funding, the thousands of missing folks who shaped the city's culture.

Somewhat miraculously though also sort of predictably, the music had trickled back. Plenty of it. Already the music section of *Gambit Weekly* listed local clubs hosting favorite bands. Kermit Ruffins was back on Thursday nights at Vaughan's, the wonderful Bywater hole-in-the-wall joint where the crowd always spilled out onto Lesseps Street.

Donna's Bar and Grill, a charmingly run-down corner bar across the street from Armstrong Park, on North Rampart Street, the dividing line between the French Quarter and Tremé, was open, its hand-painted wooden sign still missing one chunk of its upper righthand corner, as if someone had taken a bite. At Donna's, the guys who'd stopped by and sat in with drummer Shannon Powell on one Sunday night explained what it had taken to get there: they were driving in from Atlanta or Baton Rouge or Houston—wherever they'd dropped anchor after the evacuation—to make the gig. They needed the money, and they needed to play for a hometown crowd.

Uptown on Oak Street at the Maple Leaf Bar, the cavernous room next door to the bar was mostly full whenever the Rebirth Brass Band played its Tuesday gig, even though the Tulane kids had yet to return to the nearby university campus. Phil Frazier, Rebirth's leader, sat in the back near the pool table in between sets, one hand on his tuba and the other on his cellphone. His thick shoulders, on which rested his weighty instrument much of the time, drooped. He described how hard it had been to re-assemble the group while living in Houston, his band mates fanned out over four states. "I used up a whole lotta minutes," he said, looking hard at his Nokia. He and the guys were grateful for those gigs; they had houses to rebuild and kids to feed.

If the Maple Leaf gig was still irregular, it was only because the group was on the road so much: It seemed every city wanted to book a brass band from New Orleans named Rebirth just then. The band had adopted the name in the 1980s, to signal the revival of a brass-band tradition that had waned through the 1970s. And sure enough, in the years that followed, in the Ninth Ward, the Seventh Ward, and especially in Tremé, kids began to pick up brass instruments, snare and bass drums again and parade up and down the streets. They were inspired by Rebirth's fiery sound, and how Frazier's tuba playing anchored each tune with the hip authority of, say, bassist James Jamerson on Motown hits. Where would those kids live now? How would they learn tradition, without soaking it up every day, just down the block, the way Frazier had from guys with names like Tuba Fats and Frog Joseph. Most of Tremé's homes survived Katrina. But the costs of moving back were prohibitive, and the state-run Road Home assistance wasn't yet available (and would prove to be a troubled tangle of red tape once it was). Besides, the regular jobs and the schools were still gone.

"Rebirth," Frazier sighed. "What's that mean now?"

Won't Bow Down

"Have you ever seen people build a home?" Donald Harrison asked a roomful of teenagers one Monday night in March 2006 at The Music Shed studio in the Garden District. "Well, you start with the foundation. And then you've got the support beams. If all that's not intact, it won't matter what you do—the whole thing will come crashing down."

Harrison knows a great deal about constructing a solo and, just then, whether he liked it or not, more than a thing or two about building a house. As was true of most of the nearby houses, the first floor of his home in the Broadmoor section was stripped to its beams. On a corner across the street from Harrison's home, the elegant front façade was all that remained of another home, leaning precariously against three support beams.

At forty-six, Harrison had a unique perspective on the precariousness of the moment, in cultural terms, because his life and career have embraced so much of what defines New Orleans culture. In his early teens, he began playing saxophone with Ernest "Doc" Paulin's brass band, a seminal group for generations of players. He studied at New Orleans Center for Cultural Arts (NOCCA), the finishing school for a long list of jazz stars. He played in Art Blakey's Jazz Messengers, then co-led a band with another hometown hero, the trumpeter Terence Blanchard. An established jazz star who spent much of the 1980s and 1990s in New York City, Harrison is nonetheless best known to some in his hometown as a Mardi Gras Indian chief and the son of Donald Harrison Sr., who was himself a Big Chief of four different Mardi Gras Indian tribes.

"The Mardi Gras Indian rhythms and chants were really the very first music that entered my consciousness," Harrison said as he sat on his front stoop, squinting in the midday sun. "My mom remembers me tapping out the beats on the side of my crib. But I didn't get the connection between the jazz I was playing and that culture until I started coming out with the Indians again, and my dad was singing 'Shallow Water.' When I heard that again, the chanting—'shallow water / oh mama / shallow water / oh mama'—and the rhythm behind that chant, in the back of my head, I started hearing Blakey's drums. I thought, 'Wow, this is all starting to make sense.' I stopped thinking of music in boxes."

Shortly before Donald Sr. died, Harrison recorded "Indian Blues," blending New York–based jazz with the chants and drums of New Orleans–

based Mardi Gras Indians, including his father. After his father's death in 1998, Harrison assumed the role of Big Chief and named his tribe Congo Nation, after Congo Square. Harrison's childhood in the Ninth Ward was something out of a Norman Rockwell painting—specifically, *The Problem We All Live With*, Rockwell's 1964 rendering of a six-year-old black girl's being led into the all-white William Frantz Elementary School, the first such integration in Louisiana. Harrison, who was born in 1960, attended Frantz.

"That was my first introduction to the need not just for resistance but for a change in values," he said. "In America, people of African descent are taught that where we came from is nothing. We have a day to celebrate Irish American pride, St. Patrick's Day, and a great parade in New York to celebrate Italian American heritage. We have to come to grips that people of African descent are important too. So the pageantry of the Mardi Gras Indians means something."

The legacy of black New Orleans residents dressing up like Native Americans and parading on Mardi Gras Day dates back more than a century. Through costumes and rituals, it perpetuates not just an African consciousness, but also a bond with another oppressed and marginalized people, Native Americans. (There's far more to that connection, including the inspiring presence of William "Buffalo Bill" Cody's *Wild West* production and the fact that Native Americans took in runaway slaves to the history of intermarriage.) In Native Americans, these present-day "Indians" have an example of an indigenous culture that has been all but erased. Mardi Gras Indian culture is extravagant, bold, and completely subterranean: word of when and where a Big Chief "comes out" on Mardi Gras Day is shared strictly on a need-to-know basis. (That's less true these days than in decades past—some Indian practices are now publicized in the New Orleans *Times-Picayune*—but it's still not primarily a commercial endeavor.) It is the city's clearest and strongest culture of resistance. A Mardi Gras Indian would never apply for a city permit to assemble.

New Orleans was a major port of entry for Sicilian immigrants during the late nineteenth century and is still home to large Italian American enclaves. The Feast of St. Joseph is a citywide event: It's also one of three times each year that Mardi Gras Indian tribes gather en masse in New Orleans. By 7 P.M. on a warm Sunday, St. Joseph's night, the pageantry Harrison had described was on display, along with its surrounding reality.

The intersection of Washington Avenue and La Salle Street was packed with Indians, decked out in feathers and beads. Across the street, A. L. Davis Park, named for a reverend and civil rights activist, was filled with FEMA trailers housing displaced families. Looking fierce in his African-inspired green-and-red mask, Victor Harris, Big Chief of the Fi-Yi-Yi tribe, shouted, "They spit us all over this land. They told us we had to evacuate. But they didn't say we had to stay away."

Spy boys led the way. Flag boys bore identifying colors. Chiefs haltingly greeted fellow chiefs. Suddenly, the sound of the drums and the colorful wash of feathers were overpowered by sirens and flashing lights. Police cars drove straight through the procession, enacting their own now annual ritual. Some officers wore uniforms emblazoned with SWAT team logos. Representatives of the American Civil Liberties Union and the National Lawyers Guild signified too, with armbands marked "Legal Observer." Harris turned to his wild man: "We know what they're trying to say. 'You're not welcome back.'" When the cruisers had passed and the sirens died down, a few, then dozens of Indians, began singing "Indian Red," raising their voices at the lines: "We won't bow down / not on the dirty ground."

The next day, in front of the trailer in which his mother was living, next to the ruins of her home, Harrison framed the scenario. "What's happening in New Orleans right now is a test for the soul of America. If we say the cultural roots of this city are unimportant, then America is unimportant. I'm going to continue to be a Mardi Gras Indian. I'm going to play my saxophone. If enough people do their part, everything will endure. But that's the question: Will people be allowed to do their part?"

Silence Is Violence

The first week of January 2007 brought with it an alarming fact, for those who took note: more Americans had died thus far in the new year in New Orleans than in Iraq. Fourteen between December 29, 2006, and January 8, 2007. New Orleans had long vied with other cities—Newark, Washington—as this country's most dangerous. CNN used a graphic—"Murder City, USA"—when reporting on post-Katrina New Orleans; not a new sentiment exactly, but a seemingly cynical jab at a place suffering a fresh wave of violent crime in the wake of disaster.

Two murders in particular sounded a citywide alarm, and sent specific shock waves through the cultural community: On January 3, the filmmaker Helen Hill was shot and killed in her own home in the Marigny neighborhood, as her husband and two-year-old child watched helplessly. A week prior, during a nine-hour stretch in which eighteen people were fatally wounded in the city, Dinerral Shavers, the snare drummer of the Hot 8 Brass Band and a teacher at Rabouin High, was shot in his car on Dumaine Street, his wife at his side. The gunman was suspected of having been shooting at Shavers's stepson, who was in the back seat. Shavers died in surgery hours later.

The Hot 8, already local favorites, had risen rapidly and recently to more widespread attention. They'd appeared in Spike Lee's HBO documentary *When the Levees Broke*. Just after Katrina, they'd been caught by the CNN anchorwoman Rusty Dornin, in uplifting performance at a Baton Rouge evacuee shelter.

Bennie Pete, a mountain of a man and the group's leader, has a soft, high voice that belies both his size and the rippling intensity of his tuba playing. "I wasn't thinking about music or the band or nothing like that when we first met up again in Baton Rouge," he told me in front of the Sound Café, a New Orleans coffee shop that has become a center for both music and activism. "I thought about survival, about my mom and dad. But it was beautiful. We just showed up, started blowing. And people began to smile and cry and dance. That's my band! It was a healing thing."

"I remember that the news crews didn't understand why we'd bring a band in here," said Lee Arnold, a band admirer who, since the storm, had grown into the Hot 8's aggressively creative manager. "Some of the Red Cross people were like, 'These people are so sad, they don't need this now.' They thought it was silly or even wrong."

"But when we kicked it," Pete said, "they all got it—the relief workers, the MPS, everyone. The TV stations showed up. They wanted to know who we were."

For a dozen years now, ever since two young bands, the Looney Tunes and the High Steppers, merged, the Hot 8 has been called with increasing frequency in its hometown for second lines, house parties, and club gigs. They've inherited a powerful tradition, and some say it's their turn to rule the streets. A subtly significant rivalry between New Orleans brass bands plays out mostly through second lines: whoever moves the dancers best claims victory. Rebirth's Phil Frazier recalls one parade in particular. "The Hot 8 was playing so hot, coming up from behind us, that we actually marched to the side, let them through," he says. "Bennie was trying to duck down, but I said, 'You can't hide, we know you're coming on. They're dancing for you today.'"

For the Hot 8, Shavers's murder was a devastating loss. It was also the continuation of band history marked by tragedy. In 1996, the trumpeter Jacob Johnson was found shot execution-style in his home. In 2004, the trombonist Joe Williams was shot dead by police in curious and never resolved circumstances. In the spring of 2006, trumpeter Terrell Batiste lost his legs in a horrific roadside accident after relocating to Atlanta.

A sense of purposeful outrage began to take shape around the murders of Shavers, a young black man, and Hill, a young white woman. Baty Landis, a Tulane University musicologist who ran a bookstore and adjoining coffee shop, Sound Café, joined together with Helen Gillet, a cellist, and Ken Foster, a poet, and planned a public gathering. They aimed to plan a march on City Hall to demand that the city address the unanswered problem of violent crime in the city. If it was an unlikely trio of leaders, the meeting place, Landis's café, was a natural choice. The Hot 8 had regularly performed there on Wednesday nights, and Hill had frequently stopped by with her toddler son, Francis. Participants took turns voicing their ideas by passing around a "talking stick," a feather-laden Bayou Steppers Social Aid and Pleasure Club fan, of which Landis was a member.

Standing atop a piano bench, Landis announced that marchers, including the remaining members of the Hot 8 Brass Band, would gather Thursday at 11 A.M., in front of the Audubon Aquarium of the Americas, near the foot of Canal Street. They expected to reach City Hall around noon. No one was sure how many people would show up.

By 10:30 the following Thursday morning, some four thousand assembled and began their slow march, led by the members of the Hot 8 and other musicians who'd been close to Shavers. Some of the students from Rabouin, where Shavers had organized a marching band and had raised funds for instruments, were there. By the time the march reached City Hall, there were at least eight thousand people on hand. A temporary podium had been set up. Several speakers—community organizers, city council members, residents—took turns outlining their demands of Police Chief [Warren] Riley and Mayor [C. Ray] Nagin: more cops, better protection for witnesses, and more accountability by police and the district attorney. Finally, trombonist Glen David Andrews addressed the crowd:

"We are young black men of New Orleans preaching culture."

A spontaneous chant sprang up: "Music in the schools. Music in the schools."

Where else would that happen?

Right to Roll

The 2007 New Orleans Jazz & Heritage Festival kicked up on April 24— good news from a city wracked by too much bad. "Now, in a way, it's even harder," the festival producer Quint Davis told me when I dropped by his office. He'd upped the ante for the 2007 event, packing its six days denser than in past, with acts ranging from big-ticket draws to local heroes—Rod Stewart and Van Morrison to Gregg Stafford's Young Tuxedo Brass Band.

"The euphoria of destruction has passed," he said. "We're in the reality of the long-term recovery. None of this is going to get someone a check from the 'Road Home' program. None will rebuild their house or get their insurance straight. But it will do something important beyond all that." The Road Home Program, run by a private company contracted by the state to distribute federal aid to homeowners, was by all accounts a disaster, a Kafkaesque bureaucracy. Locals had taken to calling it "Road to Nowhere."

Inside the Fair Grounds, at the Jazz and Heritage Festival—second only to Mardi Gras as a tourist draw for the city—cultural traditions like the second-line parade were proudly on display. There were three listed in the festival program each day. Outside the Fair Grounds was a different story.

Just three days before members of the Nine Times Social Aid and Pleasure Club would dance their way through Fair Grounds—second-lining with the Mahogany Brass Band—they appeared in federal court. On April 25, the U.S. District judge Kurt Engelhardt heard arguments on behalf of a consortium of social aid and pleasure clubs, aided by the ACLU, in a lawsuit protesting the city's hiking of police security fees—in some cases, triple or more from pre-Katrina rates—for the regular Sunday second lines, held September through May. The suit invoked the First Amendment right to freedom of speech and expression, claiming that parade permit schemes "effectively tax" such expression.

Despite a newfound regard for the sort of catharsis offered by second lines, the tradition was now newly and pointedly caught in the crosshairs of controversy in New Orleans. A shooting in the vicinity of a historic January unified parade—several clubs, parading as one—in 2006 was the original impetus for the permit fee; more protection was needed, the police department claimed, and somebody was going to have to pay for those officers. As a result, the city raised permit fees for second-line parades.

Tamara Jackson, who had organized the Social Aid and Pleasure Club Task Force in Katrina's wake, would have none of this. "This amounts to a tax for crimes the social aid and pleasure clubs don't commit and can't control," she said. "Don't we already pay taxes that pay for police?" She approached the ACLU staff attorney Katy Schwartzmann, who filed suit on behalf of seventeen sponsoring clubs.

"Should the law not be enjoined," read the ACLU complaint filed in *Social Aid & Pleasure Club Task Force v. City of New Orleans*, "there is very little doubt that plaintiff's cultural tradition will cease to exist."

"It's a solid, core ACLU issue," Schwartzmann explained when I visited her office. "We handle freedom of speech cases all the time," she explained. "But this one is different in that the speech at issue signifies this city and an entire cultural tradition. At some point, I mean, the power to tax is the power to eliminate, right? At some point, if the government can put enough fees and enough obstacles in the way of somebody exercising their First Amendment right, then they're ultimately going to eliminate it."

Item 51 of the complaint put it this way: "Many members of the Clubs, including Plaintiffs, are working class families. They are persons struggling to return to the City of New Orleans, dealing with the loss of family unity, the loss of homes, and the loss of normalcy. The City of New Orleans, rather than encouraging their return, has instead created barriers to the resumption of an important means of expression for those returning New Orleanians. The Second Line tradition is a peaceful, nonviolent tradition. What the criminals could not destroy the City is; rather than protecting, it is punishing the victims."

Delay after delay from the city's attorney left the case unresolved for roughly a year. But the matter needed settling. And when the annual Original Pigeontown Steppers Easter Sunday parade was slapped with a permit fee of $7,560 (a price inflated yet further due to holiday pay for officers), it was time to force the issue.

On a bright Thursday morning, three-dozen club members gathered at the federal courthouse near Lafayette Square for an evidentiary hearing. But 10 A.M., the scheduled time, came and passed as Schwartzmann and another attorney, Carol Kolinchak, huddled at the end of a third-floor hallway with city deputy attorney Joe DiRosa. The city had backed down late the previous night, after a round of calls between lawyers and police: the fee would be cut by two-thirds.

Jackson walked outside the courthouse to the grassy square, and stood in front of a statue of Henry Clay, the statesman known as the "Great Compromiser." The standoff between the clubs had attracted local media attention, so there were camera crews and a small crowd awaiting her. "The Original Pigeontown Steppers will be parading this Easter," she said with a raised fist and a broad smile. "We're here to proclaim that we are reclaiming the city streets. We're going forth."

It was a qualified victory; the clubs would thereafter pay around two thousand dollars for permit fees. But it was a victory nonetheless. Three days later, after a brief rain subsided and clouds parted for a spot of sun, the Original Pigeontown Steppers made their way out of Stanley U's Lounge in suits, fedoras, and sashes of powder blue offset by pale yellow. Joe Henry, the club's president, rolled his wheelchair, bedecked with feathers that matched his suit, onto the street. "They're trying to keep us down, no doubt. But people count on this. They need it now more than ever. So here we are."

Happy Birthday, Katrina

There were fewer media folk in New Orleans gearing up for the second anniversary of Hurricane Katrina than for the first commemoration. Maybe that was a good thing—the first time around most locals seemed genuinely annoyed by the drop-in presence of so many cameras and commentators, many of whom knew little of the city and craved simply a good setup shot and a ticket out of town. I remember one Ninth Ward family who stood by and watched as an anchorwoman held her microphone in front of their devastated home: "The producer said he doesn't want us in the picture," the father told me, his baby in his arms.

Those living in New Orleans in 2007—by even optimistic estimates, around 60 percent of the pre-Katrina population level, or nearly 300,000—hardly needed to mark calendars. Every day was an anniversary, a stark reminder of nature's wrath and more so of the distinctly unnatural disasters of levee failures, insurance shortfalls, and a tide of bureaucratic red tape that rivaled even the water's ability to stall lives. Two years after the storm, only about one-third of those residents approved for their "Road Home" awards from the Louisiana Recovery Authority had received payments. The number of press on hand for the second anniversary may have been down compared to the previous year, but the politicians were out in force. And there was much discussion, a good deal of it in conferences with impressive, even hopeful, titles, such as Lieutenant Governor Mitch Landrieu's "World Cultural Economy Forum." For all the talk and all the music of the past few days in New Orleans, the most emphatic statement about post-Katrina life, and particularly about cultural economy, was silence.

A Sunday Musicians Solidarity Second Line found members of the Treme Brass Band and some two-dozen other musicians, instruments in hand, assembled for a parade. At a typical second line, a brass band or two plays, and supporters follow along, dancing and clapping out rhythms. But this time not a note was played, not a step danced. The message was clear: New Orleans's musicians need better support, lest the music that lends this city its identity one day fall silent.

That Sunday a slow, steady rain lent dramatic drips to homemade signs that read: "Living Wages = Living Music," "Imagine a Silent NOLA," "Keep Our Story Alive." But the procession never exploded into music. When it reached the French Quarter's Jackson Square, Musicians Union president "Deacon" John Moore, a guitarist who played on several seminal R&B hits during his career, addressed the small crowd. "It ain't easy in the Big Easy," he said. "Our musicians are suffering. We hate to come out here like this but we have no alternative."

Benny Jones Sr., the drummer and founder of the Treme Brass Band, had been making music in New Orleans for some fifty years. "It's always been a bit of a struggle," he said, "but now it's become a losing proposition." At issue were the pressures of a hard-hit tourism industry, the increased cost of living in New Orleans, and the need among musicians for better pay and some meaningfully nurturing initiatives during tough post-Katrina times. Several nonprofit organizations—most pointedly a dynamic new one, Sweet Home New Orleans—had risen to embrace the latter task. But while the need remained daunting, the flow of contributions had begun to ebb: An economic downturn, combined with something casually referred to as "Katrina fatigue" had set in. The director of

Sweet Home, Jordan Hirsch, estimated that of the approximately 4,500 working musicians and others in the New Orleans cultural community, "about a third are back and doing OK, a third have yet to return, and a third are here but in unstable situations."

"Historically, musicians have been taken for granted here because it's so common and pervasive," said Scott Aiges, a director at the New Orleans Jazz and Heritage Foundation and a former city government official, who walked along the parade route. "It's such an intrinsic part of our culture that, when we hear a brass band it's just another day." Aiges suggested solutions to some musicians' problems, ranging from promotional strategies to zoning ordinances, and especially tax and other incentives to those who employ musicians. The next night, in between his sets at the Snug Harbor club, Ellis Marsalis told me: "Those ideas are all well-meaning. But, see, New Orleans culture developed out of a hustle and will always be a hustle." That hustle won't suffice, it seems, during the slow crawl of recovery: Maybe some public policy *was* in order. Maybe something was in danger of disappearing below some forbidding economic red line, something that would be missed in deep but also largely unacknowledged ways.

I remembered something said at Landrieu's Cultural Economy Forum, by the ambassador of Grenada, Denis G. Antoine: "New Orleans is a perception. When we talk about safety, how safe do you feel? It's not just about crime, it's about how safe do you feel to be you?"

Hymns, Dirges, and Misdemeanors

In the fall, second-line season kicked up again. Despite the uneasy compromise in the case against the city and the increased permit fees, social aid and pleasure club members were happy just to get on with their weekly parades. Brass band musicians breathed a sigh of relief. They needed the work and, maybe as much as the money, they needed to be out in the streets. It was a brief pause between battles.

On the evening of October 1, 2007, two dozen of New Orleans's top brass band players and roughly two hundred followers began a procession for Kerwin James, a tuba player with the New Birth Brass Band who had passed away on September 26. They were "bringing him down" with a funeral procession that began as a dirge and ended with up-tempo release each night until his Saturday burial. But the bittersweet tradition ended just plain bitter—with the trombonist Glen David Andrews and his brother, snare drummer Derrick Tabb, led away in handcuffs. Twenty police cars converged near the corner of North Robertson and St. Philip streets, in the heart of Tremé. In the end, it looked more like the scene of a murder than misdemeanors.

"The police told us, 'If we hear one more note, we'll arrest the whole band,'" Tabb said two nights later, outside a fundraiser to help defray the costs of James's burial at Ray's Boom Boom Room on Frenchmen Street. "Well, we did stop playing," Andrews said. "We were singing, lifting our voices to God. You gonna tell me that's wrong too?" Ellis Joseph, drummer of the Free Agents band, was also in the Monday night procession. He walked over, leaned against Andrews's shoulder. "They came in a swarm," he said, tracing a circle with his hands. "Like we had AK-47s. But we only had instruments."

The police hadn't shut down a tourist show. They had cut short a familiar hymn, "I'll Fly Away," during a procession for one of Tremé's own. Funeral processions are an essential element of New Orleans culture, and the impromptu variety—honoring the passing of someone of distinction, especially a musician—are a time-honored tradition. For this tight-knit neighborhood community, the police had stomped on something sacred, on home turf. Tremé had a long history of embattlement. Here was one more chapter.

The New Orleans Police Department spokesman Joe Narcisse claimed the department was simply acting on a neighborhood resident's phoned-in complaint to a 911 line. He maintained that such processions require permits. Technically, they do, according to a statute on the books since 1925. But no one in Tremé, not even the regular beat cops, could recall enforcement of this regulation. Beyond all that, it was the scale and intensity, the callousness, of the police response that angered the musicians and followers. Katy Reckdahl, a reporter for the New Orleans *Times-Picayune* who lives on North Rampart Street, Tremé's southern border, had rushed to catch up with the Monday-evening procession after her two-year-old son Hector heard tubas in the distance. What she found was a flood of patrol cars, sirens blaring. Her front-page, full-banner-headline report two days later described police running into the crowd, grabbing at horn players' mouthpieces, and trying to seize drumsticks out of hands. "The confrontations spurred cries in the neighborhood about over-reaction and disproportionate enforcement by the police, who had often turned a blind eye to the traditional memorial ceremonies," she wrote. "Still others say the incident is a sign of a greater attack on the cultural history of the old city neighborhood by well-heeled newcomers attracted to Tremé by the very history they seem to threaten."

It's unclear who called the police that night. Some locals pointed to the green house on North Robertson Street with shutters that seem always closed. In any case, it was easy to sense the difference, longtime residents say, between North Robertson before and after the storm. With its proximity to the French Quarter and historic architecture, Tremé, most of which did not flood, had become newly attractive to homebuyers given the city's shrunken post–Hurricane Katrina housing stock. Home prices in Tremé had risen more than 30 percent since 2006. Meanwhile, as in most of New Orleans, rents had even more sharply increased. Laureen Lentz, who owned several properties in the neighborhood, had pumped up Tremé's development potential on her New Orleans Renovation blog with a breathless June posting: "Since Katrina, the Historic Faubourg Tremé Association has gathered a lot of steam. Our neighborhood is changing as people have begun to realize that this area is prime, non-flooded real estate. . . . So much is happening in Tremé, it's hard to convince people that aren't here. You have to see it to believe it."

To many in city administration, such transformation was one answer to the crime and drug problems that had plagued the neighborhood since the 1980s. To longtime Tremé residents, the rapid change was the latest in a series of clear threats to tradition. The intensity of the police response during the Kerwin James procession prompted a second line of print voices, so to speak, in the *Times-Picayune*'s pages.

"If somebody is blowing a horn in Tremé and somebody else is calling the police," wrote columnist Jarvis DeBerry, "only one of those people is disturbing the peace, and it isn't the one playing the music." Nick Spitzer, creator of the public-radio program *American Routes*, wrote in an op-ed piece, "In a city where serious crime often goes unprosecuted and unpunished, jazz funerals make the streets momentarily sacred and safer." The columnist Lolis Eric Elie wrote, "New Orleans Police Department declared a resumption of its war against our city's culture."

The day following the skirmish, discussions between community leaders and First District police captain Louis Colin yielded a temporary agreement. That evening, Andrews, Tabb, and other musicians were back on those same streets, leading another procession, this time protected by a permit, which some residents viewed as a disappointing compromise. "We don't need anyone's approval to live our lives," muttered Al Harris, who lived his whole life in Tremé, as he followed the musicians down North Robertson. He still couldn't believe that someone had dialed 911. He stopped and turned. "What are these people thinking? It's like if you move into beachfront property and then decide that you don't like sand or water."

The procession wove through the neighborhood, culminating on that grassy lot. Andrews put down his trombone and sang "I'll Fly Away." Tabb snapped out soft rolls on his snare. A tight circle surrounded the musicians. A middle-aged black woman in a blue housecoat turned to the man next to her. "They say they want to stop this?" she asked softly. "They will never stop this."

Ritual Matters

The Sunday before Mardi Gras in New Orleans in 2008, Donald Harrison Jr. lay on the living-room floor of his mother's house in the Ninth Ward, cutting leopard-print fur in a pattern as he spoke. Nearby, a sofa and chair were covered with beads and rhinestones, along with ostrich and turkey feathers that had been dyed a golden yellow.

In other parts of the country that year, February 5 marked Super Tuesday. All attention was focused on would-be elected leaders with practiced battle cries, competing to prove themselves fierce and attractive. But in New Orleans it was Fat Tuesday. Uptown, in the limelight, the various well-publicized krewe parades (a throng that included Hulk Hogan, that year's King of Bacchus) lorded over the city, riding high on floats and tossing down beads. But on less-traveled streets, more in the shadows and announced mostly on a need-to-know basis, Mardi Gras Indian chiefs, possessors of strictly inherited thrones, asserted their authority. Dressed in eight-foot-tall, six-foot-wide feathered and beaded suits and accompanied by "wild men," "spy boys," and others, they were introduced with drumbeats and chants, lending voice and hope to New Orleans residents who'd been all but ignored during the presidential primary season. Like the candidates, the big chiefs competed with words. And in a ritual that once frequently did turn violent, they battled to win hearts and minds, using their elaborate suits to "kill 'em with pretty." The presidential candidates were selling change, but in New Orleans, a city all but ignored by that lot (except for John Edwards, who stood in front of the Ninth Ward's Musician's Village as he dropped out of the race), the message from these local leaders was continuity. Midday, Victor Harris of Fi-Yi-Yi showed up in front of the home of Joyce Montana, the widow of Tootie Montana, the late "chief of chiefs." Around 3 P.M., Darryl Montana, Tootie and Joyce's son, came out of Joyce's front door, looking regal in his tall, broad, lavender feathered suit, which rippled gently in the growing breeze as he headed up to Claiborne Avenue, beneath the overpass for I-10, where Indians generally convene on Mardi Gras—"Under the Bridge," they call it. That phrase held a different meaning just then, as it did splashed across the cover of the *Gambit*, headlining a piece about the growing encampment of some two hundred homeless underneath the freeway, just a small portion of an estimated twelve thousand cast-out residents. And not far from view on Claiborne was the darkened façade of the Lafitte Housing Projects, its doors and windows covered with steel plates.

It seemed a cruel indignity, some mash-up of Dickens and Orwell, when, five days before Christmas, 2007, the New Orleans City Council unanimously approved a HUD-ordered plan to tear down some 4,500 units of public housing. I was in New York, watching CNN as residents assembled outside by barricades and police lines. "If you know New Orleans, you'll know how dilapidated these housing developments are," said anchorwoman Kyra Phillips. "They've been crime-ridden, very popular for drug-running. . . . According to the mayor, this is an effort to clean up the city, have better housing for folks."

Meanwhile, like some bizarre B-roll footage, we saw a live shot of New Orleans residents being turned away with pepper spray; one woman fell to the ground after being Tasered. But we heard only Phillips. The residents were voiceless, as they'd been in the debate about demolition and rebuilding of public housing in a city hard-pressed for affordable homes. On Mardi Gras morning, Gerard Lewis, Big Chief of the Black Eagles, led his tribe in a prayer outside the B. W. Cooper projects—once their coming-out spot, then slated for destruction. Later in the week, after Super Tuesday's primary results proved inconclusive, New Orleans made its way into the election year discourse. "Suddenly, candidates are paying attention," read the subhead to Thursday's front-page coverage in the *Times-Picayune*. Barack Obama spoke at Tulane University that day. He made eloquent mention of slaves at Congo Square and their "dances of impossible joy," but he didn't say a word about public housing.

The Sunday before Mardi Gras, Donald Harrison had told me he was going to wear his suit, but that he would stay close to home, holding court as it were. He wasn't going to take to the streets, to "come out." I told him I didn't believe him. "Wasn't ritual important?" I asked.

We waited and waited, a group of us, in front of the Holy Faith Temple Baptist Church on Governor Nicholls Street. Finally, near dusk, Harrison arrived, driving a yellow Penske truck filled with the parts of his suit. As the sky darkened, he made his entrance from church to street, arms folded, concealing the detailed beadwork in the image of his father, feathers rippling as he walked, chants and beats following him. He looked spectacular, and moved tall and proud.

"So you came out after all," I said.

"Yeah," he shot back. "Ritual matters."

Muddy Homecoming

Above all else it was a homecoming: The Neville Brothers performed at the annual New Orleans Jazz and Heritage Festival in 2008 for the first time since Hurricane Katrina. And there was more good news: the festival returned to its full seven-day schedule for the first time since 2005. Still more: though the heavy rains of the first weekend made a muddy mess of the Fair Grounds infield, they didn't dampen spirits or attendance much. According to event officials, nearly 400,000 people attended.

Given the emotional heft of their return, the Nevilles were the big story. Their presence built throughout the fest's final weekend: first Art, in his debut solo set, inviting Aaron up to the stage; then, Aaron, bringing many in a packed gospel tent to tears, his saxophonist brother Charles at his side; finally, all four—Art, Aaron, Cyril, and Charles—together on the Acura stage to close the festival's final day. Before that performance, the producer Quint Davis spoke of "families being torn apart, brothers separated from brothers all over New Orleans." "The Neville family's coming back together," Art said from the stage. The crowd roared. The four reprised the three decades of hits that made them such beloved stars in the first place.

It was an important symbol, no doubt. Though Charles had lived in Massachusetts for more than a decade, Aaron, Art, and Cyril all lived in New Orleans before Katrina. These brothers had been separated from each other—and from the city that identified so powerfully with them. I was struck by Aaron's son, Ivan Neville, on *Sing Me Back Home*, a CD by displaced all-star musicians recorded in Austin, Texas, six weeks after the storm; covering John Fogerty's Creedence Clearwater Revival hit, Ivan snarled, "I ain't no fortunate son!"—and meant it. (If a Neville wasn't entitled by birth, who in New Orleans was?)

As for the city's overall population, July 2005 census reports had estimated a pre-Katrina population of some 450,000—a little more than the total of Jazz Fest attendees. Estimates from the Greater New Orleans Community Data Center, based on an analysis of homes receiving postal service, yielded a 2008 population of 325,000. Yet it was impossible to determine how many within this total were new residents, and there were no reliable figures for former residents of New Orleans who still wished to return home. One thing that was clear: the changing population of the city had political implications. An April 24 *Times-Picayune* piece by Michelle Krupa cited a study by Ed Chervenak, a political scientist from the University of New Orleans, based on voter turnout in the 2003 and 2007 gubernatorial elections. The results, Krupa wrote, "confirm what election-watchers have suspected since Hurricane Katrina: the number of voters in the New Orleans area has fallen sharply, with African-Americans and registered Democrats losing the most ground." According to Christine Day, chairwoman of the Political Science department of the University of New Orleans, "It has really important implications for the redrawing of districts—congressional districts and all the way down."

These facts and figures were likely lost on those who charged from stage to stage, softshell crab po' boy in hand, at the Fair Grounds, the horse-racing track that transforms into a music stadium once each year. Yet in many ways, politics were in the air during The New Orleans Jazz and Heritage Festival Presented by Shell (as it was officially titled)— literally, at one point. While the Neville Brothers played the Acura stage, a plane circled above the Fair Grounds towing a banner: "Shell, Hear the Music. Fix the Coast You Broke."

Stevie Wonder flat-out endorsed Barack Obama's campaign at the start of his show. He decried the racism that could threaten the senator's run for the White House, then segued into "Love's in Need of Love Today," biting down hard on the line, "Hate's goin' 'round." And how's this for a slogan Obama's campaign manager didn't think of? When Mardi Gras Indians Bo Dollis and the Wild Magnolias reached the climax of their Jazz and Heritage stage set, an election-year twist on an Indian chant, best known via a 1965 recording by The Dixie Cups, could be heard a football field away: "Iko, Iko, Obama!"

Perhaps no song speaks to the Katrina experience as well as Randy Newman's "Louisiana, 1927." Written more than thirty years ago, the tune has become a contemporary anthem, its chorus—"Louisiana, they're trying to wash us away"—bearing new relevance. Yet it was Newman's "A Few Words in Defense of Our Country" that elicited the most knowing chill, especially through its closing verse:

> The end of an empire is messy at best
> And this empire is ending
> Like all the rest
> Like the Spanish Armada adrift on the sea
> We're adrift in the land of the brave
> And the home of the free.
> Goodbye. Goodbye. Goodbye.

If trumpeter Terence Blanchard's statements at the festival's jazz tent were political, they were wordlessly so, as he performed selections from his Grammy-winning CD, *A Tale of God's Will*, with his band and members of the Louisiana Philharmonic Orchestra. The music, drawn from Blanchard's score to Spike Lee's *When the Levees Broke*, called up indelible images of Katrina's aftermath and their associated emotions. Unlike several New Orleans musicians who left the city for fame and for good— Armstrong included—Blanchard moved back to his hometown in 1995, having established his reputation in New York. By now he's a defining voice of modern mainstream jazz and one of few jazz musicians to find a career composing for film. His is the musical voice of Mr. Lee's films for nearly two decades. One riveting scene of "When the Levees Broke," which Blanchard scored, showed the trumpeter escorting his mother back to her home, where he lived most of his childhood. She broke down crying in the doorway when she realized everything inside has been destroyed. Suddenly, the story being told was Mr. Blanchard's own. Yet when he sat down to translate his compositions for "Levees" into a suite for jazz band and orchestra, he heard only silence. "That's my memory of that visit to my mother's house," he told me. "No cars. No birds, no insects. Nothing. But the silence finally broke, and I started to hear voices, and the stories those voices told. I tried to give the listener an idea of all this." At the jazz tent, as on his recording, violins voiced the storm's fury, woodwinds the foreboding calm of its wake, his horn the anguished cries and later rage of those left stranded. Blanchard's requiem contains tightly composed passages but also moments during which he pushes his trumpet beyond its comfortable range. Not screeches, exactly—nothing close to Abbey Lincoln's screams on Max Roach's 1960 "We Insist! Freedom Now Suite," but angrier and more daring than any of his previous work. And, like Roach's music almost two generations ago, meant to make a point.

Among the Mardi Gras Indians at Jazz Fest, I noticed Eddie "Big Easy" Vanison, "gang flag" of the Hardhead Hunters, passing by with an elaborate suit, including one embroidered patch that could have been a news story. "Chocolate City," it read along the top. Underneath was a detailed image: a sign reading "Club Tremé," in memory of one among many long-gone neighborhood venues; a bleeding body with numbered shell casings alongside; a police cruiser and yellow police tape; Mardi Gras Indians and neighborhood kids on the sides, watching it all. In context, amid the other patches on Vanison's suit—second lines and the Superdome, among other things—it was just one element of a panorama of New Orleans life. "But it was a piece that needed to be shown," he told me later, "and that we live with."

At Glen David Andrews's performance, not long after the trombonist drifted in and out of the lyrics to Dr. John's "Right Place, Wrong Time," he dedicated the hymn "I'll Fly Away" to Kerwin James. He wasn't simply honoring a dear departed friend and beloved musician: He was referencing the evening of October 1. By then, the charges against Andrews and Tabb—"parading without a permit" and "disturbing the peace by tumultuous manner"—had been dropped, but the ante was still upped up in the fight over the city's culture. With his tribute hymn at Jazz Fest, Andrews was completing that cut-short ritual—free, onstage, employed, and empowered.

Mac Rebennack, best known as Dr. John, offered up a few songs from "City That Care Forgot," his artful 2008 rant of an album that took on a wide range of issues—from disappearing wetlands to oil-industry greed, the Iraq war to the botched response to Katrina (and connected the dots between these problems). Rebennack's deepest ire was saved for recent challenges to the culture he grew up with. He drew more than a few knowing nods with his lyrics to "My People Need a Second Line," which referenced both the October Tremé arrests in particular and the embattled parade culture in general. "You know it ain't right / to charge people for a second line," he sang. "It's something spiritual / ought to be kept out of politics / Sending 20 squad cars to stop a second line / sending musicians to jail instead of stopping crime."

Quint Davis once told me he thought of his Jazz and Heritage Festival as "this big soul-generating battery." Surely the $300 million in estimated revenue the seven-day event generated in the city didn't hurt. And apart from the national pop acts on Jazz Fest's 2008 bill—from Al Green to Tim McGraw to Billy Joel—there was a dazzling range of homegrown artistry, the breadth and depth of which was stunning. The musicians and Mardi Gras Indians and second-liners at Jazz Fest who were born and raised in New Orleans told the city's truth beyond the Fair Grounds fences, for those who cared to listen thoughtfully. And it was even possible that something necessary, perhaps instructive, some basic feeling that locals have come to understand, was conveyed during that first weekend, when the rains came sudden and hard, shutting things down for hours: we all had to slog through the mud just to get where we were going.

Yes We Can Can

The night before the 2008 Democratic Convention in Denver, Allen Toussaint played "Yes We Can Can" for a party filled with delegates. The song sounded tailor-made for the Obama campaign. But he wrote it in New Orleans, in 1970, inspired by a different era of change. No wonder. New Orleans musicians have for more than a century anticipated and articulated just what this country needs.

Toussaint was just one in a dazzling lineup of Crescent City musicians that kicked off the Democratic National Committee's week. The presence ran yet deeper when Margie Perez, a singer who lost her New Orleans home to Katrina but had since moved back, spoke from the convention stage. But Denver's resonant notes turned dissonant when some of these musicians moved on to Minneapolis for a Republican National Committee party the following week. How could Tab Benoit's "Voices of the Wetlands" possibly harmonize with John McCain's "drill here, drill now" refrain?

The larger questions posed by these convention-related performances reflected the paradox surrounding New Orleans culture even in its hometown. Did the musicians make a statement of identity tied to political purpose (the needs of communities that created and nurtured this culture)? Or were they merely a traveling "Crescent City" revue? New Orleans had figured into 2008's election season as a reminder of the Bush administration's bungled, uncaring response to Katrina. Yet amid so much talk of hope and change, on this anniversary of disaster, many in New Orleans hoped for a change of policy—the kind of federal assistance that can make a dent in crises of housing, public safety, education, health care, and levee protection. It made sense for musicians to kick-start that conversation. How closely an Obama administration would be listening and whether it could engage in a productive exchange remained an open question. But these musicians had something of substance to contribute to and to ask of his platform. Also, not that Obama needed the help, such a focus might have energized his theme, adding rhythmic emphasis: Yes we can can.

Reality TV

"Price was twelve, bruh."

"Say, bruh. Them twelve hundred was for eight pieces."

A deal was going down, yeah. Just not the sort we're used to witnessing between black men on a television show set in an American city. Certainly not a David Simon drama on HBO.

Yet before even a word of dialogue was uttered in the very first episode of *Treme*, Simon's HBO series set in post-Katrina New Orleans, came clues. A saxophonist licked, then adjusted, his reed. Slide oil was applied to a trombone. Soldiers and cops stood guard. Two little kids danced to a faint parade rhythm, which was soon supplanted by the bass booming from an SUV. An unseen trumpet sounded an upward figure, followed by a tuba's downward groove.

Back to that deal: one guy delivering those lines, an imposing-looking sort, was Gralen Banks, an actor who is also a member of the Black Men of Labor, one of some three dozen social aid and pleasure clubs operating these days in New Orleans; the other, diminutive and serious-looking, is Keith Frazier, the actual bass drummer and cofounder, with his brother Phil, of the Rebirth Brass Band. They were working out a price for eight musicians to march in and play a four-hour parade in a shattered economy. The scene recreated that first second-line parade after Katrina, the memorial for chef Austin Leslie. This was New Orleans, three months past the floods. The hulking, extinct refrigerators and carcasses of former houses looked familiar from news reports, as to some degree did the horns and drums. But now foreground and background were flipped.

The danger and dislocation in the streets of New Orleans equals if not surpasses that depicted by *The Wire*, Simon's finely detailed evocation of his hometown, Baltimore, as told through the intersecting lives of cops, drug dealers, politicians, teachers, and journalists through five HBO seasons. But there's also devastating beauty in New Orleans of a type neither found nor meaningfully understood anywhere else. Whereas *The Wire*'s title referenced a police wiretap on a drug ring, suggesting as well unseen links between street action and the corridors of power, *Treme*, which debuted on HBO in April 2010, plugged directly into the city's indigenous culture.

The pilot episode's parade under way, another negotiation took place, this one setting off what became a running comic bit: with a deft mixture of desperation, charm, and speed, Antoine Batiste, the freelance musician played by Wendell Pierce, talked down a cab fare. That score settled, he rushed up to the band and began to blow his own commentary on the tune, Rebirth's "Feel Like Funkin' It Up." It was, in all likelihood, the first opening monologue by a central character in a television series delivered wordlessly, on trombone.

In early March, at his production office in New Orleans's Lower Garden District, Simon was struggling with the fine points of a later episode's script. He was reluctant to draw a strong connection between his former series and *Treme*. Yet he described a natural progression of thought. "*The Wire* was a tract about how political power and money rout themselves," he said. "But there was no place to reference on some level why it matters, emotionally, that America has been given over to those things. This show is about culture, and it's about what was at stake. Because apart from culture, on some empirical level, it does not matter if all New Orleans washes into the Gulf, and if everyone from New Orleans ended up living in Houston or Baton Rouge or Atlanta. Culture is what brought this city back. Not government. There was and has been no initiative by government at any level to contemplate in all seriousness the future of New Orleans. Yet New Orleans is coming back, and it's sort of done it one second line at a time, one crawfish étouffée at a time, one moment at a time."

Right—that's what I've been trying to say, I grumbled to no one in particular. I grew fascinated not just by Simon's earnest focus, his show's often hip evocation of the city, and the savvy musical choices of his music supervisor, Blake Leyh, as well as by—since *Treme* is a TV drama, not a documentary—the confluence of fact and fiction. In Sidney Bechet's memoir, *Treat It Gentle*, the late, great clarinetist's real grandfather is supplanted by Omar, a fictional figure based on a folk tale, all the better to convey stirring truths about the origins of New Orleans jazz. On most evenings in the French Quarter, tourists gather on street corners as dubiously credentialed docents lead "Haunted History" tours. Real and imagined intermingle pointedly in New Orleans, in all walks of life.

And sometimes, real and imagined overlap in ironic fashion. There's a scene in episode 3 of the premiere season of *Treme*, wherein Pierce's Batiste walks through the French Quarter after playing at a Bourbon Street Strip joint—a gig he took reluctantly, out of need in a makeshift, postflood scene. He's tired, maybe a little drunk, and carrying his horn, sans case. He pauses in front of two street musicians on the corner of Royal and St. Peter streets, in front of Rouses Market. Suddenly energized by a version of "Ghost of a Chance," played by a pretty young violinist (Annie, played by Lucia Micarelli) and a gangly young pianist (Sonny, played by Michiel Huisman). He sings a bit of the lyric, nods in approval of Annie's improvisation, then turns and half-staggers into the night. His trombone grazes the side-view mirror of a police car parked nearby. Soon, in a rush, he's up against a wall, his instrument slammed to the ground by an officer. A minor beat-down and arrest follow.

Simon clearly meant to highlight the pressure-cooker atmosphere of New Orleans and especially within an undermanned and overburdened police force in December 2005, as well as to foreshadow what would become on inevitable theme coursing through his series: the tensions between the city's culture bearers and its powers that be.

If that scene had played out in real life, in June 2010, it might have gone like this: police officers approach Annie and Sonny to inform them that playing music after 8 P.M. is violation of a city ordinance. They ask the two musicians to read and sign their names and dates of birth on documents acknowledging receipt of a notice stating, "effective immediately, the New Orleans Police Department will be enforcing the below-listed ordinances": Sec. 30–1456, prohibiting street entertainment between 8 P.M. and 6 A.M. within the entertainment section of Bourbon Street, from Canal to St. Ann Streets; and Sec. 66–205, which says, "It shall be unlawful for any person to play musical instruments on public rights-of-way between the hours of 8:00 p.m. and 9:00 a.m.," unless protected by special permit.

In the real New Orleans, on June 12—as the premiere season of *Treme* drew to its close, having celebrated street musicians and brass bands of New Orleans as something like heroes—just such notice was served on the To Be Continued Brass Band. They'd set up shop, just as they'd been doing since 2003, on the corner of Bourbon Street and Canal, in front of the Foot Locker store. According to a statement issued by the new police chief, Ronal Serpas: "The New Orleans Police Department's 8th District has for many years, and as recently as within the last several weeks, received numerous complaints from residents of the French Quarter noting that musical street performers are violating existing ordinances. These complaints have also resulted in repeated request for enforcement from the NOPD."

The irony couldn't have been more pointed. The New Orleans Convention and Visitor's Bureau had just inaugurated a new series of television advertisements, urging viewers to "book your New Orleans reservations right now." At one point, trumpeter Irvin Mayfield looked straight into the camera to say: "Right now in New Orleans, you can hear great jazz in the streets of the French Quarter." Behind him was dark of night.

In 2007, a crowd of eight thousand had followed the Hot 8 Brass Band through the streets of New Orleans to make a political point. By June 23, 2010, more than thirteen thousand signed on as Facebook followers of the page, "Don't Stop the Music. Let New Orleans Musicians Play!" which was created by TBC's manager, Lisa Palumbo. In a brief interview, posted on YouTube, the TBC trumpeter Sean Roberts described his frustration. "What they're doing is slowly but surely killing the New Orleans tradition," he said. "I learned how to play trumpet on this corner."

I first met Roberts in 2007, when he sat in the back of the Sound Café, studying a collaboration between the Hot 8 Brass Band and clarinetist Michael White. White had lost not just his home in the flood of 2005 but also a personal archive of more than 4,000 books and 5,000 recordings, many obscure; transcriptions of music from Jelly Roll Morton, King Oliver, Sidney Bechet, and other jazz pioneers; vintage clarinets dating from the 1880s to the 1930s; photographs, concert programs, and other memorabilia, including used banjo strings and reeds tossed off by early twentieth-century musical heroes.

Yet even before Katrina, White had sensed a gradual fading away of the musical tradition he came up within—brass-band players clad in white shirts, ties and black-banded caps, playing everything from hymns and marches to blues and jazz, always with swinging rhythms, complex group improvisation, and specific three-trumpet harmonies. His newfound, post-Katrina link to the Hot 8, who were older than the guys in the TBC band but still of the contemporary scene, signaled a tightening of ranks and renewed sense of purpose among brass band members within a re-building city. Bennie Pete, the Hot 8's leader and tuba player, had told me that White had provided "answers to questions about this tradition I'd never thought to ask." Roberts explained to me later that he "wanted in on whatever was being passed along."

"There's a feeling among many that some of our older cultural institu-tions, like parades and jazz funerals, are in the way of progress and don't fit in the new vision of New Orleans," said White, who is also a Xavier Uni-versity professor. "That they should only be used in a limited way to boost the image of New Orleans, as opposed to being real, viable aspects of our lives."

At her law office in a MidCity shotgun house, Mary Howell—whose work inspired a character in *Treme*, civil rights attorney Toni Bernette—had recalled for me how she began defending musicians on a regular basis more than three decades ago. A nearby picture frame held Matt Rose's 1996 photograph, which ran in the *Times-Picayune*, of musicians march-ing after one such incident: There, next to a ten-year-old Troy Andrews (better known as "Trombone Shorty" these days) on tuba, is a teenage snare drummer wearing a sign: "I Was Arrested for Playing Music." The French Quarter, where tourists regularly get their first encounter with New Orleans music, has long been contested space, she explained. The ordinances covering music in New Orleans, some based on decibel levels, others based on geography or time of day or night, she said, are "vague and overbroad enough to be ridiculous. They're not enforceable, and they're technically unconstitutional." Add to this, Howell explains, that in 1974 the city passed a zoning ordinance that actually prohibits live entertain-ment in New Orleans, save for spots that are either grandfathered in or specially designated as exceptions. The very idea is mind-boggling—a city whose image is largely derived from its live entertainment essentially outlawing public performance through noise, nuisance, and zoning ordi-nances.

By 2010, New Orleans had become a new city, in quite a number of ways, one being the absence of former mayor C. Ray Nagin and the presence of a new one, Mitch Landrieu, who, as lieutenant governor of Louisiana, made "cultural economy" his signature issue. By the end of June, City Hall and a newly elected city council were sending out signals of a desire to compromise about the issue at hand surrounding the TBC band and other musicians, and to revisit these longstanding yet troublesome ordinances.

It was a moment in which attention was turned to the Gulf Coast, focused on the continuing disaster caused by BP's failed oil well—to the potential loss of an industry, a way of life, and of precious, long-abused wetlands. Trumpeter Terrell Batiste, a member of the Hot 8 band who had begun playing regularly with the TBC band too, told Katy Reckdahl of the *Times Picayune*, "People come to New Orleans for two things: food and music. Now the oil in the Gulf is threatening one of them and the city wants to take the other one away."

A thought rattled around my head, inchoate at best: since so much of the culture that defines New Orleans—from its Mardi Gras Indians to second-line parades to the city's version of jazz—developed in some subversive way, usually in opposition to authority, maybe this tension—this sense of being put upon, threatened, and prosecuted (if not persecuted)— is necessary to the thing itself. No. I'm not ready to accept that, nor did Glen David Andrews, who gathered musicians and supporters in front of TV cameras in June to apply pressure to city hall.

On August 29, 2010, the fifth anniversary of the floods that resulted from the levee failures following Hurricane Katrina, some people in New Orleans celebrated renewal. Some mourned loss. Others touted progress or lamented lingering inequity. Still others sought just another day, a regular one, in the city they call home. Nearly everywhere, the word "resilience" popped up. A poster stapled to lampposts in some neighborhoods quoted activist and attorney Tracie Washington: "Stop calling me resilient. Because every time you say, 'Oh, they're so resilient,' that means you can do something else to me. I am not resilient." Over in Armstrong Park, a statue of Louis Armstrong stood bound by ropes and secured by sandbags amid torn-up concrete and weeds, its base rusted and damaged—the unfortunate consequence of a renovation project gone sour that had been initiated by then-mayor Nagin. Both statue and plaza were due for repair, but the image was apt: In a city that has known devastation and government incompetence, could a celebrated homegrown culture once again find firm footing?

New Orleans jazz culture will endure, of that I'm convinced. It won't be precisely what it was prior to August 29, 2005. How could it, with rents doubled, public housing razed, and so many still yet or never to return? Still, I remember trumpeter Kermit Ruffins, playing "Skokiaan" at Vaughan's, not long after the flood. ("The saddest gig I ever played," he told me, "but also the happiest, because we were coming back.") And John Boutté at DBA on Frenchmen Street, singing Stevie Wonder's "You Haven't Done Nothin'," biting down hard on the line "We would not care to wake up to the nightmare that's becoming real life." And hundreds, following brass bands through ravaged streets, always for pleasure but just then to assert an uncertain right to return.

When I first got to New Orleans after the flood, I was stunned by just how much had been destroyed. And by how little I knew. I'd been writing about jazz for twenty years. Yet I was profoundly ignorant about what it means to have a living music, one that flows from and embeds everyday life. I knew but had not yet meaningfully felt the link to something fundamentally African, transplanted via the enslaved who passed through much of this hemisphere, many of whom, come Sundays, drummed and danced in Congo Square, in what is now Tremé. I keep thinking about the language of that lawsuit brought by the social aid and pleasure clubs, invoking First Amendment rights. "Should the law not be enjoined," the complaint stated, "there is very little doubt that plaintiff's cultural tradition will ceasc to exist." Just because something will not die doesn't mean you have to keep on trying to kill it. Nothing has ceased. Yet nothing will ever be the same.

Nate Chinen

(Over the) Rainbow Warrior

Israel Kamakawiwo'ole

and Another Kind of Somewhere

It begins with a dedication, exhaled more than uttered. "OK, this one's for Gabby," a voice declares, casually but meaningfully, invoking the great Hawaiian singer and guitarist Gabby Pahinui. What follows is the simplest of chordal vamps, a flutter of upbeats strummed on a ukulele. And then that ethereal sigh, that bittersweet waft of pristine "ooo-oohs" that marks and claims the song before a single word is sung.

This is the lilting solo version of "Over the Rainbow" recorded by Israel Kamakawiwo'ole, the Hawaiian music legend also known as Bruddah Iz. There's a decent chance that you've heard it somewhere. On the soundtrack to a Hollywood star vehicle like *Meet Joe Black*, *Finding Forrester*, or *50 First Dates*, perhaps. Or during a pair of emotionally charged scenes in the NBC series *ER* and *Scrubs*. Or in one of many hundreds of earnest YouTube montages. Or during the seventh season of *American Idol*, when it was performed by a popular contender, complete with ukulele. The ballad reaches straight for the heartstrings, as it was clearly intended to do.

But Kamakawiwo'ole, Bruddah Iz, brought some coded context to the song that most listeners don't begin to recognize. As an outspoken advocate of Hawaiian sovereignty, he knew the deeper shading of a song about longing for another place, where skies are still blue. His

"Over the Rainbow" is a hymn of exile and displacement, rich in meta-phorical suggestion. Its impact has reached far and wide, eclipsing its veiled intentions—but those intentions tell us much about the world in which Kamakawiwo'ole lived, and the one that he never lived to see.

. . . . .

"Over the Rainbow" was composed by Harold Arlen with lyrics by Yip Harburg, and first recorded on an MGM soundstage in 1938. Kamakawi-wo'ole would surely have known it by its movie pedigree: a barnyard, a gingham dress, a Cairn terrier named Toto. As sung by Judy Garland in *The Wizard of Oz*, the song opens with the most famous octave leap in popular music—an assertion of the tonic, a laying down of the ground-work. Her Dorothy is rooted, so to speak, in a specific place and time: rural Kansas, a place apparently bereft of felicity, to say nothing of Tech-nicolor.

"There's a land that I heard of," she sings achingly, "once in a lullaby." A world of yearning is compressed in that famous couplet, which combines the whimsy of a bedtime story with the faintest stirrings of maturity. The fabled land in the song is a place where troubles melt, and the "dreams that you dare to dream" crystallize into truth.

At the onset of the bridge—"Someday I'll wish upon a star / And wake up where the clouds are far behind me"—the melody oscillates between a perfect fifth and a major third, and then the fifth and the fourth. And it doesn't take much interpretive energy to understand that the song is a cry of disillusionment with present circumstance. Would Dorothy really need an Oz if Kansas weren't such a wash? One could pose a similar question to the generations of Judy Garland fans who recognized this alienation, eventually claiming the rainbow as their banner ideal.

But there's a nonpartisan power to this performance: who *hasn't* wished for bluebirds while standing, metaphorically speaking, in a yard full of chickens? It's not for nothing that voters polled by the Recording Industry Association of America and the National Endowment for the Arts chose "Over the Rainbow" to top their Songs of the Century list—though as it should be noted, that was a referendum on the twentieth century.

In the twenty-first, it may actually be the case that Arlen and Harburg's evocative anthem would best be carried not by a petite warbler from Middle America but by a seven-hundred-pound crooner from the middle of the Pacific. According to Jon de Mello, essentially the Rick Rubin to

Kamakawiwo'ole's Johnny Cash, representatives at EMI Music Publishing have already shifted their allegiances. "They told me that in one more generation, no one will remember that Judy Garland was the first to sing it—it will be Israel," de Mello attested. "They said that this was the most requested song they have ever, ever had." The song has been licensed to nearly thirty countries, selling everything from toys to lottery tickets. As recently as 2008 it made Billboard's Hot Digital Songs chart, just missing the Top 10.

And why not? Kamakawiwo'ole was someone who had actually resided in a land of rainbows. With his version he managed to make the song both sweeter and sadder, using it not to express pining for a paradise unseen but for a paradise lost, or more precisely, occupied and annexed: an Oz becoming Kansas, right before his eyes.

. . . . .

On the inside cover of *Facing Future* (Mountain Apple)—his landmark 1993 solo album, and the one that introduced his take on "Over the Rainbow"—Kamakawiwo'ole printed an original inscription in verse form. This is how it begins, with capitalization and line breaks as shown:

FACING BACKWARDS I SEE THE PAST
OUR NATION GAINED, OUR NATION LOST
OUR SOVEREIGNTY GONE
OUR LANDS GONE
ALL TRADED FOR THE PROMISE OF PROGRESS
WHAT WOULD THEY SAY. . . .
WHAT CAN WE SAY?

Those sentiments spill over onto "Hawai'i '78," the anthem that bookends the album, originally recorded by Kamakawiwo'ole's landmark group the Makaha Sons of Ni'ihau.

There is no way to understand his "Over the Rainbow" without considering "Hawai'i '78." That song begins with a musical setting of a meaningful Hawaiian phrase, "Ua mau ke ea o ka 'aina i ka pono O Hawai'i," "The life of the land is perpetuated in righteousness." King Kamehameha III spoke those words in 1843, to mark the end of a five-month British occupation. Two years later they appeared on a coat of arms adopted by the sovereign Kingdom of Hawai'i. And after a forced annexation by the United

States at the turn of the century, they were emblazoned on the Hawaiian territorial seal.

"Hawai'i '78" takes much of this history into account, implicitly and plainly. Written by Mickey Ioane in its namesake year, it's an indictment of the commercial development that had subsumed the islands in the years since sovereignty. After that initial recitation of the state motto, the song poses a leading question:

If just for a day our King and Queen
Would visit all these islands and saw everything
How would they feel about the changes of our land?

The following stanza magnifies the question:

Could you just imagine if they were around
And saw highways on their sacred grounds
How would they feel about this modern city life?

And the next one furnishes an urgent answer:

Tears would come from each others' eyes as
They would stop to realize
That our people are in great, great danger now

Structurally this is a Hawaiian song of protest, a *mele ku'e*. Its melody resembles that of a traditional chant—an association that de Mello's production reinforces with the synthesized approximation of an *ipu*, or gourd drum. Crucially, though, there is no heat in Kamakawiwo'ole's singing as he forms this bitter hypothetical. During the verses, he projects in a drowsy murmur, as if exchanging bedside confidences. And when he gets to the chorus, with its sudden, plaintive exhortation—"Cry for the gods, cry for the people / Cry for the land that was taken away"—his singing grows not only more forceful but also more mellifluous, rising to the loveliest part of his register. His voice, bathed in reverb, reaches the listener as if wind-carried from a point on the horizon.

Israel Kamakawiwo'ole was born on May 20, 1959: three months almost to the day before the ratification of Hawaiian statehood. The youngest of three children, he spent his adolescence in the town of Makaha, on the Waianae coast. Then as now, this was a poor community: in the 2000 U.S. Census, it was determined that roughly 20 percent of its population was below the poverty line. More recently, addressing what it acknowledged to be an epidemic, the state opened multiple homeless shelters there.

Such problems were already painfully present in the 1960s, when Kamakawiwo'ole came of age. A decade later they were addressed by a group of activists and artists that engendered what's known as the Hawaiian Renaissance. Theirs was not just a cultural resurgence but also a political movement, intended to subvert the hum of a tourist economy and counteract the polyester charms of Don Ho and *Hawaii Five-O*. The original movement, at least at its core, was less explicitly concerned with revolution than with reclamation, a proud and willful embrace of native culture and traditions.

Accordingly, the heroes of the Hawaiian Renaissance were those who preserved native language and folklore, and especially homegrown music. They were artists devoted to *ki ho'alu* slack-key guitar and *leo ki'e ki'e* falsetto singing, artists like Gabby Pahinui. The politics of the movement have since hardened into a committed and vocal radicalism, which is one reason why many of its musicians now seem wary when it comes to their Hawaiian Renaissance affiliations. "When people talk about sovereignty," said the Reverend Dennis Kamakahi, a renowned slack-key guitarist, "our music *is* our sovereignty. Because nobody tells us how to play our music. We know how to play our music because we learned from our *kupuna*, our teachers." As he spoke, Kamakahi was on the beach in Waimanalo, for an interview and *kanikapila*, or jam session, with Eddie Kamae and the Sons of Hawai'i—the group in which he succeeded Pahinui on guitar, during the headiest days of the seventies. (Incidentally, Analu Aina, the taciturn bassist currently in the Sons of Hawai'i, was an uncredited contributor to *Facing Future*.)

In any case, it was the spirit of reclamation that led Israel and his older brother Skippy to form the Makaha Sons in 1976. Among their early and enduring successes was a version of "Hawai'i '78." So any informed listener would draw immediate associations from Kamakawiwo'ole's new version of the song, as it opened *Facing Future*.

"Over the Rainbow" is a trickier case: it carries no inherently clear pang of protest, and its sound was unmistakably appealing even before the global imprimatur of all those licensing deals. A few years ago, when asked about the critical subtext of the song, de Mello himself was initially skeptical, citing the song's outright beauty as a universal truth. But he acknowledged that while Kamakawiwo'ole never once performed "Over the Rainbow" in concert, he did sing "Hawai'i 78," many times, along with "E Ala E," which means "Stand Up." (That song, the title track of the album that succeeded *Facing Future*, clearly suggests a certain Bob Marley–Peter Tosh anthem.)

Kamakawiwo'ole was known for lecturing local audiences about Hawaiian pride, and for warning against the perils of gangs (which he had seen up close) and drugs (which he had suffered firsthand). But in the spirit of the islands, he always took care to soften his tone, usually with a dollop of humor. And he was well versed in the native Hawaiian tradition of communicating in symbols and signs.

It helps to remember that tradition when considering "Over the Rainbow." *Ke Anuenue* is the Hawaiian term for rainbow, a sacred totem in many native cultures. The term also refers to the goddess of rain, who once bestowed her blessing on a young chief named Makaha, naming a valley in his honor. Obviously this bit of folklore would have been familiar to someone who named his first group the Makaha Sons of Ni'ihau.

Of course there's a broader, more casual significance of the rainbow in Hawaii, as anyone who has played tourist there can attest. Rainbows are everywhere: not just shining over Makaha Valley but also emblazoned on license plates and plastered on store windows. For many years, it was the symbol of all University of Hawaii athletic teams. That changed in 2000, however, when the university—increasingly sensitive about the association of rainbows with the gay rights movement—overhauled both its logo and its image. This was felt most dramatically with regard to the football team: almost overnight the Rainbows became the Warriors, attired not in verdant green but a severe, martial black.

The team's rituals evolved too: suddenly it came to include the *ha'a*, an intimidating chant of solidarity that got the team penalized for unsportsmanlike conduct. Kamakawiwo'ole would have savored that irony—brotherhood mistaken for brutishness—just as he would have delighted in the Rainbow Warriors' undefeated 2007 season. Certainly he would have been touched by the surge of Hawaiian pride sparked by the team's success. When the Warriors finally played their ill-fated Sugar Bowl, the only thing that went right was the halftime show, which found the University of Hawaii marching band taking the field with two emblematic numbers: "Over the Rainbow" and "Hawaii Five-O."

Kamakawiwo'ole brought a similar duality to his performance of "Over the Rainbow," a sense of anguish braided with uplift. He recorded the song in medley form, paired with "What a Wonderful World," the Louis Armstrong vehicle that had recently enjoyed its boost from *Good Morning, Vietnam*. His segue is clearly intended as both a salve and a spur: here is paradise, he's implying, all around us. That land that you dream of—it's not completely lost, at least not yet.

. . . . .

Those who were close to Kamakawiwo'ole in his last few years say that he was concerned with leaving behind some beauty. In discussing the medley, de Mello pointed out that he was in poor health at the time: on the recording, it's all too easy to detect his belabored breathing. His weight problem was such that he required an oxygen tube, spending hours each day in a swimming pool to relieve the strain on his frame.

He recorded the medley on the spur of the moment, calling a studio at 2:30 in the morning and begging the engineer to stay open for another hour. As it happened, he was done in less than twenty minutes. The take was ultracasual, true to form. As a self-taught musician, comfortable in just a couple of keys, Kamakawiwo'ole took liberties with melodies and lyrics. Some older Hawaiian artists would refer to a song as having been "Israelized." Others would simply say that he made mistakes.

A small but thoughtful book called *Facing Future*, written by the journalist Dan Kois and published under Continuum's 33 1/3 series in 2010, presents a number of keen insights on the album. One of the keenest comes from Ricardo Trimillos, a professor of ethnomusicology at the University of Hawai'i. Listening to Iz's version of "Over the Rainbow," Trimillos zeroes in on the line "Someday I'll wish upon a star / and wake up where the clouds are far behind me," providing a kind of critical annotation.

"In a Hawaiian kahiko melody, that's what happens," Trimillos says. "You have at most three pitches, and one pitch is the chanting pitch for a lot of it." He adds: "The pitches he's using are substitutions that fit harmonically in the material—much like a jazz musician does when he improvises." Is it any wonder that Louis Armstrong lurks as a phantom presence on the track? Like Israel, Pops was a flexible interpreter of popular song with a liberated approach to melody. And he similarly veiled his social critiques, bringing layers of resonance to a tune like "(What Did I Do to Be So) Black and Blue." (Is it a stretch to invoke Ralph Ellison's nameless Invisible Man, as he addresses his faceless reader: "Who knows but that, on the lower frequencies, I speak for you?")

To be fair, some of Kamakawiwo'ole's lyrical revisions feel merely capricious. He drops "A land that I heard of," skipping straight to the "dreams that you dream of" line. Then he shortens the second verse, moving on to the bridge, where he sings an open fifth, leaving out the business with the third and the fourth. Recordings tend to codify mistakes: when Jason Castro, the *American Idol* contestant, paid his homage, he was doggedly faithful to the Israelized melody. So was Jon de Mello, when he arranged an orchestral background for Kamakawiwo'ole's voice on the posthumous 2007 album *Wonderful World* (Mountain Apple), which briefly cracked the Top 50.

But the simplest and most ingenious revision in Iz's "Over the Rainbow" occurs right up front, when he sidesteps Arlen's famous octave leap and begins instead with a seventh: the most restless interval in Western music, the degree of the scale that best expresses its desire for resolution. There's a kind of yearning here that even Dorothy couldn't touch, a rootlessness that resonates on a few different levels.

Before there was really an outlet for Warrior pride, there was this bittersweet melancholy. Kamakawiwo'ole knew what he was doing when he summoned it, and probably had a few thoughts rattling around his mind: notions of sovereignty and occupation, notions of the land—the sacred 'aina—being exploited and commodified.

Still, the second half of the inscription in *Facing Future* reads as follows:

FACING FUTURE I SEE HOPE
HOPE THAT WE WILL SURVIVE
HOPE THAT WE WILL PROSPER
HOPE THAT ONCE AGAIN WE WILL REAP THE BLESSINGS
    OF THIS MAGICAL LAND
FOR WITHOUT HOPE I CANNOT LIVE
REMEMBER THE PAST BUT DO NOT DWELL THERE
FACE THE FUTURE WHERE ALL OUR HOPES STAND

It's a passage made all the more poignant by time and recent events: the fiftieth anniversary of statehood, and of Kamakawiwo'ole's birth; the installment of a United States president who used hope as his bulwark, and who spent his formative years in Hawai'i.

Of course in the end Israel did leave something beautiful behind. Invoking a mental image of rainbows, he spoke to his people in language they alone would fully understand. So it is that with promise and sadness, and a measure of quiet indignation, one phrase bears repeating one more time: There's no place like home.

Diane Pecknold

Travel with Me

Country Music, Race, and Remembrance

Isaac Hayes started a movement
You watched in 'silent revolution'
As he entered Phoenix you watched through black-filled eyes
I knew then that Blackness was your first love
—"A Simple Poem to Mae," Omari Kenyatta Tarajia
(Richard C. James III)

In 1971, Omari Kenyatta Tarajia's "A Simple Poem to Mae" appeared on Detroit's Broadside Press, one of the most prominent institutions of the Black Arts movement and home to the early writings of legendary poets such as Sonia Sanchez, Gwendolyn Brooks, Audre Lorde, and Nikki Giovanni. Like other exponents of the Black Arts movement, the literary figures who gathered around Broadside Press understood their work as a cultural corollary to the political aims of the Black Power movement, promoting an aesthetic consonant with the "necessity for Black people to define the world in their own terms" and to speak "directly to the needs and aspirations of Black America."[1] Given this context, Tarajia's allusion to Isaac Hayes, soon to be rechristened "Black Moses," was a sensible reference to an artist who was becoming an icon of Black pride in popular culture. His citation of "By the Time I Get to Phoenix," however, appears more difficult to decode. How *does* a country-pop hit, written by Jimmy Webb and recorded originally by

Glen Campbell, become a symbol of Black cultural nationalism at one of the most racially polarized moments of twentieth-century U.S. history?

The surface irony of this transformation derives from what has come to seem a timeless association between country music and the performance of whiteness (at best) or outright racism (at worst). By the late 1960s, thanks in large part to its prominent role in the campaigns of the segregationist George Wallace, country music had become the soundtrack of an unrepentantly racist segment of the white South. Richard Goldstein wrote in the pages of *Mademoiselle* that country music promoted "political conservatism . . . [and] racism," and that its popularity "damned well ought to frighten every longhaired progressive urbanite, and every black man who is not a part of it."[2] Jens Lund, a folklorist, suggested that charges of racism in the industry and in lyrical content failed to capture the music's inherently and inescapably racist nature. "Country music's distinctive 'sound,'" he argued, "reflects its conservative and discriminatory make-up, even when a given song has no overt political or religious message."[3] Evident in all of these assessments was a connection between country music and an explicitly white but otherwise often ideologically imprecise nostalgia, a dehistoricized "naive victimhood . . . at the centre of the perception of besieged-ness" that continues to characterize "the performance of white conservatism in post–World War II American cultural politics."[4]

But country also remained, as the *Village Voice* critic Carman Moore wrote, "the music of [his] super-soulful Grandma, born a few years after Emancipation, come north in the twenties and listening to it ever since to assuage homesickness."[5] For Anthony Walton's mother, a southern migrant living in suburban Chicago in the late 1960s, the loss and sadness expressed in country music signaled nostalgia, not for the South, in which even a "relatively gentle upbringing" could not protect her from the bitter insults of Jim Crow, but for childhood itself, "a time when she was with her family and when they all had the pure hope, unsullied by reality, of better things to come, in particular in the North."[6] In spite of the deepening association between country music and whiteness as both performance and privilege, in the late 1960s and early 1970s, country could still evoke a very different narrative that connected residual structures of feeling surrounding the Great Migration and resistance to segregation in the South to the emergent structures of feeling surrounding Black cultural nationalism.

Both Hayes and Tarajia used "Phoenix" in a way that invoked this narrative of transformation, figuratively positioning the song at a moment of migration and transition that simultaneously gestured to the past and ratified the future. Hayes's opening rap, which deepened the country lyrical tropes of the original, helped to fix his artistic persona at a crossroads between rustic naiveté and sophisticated urbanity, while Tarajia's allusion to it served to connect his subject's contrasting incarnations as a "sister of natural beauty" and a larger-than-life ideologue. Together, these uses of "Phoenix" point to the ways in which many Black performances of country repertoire in the 1960s and 1970s employed country—both as a musical style and as a set of tropes about rural southernness—as a sign of Black subjectivity anchored in a historically specific configuration of region, rurality, migration, and generation.

In his work on soul covers, Michael Awkward suggests that cover versions "employ songs with a discernable cultural history to negotiate aspects of the ideologically inflected public and private personae [their] singers seek alternately to project, protect, and resist."[7] Covers, he argues, allow artists to define themselves both in relation to other singers and in the landscape of popular music as a whole. They serve as "vehicles through which artists explore how they are different than other singers and who, precisely, they want and believe themselves to be."[8] Borrowing from the semiotician Robert Scholes, Awkward notes that this process is always a "two-faced activity" that both seeks the "original intent" of the text's producers and exercises "the critical 'freedom' to situate [the texts] as part of 'a textual world that is always being written.'"[9] Awkward thus imagines covering, like other intertextual practice, as a conversation between the established meanings and histories of a song, determined in part by its generic identity, and the alternate possibilities the artist envisions for both self and text.

Particularly given the circumstances in which the song was recorded, Awkward's framework seems an especially compelling one for analyzing Hayes's version of "By the Time I Get to Phoenix." When he recorded "Phoenix" in early 1969, Hayes was emerging from a period of crisis that was at once personal, professional, and ideological. The song and *Hot Buttered Soul*, the album on which it appeared, played a particularly important role in the reconstruction of his artistic persona. Both as a textual practice and as a construction of selfhood, Hayes's cover of "Phoenix" looked both backward and forward: to the original moment and meaning of the song and his own deconstruction of it; to his past as an impoverished country boy and his future as an icon of Black cultural nationalism.

When he recorded *Hot Buttered Soul*, Hayes had been at Stax records for nearly half a decade, working first as a staff musician and then as half of a songwriting team with David Porter. The story of Stax's version of the "Southern dream of freedom," as Peter Guralnick has described it, is a particularly familiar feature of popular music history.[10] Started by a white former hillbilly fiddler and his sister in a Memphis neighborhood experiencing the racial transition that characterized so many urban areas in the age of government-funded white flight, the label brought together Black and white artists in an environment of mutual creativity and respect. In later years Hayes succinctly described the utopianism of the atmosphere at Stax with the observation, "We were a family. . . . Music has no boundaries. It's a healing process and that's what brought us together."[11] Both at the time and in retrospective accounts, the early years of Stax have served as a symbol of the promise of integration and racial reconciliation.[12]

But by the end of 1967, the tenuousness of the accord that had been reached within Stax was becoming evident. In early December, a tragic plane crash killed Otis Redding, one of the label's most successful and promising artists, along with several members of his backing band, the Bar-Kays. Within weeks, the coowners of Stax, Jim Stewart and Estelle Axton, also learned that their longstanding relationship with Atlantic—which had distributed Stax releases and had brought Sam and Dave to the label—would dissolve. Not only would Atlantic reassert its contractual rights over Sam and Dave, Stax's most successful and lucrative act, but it would also control the masters for almost all of the label's back-catalogue, the rights to which had been inadvertently signed away in the initial distribution deal. The experience caused everyone at Stax to reevaluate the terms of their work. What had once seemed a family collective now could not be imagined as anything but a business. As Jim Stewart recalled recognizing for the first time, "Hey, I'm in the record business. It's not all peaches and cream."[13] And, as it had always been, that business was inflected by race. Rearranging the internal distribution of profits was part of the process of hammering out a new distribution agreement with Gulf and Western, and while Al Bell received a 10 percent equity share in the company, the rest of the profits went to Steve Cropper, Stewart, and Axton.

The souring of the relationship with Atlantic and the peremptory appropriation of the catalogue were blows to Stax's collective utopianism, but it was the assassination of Martin Luther King Jr. in April 1968 that Stax participants recalled as finally destroying the sense of boundless possibility embodied by the label's interracial organization. "The whole complexion of everything changed," recalled Rufus Thomas, "It had to."[14] Jim Stewart recalled that after the assassination, "there wasn't that mixing and melting like we had before." "It heightened the racial sensitivity amongst those of us at Stax," Al Bell remembered.[15] Though some of that pressure came from outside the studios, where Black artists might now be accosted by the police, and white and Black artists by neighborhood residents who saw Stax as yet another form of white exploitation of Black labor, the uneven distribution of profits along racial lines rankled in a way it had not before.

The shock of King's assassination was especially devastating for Hayes, who entered into a period of despondency and a prolonged creative block. He later described the anger and bitterness that kept him from working for nearly a year after the murder, and concluded with the observation, "I thought, What can I do? Well, I can't do a thing about it so let me become successful and powerful enough where I can have a voice to make a difference. So I went back to work."[16] Its position as his first artistic statement after King's assassination was one of the most salient features of the album for Hayes and it figured in his life narrative as both rebirth and salvation; as the biography on his official website described it: "He emerged in the summer 1969 with the landmark *Hot Buttered Soul*, and the career of Isaac Hayes would never be the same again."[17]

Though it was not his first solo album, *Hot Buttered Soul* clearly occupied a privileged position in Hayes's construction of his persona, and he frequently described the album as his first effort to truly express himself as an artist. Ironically, it was the loss of the Stax back-catalogue that provided him the freedom to experiment with the longer pieces and fuller arrangements that would revolutionize soul, to "express [him]self no holds barred, no restrictions."[18] The album was released as part of Al Bell's ambitious plan to assert Stax's independence and viability by releasing twenty-seven albums and thirty singles at a single sales meeting in May 1969. As a result, Hayes recalled, he "didn't feel any pressure that [*Hot Buttered Soul*] had to sell because there were 26 other albums out there."[19] Hayes invariably spoke of the album explicitly as an effort to construct a musical identity for himself as he emerged from the behind-the-scenes work he had been performing at Stax. "What it was, was the real me . . . wanting to express myself as an artist, that's what *Hot Buttered Soul* was."[20]

"By the Time I Get to Phoenix" was one of only four songs Hayes chose for *Hot Buttered Soul*, and, at almost nineteen minutes, it constituted nearly half of the record's running time. It also introduced what would become his stylistic signature: the extended introductory rap that provided a backstory for a more traditional, elliptical pop lyric. Given the freedom to fully express himself as an artist and working at a moment when his identity—both as a Black man in the United States and as a professional composer and musician in an industry where racial inequality was firmly institutionalized—was in a state of pressurized flux, why would Isaac Hayes turn to what some people might describe as a vapid, even white-bread, country-pop ballad?

In the account related by Rob Bowman in *Soulsville, U.S.A.*, Hayes described the song simply as raw material, as a found object without any significant cultural import: "I first heard 'Phoenix' on the Radio. . . . Glen Campbell was singing it. I stopped and said, 'Damn, that's great.' I bought the record and went back to the studio the next day and told Booker and them, 'Man, I heard a hip song by Glen Campbell named 'Phoenix.' Nobody showed any enthusiasm, but I felt there was something in that song."[21]

In this rendition, it seems to matter not at all that "Phoenix" was originally a country-pop song, and certainly there is nothing in the song's structure, or even its original lyrics, that makes it distinctively country. As David Brackett has pointed out, the song's identity as a 1960s pop-MOR (middle-of-the-road) hit—with its orchestral backing and Tin Pan Alley sixteen-bar form—is much easier to establish than its identity as a country tune. The original lyrics of the song make no mention of southern or country tropes. We know nothing about the singer except that he is leaving a woman, and the regional imagery is western and urban rather than southern and rural. Like other ballads of the era, Brackett argues, "Phoenix" evinced a "generic ambiguity . . . that enable[d] [its] codes . . . to be seamlessly rearticulated in varying formats."[22] Campbell's recording of the song is identifiable specifically as country-pop, rather than merely pop, in large part because of its similarity to earlier country-pop songs and because of Campbell's identity as a country singer.

The profusion of soul covers of "Phoenix" would seem to underline the generic ambiguity Brackett describes and provide a testament to the particularly malleable nature of the song. By the time Hayes recorded it, "Phoenix" was the subject of no fewer than five R&B covers, including versions by Joe Tex (*Soul Country*, Atlantic, 1968); Solomon Burke (*I Wish I Knew*, Atlantic, 1968); King Curtis (*Sweet Soul*, Atco, 1968); The Four Tops (*Yesterday's Dreams*, Motown, 1968); and O. C. Smith (*Hickory Holler Revisited*, Columbia, 1968). In fact, Hayes's version wasn't even the only R&B cover of "Phoenix" available at the 1969 sales meeting at which *Hot Buttered Soul* was released; versions by William Bell (*Bound to Happen*, Stax, 1969) and the Mad Lads (single only, Enterprise, 1969) were also on offer.

While the widespread adoption of "Phoenix" as an R&B ballad can be read as a statement of the song's lack of generic specificity, at least the versions by Joe Tex and O. C. Smith were clearly efforts to construct artistic personae with identifiable links to country as a genre and appeared on albums that featured other country material. Tex was a protégé of Nashville publisher Buddy Killen, who claimed that he had first met Tex backstage at the Opry in a purple cowboy outfit and that Tex told him he had started out hoping to be a country singer.[23] In addition to "Phoenix," *Soul Country* featured covers of "Green, Green Grass of Home," "Funny How Time Slips Away," and "Ode to Billie Joe." As Tex did with *Soul Country*, O. C. Smith, formerly a singer for Count Basie, did for his *Hickory Holler Revisited*, on which he included his version of "Phoenix," to gesture to its country influences, and "The Son of Hickory Holler's Tramp" and "Long Black Limousine." Solomon Burke's version of "Phoenix" was also part of a larger repertoire with consistent connections to country, including his breakthrough hit, "Just Out of Reach (of My Two Empty Arms)," and covers like "Down in the Valley," "I Really Don't Want to Know," "He'll Have to Go," and "Detroit City." The MOR characteristics of "Phoenix" may have made it especially conducive to crossover, but its country identity helped to define the particular crossover space in which Black artists placed it.

Hayes's rendition suggests that he was at least passingly familiar with some of the previous soul covers; his vocalizing in certain passages, for instance, recalls Solomon Burke's version. But Hayes clearly did not imagine himself as drawing on R&B repertoire when he covered the song, and he described his version as a process of racial as well as generic transformation. In later years, he invoked racialized genre distinctions in describing the dramatic content that attracted him to "Phoenix." "I always wanted to present songs as dramas: it was something white artists did so well but black folks hadn't got into. Which was why I picked those, if you like, white songs for [*Hot Buttered Soul*]."[24] He similarly described the invention of the introductory rap to a reporter for *Ebony* as a process of racialized genre translation. "I knew [the song] hadn't been introduced to black listeners," he said, so the rap was a way of "talking about a situation that could possibly have happened to the person in that song had he been black."[25]

Through the rap, Hayes personalized "Phoenix" to a greater degree than any of the other songs on the record, and made it central both to establishing his musical and vocal style and to fixing his persona. The rap was the most obvious structural location for Hayes to exercise the artistic freedom he cited as one of the most important features of the album; that he used that space to gesture to the song's country connections and deepen the country lyrical tropes elided in the original suggests that he approached it as a cover of country-pop specifically, and that its generic positioning mattered in constructing his artistic identity.

That identity simultaneously acknowledged and disengaged from Hayes's own southern rural experience. Hayes was born in Covington, Tennessee, about thirty miles south of Memphis, to a family of sharecroppers. Orphaned young, he was raised by his maternal grandparents, who moved to the city of Memphis when Isaac was seven in an effort to escape the grinding poverty to which the economic inequalities of Jim Crow in the rural South consigned them, and which persisted after their move. Throughout his life, Hayes emphasized his identity as a rural-to-urban migrant, noting in his official online biography that his grandparents "instilled love in [him] for the simple pleasures of country life," and describing how they raised their own crops, cattle, and pork. "When we came to the city of Memphis, we didn't have anything to compare it to," he reminisced.[26]

In describing his early childhood, Hayes sometimes made reference to his grandparents' affinity for country music and spoke particularly about listening to the Grand Ole Opry, a background he shared with many of the first wave of Stax artists with whom he would work as an adult.[27] "Where I grew up in Tennessee, that was about all you heard on the radio," he told one interviewer.[28] His partner David Porter attested to the continuing influence of country music as Hayes began his songwriting career: "[We] studied country and western tunes because we discovered that some of the greatest lyrics in the world came from these. . . . Hank Williams was someone whose stuff I studied and whose emotionalism was a great inspiration for me."[29] But Hayes was far more likely to emphasize as musical influences his singing in church, his early work with a local doo-wop group, and the impact of hearing Nat D. Williams's "Sepia Swing" show on WDIA.[30] It seems unlikely, then, that he approached the cover as a form of homage to country music, as a means of connecting himself to country's generic pedigree, or as an exercise in the kind of nostalgia for a simpler rural past with which the genre has been associated.

Instead, the "country-ness" of "Phoenix" served as a point of departure for and differentiation from the sophisticated, self-possessed masculinity that would become the central feature of Hayes's "Black Moses" persona. Hayes's opening rap deepens the song's country imagery and provides a back-story for the protagonist that essentially makes him a stand-in for the artist. Hayes immediately reframes the main lyric as the story of a man, like himself, "raised in the hills of Tennessee" who moves to a city on the West Coast. Though "he worked every day and sometime he pulled overtime, double time, triple time," he comes home sick from work one day to find his wife cheating on him. While Jimmy Webb's original song is a generic story of romantic loss, Hayes's rap positions that story in one of the classic honky-tonk country narratives: the displaced rural-to-urban migrant lamenting the disappointments of hard work and faithless women far from a country home.

Hayes thus used "By the Time I Get to Phoenix" as a vehicle for presenting himself as a romantic, vulnerable country boy who became an urbane black contemporary artist. In many ways, these two identities seemed to be inextricable for Hayes. Asked in 2005 what had "allowed [him] to be in the forefront of so many things," he paradoxically looked backward: "Well I'm a country boy. And when I was picking cotton I learned just keep pushing forward, just keep moving. Keep pushing forward."[31] By inventing a specific back-story for the original song's somewhat ambiguous presentation of a man leaving a woman, by lyrically emphasizing the protagonist's country roots, his simplicity, and his sense of loss, all while backing the lyrics with a symphonic but nonetheless clearly R&B arrangement, Hayes allegorized his own biography and made his country roots the starting point for his persona as an icon of Black pride.

The opening rap can also be read as a more assertive statement of Black artistic and aesthetic autonomy. Hayes consistently described his approach to "Phoenix" as a form of dissection and reconstruction. In the early 1990s, he told Rob Bowman that when he recorded the covers on *Hot Buttered Soul* he "took them apart, dissected them, and put them back together and made them my personal tunes. I took creative license to do that."[32] More than a decade later, he repeated that description of the process almost verbatim. "I was a songwriter and as a songwriter, you can dissect things," he told journalist Ed Gordon. "So I took it apart, I took license. . . . I just took 'Phoenix' apart and put it back together."[33] In personal and professional terms, "Phoenix" was obviously a statement of artistic freedom. But if we are to take *Hot Buttered Soul* also as a statement of Hayes's reformulation of "the place of race in black music creation and distribution," his repeated emphasis on taking license evokes a deeper discourse that claims the right to recover Black experience and autonomy by rewriting standard narratives, and that signifies on and overturns the history of whites taking license with Black music ever since Daddy Rice hit the stage as Jim Crow in the 1820s.

The lyrics of the rap explicitly drew attention to this process of repossession. The early sections draw the listener's attention to the origins of the song, acknowledging Jimmy Webb as "one of the great songwriters of today," and gesturing to the notion of covering generally, particularly across styles. After telling the listener that "everybody's got his own thing; everybody's got his own way of doing a thing," Hayes declares, "I shall attempt to do [the song] my way. . . . I'm gonna bring it on down to Soulsville." At the outset, then, Hayes invited the listener to recognize the country-pop origins of the song, indexed its transformation into symphonic soul as a statement of his artistic identity, and asserted his prerogative to take possession of the song and do with it what he liked.

His cover of "Phoenix" was not the only occasion on which Hayes used country music to weave together his rural southern past and his cosmopolitan future. The sessions for *Black Moses* produced two more covers of country songs: Kris Kristofferson's "For the Good Times," which had been a number 1 country hit for Ray Price, and Hank Williams's "I Can't Help It (If I'm Still in Love with You)," which was released as the backing track to the single of "I Never Can Say Goodbye." Hayes's repeated use of country repertoire to reconstruct his artistic persona signals the importance of regional and rural pasts in the construction of his identity as a Black man, and gestures to the importance of the parallel but very different Black and white experiences of rurality, southernness, and class at mid-century.

Isaac Hayes in his iconic shirt of gold chains. Hayes's cover of "By the Time I Get to Phoenix" used country music as a point of departure for constructing a version of black masculinity that insisted on the continuing presence of the past. Image courtesy of Photofest.

Omari Kenyatta Tarajia's allusion to Hayes's version of "By the Time I Get to Phoenix" suggests that we might see Hayes's use of the song, and other country covers, not simply as a personal quirk or individual eccentricity, but as representative of what Raymond Williams would characterize as a structure of feeling in the first post–Civil Rights generation.[34] Tarajia remains substantially true to Hayes's expression in his use of the song, using it to connect urban and urbane black cultural nationalism with a sense of rurality and natural simplicity.

At the outset, "A Simple Poem to Mae" establishes its subject as someone working toward self-love particularly as a Black woman. The line "I knew then that Blackness was your first love" recurs over the course of the poem, fixing Jackson primarily in relation to blackness and to notions of self and nation. But through the allusion to "By the Time I Get to Phoenix" Tarajia transitions from that forward-looking sense of Black identity to an implicitly southern rural past that provided one of its most significant cultural foundations. Before she "watches" the story of "By the Time I Get to Phoenix," Jackson is "not human," merely "a Goddess with pen wings," but listening to the song transforms her into "a sister of natural beauty," not a faux "bourgeois revolutionist with a one-hundred dollar dashiki" or a "megalomaniac." The song invests her with a simplicity that is potentially specifically southern, as implied by the "the streets of a northern ghetto" in which she seems so out of place, "a lovely chrysanthemum" growing in "a crack in the cement."

Like Hayes, Tarajia invokes "Phoenix" as a connection to the tropes of naturalness and simplicity that have been country's primary aesthetic mode, but he does so in a historically specific way that positions the genre's standard rural nostalgia in relation to narratives of Black migration, and the move from southern segregation to northern ghetto. Whether or not Tarajia was aware of the song's origins as a country-pop tune, he incorporated wholesale the elements of Hayes's rendition of it that capitalized specifically on country's generic identity.

The country associations of "Phoenix" helped Hayes establish a biographical and artistic identity that linked his own experience to that of millions of migrants in the Civil Rights generation, both Black and white. At the same time, those associations allowed him to mark out the limits of shared Black and white experience. Michael Awkward has suggested that the murder of Martin Luther King Jr. prompted Hayes "to reformulate his notions of the place of race in black music creation and distribution."[35]

That reformulation no doubt connected violent massive resistance to integration with Atlantic's appropriation of the entire Stax catalogue; both demonstrated that racism was an economic structure at least as much as it was a set of cultural habits. Hayes viewed *Hot Buttered Soul* not only as his first opportunity to fully express himself as an artist, but also as the act of will through which he moved beyond the shattering pain of Martin Luther King's assassination. The story Hayes tells in the opening rap is ultimately one of disillusionment, the move from naiveté to bitter experience. In the context of the creative crisis *Hot Buttered Soul* ended, this narrative can be understood as two-sided, expressing through its protagonist's romantic loss Hayes's own response to the King assassination.

With its single droning organ note and its homiletic cadence, the rap is as much sermon as story. "I'm talking about the power of love now," Hayes begins, recalling King's famous encomium to "meet the forces of hate with the power of love."[36] But if Hayes understands "Phoenix" as "a deep tune because it shows you what the power of love can do," he has none of King's redemptive vision in mind. In "Phoenix," love is the source of the speaker's humiliation, pain, and powerlessness. He leaves in defeat rather than triumph, having sacrificed his heart for love and gotten nothing in return. When he says that "you can take love and kindness sometimes for weakness," Hayes delivers an ideologically loaded warning in the context of a simple pop song about a man leaving a woman.

In the same way that "Phoenix" connects a rural past with an urban future, it speaks to the transformation of the nonviolent, integrationist Civil Rights movement into the Black Power movement, and it is in this guise that it served as the point of departure for another journey in Public Enemy's "By the Time I Get to Arizona" some twenty years later. That song is a condemnation of Arizona's refusal to celebrate Martin Luther King Jr. Day, and it recontextualizes the role "By the Time I Get to Phoenix" played in Hayes's symbolic response to King's assassination. In it, Chuck D follows Isaac Hayes's injunction in the opening rap of "Phoenix" to "use your imagination . . . to travel with me," but he traces a very different voyage from California to Arizona. Prefaced by the sound of an airplane engine, in intertextual opposition to the 1965 Ford in which Hayes's protagonist agonizingly wends his way down the highway toward Phoenix, Chuck D declares: "I'm on the one mission / To get a politician / To honor or he's a goner / By the time I get to Arizona" and punctuates the phrase with an organ sample that recalls the song's namesake.

Hayes's "Phoenix" rap made a romantic metaphor of the political and moral frustration prompted by massive resistance: "The heart can take so much . . . you can kick a dog around for so long and he'll get tired, he'll turn." Public Enemy gives newly politicized meaning to that romantic disappointment. Chuck D's intertextual invocation of "By the Time I Get to Phoenix," is a dual commentary that simultaneously hails and rejects Hayes's position in what Pete Daniel describes as "the last generation of sharecroppers."[37] His is not a slowly developed, painful conviction that unfolds over miles of highway, but a jet-fueled revolt; not a reflection on the power of love but on the powers that be. Here, "Phoenix" no longer functions as a vehicle for narratives about rural-to-urban migration or the connections between simplicity and sophistication—the structures of feeling that dominated both Hayes's rendition and Tarajia's allusion to it—but instead marks the gulf between that generational position and Chuck D's own.

Black performances of country music are routinely dismissed as a form of bizarre racial dysphoria or sutured into a longer tradition of Black country repertoire that stretches from the Mississippi Sheiks and DeFord Bailey to Ray Charles and Darius Rucker. Far less frequently is country imagined as a reservoir of significations that can be tactically deployed by Black performers in registers that transcend irony or parody. Through his rendition of "By the Time I Get to Phoenix," Hayes measured his own journey from a childhood impoverished by southern apartheid to his reincarnation as "Black Moses." In doing so, he transformed country's nostalgic cast into a politically charged melancholia, refusing either to celebrate or to forget the past.

Notes

1. Larry Neal, "The Black Arts Movement," *Drama Review* 12, no. 4 (Summer 1968): 29.

2. Richard Goldstein, "My Country Music Problem—And Yours," *Mademoiselle* (June 1973): 114–15.

3. Jens Lund, "Fundamentalism, Racism, and Political Reaction in Country Music," in *The Sounds of Social Change: Studies in Popular Culture*, ed. Serge Denisoff and Richard A. Peterson (Chicago: Rand McNally, 1972), 91.

4. Geoff Mann, "Why Does Country Music Sound White? Race and the Voice of Nostalgia," *Ethnic and Racial Studies* 31, no. 1 (January 2008): 89.

5. Carman Moore, "This White Southern Music Is Mulatto," *New York Times*, June 3, 1973, D15.

6. Anthony Walton, "Chicago as the Northernmost County of Mississippi," *Southern Cultures* 8, no. 1 (Spring 2002): 54.

7. Michael Awkward, *Soul Covers: Rhythm and Blues and the Struggle for Artistic Identity* (Durham: Duke University Press, 2007), xv.

8. Ibid., xxvi–xxvii.

9. Ibid., 6.

10. Peter Guralnick, *Sweet Soul Music: Rhythm and Blues and the Southern Dream of Freedom* (New York: Perennial, 1994).

11. World Café, "Isaac Hayes: Remembering Soulsville's Main Man," August 11, 2008, interview by David Dye recorded May 2003, at http://www.npr.org.

12. Guralnick, *Sweet Soul Music*; Brian Ward, *Just My Soul Responding: Rhythm and Blues, Black Consciousness, and Race Relations* (Berkeley: University of California Press, 1998), 218–25; *Respect Yourself: The Stax Records Story*, dir. Robert Gordon and Morgan Neville (Concord Music Group, 2007); Paul A. Bernish, "Memphis Hopes Boom in Recordings Will Aid Local Racial Harmony," *Wall Street Journal*, March 30, 1970, 1.

13. Guralnick, *Sweet Soul Music*, 357.

14. *Respect Yourself*, dir. Gordon and Neville.

15. Rob Bowman, *Soulsville, USA: The Story of Stax Records* (New York: Schirmer, 1997), 146.

16. Ibid., 144.

17. "Biography," 2008, at http://www.isaachayes.com/bio/bio-2.html.

18. Bowman, *Soulsville, USA*, 182.

19. Ibid., 181.

20. Ibid., 182.

21. Ibid.

22. David Brackett, "Questions of Genre in Black Popular Music," *Black Music Research Journal* 25, nos. 1–2 (Fall 2005): 82.

23. Buddy Killen, *By the Seat of My Pants: My Life in Country Music* (New York: Simon and Schuster, 1993), 158.

24. Lloyd Bradley, "Isaac Hayes on Isaac Hayes," *Mojo*, July 1995, at www.rocksbackpages.com.

25. Ebony, "From the Vaults," and "Isaac Hayes on Phoenix Rap 2/18/87," http://www.youtube.com.

26. "Biography," http://www.isaachayes.com.

27. Bowman, *Soulsville, USA*, 51.

28. Barney Hoskyns, *Say It One Time for the Brokenhearted: Country Soul in the American South* (London: Bloomsbury, 1987), 72.

29. Ibid.

30. "Biography," http://www.isaachayes.com; Bowman, *Soulsville, USA*, 51.

31. "Ultimate Isaac Hayes: Can You Dig It?" *News and Notes*, November 14, 2005, www.npr.org.

32. Bowman, *Soulsville, USA*, 182.

33. News and Notes, "Ultimate Isaac Hayes."

34. Raymond Williams, *Marxism and Literature* (Oxford: Oxford University Press, 1977), 130–34.

35. Awkward, *Soul Covers*, 221.

36. Martin Luther King Jr., "An Experiment in Love," in *A Testament of Hope: The Essential Writings and Speeches of Martin Luther King, Jr.*, 2nd edn., ed. James H. Washington (New York: Harper Collins, 1991), 17.

37. Pete Daniel, *Lost Revolutions: The South in the 1950s* (Chapel Hill: University of North Carolina Press, 2000), 1.

Oliver Wang

The Comfort Zone

Shaping the Retro-Soul Audience

Prior to 2007, singer-songwriter Amy Winehouse was largely unknown outside her native Great Britain. Her 2003 debut CD, *Frank*, was what one might call a contemporary torch song album, mixing a few standards ("Moody's Mood for Love") with some Winehouse originals ("Fuck Me Pumps"). Producers such as Salaam Remi and Jimmy Hogwarth combined touches of older pop styles (the big-band era horn samples on "Help Yourself," for example) with current, hip-hop-influenced beats. As for Winehouse herself, music critic Sasha Frere-Jones situated her warbling voice within a mish-mash of both vintage and contemporary styles, comparing them to a "denatured version of jazz vocals, sung by someone channelling Lauryn Hill and resorting to wobbly flourishes when stuck for an idea."[1]

By 2006, Amy Winehouse had remade her image— and sound. Now sporting a towering beehive coif, Winehouse recorded and toured for her sophomore album, *Back to Black*, with members of the Brooklyn-based soul-funk band, the Dap-Kings. Produced exclusively by Remi and Mark Ronson, *Back to Black* eschewed the smoky jazz ballads and mellow neo-soul aesthetic of *Frank* and went heavy into 1960s girl group and R&B styles instead, mining the sounds of Phil Spector and Holland-Dozier-Holland to the tune of double-platinum sales and five Grammy awards. That success—coupled with tabloid-fueled controversies around drug and alcohol abuse—turned Winehouse into a short-lived star.

As a twenty-something Jew from South London who cameoed with rap acts and scored her biggest hit singing about rejecting rehab, Winehouse wasn't exactly a new-era Pat Boone sterilizing Little Richard tunes for "respectable" middle-class audiences. Yet Winehouse's success, especially as a younger, white soul singer, became a favored topic of discussion in the media, especially because of the African American, fifty-something singer that the Dap-Kings normally play with: Sharon Jones.

The Dap-Kings (then called the Soul Providers) first discovered Jones in the late 1990s when she was working as a corrections officer at Riker's Island prison and gigging as a wedding singer. This native of Augusta, Georgia, briefly sang on tour with the R&B group Magic Touch in the early 1970s but never recorded with them. Her pairing with the Soul Providers/Dap-Kings proved a boon on both sides: for Jones, it allowed her to revisit a singing career she thought was long past her and for the band, they found a vocalist with the chops and sense of history that fit with their own revivalist aesthetic. Their 2002 debut, *Dap-Dappin'*, heavily mined soul and funk styles from the late 1960s through early 1970s. If Winehouse, Ronson, and Remi borrowed from the Shirelles and Supremes, Jones and the Dap-Kings initially used Marva Whitney and Sugar Pie Desanto as points of departure.

Both *Back to Black* and all of Jones's albums play with a style of R&B collectively and colloquially known as "retro-soul."[2] Broadly speaking, retro-soul can be defined as R&B and funk music made by *present-day* artists that sounds exactingly loyal to *past* styles, especially those from the early 1960s through mid-1970s. To be sure, popular music, in general, is dialogic with its own past but in retro-soul's case, styles of yore do not merely "influence" genre, they are a template artists try to follow as accurately as possible, within varying degrees.[3]

Equally important, retro-soul is also defined by those who belong to a community of different artists around the world, many of them linked not only by similarities in sound, but by interpersonal or professional relationships via a small number of artists and record labels invested in this niche market. This community has existed since at least the late 1990s, on at least three continents, but largely flew under the proverbial radar. When Amy Winehouse mined the retro-soul sound for *Back to Black*, what had once been largely obscure from the pop mainstream suddenly crossed over. Therein lay part of the rub.

Given that Dap-Kings members backed both Winehouse and Jones on albums released within half a year of one another (Winehouse's first), a narrative practically wrote itself: "Amy Winehouse steals Sharon Jones' sound *and* band." Winehouse became, in the words of Ben Sisario of the *New York Times*, "an elephant in the room at the Brooklyn headquarters of Daptone Records—a skinny, British elephant with an enormous beehive hairdo."[4] *Back to Black* went double platinum while *100 Days, 100 Nights* did not.[5] Winehouse was white, young, and thin while Jones is not. For some pundits, that second set of differences explained the first.

For example, Kandia Crazy Horse, writing for the *San Francisco Bay Guardian*, described Winehouse's performance as "borderline minstrelsy," while casting Jones and other black singers as artists who "can *sang* but whose efforts render them invisible in a field overwhelmed by white soul saviors."[6] In *The Nation*, Daphne Brooks took a no less trenchant tack, excoriating Winehouse's "pseudo-inebriated singing" as "more like a caricature of *Amos 'n' Andy* meets one of Billie Holiday on heroin"[7] and, at the 2009 Pop Conference, describing Winehouse's vocal style as "archival aural blackface."[8]

Crazy Horse and Brooks are referencing far deeper histories around race, culture, and appropriation than just Winehouse's and Jones's, ones that Ann Douglas has summed up as "blacks imitating and fooling whites, whites imitating and stealing from blacks, blacks reappropriating and transforming what has been stolen, whites making yet another foray on black styles, and on and on: this *is* American popular culture."[9] That cyclical, discursive relationship is certainly no stranger to soul music in particular; Gayle Wald tackled an earlier era for "soul revivalism" in an essay that examined the popularity of white American and British soul projects/ artists from the early 1980s through early 1990s. In particular, in looking at the success of the 1988 R&B album *Faith*, by the British singer George Michael, Wald raises similar questions that contemporary pundits and scholars have continued to do with retro-soul: "Michael's success in resurrecting a black cultural practice (soul) associated with asserting black difference and expressing black resistance thus raises issues not only of what it means to revive or recall the past, but of what it means to do so within the highly charged context of cultural 'borrowing.'"[10] It goes without saying: this is tricky terrain to navigate and I always think of the well-nuanced approach that George Lipsitz has taken in regards to the slipperiness of engaging cross-racial/national/historical borrowings: "To think of identities as interchangeable or infinitely open does violence to the historical and social constraints imposed on us by structures of exploitation and privilege. But to posit innate and immobile identities for ourselves or others confuses history with nature, and denies the possibility of change."[11] In acknowledgment of that complexity, I suggest it's best to think of retro-soul as a terrain upon which issues of race, appropriation, and community are contested but not easily resolved.

When I originally began my research on contemporary retro-soul artists, I assumed I would be probing the cultural politics of the music and its most visible artists, but something nagged at me regarding the conventional critiques lodged against Winehouse. The argument that she was an exploiter while Jones was an originator seemed to rest on a narrow premise, one that focused almost solely on the singers at the expense of all the other people surrounding them. For example, as someone who has attended concerts by both artists, I have noticed how predominantly white the audiences have been. This point has been reported upon at times, whether matter-of-factly, as when Dave Gil de Rubio observed in the *East Bay Express*, "This recent soul revival seems to have struck a chord with a largely white following,"[12] or less charitably, as when Siddartha Mitter in the *Boston Globe* made the following remark about one 2005 Jones/Dap-Kings show at Cambridge's Middle East: "That scene is young, self-conscious, and overwhelmingly white. It felt as if Williamsburg had invaded."[13] This trend is neither unique to the Dap-Kings nor is it confined to recent years; Los Angeles's Breakestra formed in the late 1990s, making them one of the earliest retro-soul bands on the West Coast, and when they were signed to Stones Throw Records, the label's comanager Eothen Alapatt recalled that in the late 1990s, "there might have been a smattering of black faces in the crowd but on stage, I saw more black people in the band than in the crowd."[14]

Moreover, these bands are not simply playing to predominantly white crowds; their line-ups are also predominantly white (be it American, European, Australian, or other). That's as true for the Dap-Kings as it is for Breakestra as it is for Helsinki's Nicole Willis and the Soul Investigators, London's Quantic Soul Orchestra, Australia's Bamboos (Melbourne) and Cookin' On 3 Burners (Victoria), Munich's Poets of Rhythm or Milwaukee's Kings Go Forth.[15] Brooks actually makes note of this in her article, describing the Dap-Kings' musical approach as having "resuscitated the sound as well as the aura of black culture circa 1964—yet it was played by a predominantly white group of musicians."[16] This observation is left adrift however; Brooks singles out Winehouse for scrutiny but doesn't ask similar questions of the band even though, as her own description captures, the Dap-Kings are a predominantly white set of musicians recreating a musical style indelibly attached to a historical moment of African American political liberation and cultural empowerment. Given that, questions of race, identity, history, and community would seem clearly relevant beyond just the lead vocalists.

I want to emphatically state that I am not suggesting there is something "strange" or "wrong" about this abundance of nonblack fans or participants, nor about the absence of black fans or participants. As Craig Werner has chronicled, soul music is "grounded in the specifics of African American life but open to anyone willing to answer its call for change" and that "unsurpassed vision of shared possibility" has long been part of the genre's cross-cultural appeal.[17] However, it's equally important to acknowledge that R&B's popularity through the decades has been possible *despite* the pernicious legacies of American race relations, not in the absence or erasure of them. For example, even the most popular black rock 'n' roll and R&B acts of the 1950s and 1960s had to contend with the treacherous realities of segregation while on tour,[18] while the very R&B charts that measure soul music's penetration into the mainstream are themselves a remnant (and perpetuation) of a forced segregation between black and white artists.[19] In short, the specter of race has been an indelible part of soul music's heritage and it has proven no less relevant in the present. Indeed, when Jones and the Dap-Kings sold out a fall 2007 date at Harlem's Apollo Theater—arguably the most famous black musical venue in America—to celebrate the release of *100 Days, 100 Nights*, Jones was later confronted by people asking "why there were so many young white people at the Apollo."[20]

One can debate whether that question is fair or relevant but the very fact it's even asked suggests the persistence of racial concerns within the retro-soul scene. This is an admittedly challenging area to explore, especially given a dearth of data; the racial composition of retro-soul bands and audiences has been observed often enough, but only anecdotally. That has not prevented pundits from trying to theorize the phenomenon, however.

Mark Reynolds's 2008 essay for Popmatters.com addressed the opposite side of the "Apollo question": where are retro-soul's black fans? Reynolds's theory: "While Daptone and its peers do an excellent job of trafficking in black music of yore, black music's audience of today isn't particularly interested in revisiting the previous generation—and never has been."[21]

Reynolds attributes this to two cultural factors within the black community: an ambivalence toward revisiting the past and a focus on the present/future. In his words, "In the black pop mind, 'now' represents the reality of the current day and the hope for, or promise of, better days to come, while 'then' represents an unwelcome reminder of harder times and oppression left in the dust." In contrast, amongst nonblack listeners, Reynolds argues that retro-soul "does not connote difficult memories of difficult days, or of a black culture less advanced and self-assured than the current world. Unburdened by intimate attachments to, and uncomfortable memories of, the history beyond the music, they're much freer to accept the music on its own terms."[22]

The relationship between race, nostalgia, and history is a rich one to probe, but Reynolds not only paints with a broad brush of essentialist generalizations, his arguments also seem undermined by a wealth of countervailing evidence. For one, many mainstream R&B artists have forged deliberate dialogues (musical or otherwise) with the past, whether Alicia Keys covering Donny Hathaway or sampling the Main Ingredient,[23] Erykah Badu's controversial "restaging" of the Kennedy assassination,[24] or Beyoncé playing both Etta James and a Diana Ross doppelgänger in *Cadillac Records* and *Dreamgirls* respectively. In addition, the existence of a regional southern blues / R&B scene, heavily seeped in 1960–70s soul traditions, suggest that nostalgic connections to black music of the past is alive and well among a predominantly black audience that includes both the young and old.[25]

None of this is to deny that cultural trends—including musical preferences—are inherently subjective and influenced by social norms formed and sustained with any given community (racial or otherwise). However, in the case of retro-soul, I would argue that rather than privilege explanations based around generalized cultural preferences, we also need to examine how decisions made by retro-soul artists and their labels have contributed to the formation of those audiences.

In this essay, I analyze retro-soul's growth by discussing how artistic and especially organizational or business decisions have shaped how the music has reached certain audiences (but not others).[26] Specifically, I am interested in exploring how retro-soul's outreach to its audience or consumer base has been impacted by selective aesthetic choices and marketing strategies. As I will argue, those decisions have an important influence on the relative homophily of the audience they reach.[27]

In the midst of analyzing my research, I was initially drawn to a loose constellation of work on the diffusion of innovations, in part linking back to Everett Rogers's classic research on the topic, but also including more contemporary adaptations by Leah Lievrouw and Janice Pope and "creative marketing" analysts such Rob Walker and Malcolm Gladwell, all of whom have tried to apply ideas originally designed to explain technological adoptions in the aesthetic realm.[28] However, in the end, I found that the most useful model has been Keith Negus's extensive analysis of "genre cultures" in popular music. Especially given that retro-soul is a newly emerging genre, I was drawn to Negus's description of "genre cultures" as "an unstable intersection of music industry and media, fans and audience cultures, musician networks and broader social collectivities informed by distinct features of solidarity and social identity."[29] This raised not only the important—though often overlooked—role that retro-soul labels have played in constructing their identity and audience, but also the broader set of social relations that, in turn, influence what one might call the emerging "retro-soul industry."

My research draws from interviews with various retro-soul musicians and label personnel as well as my personal experiences of marketing/publicity campaigns as a college radio DJ and a music journalist.[30] Through these, I will attempt to show how the aesthetic decisions as well as interpersonal and professional networks amongst retro-soul artists and labels influenced marketing strategies that were more likely to expose their music to specific demographic audiences, namely younger, middle-class, white listeners. I conclude with some thoughts about how some of these dynamics may be evolving in the wake of Winehouse's and Jones's watershed year in 2007 and what this may mean to questions around retro-soul, race, and audience.

. . . . .

"Shitty Is Pretty": The Aesthetics of Retro-Soul

In the early 1990s, Lyrics Born (né Tom Shimura), a producer-rapper from the Bay Area, traveled to New Orleans to look for vintage soul and funk records. There, he came across a seven-inch single released on Hotpie & Candy, an imprint he was unfamiliar with. As he recalls, "I was totally convinced this was a 45 from the early 70's based on the title, the way it was mixed, the instrumentation, and the arrangements."[31] As Shimura later learned, his mystery single was actually new and had been secretly left there by members of Munich's Poets of Rhythm who had seeded American record stores with their singles as an experiment in "passing" for vintage.

The Poets were formed in the early 1990s by brothers Jan and Max Weissenfeldt, along with Jan Krause and Boris Geiger. Their first singles — deliberately released only on seven-inch records — such as "Funky Train" (1992) and "Augusta, Georgia" (1993) and their 1993 debut album, *Practice What You Preach*, were molded after the spartan, boogaloo funk style pursued by hundreds of post–James Brown bands of the late 1960s and early 1970s. Arrangements were kept simple but aggressive, with a heavy focus on polyrhythmic drum breaks, angular guitar work, and blaring brass punctuation.

The Poets were not the only funk recyclers; the acid jazz movement had been under way since the late 1980s and built its sound around jazz fusion albums on labels such as Blue Note and Prestige, also from the same late 1960s/early seventies. However, for a group like the Poets, acid jazz became an aesthetic foil. Jan Weissenfeldt described the genre as "emotionless crap" and argued, "that polished, pseudo sophisticated attitude that acid jazzers thought of themselves [just] because they wore suits and took inspiration from 70's funky fusion but the sonic result was mostly not much different than Kenny G. It was the opposite of what I wanted to hear in music, which was warm, analog and raw."[32] The hostility toward acid jazz by a group of funk revivalists is interesting here, especially since both movements were revisiting the funk-influenced aesthetics of the late sixties. However, despite that common cultural source, Weissenfeldt emphasizes how acid jazz lacked the "warm" sound commonly associated with analog production and more importantly, the absence of "rawness" in acid jazz. Like terms such as "gritty" or "rough," "rawness" connotes a conventional ideal of "authenticity." Indeed, the invocation of Kenny G, whose very name has become shorthand for schlocky, commercial pop music, deliberately implies that acid jazz was the antithesis to "raw" (read: "real") music.

The Poets were not the only ones to draw daggers on acid jazz. In 1995, recording engineer Gabriel Roth and Phillipe Lehman, a record collector, met in New York and formed Desco Records, the precursor to several later retro-soul labels, including Daptone. Roth developed a reputation for engineering Desco's recordings to sound "authentically" from the past (the Poets won similar praise), and the British music magazine *Big Daddy* invited him to write a pair of articles describing his approach. Entitled "Shitty Is Pretty: The Anatomy of a Heavy Funk 45," the articles doubled as both a recording manual and manifesto against what Roth described as "this bullshit acid-jazz, smooth R&B method. . . . They call it professionalism. I call it bullshit. If your [*sic*] going to try to record Funk, you got to have enough balls to make it rough."[33] Lehman added, in a separate article for *Big Daddy*, "If it's rough funk you're after and you are trying to record with Acid Jazz & P Funk playing motherfuckers you can forget it. It will sound like shit."[34]

Notably, these figures were simultaneously celebrating certain eras of black musical practices—especially "gutbucket" funk and southern soul of the late 1960s and early 1970s—while dismissing others, including the Parliament-Funkadelic (aka "P-Funk") sound.[35] In essence, the retro-soul aesthetic was as much oppositional—defined by what it was not—as it was aspirational. This passage, in which Roth explains what kind of musicians he looks for, is especially telling: "It is best to get time-machine players. That is: genuine old-school players that think they are still in 1971. If this isn't possible, your second choice is to get musicians who are so into rough old shit that they can *willfully deny the influence of the last 30 years of music*" (emphasis mine).[36]

I was always struck by this idea that "the last 30 years of music" would be worthy of such antipathy but it certainly aligns with retro-soul's raison d'être in valorizing a distinct musical era via an oppositional attitude. For its creators and fans, retro-soul is "good" partially because it rejects those other movements deemed "bad," a belief easily found in critical and consumer comments.[37] I will return to this point in the conclusion, but suffice to say for now that retro-soul's popularity has to be at least partially understood via a larger set of tensions with other forms of pop music, especially contemporary R&B.

In 1996, Roth and Lehman released Desco's inaugural LP: Mike Jackson and the Soul Providers' soundtrack to the *The Revenge of Mr. Mopoji*. Like the Poets of Rhythm's singles, the music brought together a "best of" mix of early 1970s instrumental funk styles that included tightly wound guitar riffs, whirling organ vamps and darting flute arrangements that managed to recall the likes of Don Julian, Archie Bell, The Meters, and of course, James Brown. However, though the music was real, everything else about the album was elaborately fabricated to make it appear to be a reissue of some long-lost blaxploitation/kung-fu era soundtrack. Here's Roth explaining their thinking:

> We made up the story of an old kung-fu movie from the '70s called *The Revenge Of Mr. Mopoji*. A total fake film, but we had a plot and we even gave it a kind of history, with production in Hong Kong. We put the "soundtrack" out as a reissue and took it around to record stores. These stores would never have touched a funk or soul record by a new band, but when they saw a "reissue" they scooped it up. We heard people saying, "Oh, yeah, my cousin had that movie on VHS."[38]

I came across the album circa 1996 and if hazy memory serves, bought into the invented backstory. The packaging and especially, the music, helped sustain the illusion. If the ambition was to create a sound that was aesthetically "authentic" with the musical conventions of the blaxploitation era, the Soul Providers provided.

However, as Roth's recollection suggests, there was a practical angle here too. Desco wanted to get their music into retail stores but sensing listener resistance to newly recorded funk and soul, they gambled that a fake reissue would gain more traction. Those kind of marketing and promotions decisions, however spurious or strategic, are important to how retro-soul, as a newly shaping style, would become exposed to a larger public.

Specifically, Desco and the Poets of Rhythm were literally banking on their ability to recreate the aesthetics of a "vintage" soul/funk recording in the hopes that this would strike a favorable chord with a particular kind of audience invested in those same aesthetics. This included not only consumers but a larger network of likeminded soul enthusiasts among retailers, DJs, and journalists—all of whom would be in a position to further bring their labels and/or recordings into greater public prominence.

As noted, these early recordings not only were informed by a politics of inclusion—what these artists stood for musically—but also exclusion—what they didn't represent. Thus, acid jazz was considered too "smooth" and insufficiently "rough enough," and these retro-soul recordings were partially aimed at audiences who shared those same judgements.

This notion of what one might call "aesthetic compatibility" is common amongst testimonials from other retro-soul groups. For example, Helsinki's Soul Investigators formed in 1998 and by the mid-2000s, began working with American transplant Nicole Willis as their lead vocalist. In 2007, Willis explained part of what drew her to collaborate with the Investigators:

> I like working with these guys and have a great appreciation for what they do. They're kind of raw. They don't ever get polished in a way that would ever compromise the style of the music. I love hearing the horns and the sound of real drums rather than a drum machine. I think that's super important. People do not want to sit and watch musicians using drum machines and laptops, and we don't want to make records like that.[39]

What Willis describes here is a series of shared values she sees among herself, the Investigators, and their audience: live instrumentation over mechanical synthesis, rawness over polish. These kinds of aesthetic decisions, in her estimation, connect audiences to her group and vice versa.

As much as these musical choices help connect retro-soul with specific audiences, they have also served as a point of criticism, namely over the idea that retro-soul represents a form of musical retreat rather than innovation by so loyally revisiting the past. There's certainly a legitimate line of critique here, especially given the contempt that some retro-soul artists have toward other forms of music (pity P-Funk and acid jazz). However, to suggest that retro-soul is overly mired in a particular set of conventions is to overlook the ways in which familiarity versus innovation is a constant tension in practically any pop music genre. Negus takes special pain to suggest that

> genres are more than musical labels: they are social categories. When someone performs or listens to a "trite or clichéd" country ballad or feels moved by sentimental "salsa lite" or plays one more time with rock's "tedious beat and cries for freedom," they are not responding intellectually or simply aesthetically to tired musical codes, but emo-

tionally, within a context of multiple recognitions, reverberations and appropriations that are generated by and come with belonging to particular genre cultures.[40]

Retro-soul, especially, is a genre premised on generating "multiple recognitions" of styles for their primary audience, ones that validate the shared, aesthetic values and, in the process, provide a form of meaningful, emotional satisfaction and comfort through those reproductions. However, as important as aesthetic decisions are in bridging retro-soul to a larger community of like-minded listeners, there are also professional/business decisions that impact who is more likely to gain exposure to a particular innovation.

. . . . .

Comfort Zones: The Marketing of Retro-Soul

Desco's first release, on both vinyl and CD, was the Sugarman 3's *Sugar's Boogaloo* (1999). Bandleader Neal Sugarman (who later cofounded Daptone Records) explained that part of that album's marketing campaign lay in "making sure they were put in the right record shops, where the DJs were shopping, real speciality kind of stuff."[41] This suggests that Desco had a particular consumer in mind—funk/soul DJs—and they had an idea of how to reach them, via "speciality" record stores known to carry vintage, collectible soul/funk vinyl records.

However, Desco also engaged the services of music professionals to help get the word out. Sugarman explained:

> There was a small press campaign; we had a friend who was a publicist and there was a radio promoter. It was a small project for a distributor like Caroline. We had friends who were working there. It was a labor of love for them. We were also rolling a lot of records through Fat Beats, who were probably responsible for getting them into a lot of the specialty vinyl stores. [We also made sure] Keb Darge and Snowboy and all those soul DJs that were touring around and had big mouths . . . were talking about that record.[42]

What Sugarman describes here includes both the organizational channels through which the band's product reached larger audiences as well as the key interpersonal relations that abetted that dissemination. The extent of that interconnected patchwork is complex, including retail stores, radio stations, publications, night clubs. In each of these cases, Desco had personal and professional relationships with personnel such as radio promoters, publicists, and distributors, not to mention influential tastemakers such as the United Kingdom's Keb Darge and Snowboy, DJs who could spin their records in clubs and talk about them with peers, helping disseminate awareness of Desco's music to their individual communities of fans and colleagues.

The interpersonal relationships here are especially relevant. Desco's publicist was a friend of label staff. The people at Caroline Distribution were friends too. Record collectors such as Phillipe Lehman would have known fellow record hounds such as Keb Darge and Snowboy. These different players—all of whom linked back to Desco staff in personal ways—constituted what Sugarman described as "our network," an apt term to highlight the interconnected units working together for the goal of bridging product with audience.

It should follow then that the composition of that network would impact the band's consumer exposure, given who reads what magazines or listens to which radio stations or patronize which DJs. I want to be careful not to overgeneralize here—none of these outlets constitutes closed, fixed circuits when it comes to consumer demographics. Nonetheless, outlets such as speciality vinyl stores, college radio, and alternative music magazines are neither universally accessible nor popular with all audiences; in the United States, at least, they are perceived to skew toward younger, white, middle-class consumers. Moreover, the front wave of retro-soul consumers have also played a key role in becoming influential tastemakers in their own right. For example, Sharon Jones was quoted as saying, "It's been the young white college students who got us started in the last twelve years by getting us played on the college stations."[43] What's described here is a feedback loop where demographically specific outlets and consumers influence one another to magnify the exposure of an innovation among likeminded consumers.

Importantly, once these networks prove successful for one label, it increases the likelihood that other labels will follow the same paths, thus helping entrench particular marketing strategies. This was especially relevant in New York, after creative differences lead to Desco's folding in

2000. In their four years, the label not only released a prodigious catalog constituting some three dozen 45s, LPS, and CDS, but they also laid the groundwork for an emergent community of retro-soul musicians and labels. The post-Desco family tree is complex enough to require a flowchart to properly map, but it includes both subsequent record labels (Soul Fire, Truth and Soul, Daptone) and a slew of artists, including (but hardly limited to) Sharon Jones and the Dap-Kings, the El Michels Affair, the Budos Band, Antibalas Afrobeat Orchestra, Lee Fields and the Expressions, Naomi Watts and the Gospel Queens, and the Menahan Street Band.

However, retro-soul was hardly limited to Desco-related artists, nor was it purely a New York phenomenon. Japan's Osaka Monaurail began as a James Brown–influenced funk and jazz band in 1992 and started to garner national attention by 1998 once they began headlining the SHOUT! party series in Osaka. In 1997, Los Angeles DJ and bassist Miles Tackett brought together a group of soul/funk-minded DJs, musicians, and rappers that evolved into the Breakestra band. In 2000, The Poets of Rhythm signed up with the Bay Area hip-hop label Quannum Projects to release their second album, *Discern/Define*. By mid-decade, retro-soul bands could be found throughout the world, including many of the groups already mentioned, such as the Soul Investigators, Quantic Soul Orchestra, the Bamboos, and Kings Go Forth. (This says nothing of the incredible wave of post-2007 retro-soul artists, some of whom I will discuss in the conclusion.)

As retro-soul began to flower, many of these early generation bands followed strategies similar to Desco's in that they too relied on familiar networks to help "get the word out." This was especially true for two California-based record labels at the forefront of promoting retro-soul in the late 1990s and early 2000s: Quannum Projects and Stones Throw.

As I noted earlier, Lyrics Born, a Quannum Projects cofounder, discovered the Poets of Rhythm in the early 1990s and he was so impressed by them that he convinced the group to release their second album, *Discern/Define*, through his label. At the time however, Quannum had very little experience with R&B, though they were well acquainted with underground and independent hip-hop. The then general manager, Isaac Bess, explained that while the Poets were the first nonrap act on the label, they made the decision to pitch *Discern/Define* along many of the same avenues that had proven successful with their hip-hop stable: "We focused on the more crate-dig portion of our existing fan base, running ads in places like *Wax Po[etics]* and pushing for reviews in mags like *The Wire* . . . [p]laces where our *repeat business and existing support* would carry some weight" (emphasis mine).[44]

What Bess describes here is a similar strategy of utilizing existing knowledge and partnerships based around their hip-hop industry expertise, just as Desco's staff relied largely on existing, interpersonal relationships with publicity and distribution partners. In particular, Bess highlights specific publications that Quannum deemed most useful. That includes *The Wire*, a British music publication that bills itself as focusing on "modern music—improvisation, electronics, avant garde," as well as *Wax Poetics*, an American magazine that caters to soul/funk/jazz/hip-hop record collectors. Both magazines trend toward specific readership demographics—predominantly, though not exclusively, young, white, middle class, and urban; the same demographic among whom Quannum's hip-hop roster was already popular. In essence, Bess and Quannum gambled that they could pitch the Poets to that same consumer base and, therefore, followed the same marketing plans that had proved effective with their hip-hop releases.

One of Quannum's main peers and competitors was another hip-hop label, also started in the Bay Area: Stones Throw. Eothen Alapatt is one of the label's comanagers and was responsible for working with Breakestra back in the late 1990s.[45] Breakestra's musical style was similar to that of Desco and the Poets of Rhythm, but they were also highly influenced by hip-hop samples; their early songs were often covers of funk tunes made famous by rap songs that sampled them.[46] Given both Breakestra and Stones Throw's hip-hop connections, Alapatt—like Bess at Quannum—first pitched the group to the same consumers who supported the the label's hip-hop clientele and strategized how to expand from there: "We tried to sell it to the hip-hop audience and then tried to cross over to the thirty-something, white crowd that listened to Medeski, Martin, and Wood. It was just a hunch that it would work—based on some MMW shows I went to to see DJ Logic play 'breakbeats' in the late nineties. The audience seemed to eat it up."[47] Alapatt's marketing strategy was based on a personal hunch—that his knowledge of the fan base behind an "avant-groove" jazz band such as Medeski, Martin, and Wood could also be targeted to sell Breakestra's records too. Race here is neither completely intentional nor incidental. Alapatt was not trying to deliberately target white consumers in going after MMW fans; however, he was also aware that in going after those fans his target base would be largely white.[48]

Alapatt and Bess's familiarity with hip-hop marketing channels was also paralleled by a lack of familiarity in reaching audiences beyond the collegiate rap scene. For example, I asked Alapatt if he had made attempts to pitch any of Stones Throw's funk/soul-related projects to older, black consumers—the demographic that might have grown up with those styles in their households. He replied, "At first, we didn't even know how to reach [older soul listeners]. The first Breakestra album came out when I was twenty-one. I knew how to talk to a twenty-year-old, I had no idea how to talk to a forty-year-old." And even as Alapatt got older, he still felt it was difficult to find ways of reaching older R&B fans, especially given the means of communication. He explained, "We've always gravitated to the new medium of communication and shied away from the old, largely because we couldn't afford the old: print advertising, radio, billboards. That's not to say we haven't tried to cross over to an older audience, it's just that we haven't been able to afford the luxury of trying to do it by a racial line."[49] Likewise, Bess also acknowledged that when it came to promoting the Poets of Rhythm,

> for us it was largely a question of cost and familiarity, but with the benefit of hindsight and some reflection, I would say instinctually that hawking new music to older folks of any background is an extremely tough sell . . . and those successes tend to be more in repackaging older artists than breaking new ones. But frankly, I didn't spend much time at older, traditionally black venues as a twenty-seven-year-old label manager. I was definitely working within my comfort zone of record nerds.[50]

We should not universalize Alapatt's and Bess's experiences, but it seems relevant to think of how this notion of a "comfort zone" again highlights how, within the small retro-soul community, personal networks and individual knowledge impacted marketing strategies that targeted some audiences in favor of others (i.e., those who lay outside of the "comfort zones").

It has to be said that there are practical, economic reasons for these decisions, not the least of which is that a marketing campaign targeting a broader, more diverse (i.e., more heterophilous) audience usually requires a far greater commitment of scarce financial resources, whether in expanded advertising costs or hiring outside personnel with specialized knowledge in reaching other audiences. In this sense, there is also a cost-benefit comfort zone. Until very recently, retro-soul has never been a lucrative genre to pursue; it has been a niche style with a niche following. As such, the limited budgets allotted to promoting these groups have meant that labels have had to make difficult choices as to what marketing strategies to pursue. For example, as Alapatt noted, reaching older audiences, including those in traditionally black neighborhoods, calls for more expensive forms of publicity, such as billboards or print advertising.

Sugarman has faced similar challenges. At the time of the first Sharon Jones album, he recalled, "We were talking down marketing proposals from Caroline, who said we could pay five thousand dollars to get into a program at Barnes and Nobles or Borders, which at the time, not only seemed like payola but [we wondered] is that really where we're going to sell records?"[51] What's notable was how the uncertainty in the potential success of certain strategies played back into the decisions to stay within "comfort zones." Besides his ethical concerns around paying for placement in retail stores, Sugarman also wasn't certain if bookstores were the best venue for selling their album; given their limited resources, it wasn't a strategy he deemed worthy of testing.

Sugarman expressed similar sentiments with a more recent Daptone release, *What Have You Done, My Brother* by Naomi Watts and the Gospel Queens (2009). Unlike the more up-tempo, funk-driven style of Sharon Jones and the Dap-Kings, Watts and the Gospel Queens recorded a traditional, soul-influenced gospel record, one that wouldn't be out of place on any number of Sunday morning gospel shows heard around the country. According to Sugarman, "We did our best to get them into blues magazine kind of places that are specializing in that kind of music," referring to a network of different newsletters, websites, and other outlets devoted to fans of southern blues/R&B. However, Daptone failed to make much headway within that network, and Sugarman explained how the budget for the album created limitations and uncertainties: "I knew what our expectations were on that record, sales-wise, and quite frankly, I have to budget the record based on that. To start throwing crazy money into ads in magazines, which is sometimes what it takes, I couldn't responsibly do that. Maybe that's what it would take? I don't know."[52] With both Watts's and Jones's releases, Sugarman realized that there were other avenues Daptone could have pursued to potentially create a greater awareness for their records, but given limited resources—and an uncertain result—they chose the more conservative approach to stay within the communication networks they were most familiar with. Especially with the Watts album, Sugarman explains, "We were working this label services company for some back end on the record. The records they were putting out were [Britpop musician] Jarvis Cocker records. Their specialty was working European records in the U.S. market. It was a network that we were all familiar with but certainly [they had] no experience in [the southern blues] market." Once again, we can see how relevant the choice of outside staffing can be in terms of which outreach strategies are pursued and which are not. Daptone's outside partners may very well have been useful for promoting other releases, but in this case, they seemed to have lacked the knowledge to effectively promote something like Watts's album to southern blues/R&B listeners.

Thus far, we have mostly focused on radio and print publicity but venue bookings play another key role. Especially for groups with a limited advertising budget, the strength and frequency of live performances can make a huge difference in terms of public awareness. As Sugarman explained, "What still sells a lot of our albums . . . [is our live act]. That was probably our biggest mouthpiece as far as marketing."[53] More relevant to our discussion, is how the choice of venue—coupled with ticket prices—can have a major impact on which audiences are likely to appear. For example, this issue has become an issue amongst independent hip-hop artists, where Bakari Kitwana has reported a trend in which "hardcore, political" black rap artists such as The Coup and Zion I find themselves performing to predominantly white crowds. "My audience has gone from being over 95 percent black 10 years ago to over 95 percent white today," laments Boots Riley of the Coup. "We jokingly refer to our tour as the Cotton Club," he says, invoking the Harlem jazz spot where black musicians played to whites-only audiences through the 1920s and 1930s.[54] Underground rap artists may differ musically from retro-soul artists but, as I've tried to detail, both have utilized similar outreach networks and that can include booking agents and performance venues. Even a cursory examination of different retro-soul artists' American tour schedules reveals that the majority of their venues are geared for alternative/indie music and/or college crowds and rarely do they seem to be booked in traditional, African American neighborhood venues.[55] Again, none of this is to say that there aren't black patrons in the indie music scene or that black neighborhood venues attract only African Americans, but factors such as geography, ticket price, and venue reputation/tradition certainly correlate with trends in audience composition.

Talking about the present-day experiences of Sharon Jones and the Dap-Kings, Sugarman mentioned that Daptone hired "a booking agent that books [Australian alternative rock band] Nick Cave and the Bad Seeds. It's just real different than working with some production company that does those chitlin' blues tours. It would have been a different route to get us to where we are now, potentially."[56] That last comment means that, theoretically, Jones and the Dap-Kings could have begun their career by following the southern blues circuit but would likely have ended up taking a different route in terms of exposure. These days, the band enjoys high-profile bookings on late-night television, such as David Letterman and *The Colbert Report*, and in international music festivals such as France's Nice Jazz Festival and the Newport Folk Festival in Rhode Island. It is impossible to know in hindsight if a different venue strategy would have altered that path, but what is certain is that the success the group has enjoyed makes it likely that future retro-soul artists would seek to follow the same routes. As I have stressed throughout, in a community as small as retro-soul, labels and artists learn from their peers. What "works" for one is likely to create a pathway that others travel down as well, thus expanding the membership of the "comfort zone."[57]

. . . . .

The Road Made by Walking: The Future of Retro-Soul

Few figures are more representative of both retro-soul's close-knit community and the genre's mainstream, crossover potential than Thomas Brenneck. In 2003, Brenneck and several other friends from Staten Island formed the Budos Band, a soul/funk outfit heavily influenced by Nigerian Afrobeat and Ethiopian jazz. The group members had grown up watching Desco and then Daptone take off and eventually signed with Daptone, releasing their first full-length album in 2005. Brenneck then joined the Dap-Kings as one of their lead guitarists and in 2006, created the Daptone subsidiary, Dunham Records, as a way to release music for his new Menahan Street Band.

Menahan's first single, "Make the Road by Walking" came out exclusively on seven-inch single in 2006, limiting its potential audience to, at most, a few thousand vinyl collectors. By 2007 however, the song had gone global, in a manner of speaking. Four bars, taken from the bridge of the single, were sampled by hip-hop producers LV and Sean C. (aka "The Hitmen") to create the track for "Roc Boys (And the Winner Is . . .)," the first single from rapper Jay-Z's *American Gangster* album. In essence, one of the most famous pop stars in the world took a relatively obscure retro-soul single and suddenly turned it into one of the biggest pop hits of 2007.

The success of Jay-Z's single didn't necessarily translate into a new influx of fans for the Menahan Street Band. As Brenneck surmised, "Maybe some DJs, hip-hop sample heads and such discovered the [Menahan Street Band] from the Jay-Z sample. That's probably a small, diverse group of people."[58] However, there was one important new fan. "A principal of a predominantly black elementary school in Fort Greene/Clinton Hill [P.S. 20] had his school band learn and perform 'Make the Road by Walking,'" said Brenneck. "He invited us to the concert as well as to the school to teach a music class. That never would have happened had it not been for that sample."[59]

There are at two points I want to make in regard to this anecdote. First of all, in this case, the homophily of Daptone's interpersonal networks actually proved crucial in helping the Menahan single "jump" to a more heterophilous network than it may have typically enjoyed. Though hip-hop producers such as the Hitmen typically scour a variety of sources to find sample material—family collections, used record stores, distribution warehouses, and so on—in this case, it was Jared Boxx, proprietor of New York's Big City Records, who personally handed them a copy of the Menahan single and urged them to take a listen.[60]

Big City is a boutique shop specializing in soul and funk records, the exact kind of store that Desco would have pitched *The Revenge of Mr. Mopoji* to. Not only that, but Boxx is close friends with several Daptone staff, another link in their interpersonal network. In other cases, that insularity could have limited the song's audience, but the intervening factor here was that while Boxx and Big City were part of Daptone's network, the store was also part of the Hitmen's regular stomping grounds. In other words, Big City represented a nexus between different communities and, as a result, Boxx was able to help push the Menahan single to new liseners, which included, for example here, rap producers looking for new source material. Moreover, the Hitmen, in creating the beat and taking it to Jay-Z, then brought the original song to an even broader audience, which, in turn, helped expose the original song to a listener such as that P.S. 20 principal. This leads into my second point.

As unusual an example as "Make the Road by Walking"-"Roc Boys" may seem, in the wake of the attention shed on Winehouse and Jones in 2007, retro-soul's crossover into mainstream pop production has become more and more common. For example, in 2010, Atlanta rapper Cee-Lo hired the Menahan Street Band to produce his new single, "Georgia," while Los Angeles rapper Snoop Dogg reached out to Stones Throw's latest retro-soul star, Mayer Hawthorne, to remix his song, "Gangsta Luv."[61]

Meanwhile, several contemporary R&B stars have also turned to retro-soul for recent efforts. That includes Raphael Saadiq, former frontman for Tony Toni Toné, whose *The Way I See It* (2008) showcased a mastery of any number of past R&B styles, including those out of Memphis, Muscle Shoals, Philadelphia, New Orleans, and of course, Detroit. Joining Saadiq in 2008 was Solange Knowles (younger sister of pop/R&B star, Beyoncé). Her sophomore album, *Sol-Angel and the Hadley St. Dreams*, was also drenched in retro-soul aesthetics: the album's lead single, "I Decided," mirrored the foot stomps and hand-claps of Diana Ross and the Supremes' "Where Did Our Love Go," while "6 O'Clock Blues" was produced by *Back to Black*'s Mark Ronson and directly samples a Sharon Jones and Dap-Kings' instrumental. These artists are just the tip of the iceberg; other, newer retro-soul artists include Los Angeles's Nikki and Rich, Brooklyn's Little Jackie, Iowa City's Diplomats of Solid Sound, Jersey City's The One & Nines, and Chicago's J. C. Brooks and the Uptown Sound, to say nothing of new bands forming outside the United States.

Meanwhile, Jones and the Dap-Kings have enjoyed their most successful release to date with 2010's *I Learned the Hard Way*. For a group that once relied on specialty magazines and college radio shows for exposure, the group has crossed over—at least for now—into mainstream prominence through any number of different venues: National Public Radio, Oprah Winfrey's *O Magazine*, BET's *The Mo'Nique Show*, the CBS *Evening News*, and *Up in the Air* (nominated for Best Picture in 2009), which uses the group's 2006 cover of Woody Guthrie's "This Land Is Your Land" as its opening song.

As the group has gained broader mass media exposure, Dap-Kings members have noticed that their concert crowds have begun to change as well. "I think we're more mainstream now and reaching more people and audiences . . . young and old, black and white. . . . Our audience is growing and more different kinds of people are getting involved in it," says Sugarman, while Brenneck jokes, "I've seen the audience slowly change from young and hip to older and less hip," though he adds it's "still predominantly white." Somewhere between the two men's observations is one common notion—their audience may be changing as a result of retro-soul's slow rise within broader popular culture. Much of that credit is due to the label's perseverance, but they've also reached a point where media outlets are soliciting them rather than the other way around. That is not a benefit enjoyed by similar groups, but Jones and the Dap-Kings' mainstream exposure at least creates the potential through which retro-soul music can reach broader communities of consumers beyond their traditional audience.[62]

I want to end with some speculative thoughts on a crucial part of this discussion, which I acknowledged would be understudied: the agency of retro-soul audiences themselves. While I have tried to illuminate the impact of decisions made on the production side of retro-soul, none of these, of course, are guaranteed to create or correlate with intended audiences. There can be any number of reasons why consumers gravitate toward or away from retro-soul that have little to do with how the genre markets itself. For example, a point I made early on is that retro-soul embodies values compatible with listeners who, like Roth back in the late 1990s, would also prefer to "willfully deny the influence of the last 30 years of music."

For example, if online fan comments are any indication, retro-soul is frequently cast against mainstream, pop chart R&B. For example, someone who signed her comment as "soulsista" wrote on my site (www.soul-sides.com) that Amy Winehouse was "going against the mainstream grain that we have been consuming in the past,"[63] while a different commenter, "sam," wrote in reply to a post about Nicole Willis and the Soul Investigators' album, "Why cant [sic] we get this record here in the USA? Instead we have to listen to crap like Beyonce and Rhihanna [sic]."[64] I don't want to overstate this—there are likely many consumers who are fans of Beyoncé, Rihanna, *and* Sharon Jones and Amy Winehouse; whatever aesthetic differences may separate them are not mutually exclusive—it depends on the ear of the listener. Nonetheless, it would be worthwhile for future research to poll retro-soul listeners on whether their interest in retro-soul is conditioned by their interest (or lack thereof) in contemporary black music styles, especially R&B and hip-hop.

It should also be said that insofar as retro-soul was a relatively niche phenomenon until recent years, part of what draws audiences to it hasn't just been compatible aesthetics, it's also the cachet of enjoying a style outside of the mainstream. The marketing analyst Rob Walker offers a succinct example in talking about fans of the indie rock band Sleater-Kinney:

> What I see . . . is a shift from fandom in the form of devotion to and alliance with a particular artist or artists, to something more like showing off personal taste. A Sleater-Kinney T-shirt just says I like Sleater-Kinney; a playlist filled with obscure stuff you've never heard of, including maybe one overlooked/under-appreciated Sleater-Kinney gem, says something different. Ideally, if you listen to and like the playlist, then it says I have awesome taste. The goal isn't to make you a fan of the Sleater-Kinney. It's to make you a fan of me.[65]

Especially given the traditional antagonism displayed between retro-soul and other music genres, it's reasonable expect that, for some consumers, retro-soul offers a kind of identity marker. Interestingly, Brenneck references this in discussing why he perceives that Jones and the Dap-Kings' audience has become "older and less hip": "10 years ago the soul and Afrobeat revival was hip. Now, it's FELA! on Broadway and Sharon in Starbucks. Not hip. . . . Mainstream goes up, hipness goes down. I guess that's natural."[66] Therefore, if retro-soul continues to penetrate further into the mainstream, it will be interesting to see how that may impact future fans as well as longtime supporters who may not derive as much satisfaction from a style that is steadily becoming more mainstream rather than staying a cultural outlier.

Last, if the growing popularity of retro-soul is helping to diversify its audience, it's worth considering the historical power of soul music to forge "crossover" audiences. As I noted at the beginning, it's problematic to uncritically celebrate R&B's popularity as a sign of racial harmony in the face of unequal institutional conditions. At the same time, though, I believe it's important to emphasize the social power of music to literally bring different people together—in physical spaces for the consumption and enjoyment of music, as well as in the symbolic sense of having common cultural markers among different communities of fans. Especially with an emergent style of music—even one based so studiously on preexisting genres—Negus reminds us that allegiances/interests in genres are not random or inconsequential. As he argues, "Moving within or across musical genres is more than a musical act: it is a social act. More than a struggle for new musical relationships and sounds, it can also involve a desire for new social relationships and harmonies. Crossing genre worlds and bringing new genre cultures into being is not only an act of musical creation, it is also an act of social creation, of making connections, of creating solidarities."[67]

The current state of retro-soul seems to be at a crossroads as it breaks beyond niche status. In doing so, it also seems at the cusp of expanding its connections and if the diversifying crowds at Jones and the Dap-Kings' shows are any indication, the potential for new solidarities may yet fulfill retro-soul's ambitions to recreate some of the more productive and progressive parts of R&B's past beyond just its musical dimensions.

Notes

1. Sasha Frere-Jones, "Amy's Circus," *The New Yorker*, March 3, 2008. Winehouse passed away at the age of 27 in July 2011, just as this anthology was going into the final stages of publication.

2. The term "retro-soul" is popular with the media and audiences but less so with artists themselves. The label most associated with the retro-soul genre, New York's Daptone Records, issued a press release that stated, "Some people don't know the difference between 'Retro' and Old School so I will tell you now. 'Retro' is a trend. Old School is an attitude; it's about doing things the way they're supposed to be done." See "Binky Griptite Press Release," Daptone Records, February 25, 2009, at http://www.daptonerecords.com.

3. This is one of the separating lines between retro-soul and the so-called neo-soul movement of the late 1990s that began with artists such as Maxwell, Erykah Badu, and Jill Scott. Neo-soul clearly draws on aesthetics from the past, especially R&B of the 1970s, but it does not aspire to replicate them *in toto*. Whereas the music of a neo-soul artist like D'Angelo may bear traces of Smokey Robinson's influence, a retro-soul artist would attempt to record something that credibly sounds like Robinson actually produced and recorded it.

4. Ben Sisario, "She's Not Anybody's Backup Act," *New York Times*, September 9, 2007.

5. *100 Days, 100 Nights* did, however, sell upward of ninety thousand units, which is six times greater than their previous album. According to the Dap-Kings' guitarist Tom Brenneck, that higher sale figure "completely has to do with . . . the exposure that the band got from Amy Winehouse, along with a couple other things, but I'd say mostly that." Tom Brenneck, personal interview, May 27, 2008.

6. Kandia Crazy Horse, "Digital Venuses," *San Francisco Bay Guardian*, May 9, 2007.

7. Daphne Brooks, "Tainted Love," *The Nation*, September 10, 2008.

8. Daphne Brooks, "Walk Hard: The Ballad of Amy Winehouse," Experience Music Project Pop Conference, Seattle, April, 2008.

9. Ann Douglas, *Terrible Honesty: Mongrel Manhattan in the 1920s* (New York: Farrar, Straus and Giroux, 1995), 76.

10. Gayle Wald, "Soul's Revival: White Soul, Nostalgia, and the Culturally Constructed Past," in *Soul: Black Power, Politics and Pleasure*, ed. Monique Guillory and Richard Green (New York: New York University Press, 1998), 140.

11. George Lipsitz, *Dangerous Crossroads: Popular Music, Postmodernism, and the Poetics of Place* (New York: Verso, 1997), 62.

12. Dave Gil de Rubio, "Don't Call It Neo Soul," *East Bay Express*, December 5, 2007.

13. Siddartha Mitter, "Jones's Soul Revue Is Stuck in Overdrive," *Boston Globe*, November 19, 2005.

14. Eothen Alapatt, personal interview, March 3, 2009.

15. Of all the best-known retro-soul bands, only Tokyo's Osaka Monaurail has a majority nonwhite line-up.

16. Brooks, "Tainted Love."

17. Craig Werner, *Higher Ground: Stevie Wonder, Aretha Franklin, Curtis Mayfield, and the Rise and Fall of American Soul* (New York: Crown, 2004), 4.

18. Peter Guralnick, *Dream Boogie: The Triumph of Sam Cooke* (New York: Little, Brown, 2005).

19. Catherine Squires, *African Americans and the Media* (Malden, Mass.: Polity, 2009), 176–79.

20. Jon Bream, "Sharon Jones & the Dap-Kings Take Vintage Soul to the Mainstream," at http://www.popmatters.com, November 20, 2007.

21. Mark Reynolds, "Retelling the History of Black Music: Adventures in Retroism," at http://www.popmatters.com, March 7, 2008.

22. Ibid.

23. Keys covered Hathaway's 1973 composition, "Someday We'll All Be Free," for a post-9/11 telethon performance in 2001, while her 2003 number 1 Billboard hit, "You Don't Know My Name," extensively sampled and interpolated the Main Ingredient's 1974 song, "Let Me Prove My Love to You."

24. "Erykah Badu's New Music Video Stirs Controversy," *All Things Considered*, National Public Radio, March 30, 2010.

25. Preston Lauterbach, "Chitlin' Circuit," *Memphis Magazine*, July 1, 2006. The southern blues/R&B scene represents an important and compelling contrast with the retro-soul scene. It's beyond the scope of this essay to properly address that contrast but the main similarity they share is a common cultural source—R&B of the 1960s and 1970s—but from there, the two scenes have developed in very different ways in terms of questions of venues, audience, marketing and artists. They exist, by and large, in different social worlds in terms of geography, class, and race. The

only exception is Lee Fields who has fashioned a successful career in *both* retro-soul and southern blues and notably, his musical aesthetics change distinctly depending on which genre he's recording for.

26. Investigating the racial composition of retro-soul *bands* (as opposed to audiences) is a worthwhile endeavor but beyond the scope of my research. In my interviews with retro-soul musicians themselves, they are at a loss to explain the phenomenon, except to posit—like Reynolds—that younger black musicians are less interested in revisiting older styles than in working with newer ones. However, in an interesting countertrend, many hip-hop artists, including Jay-Z, Common, and, most famously, the Roots, tour with live bands featuring mostly young black musicians playing, in essence, funk and soul riffs. Further research is needed to explore where a disconnect may lie between these musicians and the existing retro-soul bands.

27. Everett Rogers, *Diffusion of Innovations*, 5th ed. (New York: Free Press, 2003), defines homophily as "the degree to which two or more individuals who interact are similar in certain attributes, such as beliefs, education, socioeconomic status, and the like" (the opposite of homophily is heterophily). Homophily is important to the spread of ideas because it is assumed that the more similar two parties are, the more they are likely to influence one another. However, if two parties are too homophilous, while communication may be easier, there is less likely to be *new* information exchanged between them.

28. Rogers, *Diffusion of Innovations*; Leah A. Lievrouw and Janice T. Pope, "Contemporary Art as Aesthetic Innovation: Applying the Diffusion Model in the Art World," *Science Communication* 15 (1994): 373–95; Rob Walker, ed., *The Journal of Murketing*, at www.murketing.com/journal; Malcolm Gladwell, "The Stickiness Factor: *Sesame Street*, *Blue's Clues*, and the Educational Virus," in *The Tipping Point: How Little Things Can Make a Big Difference* (New York: Little Brown, 1994), 89–132. Though Rogers's original diffusion theory applied mostly to technological innovations, scholars and writers have made a convincing case that aesthetic innovations—whether contemporary art (Lievrouw and Pope) or children's television programming (Gladwell)—travel along similar networks as scientific ideas and consumer product.

29. Keith Negus, *Music Genres and Corporate Cultures* (New York: Routledge, 1999), 174.

30. Disclosure: as a journalist, I have written extensively about various retro-soul groups, including Willis and the Soul Investigators, Breakestra, Jones and the Dap-Kings, and others. I have also been the opening DJ for Jones and the Dap-Kings on two occasions (hired by the venue, not the group).

31. "The Poets of Rhythm: History," *Quannum Projects*, February 3, 2009, at www.quannum.com.

32. Jan Weissenfeldt, "A Few Questions about the Poets Early Years?" email to author, February 6, 2009.

33. Gabriel Roth, "Shitty Is Pretty: Anatomy of a Heavy Funk 45," *Big Daddy*, no. 4 (1999): 72.

34. "Soul Fire," *Big Daddy*, no. 5 (2000): 76–79.

35. Roth went after one of the main conventions of P-Funk—slap bass—by writing, in full caps no less, "NEVER UNDER ANY CIRCUMSTANCES 'SLAP' OR 'POP' THE STRINGS OF A BASS. THIS IS NOT FUNKY OR COOL. IT IS TASTELESS AND EMBARRASSINGLY STUPID." Roth, "Shitty Is Pretty," 73.

36. Ibid., 72. In the same article, Roth also writes, "Funk is necessarily raw and straight from the soul. It doesn't come from thinking real hard about counterpoint, odd-time signatures or new theories of harmony. It must be simple so that when folks hear it they want to get down, not ponder its significance in music class."

37. For example, this blog entry posted on the website for Arizona's Zia Records expresses a common frustration with contemporary R&B among fans of retro-soul: "For few fleeting exceptions, the great soul tradition was hemorrhaging bad by the 80's, reduced to little more than a chasm of gutless ballads that promised everything, including everlasting love, but failed to deliver those truly raw soul driven vibes that carried this music to heights that deeply connected the human experience. . . . By the 90's, the great soul tradition was a veritable corpse." See "Daptone Records: Git It In Your Soul," *ZIA Records Blog-o-rama*, December 13, 2009, http:// ziarecords.blogspot.com.

38. Dan Daley, "Gabriel Roth: Recording For Daptone Records," *Sound on Sound*, June 2008.

39. Andy Tenille, "Nicole Willis and the Soul Investigators: Reachin' for Gold," *Harp*, November 2007.

40. Negus, *Music Genres*, 180.

41. Neal Sugarman, personal interview, May 17, 2010.

42. Ibid.

43. De Rubio, "Don't Call It Neo Soul."

44. Isaac Bess, "Soul of the New Machine," email to author, March 7, 2009. By "crate-dig," Bess is referring to "crate diggers," hip-hop and funk-influenced record collectors who would be familiar with the retro-aesthetic of the Poets' compositions.

45. Stones Throw and its subsidiary Now-Again have also worked with two other notable retro-soul outfits: Connie Price and the Keystones in the mid-2000s and Mayer Hawthorne since 2008.

46. Reynolds, "Retelling the History of Black Music," highlights the important relationship between hip-hop and retro-soul by noting, "As hip-hop sampling has brought all manner of obscure beats back into view, a network of djs, collectors and other obsessives has emerged to celebrate those funky sounds excavated from attics, second-hand stores, and wherever else old vinyl has accumulated." Breakestra was one of the first retro-soul groups to make these linkages more explicit by rerecording songs made partially famous by their samplings, including James

Brown's "Funky Drummer" or Third Guitar's "Baby Don't Cry." Other retro-soul groups have made these connections even more explicit—Connie Price and the Keystones backed rappers like Big Daddy Kane and Percee P, while the El Michels Affair has released several singles since 2006 that have either featured instrumental remakes of Wu-Tang Clan songs or included Wu-Tang rappers over their tracks. This relationship between hip-hop and retro-soul is not just aesthetic but, as I have suggested, is one dynamic in the homophily of a retro-soul audience targeted by labels with extensive underground hip-hop marketing experience.

47. Eothen Alapatt, personal interview, March 3, 2009. Also Eothen Alapatt, "Re: Follow-up Question," email to the author, March 16, 2009.

48. In our interview (March 3, 2009), Alapatt also noted that Stones Throw's most popular hip-hop acts, such as Madlib, appeal mostly to white rap fans but he was unsure why.

49. Ibid.

50. Bess, "Soul of the New Machine."

51. Ironically, the group's latest album, *I Learned the Hard Way* (2001), has attained that holy grail of alternative music, retail placement in Starbucks.

52. Sugarman, personal interview, May 17, 2010.

53. Sugarman suggested that one reason why Watts and the Queens may have had more difficulty in gaining wider awareness is that they don't tour as extensively as Jones and the Dap-Kings.

54. Bakari Kitwana, "The Cotton Club: Black-Conscious Hip-Hop Deals with an Overwhelmingly White Live Audience," *Village Voice*, June 21, 2005.

55. For example, I examined the winter–spring 2009 American tour schedules for the Budos Band (a Daptone-affiliated band), Alice Russell (a U.K.-based soul singer), and Chicago's JC Brooks and the Uptown Sound. I cross-checked the venues they were performing in with other acts performing in the same venues.

56. This is the same southern blues/R&B circuit previously mentioned in Lauterbach, "Chitlin' Circuit." Ironically, Reynolds, "Retelling the History of Black Music," surmised: "One senses that if the 'chitlin' circuit' of black nightclubs and theaters still existed, Daptone would take to it like Muslims make pilgrimages to Mecca." Indeed, while that circuit actually still does exist, based on Sugarman's testimonial, Daptone chose not to pursue it for the Dap-Kings' touring decisions. Sugarman, personal interview, May 17, 2010.

57. In an email, I asked Jan Weissenfeldt why he thought the group had traditionally a white following and he replied, "We are a white band, which is most likely less appealing to a black audience." I may not agree with his logic here but I think it is interesting that this was his perception. It may be that presumptions like this would unconsciously bias groups and labels from marketing to audiences they already assumed would be ambivalent about them.

58. Thomas Brenneck, "Re: Cee Lo & Menahan Street Band," email to the author, June 3, 2010.

59. Ibid. A video of the Clinton Hill Wind Ensemble's performance of "Make the Road by Walking" can be found at www.youtube.com.

60. Tim Perlich, "Thomas Brenneck," *Now* 21, October 2008.

61. Mayer Hawthorne is an intriguing example of a latter-day retro-soul artist. Andrew Mayer Cohen is an Ann Arbor native who relocated to Los Angeles to pursue a hip-hop career as DJ Haircut. However, as a lifelong fan of Detroit R&B, he recorded several sweet soul ballads in the style of Smokey Robinson and Curtis Mayfield under the name Mayer Hawthorne and circulated them among friends and family. A copy of his songs ended up in the hands of Stones Throw Records, who successfully released two of Hawthorne's singles before putting out his full-length *A Strange Arrangement* in 2009. He has since drawn favorable support from any number of pop figures, not just Snoop Dogg but also the rapper Ghostface and the rock singer and guitarist John Mayer. See Hobey Echlin, "Eminthen?" *Metro Times*, September 23, 2009.

62. It must also be said that the more successful a group gets, the more their success can *limit* their potential audience. For example, the first time I saw Sharon Jones and The Dap-Kings was in 2003, at a small San Francisco club, the Elbo Room, capacity about two hundred, ticket price ten dollars. The last time I saw them was in 2009, at Club Nokia in Los Angeles, capacity twenty-three hundred, ticket price $29.50. As Sugarman lamented in our interview, "It's a bigger band, expenses are much higher, the venues are much bigger, the tickets are more expensive. It alienates a lot of the young audience, whether it's black or white. It definitely has to be an audience that has to be able to shell out forty bucks for a concert ticket."

63. Soulsista, "When Talking about Music," weblog comment, October 24, 2007, on "Sharon Jones and the Dap-Kings: Long Time Coming," posted by O.W., October 6, 2007, at www.soul-sides.com.

64. Sam, "Great ALbum," weblog comment, July 8, 2007, on "Nicole Willis & the Soul Investigators: A Perfect Kind of . . . ," posted by O.W., October 18, 2006, at www.soul-sides.com.

65. Rob Walker, "Expressions of Music Fandom in the Digital Era," *Journal of Marketing*, September 16, 2008. What Walker is describing here is, essentially, a variation on Pierre Bourdieu's notion of taste: "Taste is the basis of all that one has—people and things—and all that one is for others, whereby one classifies oneself and is classified by others." Pierre Bourdieu, *Distinction: A Social Critique of the Judgement of Taste* (Cambridge: Harvard University Press, 1984), 15.

66. Brenneck, email, June 3, 2010.

67. Negus, *Music Genres*, 183.

Carlo Rotella

Within Limits

On the Greatness of Magic Slim

orris Holt, the septuagenarian bluesman known as Magic Slim, is easy to place on the map: he was born in Mississippi and flourished for many years in Chicago and now lives in Lincoln, Nebraska, and he still travels around the nation and the world playing Chicago blues. But it is getting harder to place anybody else next to him on the genre map of American popular musical styles, since he's one of the few Chicago blues players left who colors entirely inside the genre's traditional lines. And these days it's harder to locate Chicago blues itself among the genres in a way that doesn't suck the life out of it by turning it into archival roots music that matters only for historical reasons—that is, as a source of more popular genres, or as a record of black history and industrial urbanism.

The paradox of Magic Slim is that he's as historical as they come right now, having hit on a style several decades ago and pretty much stuck with it, and yet he's currently the strongest argument for Chicago blues as a living genre. Putting him at center stage gives us a chance to explore what happens when you push to the margins the conventional genre-hero auteur virtues, like originality and technical brilliance and influential departure from norms, and foreground different virtues, like competence, consistency, fidelity, and the willingness to be influenced by the right precursors. That suggests greatness

Magic Slim at the Checkerboard Lounge, June 14, 1982. © Marc PoKempner.

of a different kind, and an expanded definition of virtuosity. Because we tend to equate virtuosity with coloring outside the lines of expectation and tradition, we undervalue the kind of virtuosity that consists of coloring inside the lines. But both kinds are necessary, and necessary to each other, if a popular genre is to persist and flourish.

. . . . .

One way to introduce Magic Slim, oddly enough, is with his contribution to a Led Zeppelin tribute CD. In 1999, House of Blues put out *Whole Lotta Blues: Songs of Led Zeppelin*, part of its This Ain't No Tribute series—with others devoted to the Rolling Stones, Janis Joplin, Bob Dylan, and Eric Clapton—all intended to squeeze some of the remaining financial and artistic juice out of the aging blues-rock combine. Blues musicians were invited to explore the circle of influence in which blues helped give rise to classic rock, which then, once it became the major partner in the combine, reflexively reshaped blues and its audience.

Whole Lotta Blues doesn't want to be a simple tribute. While some of the guitar players try to prove that they can trade broadsides with Jimmy Page, many of the covers make a point of falling into one or another more contemporary genre of what's generally regarded as black music: soul blues, funk blues, and even smooth jazz (from Otis Rush, of all people). The earnest intent behind the gimmicky concept is to explore the web of musical connections that give shape and depth to the canonical narrative concisely summarized by Willie Dixon as "the blues is the roots, all the rest is the fruits." House of Blues wants to embed Led Zeppelin's brand of blues-rock in the blues tradition as one significant historical development among many, on a par with Delta and Chicago and other styles it drew on, and interacting with other styles—other fruits—that came after.

But there's one tune on the CD, Magic Slim's rendition of "When the Levee Breaks," that just doesn't get with the program—not because it acknowledges and resists the program, or because it couldn't be made to fit with the program, but because it isn't interested in the program. Magic Slim makes no special effort to trace the circle of influence or the web of connections, or to either retell *or* contest the standard story of roots and fruits. There's no hushed quality of homage to the rock gods, nor is there any of the contrary sense of a self-consciously authentic bluesman retaking possession of his music by showing the rockers how to do it right. He just plays it in straight Chicago style as a Magic Slim tune—or as close as he can get using session musicians, including harp and slide, which for him amounts to a lush, overproduced symphonic arrangement.

If Magic Slim shows no sign of bending toward Led Zeppelin's version of the song—which he told me the producers sprang on him at the last minute, leaving time for little more than a quick listen to get the words down—he also shows no sign of bending toward the Memphis Minnie song of the same name, or toward the other classic blues in the young Robert Plant's record collection from which Led Zeppelin assembled its tune. Magic Slim just gets the session men lump-de-lumping, as they say, in a Chicago groove, and charges right through it in his usual way— talk-singing hoarsely and playing his Jazzmaster mostly right on the beat and in the groove, marrying the churning attack of first-generation heavy-strings players like Muddy Waters to the bite and crang of second-generation string-squeezers like Buddy Guy and Otis Rush. Because he's playing with session men and not his own band, the Teardrops, he plays it extra-straight and doesn't even indulge in one of his rhythmic habits, which is to arrive just before the band at the turnaround so that they crowd in behind him and bang and scrape a bit as they get sorted out to go all together into the next chorus, a signature expression of the core blues principle of tension-and-release that usually sends a happy ripple through the dance floor and along the bar, making everybody feel suddenly twice as drunk. He doesn't even do *that*; you couldn't ask for a cleaner Chicago reading of the song.

You get the sense that if House of Blues had asked Magic Slim to do "Kashmir" instead, he would have learned the lyrics on his first listen, then counted it off, pointedly doubled the rhythm guitar with his own on the first chorus to situate the band in a solid groove, and launched into singing: "Oh let the sun beat down upon my face, y'all." He would have nailed it in one take, gotten paid, and gone home, having supplied the most satisfying blues on the CD.

. . . . .

I've heard people (including myself) complain off and on over the years about coming away dissatisfied from seeing Buddy Guy, Otis Rush, and the rest of the certified Chicago blues geniuses of Magic Slim's generation, but I've never heard anybody complain that going out to see Magic Slim play live did anything less than satisfy their urge to hear Chicago blues. Going back to when I was thirteen, when Magic Slim and the Teardrops played Tuesdays and Thursdays at the Checkerboard Lounge and it cost two dollars to get in, I've never heard anybody say that he was disappointing, or uneven, or had an off night, or showed off, or played too much guitar, or otherwise failed to deliver the goods.

The best way to appreciate Guy or Rush has been to see him on an especially inspired night, which might just change your life, and you will put up with a few or even a lot of subpar nights to get it. But the way to appreciate Magic Slim, today or at any time in the last forty years, is to see him every night for a month. He still tours steadily year-round, so it's possible to hear a lot of music in that month. No single one of those nights will change your life, and his musical athleticism is not in the others' league, but that month will bring you closer to the genre's vital ideal—and closer to a sense of the historical conditions and internal dynamics that enabled the genre's development in the first place—than could either Guy or Rush at his terrifyingly impressive best. And being satisfied in a particularly Chicago blues way every time out for a whole month is no small thing in itself—and is, in fact, fantastically rare these days. In 1957 or 1965, you could scratch that itch by going out to one of several clubs in several different neighborhoods in Chicago. In 1972 or even 1982, you could still manage it if you picked your spots with care and were willing to travel across town. In the twenty-first century, your best bet has been to follow Magic Slim.

On the other hand, nobody's going around claiming that Magic Slim is a genius for the ages. He's not on the typical short list of the genre's heroes, the era-defining talents who set and reset its course over the decades. If Guy is Muhammad Ali, radiating talent but sometimes too caught up in the theatrics of his own greatness to attend to his craft as he should, and Rush is Sonny Liston, maybe the most gifted of all but undone by a toxic streak somewhere inside him, and Muddy Waters is of course Joe Louis, then Magic Slim is the Larry Holmes of Chicago blues—adept, but not wildly gifted, and wise enough to have invested himself not in ecstatic displays of pure talent but rather in his trade, in playing it right as "playing it right" was defined in Chicago in the 1950s and 1960s. (And I recognize that I'm talking about singing guitar players here and throughout this argument, a bias I'll just cop to, although I share it with many others.) Magic Slim's kind of greatness, the kind that comes of operating within chosen limits, exemplifies what the Hollywood historian Thomas Schatz called "The Genius of the System"—the system, in Slim's case, being the golden-age Chicago blues order. Like Michael Curtiz—and exactly not like, say, Orson Welles—Slim's a master journeyman in the best possible sense of the term, who raises competence and consistency and fidelity to his trade to such a high level that he crosses into significant artistic achievement.

. . . . .

No matter who's in the Teardrops, the band always sounds exactly the same because Magic Slim knows exactly what he wants—a spare, straight-ahead, churning and clanking sound lacking entirely in fuss or flash.

Magic Slim and the Teardrops play substantive party music, even in concert settings, which means that, perhaps uniquely among current practitioners of Chicago style, they make shuffles sound fresh and func-tional, and never dutifully folkloric or archival or simply there to solo over. They play most everything as a shuffle, including most slow blues, for which they just crank down the lump-de-lump rate. The second guitar player does a lot of work in the Teardrops, doubling lines, singing, trading off leads, but when John Primer, a fine bluesman in his own right, played second guitar in the Teardrops, the band sounded no better and no worse than when Junior Pettis, a barely competent sideman, played second gui-tar. Were Magic Slim to do one of those gimmick CDs of duets with rock and pop stars, the best possible outcome would be that John Mayer or Slash or whoever would fit himself so completely into the band that he sounded just like Pettis or Primer. What would be the point?

Now, Magic Slim is a famous one-listen song sponge, and he'll play en-tirely different set lists on different nights. He does all kinds of songs, in-cluding, for example, a wholly convincing cover of Merle Haggard's "Today I Started Loving You Again." But, as with "When the Levee Breaks," every-thing passes through the one-way filter of the Teardrops' sound. When I asked him about it, he put it this way, "I listen to country and western, and bluegrass. I listen to rock. But I don't never try to play it, and I don't want nothing like it from nobody who plays with me. I don't want that doop doop doop shit. I play the blues, in the pocket."

You could see this as a problem, even as *the* problem. Why is it good that Magic Slim is a stylistic black hole who may listen to other blues-related genres but doesn't register their influence in the music he makes?

Compare him to Buddy Guy, whose playing cites a whole range of players, from Hendrix to Prince, who were influenced by him and whose influence he registers in return. Once, during an interview, Guy told me that when we were done he was going in the back to see if he could find a note on his guitar that he'd heard Jonny Lang play earlier that day. Lang, a teenager, had learned from players who learned from players who learned from Guy, who was closing in on seventy years old. We should all be so artistically supple and alive at that age. So if I'm making Magic Slim, and not Guy, the exemplar of the genre, you could argue that he exemplifies stasis, a negative trait. The style's not going to grow or change in his hands, and you can argue a popular genre begins to die when it gets locked into an unchanging form. The alternative to innovation is stagnation, then dessication.

But that's not always or entirely the case. A popular genre can also begin to die when there aren't enough—or any—hardcore practitioners who define its shape by working inside the formal lines of orthodoxy. When that orthodox center disappears, the genre can begin to lose its cohesion, which allows its various elements to drift toward neighboring genres and be absorbed by them. The result may be that the genre mutates out of existence—or, since nothing ever disappears entirely, mutates into a more purely historical style, preserved under glass, interesting mostly to revivalists and samplers. That's what's happening to Chicago blues. Although—or *because*—its DNA can be found all across the ever-changing pop soundscape, Chicago blues is almost played out as a living genre that flourished in a historical encounter between people and place—the music made by black southern Protestants in the industrial urban north.

. . . . .

When I listen to Magic Slim and wish there were a dozen more master journeymen like him out there, I think that maybe the problem with Chicago blues today isn't stasis. The typical stasis beef is that the tourist audience doesn't demand enough innovation, so the genre's turning into electric Dixieland: an endless repeating chorus of "Sweet Home Chicago." But I would say, one, there aren't that many bands that actually know how to play good shuffles all night (so what you get is a sort of funky, sort of rocked out "Sweet Home Chicago" that doesn't fully scratch a Chicago blues itch), and, two, a little stasis would be all right, and in fact would instead amount to classicism, if it happened in the middle of a robust genre with a strong sense of itself and enough edge practitioners attempting purposeful change at its boundaries.

Maybe the problem is not stasis but a passive form of innovation-by-default, by which I mean the drift of Chicago blues toward rock and R&B styles that drew on it, command a larger market share, and have recruited most of its current audience. It's not like blues musicians are saying, "You can find so much that's fresh in our music if you apply the visionary lessons in reflexive influence taught by Mahogany Rush and Anita Baker," and actively experimenting to stretch the bounds of the form; rather, most of them are more passively registering the pressure of what's generally understood to be What People Really Listen To (especially if by "people" you mean baby boomers, who still dominate the blues audience).

Bruce Iglauer, the thoughtful fellow who has run Alligator Records for four decades, proposed to me a few years ago a taxonomy of three basic schools in twenty-first-century Chicago blues. First, there are traditionalists, like Magic Slim, his former sideman John Primer (who also played with Muddy Waters), the fifties-style grinder Lil Ed, and self-conscious revivalists like Nick Moss or Billy Flynn. Second, there are soul- and Stax-influenced players like Jimmy Johnson, Lonnie Brooks, or Maurice John Vaughn. Third, there's what Iglauer calls "the more rocked-out crowd," dominated by five-minute screaming guitar-solo types whose singing rarely matches their fearsome instrumental chops, like Ronnie and Wayne Baker Brooks, Toronzo Cannon, Rico McFarland, Melvin Taylor, Chico Banks, and Carl Weathersby, who may be the best of this bunch because he's the best blues singer and usually plays guitar that talks back to his singing.

If there has been a dominant synthesis in the genre over the past generation that you could hear again and again in the clubs, it would be the pairing of wailing blues-rock guitar with funk rhythms. The compressed platonic model for it might be the guitar break played by Brian May of Queen over Alphonso Johnson's bass on Jeffery Osborne's mid-eighties soul hit "Stay with Me Tonight." This slightly harder cousin of smooth jazz sounds all right under blues singing, but as a style-epoch of Chicago blues, a phase in the genre's development, it isn't really going anywhere with purpose, or doing much. Drifting rather than exploring, it performs a holding action as a semicontemporary-sounding way to play the blues that will do until something better comes along. It sounds like a compromise, really, that sends everybody home sort of satisfied and sort of not.

This style tells a story similar to that told by the Led Zeppelin trib-ute CD: if the roots beget the fruits, one way to revitalize the roots is to put together different kinds of fruits—like funk bass and rock guitar—to achieve fresh syntheses. But there's a catch: if nobody can play the roots, then the synthesis turns into a terminal, seedless fruit—a mule, to shift the metaphor of propagation, that can't reproduce Chicago blues. With-out the center defined by Magic Slim and his handful of stylistic allies to connect the genre to its living roots, the various schools and tendencies in Chicago blues tend to drift off toward neighboring genres that exert a stronger pull. Bass players, chafing at the usual 1–4–5, tend to drift toward funk, which gives them more to do. Guitar players, chafing against the constraint of doubling and answering and extending the singing voice that constitutes a basic element of Delta and Chicago blues styles, tend to drift toward rock and other genres that let the guitar off this leash to wail. Both tendencies have the long-term effect of eclipsing blues singing, which further weakens the core as subsequent generations of musicians then further devalue singing to concentrate on their playing, and so on.

One fantasy short-term policy fix for Chicago blues would be that every-body—and especially everybody who wants to sing, play guitar, and lead a band in Chicago—has to serve a year-long apprenticeship in the Teardrops under Magic Slim. A year of toeing his line, straining to curb your urge to blaze, would be exactly the training that guitar hotshots, especially, need most. Had my Teardrop Tour of Duty Rule been instituted in 1980, you'd now have a generation of monster guitar players who *also* know how to sing the blues, how to treat a blues song like a *song*, and who could then go off and work the genre's various edges according to their inclinations, but with a strong connection to the center, even if they defined that cen-ter as a stock formula they were intent on transcending. The severe limi-tation, the genre-*blindness*, of Slim's one-way filter and his "no doop doop doop" ideology, which would be a sure inducer of deadly stasis if there was too much of it, would under these conditions work to ground unwilled change and make it purposeful, giving the genre more inner life.

That's why I think you can plausibly cast Magic Slim, rather than the virtuosic usual suspects, Guy and Rush, as the last of the great Chicago bluesmen. He's the only major figure left in Chicago blues who could have served that function as my mandatory trainer of genre apprentices—not because he's so amazingly gifted, and not because he took the music in new directions that influenced so many others. In fact, for the opposite reason: because Magic Slim's greatness resides mostly in directing his ablities, and those of his band, to playing it right, within limits, as playing it right was defined way back when Chicago blues emerged with such force and power that it began spreading its influence throughout the soundscape.

Brian Goedde, Austin Bunn,
and Elena Passarello

Urban Music in the Teenage Heartland

You know who's from Iowa? Jazzman Bix Beider-
becke. And nineties arena rock would be nothing
without Slipknot from Des Moines. Mason City is
the backdrop for *The Music Man*, and up by Clear Lake is
where the plane crashed on "The Day That Music Died."
And, well, that's about it.

The Tall Corn state is even less accomplished when
it comes to hip-hop, but here, like anywhere in mid-
America, you find the young and white listeners that
comprise the largest portion of the hip-hop/R&B fan base.
What does music exported from "the urban jungle" do
for a teen in a town with one stoplight? How is urban,
minority culture absorbed and reexpressed in the lives of
its American antithesis?

In the mode of documentary theater, we interviewed
Iowan hip-hop fans and fashioned three monologues
from the transcripts. First, you'll hear McKeen reminisce on his hip-hop education from the only black kid
in his school. Then, Laura, a freshman at the University
of Iowa, explains the seasonal uses of hip-hop in her tiny
hometown. Finally, an MC from Cedar Rapids makes a
case for Iowa's place on the hip-hop map and nominates
himself as the one to make it. While each admits that
hip-hop doesn't seem to want to represent them, in the
heartland they represent hip-hop.

. . . . .

(The beginning of "Children's Story" by Slick Rick plays, then fades out when Slick Rick begins rapping.)

MCKEEN—White, mid-thirties. No accent.

We're in *rural Iowa*, man, we have *nothing* in terms of culture. With Jason, I wanted that culture, I think. Or: I wanted *a* culture. I mean, he wore baggy mint green chino pants with black suspenders over the top of a wife beater with a red fedora? Come *on*, man! I'd never seen colors like that in my goddamn life. I'm wearing Levis, white high-tops, buttoned-down collared shirt, jeans jacket. Waaay too much denim.

Jason was/is, for all practical purposes, black. He was adopted, so no one's quite sure: people say his dad was a University of Wisconsin basketball player and his mom was a white cheerleader. Anyway. He moved to town, and you know how we were that kind of free-to-be-you-and-me culture where all the kids like kinda fight to show how *not* racist we are? You know? So everyone had to be friends with the black kid, at least for a while, and I started to get to know him. I invited him out to spend a night at our house. I told him to bring his albums, so after track practice he tied a stack of his albums to the back of his yellow piece-a-shit bike and we rode the five miles to the farm. He was like, "What the fuck." We were like three miles away on a parallel road and I was like, "See the top of that hill over there? That tree? That's where we're going," and he was like, "*Fuck* you!"

But anyway, first he played me UTFO—but he only brought that over because UTFO is a band that doesn't swear and he knew he'd probably be playin' that shit in front of my parents. Lisa Lips, Run-DMC—I basically got rap explained to me in one night and I was like, "This is *way* better than Duran Duran!"

It's just the whole rap *world* I dug. One thing he explained to me was how everyone has a persona; you have to have a persona. See, we don't have that. Everyone just wants to be "American." Everyone just wants to . . . melt.

Another thing Jason explained was that there's all sorts of collaboration, it's not about one band going up against all other bands competing for the same market, you know? Run-DMC is on Kurtis Blow's albums, and there's the whole Grandmaster Flash and the Furious Five—ah man, I wish I could show you his Grandmaster Flash album because it's like seven dudes, just sittin' there, with like transparent jerry-bags on their hair, just sittin' on the stoop? That's the other thing about Jason is that he carries around this yellow backpack and inside it he has like some sort of spray-on moisturizer and this curl activator? Or deactivator, or something? Because he has this like . . . The Cockroach on the Cosby Show. You know Theo's friend, The Cockroach? With the fade but in the front it sticks out and gets kind of poofy? So Sweet has it *way* poofy and pulls it down like [*trying to remember the name*] El DeBarge. You know El DeBarge? That "can you feel the beat in the rhythm of the night, na-na-na-nana," that guy. He married Janet Jackson when she was like fourteen and shit. Maybe she was eighteen. But I think she was sixteen. Anyway.

So me and Jason started learning the raps we listened to: "La-di-da-di, we like to party / we don't cause trouble, we don't bother nobody / we're just some kids that's on the mic / and when we rock the mic we rock the mic, *right?!*"

He's the one who had the idea to turn "McKeen" into "MC Keen," which is so stupid it's irresistible. But his last name is Sweet, so Jason Sweet, so fuck him, he had it easy. And we wrote a few raps I don't really remember . . . but I remember what we wrote about: There was this kid, Jason Modernock, with this *gigantic* nose he breathed through all the time. His dad was an engineer or something, and he did a bunch of math and determined that the rapture was going to happen on like September 18. He even went on TV and warned everyone to get ready. He even called in and *excused his kids from school*, for the Rapture. So Sweet and I rapped, like rhymingly taunted him for not having been sucked up in the Rapture. And then we also had some rhyme about his dad.   .

But then Jason moved to Waterloo East, because there were black people there, and, uh . . . so I'd ride my bike over there, and play basketball, and I'd listen to him—by then he was in his own little band . . . I can't remember what their name was. But Big Head Earl was in it. I had met Big Head Earl a couple years before that, but now he was Jason's beatbox guy. So I still saw him, but . . . then the next year I moved to Des Moines, which was hell. And I never heard from Jason after that.

. . . . .

(The chorus of Huey's "Pop, Lock & Drop It" plays, and fades out.)

LAURA—late teens, Midwestern farm girl accent

If we're getting ready to go out or something we always turn on some music that'll get us all excited. And this is the music we always hear at the bars, so . . .

Wait—when you say hip-hop; you mean like [*arms in air, bumpty-bump*] Right? So, if I can dance to it, I guess? Cuz that's what I think of. Just if it has a good beat; I don't have to know the words. You don't have to know the words just to [*unsure of term*] pop-and-lock?

Hey—are the Black Eyed Peas considered hip-hop? Because, like, the other day I was listening to them and they were talking about how they're a hip-hop band. But I don't know. Do you think they are? Sometimes I can't—I don't know how to like, *classify* certain things. Because it's not like my favorite kind of music or anything; even when I'm dancing to it I'm really not paying attention to it, but, like, whenever I hear a song my roommates'll be like, "Oh, yeah, they always play this song at Martini's" or something and I'm like, "Oh yeah, that does sound familiar," and then I download it because then next time I'm at the bar, I'll hear it, and be happy that it's on. Like "Sweet Escape" by Gwen Stefani—I don't like her, but I like that song, and I heard it the first time at the bar. It's my ring tone, actually. Wait, is she hip-hop? See, I don't know!

I'm more into country . . . actually, I flip-flop back and forth. I was into country first—I wanted to get that "tough farm girl" look. And then my brother went off to college and brought back this rap stuff, and I was like, oh, OK, I kind of like this, you know, it's kind of rebellious, I guess. And all the guys in my high school thought it was really cool to listen to like, [*with the R*] "gangster" and stuff.

It depends on what mood I'm in, if I'm in a good mood, when I'm feeling good about myself. I know it sounds corny or whatever, but I'm always in a better mood when it's sunny out, and I always, like, have more of a bounce to my walk? So I listen to hip-hop when I'm like, "Yeah, *look at me*." But then, you know, in the summer, with the fair, the Greene County Fair, you know, you show the cattle and the pigs and everything, and everybody comes in, does that, I think that's when I switch to country and get back with the whole farm-girl scene. In summer you slow down, it's just very mellow, like, laid-back. I feel like during the school year everything is moving so quickly and I guess that's kind of how hip-hop is—dancing, moving quickly.

And even at the dances during the school year the slow songs are country, because, well—I have the stereotype that country singers have better slow songs? They just feel like they're more meaningful? And then the hip-hop, you know, break-it-up and slappin-this and blah-blah. Yeah. That was one of the things that made me feel rebellious, because they were talking, you know, "F" this, and all that stuff. And I guess when I'm dancing I don't really think about it, I'll probably just sing it, but if I'm not on the dance floor and am just listening to this song I'm like, "Oof, that's not the nicest thing to say."

My sister likes that stuff more; she really likes Eminem. I don't know if you've ever heard of that concert, the Anger Management tour? My mom was like, "You have to take your sister; she would love it." So me and four of my friends drove to Chicago to the Anger Management concert. It was like, Eminem, and [*with both Fs*] 50 Cent, and Young Buck and all these people, and people were like *out of their minds*. There were drugs everywhere, and people were falling over drunk and doing that whole "raising your arm" like that [*does it, side to side*] you know, to the music? So that was quite the experience. But it was one of the best concerts I've ever been to, just 'cuz it was so different. My friends still talk about it—like, "that was so fun." And I didn't used to like Eminem until that concert, so that's an interesting fact. Because, you know, we don't have too much goin' on in Scranton . . . you know, one stoplight. And the roller rink, but that's technically in Jefferson, and they don't play hip-hop, they play oldies. Actually our stoplight is technically in Jefferson too.

· · · · ·

(*"Eruption" by II MC's plays, fifteen seconds before the chorus.*)

KRUMMIE—white, late twenties, talks "black"

Yo yo yo, check it. This is our anthem. [*Raps over the chorus of his own song*]
     "You don't wanna mess with IA. / You don't wanna test the boys from IA. / Tell it to our face if there's something to say. / You can find us in our state, I-O-W-A."

("Eruption" fades out.)

Yeah, I know, we copied N.W.A on that i-o-w-a thing. But look at the postcards because the postcards are sweet. That's the Five Seasons Monument. On the postcards. If you were wondering. It's in downtown Cedar Rapids where we grew up. They say we have five seasons here. It's like the four regular ones plus one that smells like Fruit Loops because the Quaker Oats factory is here. I'm telling you, it's *impossible* to find good visuals in CR. There's no real stuff to be cool next to in Crapids. For the album, me and BearCat climbed a tree outside the public library.

We made up that "Iowa Hip-Hop, Love it or Hate it" because it's hard here. It's hard because we get stereotyped. They're like, "Oh, *Hiphop*." I remember in the bars trying to sell the album and people would say, "Nah, man; I've already heard Vanilla Ice." People think that because we're from Iowa and we're white we'd be more accepted. But I think we get discriminated on by white people as much as others.

We started in high school, doing parodies. We'd take songs; I wouldn't say it was like Weird Al—it wasn't that bad—but we just off-the-wall kind of different, on the humor side of things. We had this single, "Who's to Blame." It was us talking about how you don't have to be a thug or a gangster or be strappin'; just be yourself. The B side was called "Beyatch." Remember, BearCat, how your dad would flip it so much when he heard it? "Clean it up, clean it up." And you're like [*teenager whine*] "Dad, shut *up!*" We were hearing ourselves on the mic for the first time, just two white boys being crazy.

We did our first show in Waterloo, and we brought in like 150 people from Cedar Falls, 'cuz we both went to UNI. And it was a kinda rocky show, to be honest. We just thought about it wrong. We thought it was supposed to be a rock show, where like, you start at 11 and you rock until the bar closes. So we thought, we've got to ROCK *for three hours.* So we rocked for an hour and a half and took a fifteen-minute break and then rocked for another hour and a half. But with hip-hop, you can NOT do that. Now our sets are like thirty minutes long; forty-five maybe.

Last year, we both went down for the auditions for that MTV show *White Rapper* in Cincinnati, and it was basically *American Idol.* In Cinci, it was just one chick and a camera man. She asked us a few questions and then you had to spit a sixteen-line verse, just a capella, and then she asked us to freestyle about our trip up there. It only lasted like ten minutes. My freestyle was pretty much garbage. I said something about the drive, the hotel, "the mayo"—pretty worthless. I spit four bars and I said, "I'm done."

But I made the top twenty-five and they said, "Pack your bags. Pack. Your. Bags." They did this background check that took forever and I couldn't figure out if they wanted people with stuff in their backgrounds or not. I don't have anything. I've got a kid. I have a girlfriend. I'm from Iowa.

In New York, I only did one audition that was on an actual set. It was MC Serch and Prince Paul watching me and they asked a bunch of questions and made you spit again, and then I had a one-on-one interview with one of the guys from Ego Trip. And we had to do this psychology test; we had to fill out like a *thousand* bubbles and then you had to meet one on one with a psychologist. Make sure you weren't crazy. Make sure weren't going to knife people. On TV. But I didn't make it. So that's my story.

Last year, we were going to move to New York, just because there's more people. And because it wasn't as cliché as L.A., which was totally out of the question. I've never been to L.A. but I have my image of what L.A. would look like. Like South Beach—fast-paced. And we could've done Atlanta Crunk, "Does Your Chain Hang Low," but no way. If we were to go down to Texas or Atlanta and perform, they don't want to hear it unless it's crunk. So then we decided Chicago, and it was going to happen. If I hadn't had my son, we'd probably be in Chicago. We were ready. We were at a point where we were waiting for somebody to go, "Hey, we'll give you a signing bonus of 50,000." Or probably more than that. A million. And it'd be like, "OK." But you know what? You do what *they* want from then on.

So I ended up staying and I'm glad we didn't go because we were looking at it the wrong way. If we went to New York we would have been looked over harder than anything. I think the best plan for us is to take over Iowa. Which we've been doing a good job doing: take over the Midwest. Because out here, you're not seeing promotion or TV. If you hear something and you like it you're going to listen. There's nobody to tell you that it's cool or not. You could just walk into the Sam Goody—well, you can't now, it's closed—but you coulda walked in there and just get stuff. Because out here hip-hop is pure. Iowa hip-hop is *pure*.

Michelle Habell-Pallán

"Death to Racism and Punk Revisionism"

Alice Bag's Vexing Voice and the Unspeakable Influence of Canción Ranchera on Hollywood Punk

I wasn't consciously doing any kind of ranchera music when I was doing punk, but I think part of how I projected was very . . . I don't know if you're familiar with ranchera music but it's . . . very emotional and big and part of my personality on stage did go to "emotional and big" and maybe that's where it came from.
—Alice "Bag" Armendariz Velasquez, 2008

Death to Racism and Punk Revisionism.
—Brendan Mullen, 2008

It would be surprising to find an aficionado of Hollywood punk who did not know Alice Bag, cofounder of the infamous Bags.[1] Alice's presence in Penelope Spheeris's 1981 scene documentary, *The Decline of Western Civilization*, is an unforgettable illustration of how the vocal texture of that moment came to fruition in her piercing, primal shrieks.[2] Alice has also been featured in two recent museum exhibits, *American Sabor: Latinos in U.S. Popular Music* and *Vexing: Female Voices from East L.A. Punk*.[3] While *American Sabor* situates her punk performances inside a continuum of Latino communities' musical practices, *Vexing* highlights the influence of Chi-

Alice Bag, Pat Bag of The Bags, 1978. Photo by Ruby Ray.

canas, including Alice, on the local Los Angeles punk scene. *Vexing* generated unexpected controversy when the exhibit received coverage in the *Los
Angeles Times* by Agustin Gurza.[4] What Gurza had highlighted was the uncomfortable fact that *Vexing* associated Alice Bag with a new punk scene
that emerged *after* the 1970s Hollywood scene and whose performance
epicenter, Club Vex, was located in the historic Mexican American community of East Los Angeles. For Alice Bag to move, symbolically, to East
L.A. created a narrative crisis for fans and producers who wanted to keep
their 1970s musical uprising, to cite the cemetery where guitarist Johnny
Ramone is buried, Hollywood Forever. For those not familiar with West
Coast punk, a debate over the placement of Alice Bag may read as "inside
baseball." Yet these passionate discussions of the minutiae of local punk
scenes of thirty-plus years ago are important for understanding how the
sound of the music developed, and equally important for understanding
how, why, and when narratives of U.S. cultural production made space for
women of color, specifically Chicanas, as "agents of musical history and
cultural change." *Vexing*, in opposition to how Alice Bag's ethnicity was

undefined in the Hollywood punk scene, clearly marked Bag as a racialized subject who was part of an ethnic Mexican community.

Hollywood punks remember their scene as fervently accepting of difference—open to any social outcast regardless of musical training, age, race or ethnicity, class, gender, or sexuality. Alice herself has talked about the creative openness of the Hollywood scene.[5] But by merely repeating a common assertion in an interview that East L.A. punk developed after the Hollywood scene became closed and unwelcoming, Alice Bag found herself accused of a racism that one scenester equated with "punk revisionism."

Both museum exhibits attempted to show that though two distinct punk scenes existed, they were not hermetically sealed. In particular, *Vexing*'s claiming and relocation of Alice Bag to the East L.A. scene created a productive disruption that traced the movement of musicians between the two scenes. Crossing did occur, and Chicanas influenced both scenes. However, those crossings were not without tensions. Who could cross, and under what conditions, were questions that remained unresolved and would resurface decades later, in a defensive response by Brenden Mullen to Gurza's review of *Vexing*.[6]

The controversy I have outlined is worth examining in tandem with an analysis of Alice Bag's performance style because it allows us to explore the cultural stakes of reconstructing Hollywood punk culture, including the racialized tensions that surrounded those scenes, and to utilize an analysis of the body in performance as evidence of the influence of Mexican musical culture on Hollywood punk. Music criticism of the kind I am offering in this essay, that is, a criticism informed by Chicana feminisms, suggests that punk's contradictions and messy politics lead to unexpected musical creations. This criticism also allows for a fuller reconstruction of the archive of Hollywood punk culture, one that focuses on the bodily, sensual, and gestural influences of women in punk.

My invocation of the controversy underlines the importance of public exhibits that retell the story of U.S.-produced music from new perspectives. Mullen's vigorous stand against the reconstruction of punk history, and his desire to leave undiscussed the implications of racialized difference in the punk scene (despite his invocation of racism), illustrate why it has been difficult to narratively "speak" the influence of Chicanas in the making of the scene. However, by examining Alice Bag's sound and gestures, we can begin to reconstruct that history in a way that satisfies

Mullen's desire to stay true to his race-neutral version of the scene and yet shows how much of the scene's richness was due to the creativity and generative difference of its racialized subjects. Alice Bag's performance style provides evidence of a strong Mexican influence in Hollywood punk, yields a more nuanced picture of the scene, and indicates a more sophisticated racialized discourse in narratives of Hollywood punk than has been noticed until recently.

.....

Though Alice Bag had roots in East L.A., she did not, thirty years ago, proclaim Mexican or Chicana identity, as did performers in the East L.A. scene. But Alice realizes now that, without conscious intent, she did bring the influence of Mexican/Chicano musical culture to the Hollywood punk scene via what she herself recently identified as the Mexican genre of *canción ranchera*—"country song." The adjective *ranchera* derives from *rancho*, the ranch of the rural Mexican countryside. Canción ranchera became closely associated with mariachi ensembles after the 1930s as they became commercialized and popularized, nationally and internationally, through Mexican cinema. The postrevolutionary Mexico state promoted canción ranchera above a multitude of other regional genres to construct a sense of shared national culture in a nation profoundly defined by region. In its lyrics, the genre often professes a deep love of the Mexican countryside and its culture. It is no accident that audiences identify the mariachi ensemble playing canciónes rancheras as the official sound of Mexico.[7] If we look closely at Alice Bag's performance style in the Hollywood punk scene, we see how Alice infused the sound of Hollywood punk with elements of cancíon ranchera's vocal aesthetic, *estilo bravío* (wild style)—an influence that is hard to deny, even though this interpretation flips the script of received narrative of the West Coast punk scene.

I acquired the soundtrack of Spheeris's documentary *The Decline of Western Civilization* sometime in 1982 or 1983, and though I wore out the grooves listening to the LP, I never had an inkling that Alice was Mexican American or grew up in East L.A. Alice herself took decades to openly bring her punk performances into dialogic confrontation with canción ranchera's intrepid estilo bravío, the wild and rough vocal aesthetic in which women sing with aggressive, fearless, and bold expression, appropriating so-called masculine traits.[8] Others may have known about these connections from the start. Sean Carrillo, who would later open up a performance venue, Café Troy, with his wife Bibbe Hansen (mother of Beck and an important player in the punk scene), remembers hearing the Bags on local radio. "It gave me a sense of pride and a sense of ownership because coming from East L.A., it was a unique experience to know that the punk rock music that people were coming to clubs and paying money to hear . . . was made by people I went to school with."[9]

During her punk years, Alice resided at the infamous Canterbury Apartments in Hollywood with, among others, Jane Wiedlin and Belinda Carlisle, capricious young women who would later form the wildly successful eighties all-girl group the Go-Gos. Although these women may have influenced Alice in some ways, she credits her mother for her "weird" fashion sense.[10] In a recent blog Alice wrote about learning the art of making do with limited means from the way her mother challenged fashion norms as a young girl growing up in L.A., hemming her skirts to a fashionable length on her way to school and quickly unhemming them before returning home.[11] This fashion practice is reminiscent of young Mexican American *pachucas*, the young women zoot-suiters of 1940s Los Angeles, who customized their outfits to project feminine sexuality and toughness.[12] Surprisingly, Alice's traditional-style father, who would not allow his children to speak English at home, was very supportive of her punk band. After a rambunctious performance at Madame Wong's in Chinatown, he commented, "I don't know what you were singing about, but I loved the way you were doing it."[13]

Alice's Mexican cultural background did not detract from her invention of a particular performance of punk. Indeed, it helped in its creation. But to understand or even detect this we must move toward the embodied knowledge residing in physical movement.

. . . . .

Part of what made the Bags noticeable was Alice's furious onstage power. In 1978 Kristine McKenna wrote in the *L.A. Times*, "Vocalist Alice Bag jerked across the stage in a convulsive rage, spitting out indiscernible, shrew like screeches that were oddly engaging."[14] Later that year McKenna called her "a brash steamroller of aggression. . . . Lyric and melody are mostly irrelevant there. Bags is an exercise in pure energy. The message comes through loud and clear."[15] Bibbe Hansen remembers: "Alice performed with a vengeance and up until that time, I'd never seen women perform like that."[16]

Alice Bag, The Bags, 1979. Hong Kong Café. Chinatown, Los Angeles, California. Photo by Louis Jacinto. For more photos of Alice Bag, see Louis Jacinto's *Punk Los Angeles* (onodream Press, 2007).

"Alice Bag," Alice Armendariz Velasquez's alter ego, was born to fashion-conscious Mexican parents of modest means who immigrated to working-class East L.A. But Alice emerged at the grimy underground club Masque located in an impoverished section of Hollywood, ground zero for the misfit artists, musicians, and fans that were the Hollywood punk scene. The punk chronicler Dave Jones calls Alice the inventor of the West Coast hard-core punk sound.[17] A prime example of this sound is the Bags' 1978 track "Survive," cowritten by Alice and fellow band cofounder Pat "Bag" Morrison, in which her vocals "rise up over distorted electric guitar and sped-up bass and drums, to create a thick, dissonant texture, a trademark of early punk."[18] At the time, Alice's unique style was equated with a particularly feminine brand of aggressiveness: "When Alice takes the stage in torn fishnet hose and micro-mini leopard-skin tunic, she explodes into convulsive, unintelligible vocals. The effect is a raw sexuality not for the fainthearted," wrote McKenna.[19] The *Times* critic, describing Alice along with Diane Chai of the Alleycats and Exene Cervenka of X, hailed these unconventional young women for demolishing models of "women in rock" as coy sex kittens or wronged blues belters. While Alice's Mexican American musical cousin Linda Ronstadt was burning up the charts with velvety vocals, Alice's confrontational style was inciting small riots.

Alice locates her stage rage in the anger and helplessness she felt witnessing domestic abuse within her family. However, when she speaks about her family, her words acknowledge ambiguity. "My father was just incredibly important and I loved him like I had never loved anyone else. He would beat up my mother on a regular basis."[20] Alice's complex emotions were fully released in performance. If she felt helpless to protect the ones she loved, in the persona of Alice Bag she controlled the stage. She recalls a show in San Francisco when "all of a sudden, I see this guy and he's just flipping me off for three or four songs, and I just got so angry. . . . He had wire-rimmed glasses and I just, like, took 'em and I twisted 'em and then I stomped on them on the stage and I threw them back at him.[21] All the violence that I'd stuff down inside of me for years came screaming out . . . all the anger I felt towards people who had treated me like an idiot as a young girl because I was the daughter of Mexican parents and spoke broken English, all the times I'd been picked on by peers because I was overweight and wore glasses, all the important rage that I had towards my father for beating my mother just exploded."[22]

. . . . .

Dressed in a pink, 1960s-style, one-shouldered thrift store dress, with white pointed pumps and her signature dramatic cat-eye *chola* makeup, Alice performs "Prowlers in the Night" in *The Decline of Western Civilization*. As she sings, an eager mosher tries to jump on stage. Alice eggs him on by leaning toward him, puffing out her chest, and flipping her head back, daring him to take her on and switching her microphone to her right hand as if readying it to use as a weapon of self-defense. This is just the beginning.

"Gluttony" is an equally scathing and campy song about adding "pounds to hide the tears." While she performs it, the young men in the crowd mimic her body as it jerks, jumps up, and twirls, the sound of her guttural screams encouraging them. Alice impressively manages to keep singing as she pushes away the swings of a boy mosher whose violently flailing arms and legs have knocked down a female fan dancing onstage. She reaches out as if to block the dancer from the mosher's blows and catches the woman, who is knocked on her back and later practically knocked offstage. This incident seems to add fire to Alice's performance. Before she snaps her head back in a frenzied dance, she takes a deep breath and bares her teeth. The film cuts to the mosh-pit pulsating with young men shoving each other. This performance captures Alice's almost painful piercing scream as she sings, at the top of her lungs, "it's more mad gluttony," starting in a low pitch and drawing out the last part in a piercing high-pitched punk rock *grito*.

What clues does this clip of *Decline* provide for making sense of Alice's aesthetic connection to estilo bravío of the canción ranchera? Like many children of immigrants, Alice grew up listening to her parents' music, and the Mexican canción ranchera was part of her cultural formation. It is a genre both transnational and urban. In Los Angeles County, and other locales in the Southwest where large communities of Mexicans and Mexican Americans reside, canción ranchera is in the air to this day. Diners who step into L.A.'s taquerias and Mexican restaurants, Latino or not, are exposed to the canción ranchera, even if they cannot name the genre. The music has been broadcast on L.A. radio stations since at least the 1930s, and during Alice's youth Mexican movies featuring canciónes rancheras were broadcast on Spanish-language television.[23]

Canción ranchera as a genre is generally associated, as noted above, with the mariachi ensemble. As the ethnomusicologist Cándida F. Jáquez explains, the "urban mariachi tradition emerged as a symbol of Mexican identity in the post-revolutionary period of the 1920s. . . . [I]t was a bold rejection of earlier attitudes that had valorized European culture." In the project of modernity in Mexico, she tells us, the urban mariachi came to "officially represent the tri-ethnic heritage (European, in particular Spanish, indigenous and African) of rural mestizo musical forms" at the expense of other regional genres "differentiated by instrumentation, repertoire, and rhythmic organization."[24]

What is exceptional in canción ranchera as a genre within the Mexican musical repertoire is that it permits women vocalists to perform in bold, brash, unapologetic, and aggressive ways, or what is known as estilo bravío. Most English-speaking audiences in the United States were first introduced to estilo bravío via Linda Ronstadt's 1989 *Canciónes de mi Padre/My Father's Songs*. Ronstadt has long proclaimed her admiration for the famed estilo bravío interpreter Lola Beltran, asserting that Beltran's aesthetics shaped the sound of her rock singing.[25] And Beltran herself had adapted estilo bravío from the great Lucha Reyes, who is credited with developing the style.[26] Quite literally, "estilo bravío" means bold and aggressively, like a man. For Lucha Reyes, it is an act of gender transgression.[27] In Alice's performance, we can see that she brings the intensity of boldness, fearlessness, roughness, and the gender transgression aspect of estilo bravío, to the punk arena.

The song "¡Ay! Jalisco No Te Rajes" ("Jalisco, don't retreat!"), featured in the 1941 film of the same name,[28] is an iconic example of Lucha Reyes's estilo bravío.[29] Set against the backdrop of the Mexican Revolution and the imagery of the charradea or rodeo, Reyes, with her chin up, forcefully captivates her audience by belting out for four counts "Ay," then quickly and volcanically exhorts "Jalisco no te rajes." Even through the relatively flat sound of a YouTube clip, one can feel the resonant power of Reyes's commanding voice. Reyes sounds like a woman commander of the Revolutionary Army as she tells the state of Jalisco not to back down in its revolt. Her voice moves from low-pitched vibrato cry to a growl, then to high-pitched gritos, and then, in the song's final cadence, back to a vibrato resolution.

Because Reyes knew it would distinguish her from other vocalists at the time, she became one of the first women to sing canción ranchera with a mariachi ensemble as accompaniment. Reyes's voice required a special force to be heard, without amplification, above the trumpets of the fairly large mariachi ensemble that included violins, vihuelas, trumpets, and large guitarron. Reyes's volcanic rises in pitch over the ensemble create a dynamic tension whose intensity is impossible to ignore.

It is no accident that Reyes's voice, and her *ademanes*, or facial and hand gestures, seemed to possess the power to command troops. Antonia Garcia-Orozco, an expert on estilo bravío, suggests that Reyes adapted the dramatic, resolute, and masculine facial and hand gestures of the generally belittled revolutionary *soldaderas* (women fighters), who, in the early part of the twentieth century, documented their battle experiences in songs. According to Garcia-Orozco, the singer Chavela Vargas, a contemporary of Reyes, confirms that the style of women vocalists boldly "taking the stage, putting your hands on your hip (like jar handles), throwing your voice . . . talking tough and having a style that was anti-machismo" was generated from soldadera imagery.[30] We can clearly see Reyes's performances of these particular gestures in the clip. As Reyes struts across the screen with hands on hips in her performance of "¡Ay! Jalisco No Te Rajes," she demonstrates many of the characteristics of estilo bravío attributed to her by Garcia-Orozco (there are ten in all):

> A woman's adoption of a powerful presence on stage, an unwillingness to allow the audience to disrespect her, demanding respect as a professional musician from other musicians; changing the pronouns of the songs, changing the intent of the lyrics, creating alternate interpretations of the song, questioning male privilege, mocking male privilege, challenging sexual norms, and interweaving personal narrative with performance.[31]

In the clip, Reyes takes command of her sexuality by slightly lifting her skirt as she sits and sings to three men. However, when the men, exaggerating for the camera, with their tongues hanging out, attempt to grab her derriere, they cross a sacred boundary. Almost out of the blue Reyes turns around and forcefully goes for the throat of one of the men and yanks his collar, meaning to communicate with intimidation, "Don't mess with me." She demands respect from her audience, challenges sexual norms, and mocks male privilege by appropriating it for herself.

In vocal delivery and gestural style, Reyes completely transgressed all protocols for proper women singers of the time, who were expected to be demure, exude passivity, and minimize physical movement. Yet she sang the estilo bravío in the requisite canción ranchera's *China poblana* costume, a feminine costume which aligned with the postrevolutionary culture of modernity in Mexico in promoting deeply traditional and patriarchal roles for proper women and men.[32] Still, in no way did Reyes's feminine dress overpower the message carried in her vocal delivery. For Reyes, like Alice Bag, femininity was not to be equated with passivity. In many ways the contrast between Reyes's vocalization and her costume represents the struggle against the culture of modernity that radical feminists of Mexico's early feminist movement waged during Reyes's childhood.[33] Garcia-Orozco's observation that "Reyes's *estilo bravío* became the only way for women to sing canciónes rancheras for any folkloric singer to have merit or worth" (108) is important to note because it indicates the high likelihood that Alice Bag would have encountered estilo bravío whether or not she encountered the music of Lucha Reyes; Reyes's version of estilo bravío had long since become the standard.

. . . . .

Alice's voice and physical gestures were noted for their raw, "shrewish" power, which meant that reviewers did not need to understand the lyrics to "get the message." By not relying on lyrical narrative to express her punk aggression, Alice performed in the spirit of Lucha Reyes. As the canción ranchera expert Yolanda Broyles-Gonzalez explains,

> Among the unique characteristics of the canción ranchera is its boldness and directness; admired performances have the ability to hit at the roots of an highly charged emotion, to capture a sentimiento . . . the ranchera emotes without much narrative; you fill in the blanks with your own desires. There is a powerful engagement of passion, a release of deep happiness or deep sorrow, love, hatred, or unmitigated enjoyment.[34]

Similarly, and as can be seen in *The Decline of Western Civilization*, Alice would drive her audiences into a frenzy with her vocal power.[35] Her primal shrieks punctuate her songs to create emotional drama. As Broyles-Gonzalez reminds us, the primal shriek holds a special place in ranchera, where "songs serve as a momentary and autonomous space of rehumanization, often culminating in the ritualized grito or piercing primordial scream which powerfully releases emotions through the body or (bodies) and soul."[36] Alice's punk performances were meant to ignite a cathartic release and in a sense, they prevented the violence swirling in her life from breaking her spirit.[37]

Alice's use of dramatic facial and bodily gestures is also reminiscent of canción ranchera's estilo bravío. As Olga Nájera-Ramírez, an anthropologist, explains, "The ranchera performance style includes not only a vocal display of emotions but ademanes (facial, hand, and body gestures) and even tears. Such displays of emotion render the performance one in which the singer, in the words of many ranchera performers, 'vive lo que canta' (lives what he or she sings)." Importantly, Nájera-Ramírez asserts that it is not that "rancheras transparently express what the singers (and their audiences) live but instead the ranchera singers claim they live what they sing as they perform, thus emphasizing the fact that it is a performance."[38]

. . . . .

By taking estilo bravío out of the mariachi ensemble and placing it within a punk ensemble, Alice both punkified estilo bravío, and estilo bravío–fied punk, creating a brand-new subgenre of punk. At the time Hollywood punk was still in its early stages, with no set formula. Alice capitalized on this and gave voice to all the unconscious influences living inside her. By forging what could be described as a dramatic and traumatic performance style, Alice's vocals constitute an undoing of form, albeit a creative undoing that pierces through limited definitions and social narratives of womanhood, ethnicity, and even music. The Chicana feminist Chela Sandoval describes punk as able to "puncture through the everyday narratives that tie us to social time and space, to the descriptions, recitals, and plots that dull and order our senses." Thus Alice's intractable performances embodied a conduit to what Sandoval theorizes as "differential consciousness," that which "is linked to whatever is not expressible through words. It is accessed through poetic modes of expression: gestures, music, images, sounds, words that plummet or rise through signification to find some void—some no-place—to claim their due."[39] Alice's ungovernable performance reached a new level of consciousness of being, of meaning outside of narrative. It performs a state of what has yet to come—what Sandoval describes as a move toward the decolonial.

. . . . .

During a recent lecture, Alice recounted that it wasn't until she started rehearsing for a show for the opening of the *Vexing* exhibit that she made the visceral connection between punk and ranchera in stage performance. This prompted a decision to fuse these two genres that she loved, one she helped to create and one she grew up with in her immigrant parents' home, into a new genre called punk-chera in which she performed traditional Mexican rancheras in a raw and aggressive way. She remembers how in one of her first rehearsals for the *Vexing* show, as she began to sing punk-chera, she realized that she had been channeling the same energy that she experienced in singing canción ranchera to fuel her earlier punk performances. This was a powerful, albeit thirty-years-in-coming, realization for her.

In Alice's punk-chera performance of the cancíon ranchera "El rey" ("The king"; lyrics by José Alfredo Jiménez) we clearly see an explicit punk interpretation of the estilo bravío. The intensity of Alice's performance in *Decline* is present also in her rendition of this classic ranchera. Alice, with clenched fist and commanding gestures, could not have picked a song that better explicated the estilo bravío aesthetic. As Jiménez wrote them, the lyrics read:

"El rey"
Yo sé bien que estoy afuera.
Pero el día que yo me muera,
Sé que tendrás que llorar
(Llorar y llorar, llorar y llorar).
Dirás que no me quisiste.
Pero vas a estar muy triste.
Y así te me vas a quedar.
Con dinero y sin dinero,
hago siempre lo que quiero.
Y mi palabra es la ley.
No tengo trono ni reina,
Ni nadie que me comprenda,
Pero sigo siendo el rey.
Una piedra del camino,
Me enseñó que mi destino
Era rodar y rodar
(Rodar y rodar, rodar y rodar).

Después me dijo un arriero,
Que no hay que llegar primero,
Pero hay que saber llegar.

I know very well that I'm on the outside.
But on the day I die,
I know you'll cry
(cry, cry, cry, cry).
You say you don't love me.
But you'll be very sad.
And that's how you're going to stay.
With money or without money,
I always do what I want.
And my word is the law.
I have no throne, nor queen,
nor anyone who understands me,
but I continue to be the king.
A stone in the road
taught me that my destiny
was to roll and roll,
(roll and roll, roll and roll).
A horseman also told me
that you don't need to arrive first,
but you need to know how to arrive.

"El rey," written from the perspective of a scorned male lover, performs a self-centered arrogance that masks emotional vulnerability. That Alice chooses not to change the lyrics to "I continue to be the queen" in her punk-chera version of "El rey" demonstrates Broyles-Gonzalez's assertion of the elasticity of the ranchera's estilo bravío to contain the musical contradictions Alice brings to her performances: "The symbolic ranchera cultural archive serves up a heterogeneous vision of human possibilities and impossibilities. The singer and listeners of each song rehearse strategies of personhood or selfhood with multiple fractures, contradictions, maskings, differences, and affirmations, each song offers a shift in the articulation of identity. The range of possible moves is encyclopedic."[40] Alice herself asserts that replacing "king" with "queen" negates the song's message. In a lecture she gave at the University of Washington in 2008, she queerly jokes that when embodying the power of the masculine king while singing "El rey" she often asks herself, "Did I just grow testicles!?"

. . . . .

Both the *American Sabor* and *Vexing* exhibits addressed and reconstructed a received narrative about West Coast punk that had not previously registered the influences and presence of Chicanas or U.S.-born Mexican American women. *Vexing*'s title was not just a word play on the vexing effects of the voices of Chicanas on punk scenes. It was a reference to Club Vex, the venue that became the center of the 1980s East L.A. punk scene. Club Vex was established at Self-help Graphics by young musicians from East L.A. who felt excluded by the Hollywood scene.[41] The revisiting of that exclusion in the *L.A. Times* article of 2008, as noted above, was what created the crisis in the narrative of Hollywood punk.[42]

Hollywood punk has understood itself as against the status quo, colorblind, and democratic in that it did not exclude social misfits, amongst them young women, untrained musicians, and queer youth (some of them people of color).[43] Generally within Hollywood punk, creative originality or uniqueness, supported by a discourse of individualism, was prized more than ethnic or racial identity and one was accepted if one did not highlight one's racial or sexual difference. The scene was colorblind in the most basic sense—it did not exclude based on skin color or perceived racial difference. Alice herself has commented on the ways the Hollywood punk scene served as a liberating, even if contradictory, social space, one that nurtured, rather than suppressed an incipient feminist consciousness.[44] According to the American studies scholar Daniel Traber, white participants in the L.A. punk scene could understand themselves as nonracist by "fitting themselves into public discourses surrounding nonwhite" in their quest to realize "their version of white insurgency."[45] Traber, somewhat unimpressed with the diversity of the scene, notes that "one finds nonwhites participating in the L.A. [Hollywood] punk scene, paralleling Los Angeles's multicultural population as whites, blacks (Black Flag's producer Spot), Chicanos (the Zeros, the Plugz, and Suicidal Tendencies), Asian Americans (Dianne Chai, bass player for the Alleycats, and Kenny, a teenage fan interviewed in *Decline*), and others gather in the same social spaces."[46] But Traber concludes that white punk's naive identification with racialized communities, in order to reject the benefits

associated with white middle-classness, did not go far enough and produced "an unintended contradiction . . . as punk drifts toward essential-
izing both whiteness and nonwhiteness." The music critic Don Snowden,
in *Make the Music Go Bang*, writes that Chicana/o bands like the Brat and
others were "barrio-ized by clubs into playing East LA" clubs solely, except
when "bands like X used their power and had them open gigs."[47]

Understanding the process of essentialization of both whiteness and
nonwhiteness helps us understand why Alice was accused of betraying
Hollywood punk when she participated in the 2008 *Vexing* exhibit. An
email sent to her blog charged, "I think it's kind of creepy that you'd sell
out the old scene just to be down with a couple of dink bands."[48] Alice is
a figure who highlights and mediates a previously unacknowledged narrative of difference that hinged on racialized ethnicity. But what really
caught the ire of Alice's fellow punk pioneer, Brendan Mullen, was Alice's
assertion in the *L.A. Times* that the East L.A. punk scene developed once
the Hollywood scene became closed and unwelcoming, making it necessary for some punk performers to create a new punk community. In a
Times preview of the *Vexing* exhibit, Alice muses, "What started out as a
slap in the face turned out to be 'a blessing.' . . . Because from that rejection, from that closed [Hollywood] scene, people just turned around and
created their own scene in their own backyard."[49]

Brendan took issue with both Alice, for her recounting, and Willie
Herron, cofounder of Club Vex, for what he believed was an unfair catego-
rization of the Hollywood scene as exclusionary. His response to Gurza's
article in the *L.A. Times*, which Gurza describes as "a 5,000-word e-mailed
manifesto, titled 'Death to Racism & Punk Revisionism,'" is written with
surprising animosity: "I'm reacting because basically people who weren't
there are calling something that I stood for racist. . . . All I'm asking is,
can they name one specific incident? Not like, 'Oh they might have felt
excluded.' I'm demanding more. Who exactly and where? In other words,
what is this punk scene, this abstraction, that you say excluded you?"[50]
Effectively shutting down any discussion of inequality within the Hollywood punk scene, Mullen ironically accuses Chicanos of "playing the race
card" and of "revisionist history." While addressing Willie Herron, the cofounder of Vex, he pointedly questions, "Why do desperate people always
need someone else to blame their failures on? . . . Sometimes a horrible
rock band is just a horrible rock band, Willy, no matter which way you try

to slice it with the race card." Gurza writes that "Mullen's missive also accuses me of being a professional divider of people whose meal ticket is to keep on perping racial differences. Yet, the story never mentioned race."[51]

Mullen's invocation of the "race card" performs a powerful rhetorical trick. He equates "racism" with "punk revisionism" in his phrase "death to racism and punk rock revisionism." His equation aligns with what Ralina Joseph, a communications scholar, describes as "post-identity" ideology that reflects "neo-liberal leanings."[52] The phrase dismisses those from East L.A. who claim experiences of exclusion, equates their experiences to revisionist history, and does not allow for the possibility of considering racialized exclusionary practices. His statement can be read as an enactment of how, in Traber's words, "the incongruity between positive social intention and negative ideological ramifications rarely penetrates the public discourse of [white] L.A. punks whose status allows them to be heard."[53] To be fair, in his response to the article Mullen does admit that "Chicanos were always a big part of the scene in all its manifestations, and a big reason for its success." But rather than creating a space for discussion about the racialized undercurrents in the Hollywood punk scene, Mullen labels those who have had experiences of racism within punk "racist" because they dare to mention the presence of racialized difference or ethnicity. Any discussion of racism is then deflected away from history by the scene itself.

On the same day Mullen's response appeared, Alice blogged a rejoinder of her own, noting that this controversy was happening despite the fact that "some of the individuals interviewed in the Women in Punk section of my website mentioned that they themselves had difficulty breaking into the LA punk scene in the late seventies. The fact that Eastsiders were making the same assertion was interpreted as an accusation of racism and I was accused of 'playing the race card.'"[54] Alice responds eloquently to the accusations and suggests that punk sensibility, which imagines itself disrupting the status quo, can at times reproduce it:

If whatever argument you are trying to make is predicated on perceived racial favoritism or discrimination, its legitimacy will be called into question; so most people I know will avoid bringing race into the discussion at all. Many Latinos I know would rather deal with racism in quieter ways, precisely because they don't want to be accused of playing the race card. And that is how accusing people of playing the race card effectively silences anyone from bringing up issues of racism and supports the status quo.[55]

Alice's rejoinder powerfully resonates with Joseph's critique of "post-identity" ideology. Joseph elaborates:

> In post-identity ideology manifested in the popular media, merely referencing race or gender, much less racialized or gendered discrimination or racialized or gendered "pride," is dismissed or attacked as outmoded, irrelevant, or even "racist" and "sexist." . . . [P]ost-identity is a fabricated realm where race- and gender-blind fiction supplants racialized and gendered fact. As differential outcomes and structural inequalities are silenced in post-identity ideology, they are, in effect, allowed to continue, unfettered.[56]

Mullen's discursive defense of punk falls in line with Joseph's analysis of "post-identity" ideology.

. . . . .

Alice could not erase the cultural formation she unconsciously brought with her to Hollywood from East L.A. By focusing analysis on Alice's emotive and aggressive stage performance, the body in performance can be read as an archive of embodied knowledge, and we can become more sensitive to the ways punk created an experience that exceeded the socially constructed categories of nation, race, gender, and sexuality in ways that are just beginning to be understood. Alice unconsciously channeled canción ranchera's estilo bravío emotive power and helped create a new musical and vocal sensibility in her performance of punk, thus in fact supporting claims that Hollywood 1970s punk was notably inclusive, but in ways that Mullen, in his insistence on a colorblind narrative, couldn't register. Broyles-Gonzalez's provocative speculation on the emotional, even spiritual, power of the musical practices of ranchera unites the theoretical with the embodied and hints at how the sublime effects of music as a sensory experience might move us to an intractable realm not completely governed by the constructed categories of race, genders, sexuality, and nation:

> How to understand the vibratory fields of the rhythmic and harmonious flow of the ranchera? And how does it alter the social biofield? The sensory nature of oral tradition is little understood. Beyond words,

its beats and melodies evoke deep memory and transfer subtle essences that flow and travel, like wind, water, and fire, from one person to another. That flow moves within the physical and spiritual universe. The musical beats, harmonies and words produce sublime effects: laden vibratory and auditory fields of memory, collectively validated and cherished musical fields that help define social relations and social movement.

The deeply emotional and collective charge quality of ranchera music has the ability to tap into deep levels of being. As such, it is able to bring the gap between the deep unconscious and conscious awareness in the here and now. The ineffable powers of musical flow, of musical intervals, defies description; yet they directly touch and reorganize deep levels of being, of desire, of meaning.[57]

Such esoteric theorizing on social relations in relation to the "effable powers of musical flow," begs the question of what just was being exchanged between Alice's fans, drawn to punks's emotional charge, who weren't conscious of being moved by ranchera aesthetics as they jumped, jerked, and twirled along with Alice. How were both touched and altered? This question opens up a direction for future analysis.

. . . . .

Both the museum exhibits *American Sabor* and *Vexing* can be understood as forms of "disruptive" public scholarship/public humanities that utilize Chicana feminist rock and pop criticism to compel audiences to reevaluate received narratives about the production of punk in the U.S. *American Sabor*'s centering of sound and bodily gestures deployed a decolonial methodology that permitted musical gesture, technique, and attitude to be utilized to reevaluate and remake received narratives. Focusing on the actual sounds and gestures of Alice's performance sensitizes us to the sensual aspects of music. Music implicates physical bodies and the embodied cultural knowledge that spills out in performance. Ultimately, Alice Bag's own statement that she unconsciously used the vocal gestures and affects of canción ranchera provides a way out of the conundrum for both Alice Bag and Mullen. The scholar and music critic Daphne Brooks describes it as the "the imagined subaltern sphere of independent rock culture (dubbed 'indie-rock') [that] depends on a narrow discourse of shared knowledge that largely marginalizes (if not altogether erases) the presence of women and particularly women of color in alternative music culture."[58] My analysis of Alice Bag through Chicana feminist music criticism seeks to make a parallel argument about an imagined sphere of punk culture that has used the discourse of inclusion while historically marginalizing or erasing the presence of women of color. To recognize Latinas as "agents of musical history and cultural change" is to ask not merely how they "fit in" to existing narratives, but how and why certain subjects were excluded from these narratives in the first place.[59]

Notes

This essay was completed with the support of an Associate Professor Cross-disciplinary Conversation Award from the University of Washington Simpson Center for the Humanities and the University of Washington Women Investigating Race, Ethnicity, and Difference Writing Retreat, sponsored by the Diversity Research Institute and held at the Whitely Center at Friday Harbor Labs. Thanks go to my German colleagues at the Center for Interdisciplinary Research in Bielefeld for their feedback.

1. Alice "Bag" Armendariz and Pat "Bag" Morrison cofounded the Bags in 1976. The line-up included Alice Bag (vocals), Pat Morrison (bass and vocals), Craig Lee, Terry "Dad Bag" Graham, and later, after Morrison left the band, Rob "Graves" Ritter. For a complete biography of the band, see Greg McWhorter, "The Bags Interview," at www.artifixrecords.com.

2. *The Decline of Western Civilization*, dir. Penelope Spheeris (Los Angeles, Spheeris Films Inc., 1981).

3. *American Sabor: Latinos in U.S. Popular Music/ American Sabor: Latinos en la Música Popular Norteamericana*, the curatorial team of Michelle Habell-Pallán, Marisol Berrios-Miranda, Shannon Dudley, Rob Carroll, and Francisco Orozco, the Smithsonian Institution, Ripley Center, July–October 2011; Phoenix Musical Instrument Museum February–May 2011; Bob Bullock Texas State History Museum February–May 2010; Museo Alameda June–September 2009; Miami Science Museum October 2008–April 2009; and Experience Music Project | Science Fiction Museum October 2007–September 2008. *Vexing: Female Voices From East L.A. Punk* at the Claremont Museum of Art May–August 2008; and the Museum of Art at the University of Guadalajara November 27–January 10, 2008.

4. See Agustin Gurza, "Rebels with a Cause; 'Vexing: Female Voices From East L.A. Punk' Traces the History and the Legacy of a Key Era," *Los Angeles Times*, May 10, 2008, E1; and Agustin Gurza, "L.A. Punk History Is a Serious Subject: What Transpired in Rowdy Clubs 30 Years Ago Is Capturing the Interest of Scholars," *Los Angeles Times*, May 24, 2008, E1.

5. See Alice Bag, "The Road to (and from) Claremont," May 24, 2008, at http://alicebag.blogspot.com.

6. Brendan Mullen suffered an untimely death on October 12, 2009. May he rest in peace. Randy Lewis, "Local Punk Champion, Masque Founder Brendan Mullen Dies," *Los Angeles Times*, October 12, 2009.

7. See Candida Jaquez, "Meeting la Cantante through Verse, Song, and Performance," in *Chicana Traditions: Continuity and Change*, ed. Norma E. Cantú and Olga Nájera-Ramírez (Urbana-Champaign: University of Illinois Press, 2002).

8. See Antonia Garcia-Orozco, "Lucha Villa's Erotization of the Estilo Bravío and the Cancíon Ranchera," *Women & Performance: A Journal of Feminist Theory* 18, no. 3 (November 2008): 272.

9. Sean Carrillo in conversation with Michelle Habell-Pallán, Chicana/o Punk Aesthetics Colloquium, Center for Chicano Studies, University of California–Santa Barbara, May 5, 2003, transcript.

10. See Alice Bag, "Weird Fashion Sense Runs in the Family," *Diary of Bad Housewife*, February 18, 2007, at http://alicebag.blogspot.com.

11. Alice Bag, "Cuentos de mis padres," *Diary of Bad Housewife*, March 5, 2007, at http://alicebag.blogspot.com.

12. For an excellent examination of Pachuca culture, see Catherine Ramirez, "Crimes of Fashion: The Pachuca and Chicana Style Politics," *Meridians: A Journal of Transnational Feminisms* 2, no. 2 (2002): 1–35.

13. Bag, "Cuentos de mis padres."

14. See Kristine McKenna, "L.A. Punk Rockers; Six New Wave Bands Showcased," *Los Angeles Times*, February 27, 1978, E9.

15. Richard Cromelin and Kristine McKenna, "L.A.'s Hot 12: Rockin' from Orange County to the Valley," *Los Angeles Times*, July 2, 1978, N66.

16. Bibbe Hansen, in *Chicanas in Tune*, prod. Ester Reyes for Life and Times Television,© Community Television of Southern California, broadcast on KCET public television, Los Angeles, 1994.

17. See Dave Jones, "Destroy All Music: Punk Rock Pioneers of Southern California," unpublished manuscript.

18. Script of Michelle Habell-Pallán and Marisol Berrios-Miranda, "Women with Attitude" sound module no. 2 of a 19-part series, *American Sabor: Latino Innovators in US Pop Music*, KEXP Blog, undated, http://kexp.org.

19. See Kristine McKenna, "Female Rockers—A New Breed," *Los Angeles Times*, June 18, 1978, Calendar, 78–82.

20. Alice Armendariz Velasquez, in *Chicanas in Tune*.

21. Alice Armendariz Velasquez, *Alice Bag interview* (1996), Oral History Collection, Experience Music Project, Seattle.

22. Alice Bag, quoted in Michelle Habell-Pallán, *Loca Motion: The Travels of Latina Popular Culture* (New York: New York University Press, 2005), 159.

23. George J. Sanchez, *Becoming Mexican America: Ethnicity,Culture and Identity in Chicano Los Angeles, 1900–1945* (New York: Oxford University Press, 1993).

24. See Candida Jaquez, "Meeting la Cantante through Verse, Song, and Performance," 169.

25. See Rod Davis, "Linda Ronstadt's New Old Flame- Mexican Music: 'I'm Not Good at Doing What I'm Told,'" *American Way*, April 1, 1988, www.ronstadt-linda .com. To hear the influence, listen to Berrios-Miranda and Habell-Pallán, "Women with Attitude."

26. Lucha Reyes was born María de la Luz Flores Aceves, in Guadalajara, Jalisco, Mexico on May 8, 1906. Of humble origins, her mother moved her to Mexico City and she began performing in *carpas* (tent) theaters that staged vaudeville-like performances. Reyes would perform in Los Angeles in the 1920s and eventually traveled to Berlin in 1927 to record her first recording. She lost her soprano voice after becoming ill in Berlin. When she recovered a year later, her soprano had transformed into a contralto and acquired a hoarseness that came to characterize the estilo bravío. See Yolanda Morena Rivas, *Historia de la Música Popular Mexicana* (Mexico City: Alianza Editorial Mexicana, 1989).

27. Linda Ronstadt, speaking in the role as the artistic director of the San Jose Mariachi and Mexican Heritage Festival 2009, paid homage to the music of Lucha Reyes and included in Reyes's bio that "Lucha was a lesbian. We didn't make a big deal about it, but we didn't want it to be buried, either. Being a lesbian was an important part of Lucha's life, and there was no reason why it should have been kept silent. It was something she had to struggle with." See Jenny Stewart, "Linda Ronstadt's Gay Mission," *Gay.com Daily*, August 26, 2009, at http://daily.gay.com.

28. According to Candida Jaquez, "'¡Ay! Jalisco' is often performed as the epitome of regional identity predicated upon a sense of nationalism. Its rapid polka tempo provides an exuberant introduction to what becomes a narrative in which love for a country's region is inscribed upon the body of a young women, ripe for pursuit." See Cándida Jáquez, "Meeting la Cantante through Verse, Song, and Performance," 173.

29. Ismael Rodríguez, screenwriter, *¡Ay! Jalisco No Te Rajes/Jalisco, Don't Retreat*, dir. Joselito Rodríguez, Mexico, 1941. For excellent analysis of the national and cultural significance of Mexican cinema, see Sergio de la Mora's *Cinemachismo: Masculinities and Sexuality in Mexican Film* (Austin: University of Texas Press, 2006).

30. See Antonia Garcia-Orozco, "Cucurrucucu Palomas: The Estilo Bravío of Lucha Reyes and the Creation of Feminist Consciousness via the Canción Ranchera," Ph.D. dissertation, Claremont College, 2005, 108.

31. See Antonia Garcia-Orozco, "Lucha Villa's Erotization of the Estilo Bravio and the Cancíon Ranchera," in *Women & Performance* 18, no. 3 (November): 269–86.

32. For an excellent history of the ways women challenged and negotiated the traditional gender roles via the early twentieth-century radical feminist movement

in Mexico, see Emma Perez, *The Decolonial Imaginary: Writing Chicanas into History* (Bloomington: University of Indiana Press, 1999).

33. In "Lucha Villa's Erotization of the Estilo Bravío and the Canción Ranchera" García-Orozco writes: "At the height of the Porfiriato, the ideology known as the culture of modernity rigidly cast Mexican society into categories and the virtues of Mexican womanhood consisted of economy, charity, modesty, motherhood, devotion to family, patriotism, and punctuality. The clash of the culture of modernity with the Mexican Revolution, created a nexus from which canción ranchera performers established their fan bases in live venues, revistas (theatrical shows or reviews), teatros (theatres), salones (salons), carpas (tent shows), live radio programs, palenques, and cinematic films" (272).

34. See Yolanda Broyles-Gonzalez, "Ranchera Music(s) and the Legendary Lydia Mendoza: Performing Social Locations and Relations," in *Chicana Traditions: Continuity and Change*, ed. Norma E. Cantú and Olga Nájera-Ramírez (Urbana-Champaign: University of Illinois Press, 2002), 196.

35. Craig Lee wrote a description of Alice's effect on audiences in *Decline of Western Civilization* for Flipside Fanzine, no longer available online, though the memorial site is at www.flipsidefanzine.com.

36. See Broyles-Gonzalez, "Ranchera Music(s) and the Legendary Lydia Mendoza," 196.

37. Alice "Bag" Armendariz, interview in *Chicanas in Tune*, 1994.

38. See Olga Nájera-Ramírez, "Unruly Passions: Poetics, Performance, and Gender in the Ranchera Song," in Cantú and Nájera-Ramírez, *Chicana Traditions: Continuity and Change*. Nájera-Ramírez is careful to emphasize that "we must recognize emotional excess as a deliberate aesthetic quality of the ranchera" (187).

39. Chela Sandoval, "Love as a Hermeneutics of Social Change, a Decolonizing Movida," in *Methodology of the Oppressed* (Minneapolis: University of Minnesota Press, 2002), 140, 141.

40. Broyles-Gonzalez, "Ranchera Music(s) and the Legendary Lydia Mendoza," 199.

41. For more on the history of Club Vex, see "Thank God for Punk," in David Reyes and Tom Waldman, *Land of A Thousand Dances: Chicano Rock 'n' Roll from Southern California* (Albuquerque: University of New Mexico Press, 1998).

42. See Agustin Gurza, "L.A. Punk History Is a Serious Subject."

43. See Daniel S. Traber, "L.A.'s 'White Minority': Punk and the Contradictions of Self-Marginalization," *Cultural Critique* 48, no. 1 (2001): 30–64.

44. See Alice Bag, "More Questions about Sex and Punk," February 7, 2007, *Diary of Bad Housewife*, http://alicebag.blogspot.com.

45. See Daniel S. Traber, *Whiteness, Otherness, and the Individualism Paradox from Huck to Punk* (New York: Palgrave, 2007), 141.

46. See Traber, "L.A.'s 'White Minority'," 44.

47. Don Snowden and Gary Leonard, *Make the Music Go Bang: The Early L.A. Punk Scene* (New York: St. Martin's Press, 1997), 152.

48. "I think it's kind of creepy that you'd sell out the old scene just to be down with a couple of dink bands." Alice Bag "The Road to (and from) Claremont."

49. Quoted in Gurza, "Rebels with a Cause," E1.

50. Quoted in Gurza, "L.A.'s Punk Rock History Becomes a Serious Subject."

51. Ibid.

52. For an extended analysis of "post-identity" ideology reflecting neo-liberal leanings and its framing of the "race card" in the Obama moment, see Ralina Joseph's compelling article "'Hope Is Finally Making a Comeback': First Lady Reframed" in *Communication, Culture, and Critique* 4, no. 1 (2011). "Post-identity" ideology upends and undermines U.S. civil rights discourse that had acknowledged institutionalized practices of racism, by assuming that in the current moment racialized inequities have been resolved. Any mention of race, even as a constructed category, is framed as anachronistic or worse, racist.

53. See Traber, *Whiteness, Otherness, and the Individualism Paradox*, 134.

54. Alice Bag, "The Road to (and from) Claremont."

55. Ibid.

56. Josephs, "'Hope Is Finally Making a Comeback.'"

57. Broyles-Gonzalez, "Ranchera Music(s) and the Legendary Lydia Mendoza," 196.

58. Daphne Brooks, "The Write to Rock: Racial Mythologies, Feminist Theory, and the Pleasures of Rock Music Criticism," *Women and Music: A Journal of Gender and Culture* 12 (2008); 61.

59. Sherrie Tucker asks a similar question of women in wartime swing bands in *Swing Shift: "All-Girl" Bands of the 1940s* (Durham: Duke University Press, 2001).

Scott Seward

Of Wolves and Vibrancy

A Brief Exploration of the Marriage Made in
Hell between Folk Music, Dead Cultures, Myth,
and Highly Technical Modern Extreme Metal

In my capacity as a custodian at a small island hospital off of the coast of New England, I have a host of duties to fulfill and I wear many hats. Many of these hats can be fairly smelly, and—given that I usually work by myself, and that the work itself tends to be somewhat mechanical and entirely physical—I find that I can be taken over and nearly overwhelmed at times by certain Proustian reveries triggered by the site-specific odors I come into contact with on a regular basis. Blood, urine, vomit, shit, freshly mown grass, the salt-water spray from the harbor across the street, the oppressive (on hot days almost visible) cloud surrounding the water treatment plant out back, the cleansers and waxes, the iodine and ammonia, the food from the cafeteria, and even the thick, oil-streaked coffee that my Brazilian coworkers brew nightly in the break room far from prying eyes.

All of these smells, separately and in conjunction, have the power to intoxicate me, eliciting primal, nearly forgotten memories that go back as far as the cradle. And of course it's not just the smells. The sights and sounds of birth, death, and the various bodily humiliations visited upon us in between those two milestones, to which my position affords me a unique all-access pass, can fill my

head with all manner of disorienting thoughts and connections that sometimes force sobering reflections about my own life and mortality upon me.

And then there are days when I simply dream of pie. Hot cherry pie.

It might sound a little too cute if I were to say that all of this near-
constant—occasionally alarming—stimulation provides inspirational and
creative fodder for the writing about heavy metal I do every month for a
metal magazine. But it would be true. And it might be a bit morbid if I
were to say that a blood-streaked floor sometimes reminded me of what
I love about metal. But that would be true too. I have an immediate, visceral reaction to the sounds of metal, as I do to the sight of blood, and
both serve to connect me to the past via experience and memory and to
the present via . . . what exactly?

With metal, I think it's that sense of immediacy and vitality that even
mediocre examples of the genre can conjure up simply by virtue of hyper-
bole and that striving to be the most of something. The most base, or de-
based, or most grandiose, or most gloomy, or most triumphant. I respond
strongly to unashamed displays of the will to power in most genres of any
art. At the very least, I admire those who feel as if the infinite is within
their grasp. No matter how misguided their central premise. Believing
you are a badass is half the battle when it comes to creating something
compelling.

And as far as my reactions to blood . . . well, blood is blood. It's freaky
and mysterious and hard to get out of carpets. Even a drop can send me
swooning down the rabbit hole of scabby, incandescent childhood filth
and fury.

If metal is the music that most accurately reflects my physical and
mental reactions to my surroundings, then the metal I find myself attracted to, for reasons of empathy, sympathy, and love of moss-covered
rocks in dark forests, is metal that makes the most of the past—the long
ago and forgotten past, the past of myth, the past of runes, ruins, and
revelry—and incorporates that past into a wholly modern form. I might
say the same about rock music in general (I am a rockhead and love all
its myriad guises), but modern extreme metal—the hard-to-grasp stuff,
the nasty stuff, the stuff that doesn't reach out to include you, the stuff
that lives in its own world away from the crowds, and that doesn't try to
soothe even in its beauty—reminds me more of jazz or rap or tricky modern classical music, which demand that you crack codes before they will

break bread with you and thus are more intriguing and captivating to a devourer of sound such as myself.

Rap and metal are close cousins. They rarely kiss, and when they do people often turn their heads away in embarrassment. And that's because they aren't third cousins—they live two houses down from one another and know each other well. They both have secret languages, worlds built from words and visions and fiery art filled with transcendent repetitions, monster beats, and often dour and dire predictions of harm and mishap. This, in a more general way, was jazz, too, once upon a time—dangerous, noisy, demanding, whispered about. Adored by underground Swedish hordes.

Metal and rap are still the danger sounds today, in a way that traditional and even alternative rock and roll—ever smarter, ever more bloodless and odorless—hardly ever is. There is ferment and experiment and the dedicated plowing of fertile fields in metal.

Of course, it's possible that my personality is simply better suited to the worlds that metal creates than those of other popular genres: tense, prone to delusions of grandeur, brooding storm clouds, fond of Vikings.

As I write this, I am on fire watch. The alarms are out in Wing Three and it is my job to spend the night at the hospital after my shift and search empty offices every hour for the sight of flames softly licking 'round bare wires or the acrid stench of smoke. For insurance purposes. I've set up camp on a couch in Acute Care. It's 4 A.M. and I'm blasting Orphaned Land's 2004 album *Mabool* on my headphones. I am hallucinating slightly as a result of the long day now turned to night.

Orphaned Land are from Israel and are beloved by Arabs and Jews alike. They combine their metal—which is already a combination of mid-tempo death metal and orthodox doom—with aching lyrical passages and harmonies (think of a combination of *Fiddler on the Roof* and *Jesus Christ Superstar*, if you dare) and high-spirited traditional Arabic and Israeli acoustic instrumentation, as well as a smattering of Yemenite chant and your general Old Testament–based vibe and charm.

Mabool is quite a ride. Like most compact discs, it's about twenty minutes too long, but even so, it's a striking artistic statement, and one that took all of seven years to make in between bouts of homeland insecurity and spilled blood and treasure. The acoustic folk elements are soldered seamlessly onto the electric metal chassis. Orphaned Land's metal tends to be fairly middle of the road, and even their death grunts are amiable. Not for them the extreme speed and aggression of, say, the American death metal band Nile, the Ancient Egypt–obsessed brutes who leaven their bombastic pleas to Atum or Osiris with period-appropriate serpentine constructions played on Middle Eastern instruments. Nile's self-described "ithyphallic" metal shares some of the same mythological territory as extreme archeologists and the Mesopotamia/Sumeria metal champs Melechesh and Absu, as well.

Even given Orphaned Land's relative placidness, though, *Mabool* is still an album you must give in to. Sink in to. When it comes to metal, it can be hard for literal-minded music fans to turn off their minds and float downstream. The social conditioning, the stigmas and stereotypes are so strong. I take heart in the fact that more people probably hate opera than metal (which is also a shame, and also partially vocal-based). Then there are the people who can never look beyond the juvenile and cartoonish aspects of some metal; to them the music will forever be monolithic, stupid, not worth bothering with.

The truth is, metal needs its puerile and unsavory elements to be as strong a form as it is. If you exclude the bad and the ugly from art and only focus on the good, then you are truly living in fairyland. Also, you are your grandmother. A song entitled "Strangled by Intestines" will not be to everyone's taste, but dig a little deeper and you will learn that its author, Joe Wolfe (of the group Heinous Killings), is revered by hundreds as one of the greatest low-tone goregrind vocalists of all time.

Orphaned Land has stopped whirling, and I am playing some Magane. Still no sign of fire in the building. The only thing I smell is the overripe scent of dying flowers in a vase of fetid yellow water, left on the table next to me by long-gone wishers of well. Magane are from Japan and make what they like to call Yomi metal. It is a blend of blackened death metal played with punkish zeal plus evocative strains of gagaku (ancient Japanese court music) and Shinto chants and recitations. The band draws lyrical inspiration from the sacred Kojiki text when they're not shrieking about killing Christian pigs and drinking themselves to death. Shintoism!

Many camps of folk-metal lay great emphasis on the pre-everything world. Pre-Christian, pre-Roman, the supposedly anarchic wonderland of ice and snow before the invaders showed up. Metal has always been a great place for people who don't feel they belong in the world. And metal artists go to great lengths to create a home, a place, a life, a philosophy, a religion, out of the tools of their art. Or they go out of their way to trumpet the merits of their own small patch of soil. (Again with the rap comparisons. Speaking of which, you have no idea how members of the California Latino-American thrash-metal revival movement feel about the wrong people wearing high-top Reeboks. It ain't pretty.)

I can dig the sentiment. In the 1980s, I was a big admirer of British anarcho-punks like Crass and Flux of Pink Indians, and the idea that some of these groups had punk-rock communes seemed so cool to me. In the states there was the Dischord house and the Better Youth Organization. Punk boy scouts, really. I would have looked for a like-minded place or cult myself at the time, but I've never been fond of gardening. Other than on an aesthetic basis, I can't say that I'm all that interested in Germanic neopaganism, Odinism, heathenry, mysticism, Satanism, Celtic neo-Druidism, animism, shamanism, or ritual-based Asatru worship practices, but I admire their practitioners' pep and hand-crafted leatherware — and their music, of course.

To be honest, I'm not a huge fan of the real deal ancient folke consorts that dot the landscape of music festivals and renaissance faires. Too often they lack the fierceness and meatiness of music born from blood and fire and plague. Metal bagpipers usually trump the historically accurate but noticeably timid players in the traditional music camps. One listen to Finland's Korpiklaani, who rage like the Pogues after several years of weight-training, sends me instantly back to a time when trolls ruled the woods, in a way that all the progressive, well-meaning Breton flute toodlers in the world could never manage.

I also appreciate how *modern* Korpiklaani and other folk-metal artists are. They dream of the past, but they live in the here and now and make music that reflects that. The Viking folk-metal of Falkenbach, Tyr, Moonsorrow, Ensiferum, and Einherjer recreates old Norse and Celtic battle rhythms and hymns with great liveliness and invention — they can also all play their heathen butts off — but they also never fail to bring new ideas to the world of metal and music through their deft use of modern recording techniques. Not unlike the brave — and oft-derided — seventies progressive-rock titans of yore.

Tyr are from the remote Faroe Islands, equidistant between Iceland and Norway, whose fishing communities have never entirely lost the love or feel for their Viking and Celtic heritage. Tyr even sing some of their songs in Faroese, a language based on Old Norse and once outlawed by their Danish masters (the islands are now an "autonomous region" of Denmark).

Which brings me to my next point. The nationalism, neonationalism, and even national socialism of some modern metal bands is obviously problematic, though less so when you're listening to solo music for lute and are told that the artist is "Aryan-identified." . . . *If you say so.* Luckily, most of the best artists in the folk-metal and even current neo-folk world are simply avid tree-huggers, and while I might not want to ask some of them their views on immigration or rap music, that would probably also be the case with more than one of my favorite country performers.

Even a cursory glance through the interview section of *The Convivial Hermit* magazine—an excellent chronicle and repository for the wit and wisdom of scores of kindred spirits in the metal underground—will reveal more evidence of a longing to be left alone to create in peace than of overarching theories regarding the superiority of any one race. They are all like-minded souls who appreciate the efforts of others around the world and, through their art and fandom, probably have more contact with far-flung corners of the metal omniverse, and thus everywhere, than most provincial citizens ever will, myself included.

Being of the shut-in persuasion, I can appreciate the yokelism involved in writing impassioned opuses about the mountains and terrain right outside your door. I am all for forest-identified performers. Local-color artists who may not stray far from the black and white paint on their palette, but who explore the possibilities of their limited repertoire to its fullest extent. I confess it can even make me a bit wistful. Or envious. My family has lived in New England for over four hundred years and I can't say that I know the land very well. Or that I feel I have a claim on it, or am a part of it. On the island I now call home, the pinkletink is supposedly the herald that announces the arrival of spring in our region. I'm still not sure whether the pinkletink is a bird, a flower, or a frog.

There is a tradition being passed down to young Nordic and Slavic and Asian and Russian misanthropes who are also one-man bands; they are honoring that tradition in their way and making something new and exciting out of it and learning about what makes their home unique. There is a freshness in even the most fumbling attempts to extract meaning from words and sounds and instruments that are, in some cases, thousands of years old. There is bravery in turning your back on modernity, even if only in song, and taking a walk in the woods.

I am currently writing this in Newton, Massachusetts. Don't ask me how I got here. I'm not a fan of the traffic patterns in the area, and the sprawl makes me grit my teeth. Familial warmth makes up for this, however. Not far from here is Brook Farm, that grand, doomed experiment in highbrow communal living where a few of my ancestors, as boys, learned to use a printing press and be Transcendental in every little way. In America, too—where dissatisfaction with modern life runs neck and neck with our ability to create new and often useless things to fill our lives with—there is purple mountain majestic metal that thrives on the arcane—and, apparently, bird-watching. One-man forest rangers such as Sapthuran, Blood of the Black Owl, and Celestiial.

Celestiial's debut, *Desolate North*, on the tiny Bindrune label, is a psychedelic mélange of ambient forest hush, bird sounds, gently strummed guitar, and muffled, tortured cries. It's a beautiful and unsettling journey. It would be practically New Age if it weren't for the whole tortured cry thing.

Blood of the Black Owl's main man—when he isn't harnessing masculine forest energy through funeral doom and wolf howls—has another group devoted to ritualistic drone-based pagan hypnotism. Ruhr Hunter celebrated its tenth anniversary with an elaborate box set that contains, along with a compact disc, moss and soil from the Pacific Northwest, ocean stones, crow feathers, mink bones and teeth, insects, branches, and white birch bark from the state of Maine! You know you want one.

And what did you do to commemorate Ruhr Hunter's tenth anniversary, hmmm? Plant a tree? Skin a mink?

So many of these bands and artists have been digging the nature scene for so long; they have years and years of sorrow, beauty, and brutality under their belts and are content for the most part to be ignored by everyone except the metal faithful.

None of this music is new, of course. Just new twists on old designs. And, in my eyes anyway, a certain perfection of a form. It must also be understood that most of the new music I am so thrilled about is based on newer metal subgenres such as technical death metal, funeral doom, black metal, and the like. Subgenres that came of age in the nineties. There is an all-encompassing synthesis occurring today in music that blurs the line between what is metal and what is . . . art-rock, prog, folk. All manner of genres are being assaulted by musicians who made their name with metal, but who are expanding their sounds so fast and furiously that new labels are being created daily by trainspotting weirdos working feverishly to keep up with new developments. It is a heady age.

So far I've avoided any discussion of the extremely popular and densely populated power metal/symphonic metal/progressive fantasy metal genres that have likewise been experiencing boom times in recent years. This is not because of any distaste on my part for these hirsute, virtuoso, Beowulf-gobbling, steed-riding proponents of all that is metal. Nay, it is only that these sons and daughters of the almighty Iron Maiden deserve their own lengthy scrolls to record their many deeds of valor. Germany alone counts more minions devoted to the exploits of Hammerfall, Blind Guardian, and Iced Earth than you could shake a hobbit's walking stick at. God bless their obsessively melodramatic, triumphant hearts.

Have you heard the new Therion album? *Gothic Kabbalah?* It's a double-disc set devoted to the life and work of seventeenth-century mystic and runic scholar Johannes Bureus. Yowza! Now we're talking. But as ineffably righteous as all that swordplay is, the art that truly stirs my senses lies closer to earth. And is of this earth, in its own weird way. Not that it doesn't also pay homage to what came before in the metallic realm. That is the honor and pleasure of all future metal musicians. Numerous folk-metal bands were inspired by the industrial neo-folk movement of the 1980s that involved people like Current 93, Death in June, Laibach, and Boyd Rice. Some of them, like morbid teens looking to shock, played with the totems and imagery of fascism and brown-shirt martialism.

The influence of industrial noise-rockers Swans, in their head trauma–inducing youth as well as their later apocalyptic folk-music-to-end-all-folk-music phase, can never be underestimated. But the roots of folk and fantasy and cryptic messages from beyond in metal are as old as metal itself. Even older. Born of comic books; sci-fi; horror movies; sword and sorcery epics; Poe; Lovecraft (especially Lovecraft); the British invasion of Kinks, Who, Them, Stones, Pretty Things, Beatles, Yardbirds; the garage rock that followed; ersatz-mystical sitar psychedelia; "Nights in White Satin"; "A Whiter Shade of Pale"; fairytale psych; blues myth appropriations and misappropriations; Coven; Black Widow; Black Sabbath's iron man and wizard, and drug-dream fairies wearing boots (as a kid I was so perplexed by this song—a fairy wearing boots? How is that scary? What am I missing?); the folk revival; hippie folk; the folk-rock explosion; the progressive hard rock of High Tide, Hawkwind, and a thousand unwashed others from Magna Carta to Caravan to Gentle Giant to the Nice to Status Quo to Atomic Rooster to Jethro Tull to Lucifer's Friend.

And not least, of course, Led Zeppelin, who probably could have managed the whole "future of metal" thing by themselves (well, with a little help from Black Sabbath). Their unholy mix of hard proto-metal and exquisite U.K. folk is pretty much unmatched to this day. (That and their tight grooves and swing—two things that many people bemoan the lack of in current hard-ass bands.)

Which brings us to the eighties and what would become the dominant sounds of today's modern extreme metal. The new wave of British heavy metal, second-generation U.K. punk, American hardcore punk, Venom, Trouble, Bathory, Slayer, Hellhammer, Celtic Frost, Metallica, Sodom, Kreator, Mercyful Fate, Voivod, and others would invent the future of black metal, death metal, grindcore, and doom—and they did it with a smile.

All of which brings us, lastly, to wolves. The early nineties Norwegian explosion of black metal, that disharmonic din that transformed a frosty, responsible nation seemingly overnight into a dark den for blasphemous church-burning nihilists, opened up the floodgates of creativity for a small group of outcasts and the metal world has never been the same. It certainly seemed as if death metal, which came into its own in the late eighties, would be metal's evolutionary success story for the nineties as well.

But black metal, so singlehandedly furious, more akin to the sounds of some avant-garde classical experiment in dissonant repetition and not so concerned at the time with death metal's extreme levels of technical prowess, would prove to be a do-it-yourself catalyst for many who had the fever but who lacked the flavor. Norway's Ulver were an early favorite, apart from the unholy trio of Darkthrone, Mayhem, and Emperor.

"Ulver" is the Norwegian word for wolves, and the band's first three albums were a trilogy devoted to the concept of the wolf in man. Millions of people are at least subliminally aware of Ulver, since the poster for their lo-fi black-metal masterwork, *Nattens Madrigal*, was displayed for years on the wall of Anthony Soprano Jr.'s bedroom on the popular HBO drama *The Sopranos*. Pretty tricky of whoever put it there. The wolf in man, get it?

Ulver continue to confound and beguile audiences with everything from IDM and trip-hop-based soundtrack work, massively ambitious art

Ulver, *Nattens Madrigal* album cover. Collection of Scott Seward.

rock, and other forays into the nether regions of experimental sound and vision. After the initial black metal albums they made their name with, they truly turned heads with a double-disc art-metal salute to William Blake's *The Marriage of Heaven and Hell*. They are quirky, to say the least.

For our purposes it is the second album in their trilogy that is most important here. The 1995 *Kveldssanger* is a neoclassical work of plainsong, cello, and guitar, and has enriched everyone it touches to this day. It seems like half or more of the tender spirits involved in the making of modern folk-metal—in whatever way, shape, or form that music comes in—have been possessed by Ulver's singular creation. And wolves have abounded ever since. Wolves, and woods, and ice, and snow, and more snow, and mountains, and blood, and wind, and gods, and even funny little trolls who drink too much beer in the Finnish forests. What a strange bunch.

And yet how confident they are in their torment and fury and doubt and pride and growth and love of land and primitive ghosts.

I leave the last words to Ulver, from their 1999 *Metamorphosis* EP, an experiment in techno-derived wooziness with words by Rimbaud and wolves ever on the mind, naturally.

Note: Ulver is obviously not a black metal band and does not wish to be stigmatized as such. We acknowledge the relation of parts I and III of the trilogie (*Bergtatt* & *Nattens Madrigal*) to this culture, but stress that these endeavors were written as stepping stones rather than conclusions. We are proud of our former instincts, but wish to liken our association with said genre to that of the snake with Eve. An incentive to further frolic only. If this discourages you in any way, please have the courtesy to refrain from voicing superficial remarks regarding our music and/or personae. We are as unknown to you as we always were.

Kembrew McLeod

The New Market Affair

Media Pranks, the Music Industry's Last
Big Gold Rush, and the Hunt for Hits in
the Shenandoah Valley

"The ironically named New Market, Virginia, might not seem the likeliest spot for America's most promising new music scene," *Spin* magazine observed at the height of the 1990s alternative rock explosion, "but its very remoteness may provide an important creative spark." So went the first line of an April Fools joke, a ruse that quickly took on a life of its own.

A few days later the phone began ringing at WXJM, James Madison University's student-run radio station, where I was a DJ at the time. At the other end of the line were record company A&R representatives, a term used in "the biz" that means, essentially, talent scouts. *What about this New Market scene? Any hot bands you can recommend?* The ensuing events played out like a morality play, a pitch-perfect performance that underscored the economic excesses and absurdities of the 1990s.

Although modest in scope and execution—only a few people witnessed it—this fleeting incident says much about the era that produced it. It's a comical cipher, illuminating the inner workings of our media industries, and how they have changed in just fifteen years. For instance, Jim Greer's prank couldn't work today. The most basic Internet keyword search would reveal that a club named Stinky's didn't exist in New Market, Virginia, and that bands like Sweet Draino and Faghag were mere fictions. Bloggers surely would have revealed the ruse within milliseconds, as when *Spin* published a similarly deceptive April Fools piece in 2006 (Chuck Klosterman's fake review of Guns N' Roses's *Chinese Democracy*).

Back then—prompted by little more than a ludicrous article and some phone calls to our student radio station—the major labels rushed to our neck of the woods, setting off an improbable sequence of events.

The Next Big Thing?

Jim Greer, who would go on to play bass for a while in the critically adored indie rock band Guided By Voices, wrote the *Spin* piece when he was making a living as a senior editor at *Spin*. His article, titled "Smells Like Scene Spirit," hit the newsstands of the Shenandoah Valley in mid-March, just as winter was receding from the area. "Eighteen miles north of Harrisonburg, Virginia, and a two-hour drive from Washington, D.C.," Greer breathlessly wrote, "New Market may one day supersede Seattle. The one thing that puzzles me about New Market is that there aren't *already* hordes of A&R weasels sniffing around here. I can't be the first person to hear about this scene."

The article made repeated references to Seattle, which had recently been engulfed in an inferno of hype after the commercial rise of Pearl Jam, Soundgarden, and Kurt Cobain's little band that could. "Seattle," the same magazine had declared a few months earlier, "is currently to the rock 'n' roll world what Bethlehem was to Christianity." The hunt was on for the next big thing, and *Spin* had discovered the newest scene. Sort of.

We lived next door to New Market, in Harrisonburg, a little college town near the border of West Virginia. It was one of the chicken-killing capitals of the country, and pretty much the biggest event to happen in town was the annual poultry parade sponsored by the area's largest industry. Every summer, children and adults alike rode on tractor-pulled floats dressed like chickens and other fowl (presumably right before they were to be slaughtered by the companies that sponsored the spectacle). If there was gold to be had in the hills of the Shenandoah Valley, it was fool's gold.

Even though the Greer piece pretended to be "news," there were many screamingly obvious clues that indicated it was not to be trusted. It was about a town named *New Market*, there was that "Smells Like Scene Spirit"

SPIN OUT

SMELLS LIKE SCENE SPIRIT

A&R reps, start your engines. New Market
Virginia, is tomorrow's Seattle today, and
Jim Greer got the scoop yesterday

The ironically named New Market, Virginia, might not seem the likeliest spot for America's most promising new music scene, but its very remoteness may provide an important creative spark. "Yeah, it's weird," remarks 22-year-old Ted McIntyre, singer-guitarist for New Market's current leading light, Frail. "No one really tours here, so we don't have anybody to copy. Which is cool, 'cause it means we don't have, like, a Nirvana clone or a Pavement clone. Not yet, anyway."

Eighteen miles north of Harrisonburg, Virginia, and a two-

Frail: America's *best* new band.

hour drive from Washington, D.C., New Market may one day supersede Seattle, or at least Chapel Hill, as a guitar-rock mecca. Bands such as Frail, whose feedback driven slacker anthem "Whatever," b/w "I Don't Know," was easily one of the top two or three singles of last year, and melodopunks Exit, whose excellent debut album *No* is due out this summer, have slowly begun to draw attention of indie-rock tastemakers. For good reason—the talent in this town of only 1,400 hasn't begun to be exhausted.

"We don't like to use the word

'scene,' " says 19-year-old Roger Traynor of local heroes Good Food. "It's just a bunch of kids mostly from JMU [James Madison University, a state university in Harrisonburg] who like to hang out and play music." Most days you can find a number of these kids "downtown," at the Happy Chef on 2nd Street (there's also a 1st Street, but no 3rd), scarfing down Happyburgers and sipping slowly on extra large coffees (taken, for some reason, invariably black). "The Happy Chef is cool 'cause it's, like, all ages," says Traynor. "They

don't serve alcohol and a lot of us are too young to drink."

Finding a place to play is the chief concern for most New Market bands. The night I arrived in town, Faghag, a post–Riot Grrrl all-female punk trio, which features, among other things, overamplified xylophones (crank a 'phone through a beat-up Marshall and *jaysus* what a noise), were playing for only the first time in two months at Stinky's, a three-month-old "alternative rock" nightspot on 1st Street. "It's tough," admits 19-year-old lead singer Sally Green. "Especially since we don't often get asked back

to play again." Judging from the small but enthusiastic crowd at Stinky's, the band may have found a home.

Diversity is another important key to the New Market scene. "There's definitely no monolithic 'New Market sound,' " confirms Frail's McIntyre, idly stirring his coffee the next day at the Happy Chef. "Not yet, anyway." For the most part, he's right. While Frail might bear superficial similarities to Exit, which sounds something like the Lemonheads crossbred with Cell, neither sounds anything like Good Food (pop-industrial in a Nine Inch Nails vein but friendlier). Nor do Tension (psychofolk duo), Peru's Weather (quirky They Might Be Giants–type pop), or Sweet Drano (straight grunge) have much in common besides friendship and a common inability to pay rent on time. But the fact remains, any one of these groups kicks substantial butt over most of the major-label swill I've heard lately. Can corporate sell-out be far?

"It'll probably never happen, because nobody here takes themselves that seriously," says Mark Everest, bassist for Slump, a Nirvana-tinged combo that has the dubious honor of having changed its name more than any other local band. ("We used to be Slurp, and before that Spurt," explains Everest. The band's self-run label, Flap or Soil, is derived from two previous

discarded monikers.) "Plus, I think some of the stuff going on here— the better stuff, even—is a bit too heavy for the majors."

The next day at Stinky's ("basically the only place to play now," says Good Food's Traynor, "unless you count the Sheraton in Harrisonburg. They now have Alternative Night on Wednesday"), catch a boffo matinee set from Exit then head off to a barbecue at the house of three members of Roi, a 13-person "experimental ensemble" that specializes in spacey, 25-plus-minute covers of obscure Krautrock (Can, Neu, Faust) songs.

"I was really nervous about you coming," confesses Faghag's Green at the barbecue. "I don't want to ruin what we've got here, almost don't want anyone to know about it. We'd be losing something precious if people started nosing around with bags of money. Although," she shakes her head sadly, "I guess you can't hide forever."

I guess not. Later that evening, I end up at the Happy Chef with McIntyre and Green (yes, folks, rumor has it they're an item). The one thing that puzzles me about New Market is that there aren't *already* hordes of A&R weasels sniffing around here. I can't be the first person to hear about this scene.

"We've had a few calls," admits McIntyre, "but most of the stuff I don't even know about, 'cause usually my phone's disconnected or I've just moved. We move a lot, like every couple of months, so my mail doesn't keep up with me either. About the only place anyone'd be able to find me is here, which isn't likely to happen," he says, looking around. "Not yet, anyway."

"Plus, Frail and Faghag are both breaking up," adds Green, smiling broadly. "Me and Ted are starting a new band called blot. Small 'b.' Just Bee Gees covers."

For the briefest moment I wonder if she's putting me on.

title, and the article—published in *Spin*'s April issue—ended with the line, "For the briefest moment I wonder if she is putting me on." Amazingly, none of these fair warnings stopped the culture vultures from swooping down on us.

Giant Records, Inc., Comes to Rural Virginia

Not long after wxjm received its first call, we were paid a visit from a living, breathing emissary from the recording industry, an a&r rep from Giant Records. The company's name, by the way, is not an arch literary device like, say, Big Culture, Inc.; it was in fact a division of Time-Warner. The record company man was a walking, talking cliché. Jon Bohland, wxjm's programming director from 1992 to 1994, says, "I remember the guy had some seriously moussed hair, and was really into Soundgarden and anything resembling the so called Seattle Sound." Back then virtually no one had a mobile phone, except for this jet-setter—something we all thought was pretty ridiculous.

The Giant Records man was supplemented a few days later by another a&r rep, who was slick in spirit though not in dress. There was a third, probably a fourth, and each rocked their own particular style: one wore a white linen shirt and was described as "kind of *Miami Vice*-ish"; a different one was outfitted in jeans and a hip dress shirt; and yet another dressed more casually—trying to blend in with his Doc Martens and shorts (though his silver metal briefcase made him quite conspicuous).

a&r reps performed their jobs back then—in ye olden days—using telephones and planes. Their corporate kin of today are more likely to let their fingers do the clicking by trolling for artists on MySpace, blogs, and other music-oriented web sites. Also, unlike today, the industry was flush with cash, another factor that brought these industry players into our orbit. This feeding frenzy was a sign of the times, a moment when major labels were throwing lucrative recording contracts at obscure artists. Why? "One word: Nirvana," Sonic Youth's Lee Ranaldo tells me, re-

---

(opposite) This faxed copy of Jim Greer's "Smells Like Scene Spirit" piece came from the archives of the Middle Tennessee State University's Center for Popular Music. Note the article's title, which should have been a dead giveaway that it was a prank. The same is true of the photo caption accompanying a blurry generic image of musicians rocking out: "Frail: America's *best* new band."

wxjm radio station zine and programming schedule.

ferring to the fact that Nirvana made their record company a boatload of filthy lucre. He continues, "The record companies were throwing money at 'quirky,' 'alternative' bands of all sorts, like blind men on a dark night."

Talking about the motivation for his prank, Jim Greer adds, "It was rock's last big gold rush. The fact that some people didn't get the joke not only shows how much money the companies had to blow, but also how desperate record companies were to find the next big thing." Most people I knew were well aware of this dynamic, but I'll be the first to admit there were moments when I would let my critical guard down. And there were a few good reasons for some optimism. "Something was happening in '90s music that isn't happening *anywhere* in pop culture these days, with women making noise in public ways that seem distant now," Rob Sheffield wrote in his 2007 memoir *Love Is a Mix Tape*. In his loving account of this era and his live-wire rock critic wife Renée Crist, who died in 1997, Sheffield remembers it as a time pregnant with possibilities, when real change seemed around the corner, even if it was just at the level of signification.

Kurt Cobain was alarming homophobes by French kissing his band mates and wearing a dress on MTV's macho-metal show *Headbanger's Ball*; also, women-centered Riot Grrrl bands were popping up all around us, even in the Shenandoah Valley. "It seemed inconceivable that things would ever go back to the way they were in the '80s," Sheffield writes, "when monsters were running the country and women were only allowed to play bass in indie-rock bands. The '90s moment has been stomped over so completely, it's hard to imagine it ever happened, much less that it lasted five, six, seven years."

The idea that mass culture would embrace the values of a few freaks was a dream, of course—one we woke from the day those record men arrived in Virginia with checkbooks in hand.

The Poison Dwarf

Of all the A&R reps that descended on our town, the Giant Records rep made the deepest impression. Jon Bohland and the music director of WXJM, Mike McElligott, consented to drive him up to New Market, even though the two DJs were convinced the article was a joke. "I guess Mike and I led him on a bit," Bohland admits. "I recall that once in New Market we actually stopped at a gas station or two where he got out and asked about the club mentioned in the article." Stinky's was, according to one of the "locals" quoted in *Spin*, "basically the only place to play now," adding, preposterously, "unless you count the Sheraton in Harrisonburg. They now have Alternative Night on Wednesday."

Bohland still remembers watching the man from Giant Records talking to a grubby attendant at one of the only gas stations in New Market, a tiny town known around those parts mostly for a Confederate battle-field and a big statue of Johnny Appleseed. "That was really amusing, as nobody knew what the hell he was going on about. He fully expected to find these places when we got there." Bohland adds, "The whole thing was rather surreal, and I don't think Mike or I really appreciated how bizarre it was." Upon returning to WXJM empty-handed, the Giant Records man made a call back to his corporate offices. "He was really agitated," Bohland says, "I think he was afraid of being fired."

Mr. Giant Records had every right to be concerned, given that his boss was the notorious industry hit man Irving Azoff—who managed the Eagles in the 1970s and ran MCA Records in the 1980s, before founding Giant Records. The diminutive record exec was nicknamed "the poison dwarf," and his staff was terrified of him. "I definitely knew his reputation," says Tim Quirk, whose band Too Much Joy was signed to Azoff's Giant Records—which, by the way, never paid the group a dime in royalties. "But my only interactions with him were quite polite and limited to him shaking my hand, looking me in the eye, and *completely lying to me.*"

Irv Azoff was exactly the type of old-school shark that the alt-rock explosion promised to exterminate, but didn't. Today he manages the career of pop diva Christina Aguilera, among many others, and in 2008 he became CEO of concert industry behemoth Ticketmaster, further consolidating his power base. Back in 1993, Azoff's agitated A&R man was looking to invest in the New Market bands name-checked in Jim Greer's article—"bands" like Frail, "whose feedback driven slacker anthem 'Whatever,' b/w 'I Don't Know,'" Greer wrote, "was easily one of the top two or three singles of last year." A generic, blurry action shot of three musicians rocking out was offered as evidence. "Frail: America's *best* new band," read the photo caption, with sarcasm dripping from the italics.

WXJM's Mike McElligott apparently took pity on the Giant Records rep—so he offered the guy some advice. "You know, if you really want to find the area's biggest unsigned band," Mike said, "you should drive an hour to Charlottesville and . . ." Already weary, wary, and annoyed, the record company man cut Mike off with a curt, "No *way.*" The artist recommendation? The Dave Matthews Band, which was not yet signed to a label at the time. Total DMB records sold in the United States since Mike's suggestion: thirty-three million.

The Great Grunge Prank of '92

Jim Greer's 1993 *Spin* article wasn't the first that satirized the alt-rock explosion. Four months earlier, Megan Jasper pulled off the Great Grunge Prank of '92. It was a ruse that was revealed in the pages of *The Baffler,* an independently produced publication founded by Thomas Frank, of *What's the Matter with Kansas?* fame.

Jasper masterminded this prank when she was twenty-five and working at Sub Pop Records (she's now vice president of the label). Because the company had released the first records by the "grunge" acts Mudhoney, Soundgarden, and Nirvana, Sub Pop was a magnet for journalists assigned to the youth culture beat. Fatigued by clueless queries phoned in by reporters, Jasper provided a *New York Times* correspondent with slang terms supposedly used by Seattle scenesters. You know, familiar phrases like "harsh realm," "lamestain," and the perennial favorite: "swingin' on the flippety-flop."

During the interview, the *Times* reporter would feed Jasper a phrase like "hanging out," which she had to translate it into "grunge speak." A couple, like "score" and "rock on," were commonly used by hipsters at the time, but she made most of them up off the top of her head—and a few were indigenous only to Jasper and her friends. The resulting article (published November 15, 1992) resembled the *Spin* piece, only this time it was a prank pulled *on* mass media. "I waited for the reporter to bust me," she tells me, "but it never happened. I then expected an editor to cut the section, but that didn't happen either. I was shocked when I saw it in print."

The article's credibility was immediately torpedoed by a cringe-inducing, mathematically challenged error in its opening paragraph—that *still* remains uncorrected on the *NYTimes.com* website: "When did grunge become *grunge*? How did a five-letter word meaning dirt, filth, trash become synonymous with a musical genre, a fashion statement, a pop phenomenon?" It was accompanied by the following condescending sidebar:

Lexicon of Grunge: Breaking the Code

All subcultures speak in code; grunge is no exception. Megan Jasper . . . provided this lexicon of grunge speak, coming soon to a high school or mall near you:

WACK SLACKS: Old ripped jeans
FUZZ: Heavy wool sweaters
PLATS: Platform shoes
KICKERS: Heavy boots
SWINGIN' ON THE FLIPPETY-FLOP: Hanging out
BOUND-AND-HAGGED: Staying home on Friday or Saturday night
SCORE: Great
HARSH REALM: Bummer
COB NOBBLER: Loser
DISH: Desirable guy

BLOATED, BIG BAG OF BLOATATION: Drunk
LAMESTAIN: Uncool person
TOM-TOM CLUB: Uncool outsiders
ROCK ON: A happy goodbye

The *New York Times* article offered its readers a secret decoder ring that promised to crack the code of the newest, freshest subculture. Of course, it was a faulty device that threatened to envelop anyone who used it in an impenetrable force field of squareness. Jasper's friends in Mudhoney—the Seattle band voted most likely to succeed, before Nirvana beat them to the big time—helped perpetuate the gag. She says that when the group was playing in England, "they embraced the retardation by including those words and sayings in their interviews." Mudhoney's lead singer, Mark Arm, confirms this, telling me, "Yes, we did pepper our interviews with those terms, mostly to amuse ourselves [while on tour]."

Irony-laden T-shirts emblazoned with the word "Lamestain" began popping up around Seattle, and Thomas Frank's *The Baffler* broke the story of Jasper's prank soon after. When the *New York Times* demanded a retraction, Frank replied with a snarky faxed letter that observed, "When The Newspaper of Record goes searching for the Next Big Thing and the Next Big Thing piddles on its leg, we think that's funny."

But in an irony of meta-tastic proportions, Thomas Frank's publication also fell for Jim Greer's *Spin* magazine prank. Issue number 5 of *The Baffler* included an article titled "Brain Dead in Seattle," which held up Greer's April Fools article as a sober example of how entertainment magazines didn't fact check and were, as they say, without clue. After describing how *Entertainment Weekly*, *Rolling Stone*, *Details*, and *Esquire* had systematically slashed and burned their way through Seattle, Chapel Hill, and other fertile music towns, *The Baffler* smugly stated that "*Spin* had settled on New Market, Virginia," adding, "I kid you not."

The joke, it turned out, was also on *The Baffler*.

A Special Showcase Performance

As for the Giant Records man, he was suckered twice: first, by Jim Greer's *Spin* article and, second, by a few dozen college kids informally known as the freak posse. After flying from L.A. to D.C. and then driving two and a half hours in a rental—and then returning from New Market empty-handed—the label representative was conned into attending a supposed "Special Showcase Performance." Or as the freaks called it, "The Sellout Show."

It was held in the basement of my next-door neighbor's house, which occasionally hosted touring punk acts like Nation of Ulysses and the Riot Grrrl pioneers Bikini Kill—and which housed members of a band named Cörn Röcket. Setting up for the "showcase," the band members tricked out their skuzzy basement, an underground lair marinating in spilled beer, vomit, cigarette ash, and straw. The members of Cörn Röcket— spelled with umlauts, of course—placed a La-Z-Boy in front of a bank of amplifiers, for maximum effect. Next to the leather recliner was an ashtray stand loaded with cigars because, as we all know, they are the accoutrement of choice for major label executives. No other prop works better when exclaiming, "You're gonna be *huge!*"

Their special guest barely lasted two songs. Cörn Röcket was an abrasive band that made ears and noses bleed; they were inspired equally by malt liquor, punk rock, and James Joyce. But before the man from Giant Records could leave, a freak stood in front of the door, stripped off all his clothes, and performed a full-frontal interpretive dance at close range. Ben Davis, a WXJM staffer, remembers, "Watching him grow increasingly bewildered and frustrated was amazing. It was really hard to keep a straight face."

Not only was Cörn Röcket aiming to ridicule this particular cog in the culture industry machine, they also poked fun at their peers who were all-too-ready to sign on the dotted line. "Dude, you're totally gonna be famous," friends half-jokingly told Cörn Röcket's drummer, with the decidedly un-rock-and-roll name of William Powhatan Hunt III. Billy Hunt— who has continued to play in colorfully named bands such as The Karl Rove and Straight Punch to the Crotch—doesn't remember being very thrilled. In fact, he doesn't recall much of anything. "I was pretty drunk that day," he laughs, thinking about the moment he missed his shot at the big time.

Still, Billy admits that he wasn't above being psyched, because, he says, "Pretty much every band I've ever been in thinks it'll be big. It's part of the job description, no matter how cynical you are." Other local bands were unambiguously excited about the major labels coming to town. Dave Cour, another WXJM staffer, remembers how the lead singer of a jammy alt-country group named Fried Moose stopped him with some urgency, asking how he could slip a demo tape to one of the A&R reps. John Dinsmore, the band's drummer confesses, "I do remember being astounded but excited that New Market was the next Seattle." He tells me that it took some people in town up to a month to realize that Greer's article was a gag. "I guess if you really want something to be true," Dinsmore observes, "you will readily believe it."

Reflecting back on the New Market Affair, I realize that it subtly but profoundly altered the way I look at the world, and think about media. It also confirmed for me that these kinds of media pranks can teach us useful lessons—though I should point out that by "pranks" I'm not talking about the sort of practical jokes and fraternity-hazing rituals that are merely intended to ridicule. Thoughtless practical jokes and hazing do nothing more than reinforce unfair and unequal power dynamics, and are just plain mean. A *good* prank involves cooking up a story or stage-managing an event to make a larger point, and, of course, have a little fun. In its most basic form, you could say that a prank is performed criticism amplified through media. Or, to reduce it to a mathematical formula, it might be expressed as *Pranks = Satire + Performance Art × Media.*

Executing a prank is a way of messing with media, like throwing a rock in the pop culture pond to study the ripple effect. To use a similar metaphor, it's a bit like skipping a stone across a body of water: sometimes it makes waves, and other times it sinks to the bottom (pranks often fail because of bad planning, timing, or luck, as I have personally discovered). At its most savvy, this form of trickery can help draw back the curtain, exposing how the culture machine works. A well-executed prank gives us a unique opportunity to trace a story as it moves through the mediascape. One thing that many pranksters who came before me have already learned is that when one news organization reports on an item—no matter how ridiculous or implausible—it will often be picked up by other newspapers or television stations.

If a story has been covered by another media outlet, it is legitimized, no matter how illegitimate that story is. This herd-like mentality produces repetitious, cookie cutter news items that dominate the media—a dynamic that helped spawn grunge hype. One key reason why this echo chamber exists is because of increased media consolidation over the past quarter century, in which fewer and fewer companies own more of our information gatekeepers. With mergers come redundancy, layoffs, smaller newsrooms, an increased reliance on wire services, and, therefore, nearly identical news stories. This is something pranksters often exploit, deploying minimal resources to create a powerful snowball effect.

With a well-planned deception, one can speak truth to power—or at least crack jokes that expose fissures in power's façade, often using the news media to do so. Of course, pranks won't change the world, nor do they have the same efficacy as organized direct actions, but they can have an important pedagogical value. The value of a media prank is often not in the final product or event, but in the ongoing process of educating, storytelling, and intervening in the contested world of popular culture. Pranks can also prompt unsuspecting audiences to pause and hopefully reflect—even if it's only for a few seconds. Sometimes a clever deception can help generate the conditions for an honest discussion—in this case, pulling the curtain back to reveal how "the music biz" works. Here are four short lessons gleaned from the New Market Affair.

Industry Rule 378: Don't Believe the Hype

Back when that *Spin* article was published, Glenn Boothe was an A&R representative working in the music industry. Although he laughed when I explained how his peers foolishly came to rural Virginia, Boothe admits that he almost fell for the hype surrounding another far-fetched scene/scheme: Halifax, Nova Scotia. He tells me that in 1993 he almost flew up to the "Seattle of the North" to catch the Halifax Pop Explosion music festival, though in the end he decided not to go. Boothe muses, today, "The idea that you'll find good music solely based a geographic location is pretty absurd."

Although this desire to discover and sometimes invent music scenes happened in the early 1990s with Seattle, the music industry had already descended into self-parody many years earlier. For instance, the "British Invasion" (the Beatles, the Rolling Stones, etc.) gave way to the "San Francisco Sound" (Jefferson Airplane, the Grateful Dead, etc.), which gave way to the next, Next Big Thing in 1968: "The Bosstown Sound" (um, Eden's Children, the Ultimate Spinach, etc.). It was a marketing slogan concocted to promote the nascent Boston, Massachusetts, psych-rock scene.

"The Sound Heard 'Round the World: Boston! Where the new thing is making everything else seem like yesterday. Where a new definition of love is helping to write the words and music for 1968." The ad copy concluded: "The best of the Boston Sound on MGM Records." Though it wasn't quite as ridiculous as CBS Records' 1969 marketing slogan "The Man Can't Bust Our Music," record buyers still didn't buy into MGM's hype. Commercially speaking, the Bosstown Sound went over like a lead-filled blimp.

Industry Rule 4,080: Record People Are Shady

"A&R folks had huge travel budgets and other such expense accounts," says Jenny Toomey, who played in the Washington, D.C.–based group Tsunami throughout the 1990s and cofounded the indie label Simple Machines. "These expenses are absorbed not by record companies, but by other artists signed to major labels, which is one reason why so many musicians never see a penny of royalties."

The term "creative accounting" might not have originated with the music industry, but the two go together like peanut butter and jelly. The annals of music history are littered with stories of musicians' broken dreams and shattered savings accounts—just ask the pioneering African American artists who helped turn rock 'n' roll into big business (of course, you can't talk to some because they died broke and without health insurance). "The reason why recording contracts are stacked against artists," Jenny Toomey says, using the New Market Affair as an example, "is because the major labels have to pay for the tremendous amount of waste that goes on when you have people flying off to Virginia with checkbooks in hand."

The post-Nirvana indie boom was much like the dot.com period. "It was just too good to be true," says Toomey. "In both cases there was a moment of sustained energy supporting a myth." Even though some bemoan the decline of the music industry—of course, many others want to throw a rave and dance on its grave—Toomey's example reminds us of what exactly we are losing. And it isn't pretty, sort of like a poison dwarf.

Industry Rule 6,416: The Revolution Will Not Be Televised

"Nirvana's *Nevermind*, it helped create a pop culture version of this underground thing that had been bubbling up since the 1980s," Jim Greer says. "The reason you loved it was because it was your own. And then, you know, it was just bizarre, around '92, '93, everything took off." Oklahoma City's the Flaming Lips were another relatively obscure, underground band from the 1980s that landed a major label contract, which resulted in one Top 40 radio hit—"She Don't Use Jelly." The band's lead singer, Wayne Coyne, tells me, "Our level of fame was such that we got to revel in the silliness of it all," referring to the time when he and his group made a lip-syncing appearance on the prime-time teen soap *Beverly Hills 90210*. (Sample dialogue: "You know, I've never been a big fan of alternative music, but these guys rocked the house!")

Similarly, Sonic Youth's journey through the 1990s offered them, as Sonic Youth's Lee Ranaldo tells me, "a wild, privileged vantage point for four punk flies on the wall." Not many punks guest star as themselves on *The Simpsons*, as his group did in 1996. Despite our cautious optimism, we knew in our guts that there would be no revolution—televised, recorded, or otherwise. And pretty soon, it was all over. "After Kurt [Cobain] died, stuff started to collapse," Greer says. "Bands with one hit ended up tanking on their second major label album, and what was left was a bunch of corporate-grunge bands, and then later Britney Spears and the Backstreet Boys. You know, just *total product*."

Rob Sheffield mournfully notes, "The radio has become homogenized, with practically every station around the country bought up and programmed by the same corporation, and in a shocking coincidence, the weird girls have been shoved back underground." The investments in altrock didn't pay off, and so the industry went back to pushing boy bands, teen teases, cock rock, and other safe bets. The countercultural bubble burst.

Industry Rule 9,214: Nothing Is Guaranteed

Before I get too Frankfurt School on you, I should point out that it's not as if there is some wizard behind the culture industry curtain, pulling levers that deliver guaranteed results. Music history is littered with failed million-dollar publicity campaigns, and bad business decisions—such as what happened at Irving Azoff's MCA Records in the 1980s with the group Point Blank. This generic late 1970s/early 1980s corporate boogie band remains deservedly forgotten, despite the label's best promotional efforts on the ironically titled *Airplay*, from 1979. (Their follow ups—*The Hard Way*, *American Excess*, and *On a Roll*—similarly failed to catch fire.)

Conversely, take the Dave Matthews Band, whose regional rise occurred simultaneously with the national grunge craze—heavy guitars and all. Matthews's sweeter, more upbeat sound was at odds with the prevailing trends of the day, and major labels like Giant Records initially ignored his group. It was only after the success of Matthews's independently released debut, released a few months after the New Market Affair, that he became a known commodity.

Corporations are not animated creatures with all-knowing, powerful computer brains. *People* run them, and sometimes they aren't smart enough to mount a conspiracy on consumers, like the man in the following example. Jay Zehr, who owned the only local record store in Harrisonburg, remembers that four days after the article came out a guy "straight out of central casting" came in looking for Stinky's, the club mentioned in *Spin*. He had just driven down from New Market after being told by befuddled locals that Stinky's might be in Harrisonburg. Jay recalls that he was "very pushy—a real know-it-all, big city personality who wasn't as bright as he thought he was."

Jay humored the man's delusions, and then unintentionally sent him on a fool's errand after he joked that the A&R rep should try to snag Fugazi—an uncompromising post-punk band signed to Dischord, one of America's most important, long-running independent labels. "He hadn't heard of them before, took me seriously, and got real excited about that idea, too," Jay says. "That's where he said he was going when he left."

Better Living through Pranks

We weren't the first to have our own private bohemia served back to us on a blue plate special, nor were we naive enough to think our situation was unique. Nevertheless, the New Market Affair brought a few things into sharp focus. When we discovered years ago that it was quite easy to manipulate our media system, and how easily it can manipulate us, that deeply affected our gang. Around that same time, we also watched as the entertainment industry's funhouse mirrors distorted a musical culture that we cared about.

Irreverence, irony, and pranks—a three-in-one toolkit for better living—seemed the only option left open for us, aside from driving up to New York City and throwing a brick through the plate glass windows of the Time-Warner building. It's a methodology still widely used today, and it has informed many in my aging demographic, and beyond. The New Market Affair taught me, taught us, the importance of the put-on—how pranks can be productive, instructive.

It was also a reminder of the importance of community. Away from the cosmopolitan centers, living in the geographic and cultural margins, we were left alone in rural Virginia to do it ourselves. I'm reminded of something the writer Pagan Kennedy said about the network of friends, musicians, writers, and artists who were a part of her life around this period. It's a lonely world, she writes, "a place of Personal ads, identical Burger Kings, strip malls, TV laugh tracks, lite rock. But luckily we don't need mass culture, because we can stay home and make our own fun."

We were a bunch of goofballs, misfits, slackers, overachievers, and freaks who liked spending time together *doing* and *making* stuff, and the New Market Affair provided us with an amusing playground for our experiments. When Big Culture, Inc., came calling—in person—we had fun, a whole lotta of fun, which was a life-affirming lesson I never forgot.

Bonus Track

Well, actually, I nearly did forget this ephemeral event; it was a memory that by all rights should have been erased by the sandblaster of time.

In order to reconstruct this narrative, I had to sift through artifacts pried from damaged and conflicting memories. This was made even more difficult because this story's very foundation was built on a sinkhole of deception. When I started my research, the *Spin* article wasn't included in a single electronic database index—it still isn't—and there was absolutely no mention of it on the Interweb. It's like it never happened, and I began to question whether it did.

But when I called the Center for Popular Music at Middle Tennessee State University—a place with such an unlikely name couldn't possibly exist, right?—a faxed copy of "Smells Like Scene Spirit" finally fell into my hands. My next big challenge was tracking down one or more of the A&R guys who visited Virginia fifteen years ago. After asking well over a dozen behind-the-scenes music biz types—and following many more leads in the process—I repeatedly hit dead ends.

I guess nobody wants to step forward and volunteer himself as the butt of an elaborate joke. The failed search was worth it if only for the amusement value; I acquired some colorful *Spinal Tap*–esque gossip about various entertainment lawyers and other "suits" who were working in the 1990s . . . *Good guy, though he was totally coked out during that time. . . . Yeah, he was fired after being "serviced" in his office by a female staffer with his window shades up, and he was later murdered. . . . Man, that dude nearly got kicked in the head and so he quit, but he was also on a lot of drugs . . .* etc., etc.

I said at the beginning of this essay that Jim Greer's prank wouldn't have worked in the age of the Internet. But I should also point out that I couldn't have told this story *without* it. Email and social networking sites like Facebook allowed me to tap into memories that would otherwise have been inaccessible to me in another moment in time. In digging up this story, sorting fiction from fact was hard, especially when a particularly surprising factoid seemed too good to be true. The biggest mind-blower, personally, was discovering that Jim Greer modeled the article not on the region of the Shenandoah Valley where I used to live, but on another remote place where I have resided for over ten years.

"I originally set it in Iowa City," Greer tells me, explaining that he grew fond of this college town when passing through on a road trip. "I really liked the fact that Iowa City was in the middle of nowhere, and if the joke worked, then people would have to make a very, very long trek." Greer's editor at *Spin*, Craig Marks, changed the location after he saw New Market, Virginia, in an atlas—mainly because he thought the town's name would be a dead giveaway that the piece was an April Fools joke.

Could this be true? Was I somehow propelled on a Cörn Röcket from hills of Virginia to field of dreams? Is it possible that Jim Greer's story caused a small tear in the space-time continuum, folding together the middle-of-nowhere places where I was an undergrad, then professor?

For a moment, I wonder if he is putting me on.

Carl Wilson

All That Is Solid Melts into Schmaltz

Poptimism vs. the Guilty Displeasure

S imon Frith remarked in a 2002 interview on
rockcritics.com: "Celine Dion is probably the most
loathed superstar I can remember, at least by
everyone I know, not just critics but even my mother-in-
law. . . . I doubt if she will ever be redeemed, ABBA-style,
and what seems to concern everyone is that she is just
naff."

There's no such thing as a "guilty pleasure"—that's
the mantra these days from the "poptimists," critics
and fans who have lined up to proclaim that a chunk of
bubblegum pop can shine as brightly as any rock 'n' roll
Byron's stab at significance. Delight is where you find it,
and myriad forms of pop pleasure satisfy diverse publics.
Once formulated, the proposition is self-evident. Any
vestigial vanities about high and low culture, art versus
trash, were crushed beneath Andy Warhol's Brillo box decades ago, right? Besides ABBA, recent years have seen
critics recouperate countless long-damned artists and
genres, even, as we saw at EMP last year, blackface minstrelsy. It seems nothing is beyond redemption. But what
about our displeasures, even disgusts? Should we feel a
shame in our pop blind spots to balance our liberated
pride in our enjoyments? Should there be such a thing as
a guilty displeasure?

One thing's sure: very few people seem to feel guilty
over their pleasure in absolutely fucking hating Celine

Dion. A bubbling pool of contempt for the Quebecois warbler became a tsunami in the wake of "My Heart Will Go On," her 1999 hit theme from *Titanic*. As measured a critic as Robert Christgau has referred to Celine's popularity as a trial to be endured, but more typical was the ranking of her megahit at number 3 on the Most Annoying Songs Ever list in *Maxim* magazine (fall 2005): "The second most tragic event ever to result from that fabled ocean liner continues to torment humanity years later." In 2002, Rob Sheffield in *Rolling Stone* called her voice "just furniture polish." At a more advanced level of invective, the pop culture commentator Cintra Wilson called Celine "the most wholly repellant woman ever to sing songs of love," adding, "I think most people would rather be processed through the digestive tract of an anaconda than be Celine Dion for a day." In Sarah Vowell's otherwise affectionate 1999 list of "four best Canadian jokes" in Salon, number 1 was simply, "Celine Dion."

As a Canadian I've been hating Celine years longer than you have and, thanks to the Canadian-content quotas imposed on radio there, in greater quantity. Her music always seemed to me like monotony writ huge, R&B with the sex and slyness clinically removed, French chanson severed from its wit. It's Oprah-certified chicken soup for the consumerist soul. She's even a dull celebrity, aside from her creepy royal wedding to the man who's managed her since she was a twelve-year-old child star. But rationalizations aside, her singing always made me cringe in revulsion. And it's the same with most everyone I know.

Yet where is my poptimism now? Globally Celine has sold 175 million records. She has five albums in the U.S. list of the all-time Top 100, making her the twenty-third best-selling artist ever here. She is the top-selling French artist of all time. Her legions tithe their salaries to attend her Las Vegas revue *A New Day* in a custom-built "Coliseum" at Caesar's Palace. There is even a website called Celine Dreams, where fans earnestly share stories of her cameo appearances on their nightly big screen, typically as a maternal figure or understanding friend. Overseas, from China to Ghana to Iraq, she's easily one of the three or four best-loved Western musicians, with none of the backlash.

That doesn't mean you have to like her. Unless it does. A critical generation claiming to swear off all bourgeois elitist bias seems at least obliged to account for the immense popularity of someone we've collectively deemed so devoid of appeal. Those who find Celine "naff"—British for tacky, gauche, kitschy, or, as they say in Quebec, *kétaine*—must be overlooking something, maybe starting with why those categories exist.

Tastes can be treacherous. At about age twelve, I would tell people that I liked all kinds of music—except disco and country. I lived in an overwhelmingly white, declining rust-belt city in southern Ontario, and it was only after I moved away that I saw the glaring racial and regional subtext. My perspective was mutated by social experiences and musical ones, but mainly I came to realize that my easy scorn had revealed my ignorance of other ways of life, prejudices I did not want to maintain, and I came to love disco and country. The impulse was primarily ethical, though where it led was hedonistic. Poptimism seems to assume this process always runs the other way.

Yet my earlier taste hadn't felt like a social position. It was a gut reaction. I disliked Dolly Parton and Diana Ross as cleanly and purely as I now do Celine. So how cleanly and purely is that? If in psychoanalysis your fears indicate what you want more than your conscious wishes do, so in aesthetics your hatreds might disclose more than your enthusiasms.

I am not talking about the guilty displeasure I feel about, say, not getting opera. I don't make jokes about opera. I'm aware I wasn't raised with it and haven't gotten around to cultivating an ear. Mind you, this might not be incidental to the Celine case either. With the foregrounded advertisement of her vocal chops, her duets with Luciano Pavarotti and Andrea Bocelli, and the passion-positive thrust of her music, Celine may occupy a similar point in pop that light opera did in the nineteenth and early twentieth centuries, the pop of Jenny Lind and Caruso and Callas, and the later likes of the Irish tenor John McCormack or the Italian belter Mario Lanza. Opera has always intersected with the tradition I'll call schmaltz, in which ethnic Jewish or Italian or Spanish or Irish or, say, French Canadian singers are called upon to model shamelessly over-the-top emotion for the pleasure of more vanilla audiences—perhaps as a racially palatable alternative to black music. There is a genealogy of schmaltz to be traced, but for now, suffice to say my Celine and opera barriers might be more than coincidence.

But my Celine problem seems much closer to the guilty displeasure I feel when I flinch at a noisy group of young black guys on the street at night. I'm conscious of the forces pulling the strings of my nerve endings, and feel queasy that my reflexes betray me. Because music is so tangled up with our identities, likes and dislikes seldom come without social fall-out. It's not straightforward. You might be a Juilliard graduate with a trust fund who projects coolness on to ghetto kids, hillbillies, or even teenage girls, kicking it to Mariah Carey to reassure yourself you're not stuck-up. You might be less enamoured of what you imagine about frat boys, or soccer moms, or your mom, and instinctively shun music that conjures up such listeners. And if you are a soccer mom, you may want to be a soccer mom who listens to Slayer, not one who listens to Sheryl Crow, because you don't want to be *such* a soccer mom.

In the shifting population mosaic of North America in 2006, with technology making so much music so broadly available, culture does not quite work the way Pierre Bourdieu depicted it. In his landmark socio-logical studies of taste in the relatively homogenous society of postwar France, factory workers and bureaucrats and executives each had low-brow, middle-brow, or high-brow tastes consistent with what Bourdieu called their habitus, or social sphere. In a society that puts its faith in class mobility, taste may measure direction and velocity better than position—our likes evolve along with our aspirations. What we actively dislike indicates our enemies list, which may lie closer to what we are.

When it comes to Celine Dion, the unspoken audience stereotype has been spoken with bracingly open elitism by London's *Independent on Sunday*: "Wedged between vomit and indifference, there must be a fan base: some middle-of-the-road Middle England invisible to the rest of us. Grannies, tux-wearers, overweight children, mobile-phone salesmen and shopping-centre devotees, presumably."

After reading that, I hated the *Independent on Sunday* far more than I hated Celine Dion. But they're only fleshing out the Jonathan Franzen–like snobbery I invoked with the phrase "Oprah-certified." The audience thus maligned is the sort of people who might have scrounged together tickets for the *Titanic*, only to perish in steerage. The sort of people I grew up around. If my disdain for Celine extends to them, am I pushing them out of the poptimist lifeboat?

Reclaiming abject genres and performers tends to take historical per-spective. It's harder now to hear Celine the way the future might. But hell, if music critics can sanction Muzak and the Carpenters (and they have), it seems bad faith not to try.

So I'm writing a book about the album with the *Titanic* tune on it, in a quest for my inner Celine Dion fan. It's an exercise in cultural populism, and it's still early in my deprogramming. Conventional wisdom is that you can't control what songs you enjoy, any more than you can have an inauthentic orgasm. I'm not so sure, considering some of the insufferable music I've gone to bed with out of some half-conscious sense of obligation. What seems to separate poptimism from cultural populism is that it's solipsistic: my enjoyment is always legitimate, but so is despising what you enjoy. Poptimism means never having to say you're sorry. But isn't there social value in attempting to feel the heat of other people's fires, to reconnect the demographic islands on which marketers maroon us, to build community?

In this effort it must be axiomatic that you're not seeking hidden redemptive qualities in your guilty displeasure. You can't say, "I hate the guitars and satanism, but what great vocabularies some black metal songwriters have." If you like hip-hop for its politics but not the beats, you don't really like hip-hop. And if you decide what you like about Celine Dion, as I've seen one *Village Voice* critic argue, is the vocal effects of her idiosyncratic pronunciation, you still don't like Celine Dion. You have to accept that what you hate about your guilty displeasure will be exactly what their fans enjoy.

In Celine's case, this is that she's overproduced, clichéd, bombastic, unnuanced, conformist, lacking risk and surprise. All these qualities embarrass me, and worse still I can't manage the embarrassment by listening to Celine as camp. Her excesses don't reach cathartic levels of bad taste. Instead, they are side effects of trying to be romantic, of trying, in fact, to be tasteful. She and her producers are trying to make something exquisite.

Given Celine's biography, coming from a poor fourteen-child francophone Catholic family from a working-class suburb of Montreal, this hunger for the deluxe is understandable, and it's the heart of her aesthetic. The one moment in recent history when even Celine haters had to give her props was her infamous appearance on the Larry King show last fall during the Hurricane Katrina disaster. Turning on the waterworks as only a schmaltz queen can, she righteously demanded why the U.S. government is able to fly bombs around the world to kill people but couldn't get helicopters in to help those in its own country. Then she also defended looters: "Maybe some of the people who do that they're so poor they've never touched anything in their lives. Let them touch those things for once!"

I've come to hear it as her manifesto: She wants to touch things, and the lush sonic values of her music—what you might call conspicuous pro-duction—are there to be touched. It's all about getting paid. It's an aspira-tional music the way that hip-hop can be, although Celine is more ladylike about it. But she also wants to share this plenitude with her audience—wants them to touch and be touched by the luxury item that is her voice, with its ornamental melisma and plush velvet autotuning and its many octaves like the wings of a mansion. In this way Celine is very much at home in Las Vegas. You go to this strike-it-rich spot and there is Celine, for whom luck's clearly been a lady, spewing out golden notes for you to catch like coins streaming out of a jackpot slot machine.

When she talks about her achievements, she always says "we," mean-ing her husband, producers, hairdressers, and other aides, but also her fans. This is a continuity from the communalism of French Quebec: She came up through the province's star system, a huge stock of household names utterly unknown elsewhere, a system actively promoted by cul-tural leaders there as an exercise in collective identity building, after the 1960s Quiet Revolution, in which Quebecers threw off what they saw as the colonialism of both English Canada and the Catholic Church. One of the founding texts of Quebec nationalism is called *The White Niggers of America*, modeled on Frantz Fanon. So while Celine is seen by Quebec intellectuals as very *kétaine* indeed, they still view her renown as a vital marker of the province's postcolonial triumph. Quebec has a collective stake in Celine, the way black America does in its stars, and it set the mold for her relationship to audiences: my success is yours; come touch it.

In the preshow of Celine's multimedia extravaganza at Caesar's Palace, the backdrop is a vast gilded picture frame, within which is a real-time live video of you the audience finding your seats. As show time nears, the cam-era begins zooming in on selected spectators, creating a repeated comic pantomime in which you see people realize they're being projected sev-eral stories high, shrink from the camera or mug for it—there are teen-age girls, a family in which the father is asleep, some drunk gamblers, and finally a couple still dressed in their wedding outfits. And then the frame expands, and shatters into a hundred shards of light, which all spin down and converge on Celine herself, revealed poised on a sweeping red stair-case.

In a perfect figure of music interpellating, representing, breaking, and remaking identities, here was Celine offering to mirror us back to our-selves, with all our endearing foibles but also huger, more ornate, classier, better. She put an eighteenth-century golden frame around our feelings, the ultimate in egalitarian bling, and then absorbed them all into her own body, perhaps to feed to her ravenous voice.

Yet this is no frame a "truly" cultured person would ever fix to a contemporary picture. From a remove, all Celine's attempts at class and taste go hideously wrong. With her synthesized strings and her genuine pearls, she aspires to the highbrow culture of a half-century ago, rattling at a locked door whose combination has changed. Today's upper-class markers are at least modernist. The real rich kids, the Strokes, repackage the avant-rock of twenty-five years ago. The middle-class movers hustling their fresh-minted cultural capital display the opposite pretensions to Celine's, a masquerade of downward mobility in trucker caps and ironic moustaches. Whether you want to join the bourgeoisie or épater it, it is not what it was in 1955. The ultimate U.S. bourgeois magazine, *The New Yorker*, now employs a music critic who writes about Ghostface and M.I.A. Of course there are still classical snots, but to describe them as "dominant" seems laughable, and so do Celine's attempts to cozy up to them. Which arguably is what the code switching is meant to accomplish.

For music critics, who tend not to be wealthy people but middle-class ones who have risen thanks to their skill at getting and spending cultural capital, Celine's species of cluelessness is particularly excruciating. One reason we're so fond of reflexivity and self-consciousness in music is that virtuosic symbol manipulation is our sport. These are the chops we now admire instead of guitar licks or big pipes. So when we witness an inept display of it, it nudges our concealed fear of being found out, exposed as hick frauds. And as Barbara Ehrenreich has written, middle-class people now suffer a "fear of falling" into the widening gap between rich and poor. Education and taste are defenses against such a downward spiral, so we recoil from, for instance, the shameful cultural miscues of a Celine Dion.

Yet there's something noble in Celine's failure here. It leaves an impression of conservativism, but it's also a rebuke to the dubious commandment that music innovate and subvert and contribute to a narrative of progress. Even Simon Frith, who deals comprehensively with many of these issues in his 1997 opus *Performing Rites*, comes round to saying, "In the end, I want to value most highly that music, popular and serious, which has some sort of disruptive cultural effect." Yet on an everyday level, disruption and change make up the crisis people now face. As Tom Frank argued in *The Conquest of Cool*, the countercultural privileging of constant negation and delegitimization of traditional verities turned out to be directly in line with the general needs of late capitalism, as seen in marketing and management ideology, for an individualist, decentralized, innovation-based business culture. In that sense preferring Celine over Le Tigre or even Missy Elliott could be a kind of resistance, as her music is so focused on intimacy, family, and resilience.

Not that you'd mistake her for a folk artist. Like Las Vegas, Celine does not exemplify tradition but hypertradition, not just conformity but mega-conformity. And this is the root, I think, of the complaint that she doesn't bring any interpretive nuance or personality to her songs. In part it's language—she's unmistakably more expressive in French—but it's also the most contemporary quality about her. As Joshua Clover said at a past Pop Conference, "The modality of the song-hit is not invention but intensity." Like a gambler for whom losing is as much of a rush as winning, Celine is eerily eager to disperse herself into the winds of her music, squandering more than the surplus until nothing remains but special effects. All that is solid melts into schmaltz.

"My work," she has said, "is to enter people's lives with my music. Do you think I want to disturb them when they bake? Do you think I want to disturb them when they make love? I want to be part of it. I don't want to interrupt. . . . I'm doing my job, my song, and if you want to hear this song and not that song, I have nothing to do with it."

In tending her voice as if she had nothing to do with it, she musically incarnates the masochistic devotion of the woman who takes care of everybody but herself. It would be rude to get in between the listener and the voice. And what is personality, anyway, but an assemblage of all those social influences, bricolage with no bricoleur? She is happily maximum medium, minimum message, as much a surface without depth as Giorgio Moroder's beats, a ritual sacrifice to an impersonal voice through which the luxuriant electricity of empathy passes impeded by as few circuits as possible, lighting up her fans' lives, in dreams waking or sleeping. The authenticity is in that exchange, not in her self.

This makes for an unusual absence of musical tension. As her songs rocket to their predestined climaxes, she goes along for the ride, leaning on the accelerator but never the brake. Intensity but not difference. It reminds me of nothing so much as speed metal, metal pared down to fast loud guitars, screaming, growling, and no funny business. It's been said that "pro wrestling is soap opera on steroids," so maybe Celine Dion is metal on estrogen, with nothing but the power ballads. And metal is admitted into the critical sanctum.

Of course, metal is all darkness and rebellion and Celine is all candlelight and sentiment. This is the other locus of our embarrassment, that she is so unapologetically emotionally direct. If supposedly cosmopolitan listeners have hangups about that, and I know I do, we should just get over it.

I want to end by quickly, guiltily, admitting a few misgivings about messing with guilty displeasures.

First, are you *ever* allowed to say someone else's taste sucks? It's as if, because I grasp that most Republican voters are decent human beings, I were required to give it up to George Bush. In politics, that sort of relativism doesn't wash: if you don't stand for something, you'll fall for anything. People elected Hitler. But is aesthetics a zone in which such caveats don't apply? If there's nothing wrong with Celine Dion, is there also nothing pernicious about the luxury art kitsch of the glass sculptor Dale Chihuly or Thomas Kinkade, Painter of Light™?

Second, is this just aesthetic tourism—a cheap holiday in other people's habitus? When privileged audiences embrace populist art for the sake of solidarity, it can get ugly. See "folk revival" or "conscious hip-hop."

And finally, if you are able to dismantle your socially constructed evaluative assumptions, then what? On what basis do you make any critical judgments? Do you go on thinking some punk-rock bands are better than others, and that "Only the Good Die Young" is a better Billy Joel song than "We Didn't Start the Fire"? What did it mean when Jody Rosen and I agreed last night that Douglas Wolk has good taste? I don't know. But frankly, with the hangover of several centuries of cultural elitism, a voluntary vacation from aesthetic hierarchies, even "subjective" ones, may be a necessary purgative so as to find the stomach, much less the taste, to carry on.

Postscript

Many writerly dilemmas come down to audience. Different venues demand shifts of tone, vocabulary, references, and punchlines. Since I already knew the crowd at the Experience Music Project's Pop Conference in Seattle, with its mishmash of musicians, critics, obsessives, and scholars, it seemed like the perfect place to test out ideas for the little book

I was going to write for Continuum Books' 33 1/3 Series, in which each volume centers on a single album—in my case, Celine Dion's *Let's Talk about Love*. A lot of this essay would be cannibalized for its introductory pages, while other paragraphs, for example on sentiment and subversion, ballooned into entire chapters of their own. I thought it would be a fairly quick expansion. It ended up taking another year-and-a-half of evenings and weekends.

Much of the puzzle was that my readers might well not share an assumption that critics almost hold to be self-evident: that a cultural phenomenon is inherently a metonymy, recursively containing some broader hints about society or humanity. In the pilot episode of that gorgeous mayfly of a tv teen melodrama, *My So-Called Life*, Claire Danes's character explains why she had to follow her friend's advice to dye her hair: "Because she wasn't talking about my hair. She was talking about my life." For me that's the way it is when we talk about music—with the vast array of personae, subculture, and spectacle that surround it, music just happens to be a richer storehouse of metaphor than hair (though hair's a pretty good one). My book is superficially about music and taste, but at its heart it actually is "talking about love," that is, about empathy and democracy. Music and celebrity are sexier vehicles than, for example, a seminar on ethics and philosophy. And in its specificity this approach mitigates against descending into mere platitudes.

So people who complain that thinking, writing, or talking too much about music "ruins" it or is "not rock 'n' roll" are getting it backward. Whether or not the music needs any discussion, discussion needs the music. Rock may not need discourse but discourse needs to be rocked. Mostly it's a niche activity, but now and then it breaks into the mainstream—when a moral panic breaks out about the white rapper Eminem, say, or in the overwhelming public reaction to John Lennon's or Michael Jackson's deaths. People do instinctively sense at such moments that this music or musician is standing for a larger truth or feeling, something that's changed or threatening to change. If for nothing else, such occasions make it worth keeping critics around.

When my book was finally published in late 2007 as *Let's Talk about Love: A Journey to the End of Taste*, it was gratifying to find that its odd conceit turned out to be a similar kind of opening, in a small way. Many people quickly got the idea that loving or hating Celine Dion was a good hook for a conversation about how tastes form tribes, identities, classes, places, and eras—and vice versa. (Still, it wasn't quite as good as the teaser that my fellow conference-goer Elijah Wald came up with for his book revisiting popular-music history in much the same spirit: *How the Beatles Destroyed Rock 'n' Roll.*)

Doing publicity was another kind of journey through the range of perspectives people bring to culture. Of course there were a few book reviewers and music geeks who met the book with exactly the kind of snobbery it critiques. Others embraced it but from awkward angles: on local TV or commercial radio, for example, interviewers would rhyme off various pieces of Celine Dion trivia for my reaction, deaf to my stammered protests that this wasn't what the book was really about. It was not because they're dumb, but because their point of view is that culture is an amusing sideshow to the real stuff of life (like sports), a series of isolated incidents, products, and personalities. On the other hand public-radio producers and broadcasters, with perhaps their own internal agonies about elitism versus populism, seemed to clue in right away—the CBC in Canada and NPR and PRI shows in the United States could hardly get enough of the subject. I find this fact a bit embarrassing, given the way people use "NPR music" as a term of invective and the music writer Frank Kogan described "PBS" as a form of bland-think that's rotting away society. But I am trying to own up to my uncoolness.

At the other end of the spectrum from the commercial radio people were, to my initial confusion, many musicians. The ones in "indie" scenes usually had their own cultural-theory damage to contend with (at my book launch, the Toronto solo act Steve Kado aka The Blankket [sic] covered a Dion song about domestic abuse as doom metal about the historical oppression of the French-Canadian working class). But working musicians in other forms often flatly refused to believe that any reasonable people listen to music through nonmusical filters. They'd downplay the significance of genres, for example, and quickly turn to what they admired or disliked about Dion's music technically. Their adamant denial of the metaphorical nature of culture was a defense of the autonomy of the art form (if not the business that promotes and distributes it). To them, pointing out its function as a social marker seemed like an insult to music. And fair enough.

I was pleasantly surprised to find the book being assigned in many university courses on pop culture, music appreciation, and the philosophy of aesthetics. I got to ask young people whether music in the seemingly more eclectic iPod age is still serving the unite-and-divide role it once did, and they reported that it's still a crucial maker and breaker of alliances. Those academic adoptions led to a bizarre incident in which the actor James Franco (*Freaks and Geeks, Milk, Spider-Man*) was quizzed by annoying MTV reporters on live TV from the red carpet at the Oscars about his "guilty pleasures" (i.e., which MTV reality shows did he watch?). He finally fended them off by citing my book, by full title, subtitle, and author's name. Luckily he'd just happened to read it the week before in his Columbia University nonfiction-writing MFA seminar. He told me later that after finishing it he honestly wondered, "How am I ever going to know what's good and bad again?"

That unexpected nip of the spotlight led to buying a new shirt, jetting to New York, and appearing on Stephen Colbert's nightly talk show, in which he satirizes the excesses of both right-wing punditry and knee-jerk liberalism by hosting in the persona of a conservative blowhard who nonetheless often gets the better of his earnest guests. (Backstage he's very nice, by the way, shaking hands and smiling like a 1950s TV dad.) Colbert is notorious for being mock-tough on his guests, but he was relatively gentle with me, aside from a few "hipster" jabs. I think he recognized a kinship in our premises, which are both varieties of "sympathy for the devil" exercises. Still, he was too fast for me to slip in the bit of ju-jitsu I'd planned: "Well, Stephen, the book is about whether we, somewhat unconsciously, decide what we like not as much on its merits as by what we desire to *be* like. For instance, imagine I wanted to pretend to be a Republican when I was really a Democrat—I'd immediately put on a blue suit and act like I had contempt for jazz and abstract art," as he does on the show. Ah, *l'esprit d'escalier.*

A greater disappointment is that I haven't heard much from Celine Dion fans, aside from those I interviewed. In part I blame my own subtitle about "the end of taste," whose double meaning was meant to lure in my fellow snobs who might otherwise never deign to thumb through a Celine Dion book (even then, some independent bookstores that stock other 33 1/3 titles would not deign to sell it, saying their customers wouldn't be interested). Her fans are also so accustomed to media scorn and contempt that they would doubt claims in reviews that it's a sympathetic look (especially reviews that open with a Celine Dion joke). And no matter how good my intentions, I can't deny that I too might bristle to be subjected to some kind of anthropological investigation, although in my defense I

Let's Talk about Love makes it to *The Colbert Report*.
Screen grab supplied by Comedy Central.

would argue that a greater portion of the book is about what motivates people like me to dislike Celine Dion than what drives her fans to enjoy her. As for Dion and her camp, as I'm frequently asked? No, no reactions, not even a hint that they know the book exists.

However, at the 2009 Pop Conference, I did get a chance to slip a copy to Diane Warren, the insanely successful L.A. pop songwriter who has penned a few Dion hits. Her reaction was pretty deadpan, perhaps because she doesn't have any tracks on *Let's Talk about Love*. I didn't have the presence of mind to inform her about the scene in the book in which a song she did write, "Because You Loved Me," moves me close to tears, thinking of my ex-wife, during Dion's concert at Caesar's Palace. But I do take some pride in the fact that Warren was asked to be a keynote speaker at that Pop Conference: while the open-minded curiosity (and industry connections) of the main organizers deserves most of the credit, perhaps my investigation helped warm up the atmosphere for such a mainstream figure at a confabulation of music snobs. The way the observer can change the thing observed is one of the most fraught of all these questions of audience, but now and then it's a hopeful one.

Larry Blumenfeld writes regularly about music and culture for the *Wall Street Journal*. His work has appeared in the *Village Voice*, the *New York Times*, Salon, and Truthdig, among other publications. This essay grew from his research of post-flood cultural recovery as a Katrina Media Fellow with the Open Society Institute. Blumenfeld was also awarded a 2001–2 fellowship in the National Arts Journalism Program at Columbia University Graduate School of Journalism. He is editor-at-large of *Jazziz* magazine, for which he served as editor-in-chief from 1995 to 2000. He lives in Brooklyn, New York, but heads down to New Orleans whenever possible (and especially on St. Joseph's Night).

Austin Bunn's fiction and nonfiction have appeared in *Best American Science and Nature Writing*, *The Pushcart Prize Anthology*, the *New York Times* magazine, *Zoetrope*, and elsewhere. He teaches creative writing at Grand Valley State University in Michigan.

Nate Chinen writes about music for the *New York Times*. He's also a columnist for *JazzTimes*, an independent music blogger (thegig.typepad.com), and coauthor of *Myself among Others*, the autobiography of impresario George Wein. For each of the last six years, he has received the Helen Dance-Robert Palmer Award for Excellence in Newspaper, Magazine or Online Feature or Review Writing. He was born and raised in Honolulu.

J. Martin Daughtry is an assistant professor of ethnomusicology in New York University's Department of Music. His research projects cover sung poetry in the post-Stalinist Soviet Union, post-Soviet musical nationalism, and the transformation, persistence, and attenuation of musical traditions in the wake of cataclysmic sociopolitical change. In 2007, *Music in the Post-9/11 World*, which he coedited with Jonathan Ritter, was published by Routledge. He is working on a book-length investigation of the sonic dimensions of Operation Iraqi Freedom.

Brian Goedde has written for the *New York Times*, the *New York Times* magazine, and the *Chicago Tribune*, among other publications. He is also coproducer of *Iowa*

Mixtape (Lost Footage Films, 2010), a short documentary based on the essay he co-authored in this collection.

Michelle Habell-Pallán is an associate professor in the Department of Gender, Women and Sexuality Studies and adjunct professor in the School of Music and Communication at the University of Washington. Author of *Loca Motion: The Travels of Latina Popular Culture* and coeditor *of Latina/o Popular Culture*, she has a new book, *Beat Migration: "American" Pop Music*, in progress. She curated the award-winning bilingual traveling exhibit *American Sabor: Latinos in U.S. Popular Music*, organized by the University of Washington and Experience Music Project, with an online version made in collaboration with the Smithsonian. She directs the Women Who Rock Research and Digital Oral History Project and serves as an advisory board member of American Music Partnership (AMPS), Seattle (funded by the P. G. Allen Family Foundation).

Jonathan Lethem is the author of eight novels including *The Fortress of Solitude* and *You Don't Love Me Yet*. He teaches at Pomona College, and lives with his family in California and Maine.

Eric Lott teaches American Studies at the University of Virginia. His work has appeared in a range of periodicals including the *Village Voice*, the *Nation*, *New York Newsday*, the *Chronicle of Higher Education*, *Transition*, *Social Text*, *African American Review*, PMLA, *Representations*, *American Literary History*, and *American Quarterly*. He is the author of *Love and Theft: Blackface Minstrelsy and the American Working Class*, from which Bob Dylan took the title for his 2001 album *"Love and Theft."* Lott is also the author of *The Disappearing Liberal Intellectual*. He is currently finishing a study of race and culture in the twentieth century, *Tangled Up in Blue: The Cultural Contradictions of American Racism*.

Kembrew McLeod is a writer, filmmaker, and associate professor of Communication Studies at the University of Iowa. He is currently writing a book on the history of media pranks for New York University Press, and his previous book, *Freedom of Expression®*, received the American Library Association's Oboler book award. McLeod's coproduced documentary *Copyright Criminals* aired in 2010 on PBS's Emmy Award–winning series *Independent Lens*, and his writing has appeared in the *New York Times, Los Angeles Times, Village Voice, Spin*, and *Rolling Stone*. You can read about his pranks and other work on http://kembrew.com.

Elena Passarello is an actor and writer currently living in Grand Rapids, Michigan. She has written essays and reviews for Slate, *Creative Nonfiction, Iowa Review*, and *Ninth Letter*.

Diane Pecknold is an assistant professor in Women's and Gender Studies at the University of Louisville, where she teaches popular culture and feminist studies. She is the author of *The Selling Sound: The Rise of the Country Music Industry* and coeditor of *A Boy Named Sue: Gender and Country Music*. She is currently working on a series of projects on black engagements with country music in the 1960s and 1970s, of which her essay in this volume forms part.

David Ritz has coauthored books with, among others, Ray Charles, Aretha Franklin, B.B. King, Smokey Robinson, the Neville Brothers, Grandmaster Flash, Natalie Cole, Cornel West, Tavis Smiley, Lang Lang, Etta James, Leiber and Stoller, Paul Shaffer, and Don Rickles. He is author of *Divided Soul: The Life of Marvin Gaye* and co-wrote "Sexual Healing." He's currently working with R. Kelly, Janet Jackson, and T.I.

Carlo Rotella is the director of American Studies and professor of English at Boston College. He is the author of *Cut Time: An Education at the Fights*, *Good with Their Hands: Boxers, Bluesmen, and Other Characters from the Rust Belt*, and *October Cities: The Redevelopment of Urban Literature*. He contributes regularly to the *New York Times* magazine, *Washington Post* magazine, and Slate, and he is a columnist for the *Boston Globe* and regular commentator for WGBH. His work has also appeared in *The New Yorker*, *Harper's*, *The American Scholar*, *The Believer*, *Critical Inquiry*, and *The Best American Essays*.

Scott Seward was a frequent contributor to the *Village Voice* music section from 2000 to 2006. Since 2006, he has written monthly for Decibel magazine. He also owns and operates a used record store in Greenfield, Massachusetts.

Tom Smucker has been writing about pop music and politics since the 1960s. He lives in New York City.

Greg Tate is a writer and musician who lives in Harlem. His books include *Flyboy in the Buttermilk* and *Everything but the Burden*. He is currently writing a book about James Brown for Farrar Straus and Giroux and editing the journal *Coon Bidness* when not freely conducting his band Burnt Sugar.

Karen Tongson is associate professor of English and Gender Studies at the University of Southern California, and the author of *Relocations: Queer Suburban Imaginaries*. She is currently the editor-in-chief of the *Journal of Popular Music Studies* (with Gustavus Stadler), and the series editor of *Postmillennial Pop* at New York University Press (with Henry Jenkins). By night, Karen can be found belting power ballads, flashing jazz hands, and sipping bourbon at a seedy karaoke establishment near you.

Alexandra T. Vazquez is an assistant professor in the Center for African American Studies and the Department of English at Princeton University. She is the author of *Instrumental Migrations: The Critical Turns of Cuban Music* and, with Ela Troyano, a coeditor of *La Lupe: Queen of Latin Soul*. She has published in *women and* *performance*, the volume of essays *Reggaeton*, and the special issue "The Politics of Recorded Sound" of *Social Text* 102.

Oliver Wang is an assistant professor of sociology at California State University, Long Beach. He specializes in research on popular culture, mass media, and race and ethnicity. He is currently completing work on *Legions of Boom: Filipino American Mobile DJ Crews of the SF Bay Area*. He is a frequent contributor to National Public Radio, the *Los Angeles Times*, *Wax Poetics*, and other publications. He also hosts the audioblog, soul-sides.com.

Eric Weisbard teaches American Studies at the University of Alabama, has organized the Pop Conference for Experience Music Project since it began in 2002, and is an associate editor for the *Journal of Popular Music Studies*, as well as vice president of the American chapter of IASPM. He has edited two prior Pop Conference volumes, *This Is Pop* and *Listen Again*, written a short book on the scorned Guns N' Roses albums *Use Your Illusion I and II*, and is currently at work on a study of how commercial radio formats shaped music in the United States.

Carl Wilson's *Let's Talk about Love: A Journey to the End of Taste* appeared in many lists of the best books of 2008 and has been called one of the best music books of the 2000s. He writes for many publications, is a senior editor at Canada's national newspaper *The Globe and Mail*, blogs at Backtotheworld.net and Zoilus.com, and helps run the Trampoline Hall Lecture Series in Toronto, where he lives.

INDEX

Note: page numbers in *italics* refer to illustrations; those followed by "n" indicate endnotes.

Cannon, Toronzo, 237
"Can't We Stop?" (Armstrong), 74–75
capital gain model, 28
capitalism and commercialism: culture-industry commodification, Adorno, and the Carpenters, 62–68, 72–74; gay identity and, 99–100; Orange County and, 90
"Capitalism and Gay Identity" (D'Emilio), 100–101
Carlisle, Belinda, 251
Carpenter, Agnes, 75, 76
Carpenters: Beach Boys, Lawrence Welk, and, 50–51, 54, 58; compulsory cheerfulness and sameness, 63–64, 64; control and perfectionism, 48, 49, 74–75; critical readings of, 68–69; culture-industry commodification and, 62–68; DJ persona and, 53; Karen's voice, 48, 65; Now & Then, 48–50, 53; self-annihilation of, 74–79; Singles 1969–1973, 64–65; suburban culture and family life, 47, 69–71; "Superstar," 71–73; white musical values and, 49; "Yesterday Once More," 48–49, 73–74
Carrillo, Sean, 250–51
Castro, Jason, 183
CBGB, 9, 19
Cee-Lo, 221
Celestiial, 277
Center for Popular Music, Middle Tennessee State University, 297
Cervenka, Exene, 252
Chai, Diane, 252
Chanan, Michael, 31
Chang, Jeff, 109n55
Charles, Ray, 42–44
Chicago blues, 230–39
Chicana feminism and punk. See Hollywood Punk and Alice Bag
chitlin' circuit, 219, 228n56
Chong, Tommy, 61n14
Christgau, Robert, 65, 300

Chuck D, 197–98
church of Jimi Hendrix, 40
Clinton, Bill, 61n15
Cloud 9, Knott's Berry Farm (Buena Park, Calif.), 85, 86, 91, 98
Clover, Joshua, 306
Club Vex (East L.A.), 248, 261, 262
Cobain, Kurt, 2, 283, 287, 295
Colbert, Stephen, 310, 311
combat sounds. See Iraq War, sound and listening in
Come on Over (Twain), 2
"Comunícate" (Manolito Simonet y Su Trabuco), 32–35
control: Carpenters and, 48, 49, 74–75; Lawrence Welk and social control, 50–51; as white musical value, 49
Convivial Hermit (magazine), 276
cordon sanitaire, 89, 106n22
Cörn Röcket, 291
country music: "By the Time I Get to Phoenix" and, 190, 192–93; in Iraq War, 119; prejudices and, 301; racism and, 186–87; tension in, 59n6
Coup, the, 218
Cour, Dave, 291–92
covers as textual practice, 187
Coyne, Wayne, 295
crate diggers, 227n44
Crazy Horse, Kandia, 203
Crist, Renée, 286
criticism and critics: "immanent" criticism, 67–68; knowing nothing vs. knowing everything, 27–29; Village Voice and rock criticism, 17–19; white-boy rock criticism, 16–17. See also specific critics and artists
Cropper, Steve, 188
crossover audiences, historical power of soul to forge, 223
"Cultural Criticism and Society" (Adorno), 67–68
cultural populism vs. poptimism, 303
culture, metaphorical nature of, 309

Eric Weisbard teaches American Studies at the
University of Alabama, has organized the Pop
Conference for Experience Music Project since it
began in 2002, and is an associate editor for the
Journal of Popular Music Studies, as well as vice
president of the American chapter of IASPM. He
has edited two prior Pop Conference volumes,
This Is Pop and *Listen Again*, written a short book
on the scorned Guns N' Roses albums *Use Your
Illusion I* and *II*, and is currently at work on a
study of how commercial radio formats shaped
music in the United States.

. . . . .

Library of Congress Cataloging-in-Publication Data
Pop when the world falls apart : music in the shadow
of doubt / [edited by] Eric Weisbard.
p. cm.
Includes bibliographical references and index.
ISBN 978-0-8223-5099-6 (cloth : alk. paper)
ISBN 978-0-8223-5108-5 (pbk. : alk. paper)
1. Music—Social aspects—History—20th century.
2. Music—Social aspects—History—21st century.
3. Popular music—History and criticism.
I. Weisbard, Eric.
ML3916.P673 2012
781.64′159—dc23
2011048245